D1072541

The Economic Approach
to Human Behavior

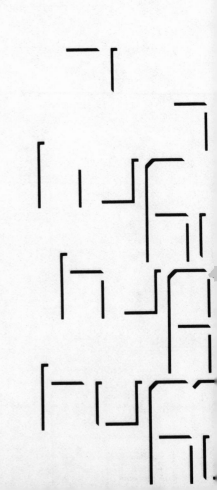

Gary S. Becker

The Economic Approach to Human Behavior,

The University of Chicago Press
Chicago and London

To Milton Friedman, H. Gregg Lewis, T. W.
Schultz, and George J. Stigler, from whom I
learned about the economic approach

HB71
·B43

Gary S. Becker is University Professor in the
Department of Economics, University of Chicago,
and Research Policy Adviser to the Center for
Economic Analysis of Human Behavior and Social
Institutions of the National Bureau of Economic
Research.
Among his previously published books are
The Economics of Discrimination (1957, rev. ed.
1971) and *Human Capital* (1964, rev. ed. 1975).

The University of Chicago Press, Chicago 60637
The University of Chicago Press, Ltd., London

Printed in the United States of America

80   79   78   77   76   987654321

Library of Congress Cataloging in Publication Data

Becker, Gary Stanley, 1930–
    The economic approach to human behavior.

    Includes bibliographical references and index.
    1.   Economics—Addresses, essays, lectures.
2.   Social sciences—Addresses, essays, lectures.
I.   Title.
HB71.B43   330   75-43240
ISBN 0-226-04111-5

Contents

Contents

Part 1   Introduction

1   The Economic Approach to Human Behavior

Economy is the art of making the most of life.
George Bernard Shaw

The following essays use an "economic" approach in seeking to understand human behavior in a variety of contexts and situations. Although
few persons would dispute the distinctiveness of an economic approach,
it is not easy to state exactly what distinguishes the economic approach
from sociological, psychological, anthropological, political, or even
genetical approaches. In this introductory essay I attempt to spell out the
principal attributes of the economic approach.

Let us turn for guidance first to the definitions of different fields. At
least three conflicting definitions of economics are still common. Economics
is said to be the study of (1) the allocation of material goods to satisfy
material wants,[1] (2) the market sector,[2] and (3) the allocation of scarce
means to satisfy competing ends.[3]

For very helpful comments I am indebted to Joseph Ben-David, Milton Friedman,
Victor Fuchs, Robert T. Michael, Jacob Mincer, Richard Posner, and T. W. Schultz.
I am especially indebted to George J. Stigler for many discussions, comments, and
much-needed encouragement, and to Robert K. Merton for a very helpful and lengthy
response to an earlier draft that provided a sociologist's perspective on the issues
covered in this essay. The usual disclaimer to the effect that none of these persons
should be held responsible for the arguments made in this essay is especially appropriate
since several disagreed with the central theme.

[1] "[Economics] is the social science that deals with the ways in which men and
societies seek to satisfy their material needs and desires," Albert Rees (1968); "[Econom-
ics is the] study of the supplying of man's physical needs and wants," art. "Economics,"
The Columbia Encyclopedia, 3d ed. p. 624; and see the many earlier references to
Marshall, Cannan, and others in L. Robbins (1962).

[2] A. C. Pigou said "[Economic welfare is] that part of social welfare that can be
brought directly or indirectly into relation with the measuring rod of money" (1962, p.
11).

[3] "Economics is the science which studies human behavior as a relationship between
ends and scarce means which have alternative uses," Robbins (1962, p. 16); "Economics ... is the study of the allocation of scarce resources among unlimited and competing uses," Rees (1968) and many other references.

The definition of economics in terms of material goods is the narrowest and the least satisfactory. It does not describe adequately either the market sector or what economists "do." For the production of tangible goods now provides less than half of all the market employment in the United States, and the intangible outputs of the service sector are now larger in value than the outputs of the goods sector (see Fuchs 1968). Moreover, economists are as successful in understanding the production and demand for retail trade, films, or education as they are for autos or meat. The persistence of definitions which tie economics to material goods is perhaps due to a reluctance to submit certain kinds of human behavior to the "frigid" calculus of economics.

The definition of economics in terms of scarce means and competing ends is the most general of all. It defines economics by the nature of the problem to be solved, and encompasses far more than the market sector or "what economists do."[4] Scarcity and choice characterize all resources allocated by the political process (including which industries to tax, how fast to increase the money supply, and whether to go to war); by the family (including decisions about a marriage mate, family size, the frequency of church attendance, and the allocation of time between sleeping and waking hours); by scientists (including decisions about allocating their thinking time, and mental energy to different research problems); and so on in endless variety. This definition of economics is so broad that it often is a source of embarrassment rather than of pride to many economists, and usually is immediately qualified to exclude most nonmarket behavior.[5]

All of these definitions of economics simply define the scope, and none tells us one iota about what the "economic" approach is. It could stress tradition and duty, impulsive behavior, maximizing behavior, or any other behavior in analyzing the market sector or the allocation of scarce means to competing ends.

Similarly, definitions of sociology and other social sciences are of equally little help in distinguishing their approaches from others. For example, the statement that sociology "is the study of social aggregates and groups in their institutional organization, of institutions and their organization, and of causes and consequences of changes in institutions and social organization" (Reiss 1968) does not distinguish the subject matter, let alone the approch, of sociology from, say, economics. Or the statement that "comparative psychology is concerned with the behavior of different species of living organisms" (Waters and Brunnell 1968) is as general as the definitions of economics and sociology, and as uninformative.

[4] Boulding (1966) attributes this definition of economics to Jacob Viner.

[5] Almost immediately after giving the broad definition of economics, Rees (1968) gives one in terms of material needs, without explaining why he so greatly reduced the scope of economics. Even Robbins, after an excellent discussion of what an economic problem is in the first chapter of his classic work on the nature and scope of economics (1962), basically restricts his analysis in later chapters to the market sector.

Let us turn away from definitions, therefore, because I believe that what most distinguishes economics as a discipline from other disciplines in the social sciences is not its subject matter but its approach. Indeed, many kinds of behavior fall within the subject matter of several disciplines: for example, fertility behavior is considered part of sociology, anthropology, economics, history, and perhaps even politics. I contend that the economic approach is uniquely powerful because it can integrate a wide range of human behavior.

Everyone recognizes that the economic approach assumes maximizing behavior more explicitly and extensively than other approaches do, be it the utility or wealth function of the household, firm, union, or government bureau that is maximized. Moreover, the economic approach assumes the existence of markets that with varying degrees of efficiency coordinate the actions of different participants—individuals, firms, even nations—so that their behavior becomes mutually consistent. Since economists generally have had little to contribute, especially in recent times, to the understanding of how preferences are formed, preferences are assumed not to change substantially over time, nor to be very different between wealthy and poor persons, or even between persons in different societies and cultures.

Prices and other market instruments allocate the scarce resources within a society and thereby constrain the desires of participants and coordinate their actions. In the economic approach, these market instruments perform most, if not all, of the functions assigned to "structure" in sociological theories.[6]

The preferences that are assumed to be stable do not refer to market goods and services, like oranges, automobiles, or medical care, but to underlying objects of choice that are produced by each household using market goods and services, their own time, and other inputs. These underlying preferences are defined over fundamental aspects of life, such as health, prestige, sensual pleasure, benevolence, or envy, that do not always bear a stable relation to market goods and services (see chapter 7 below). The assumption of stable preferences provides a stable foundation for generating predictions about responses to various changes, and prevents the analyst from succumbing to the temptation of simply postulating the required shift in preferences to "explain" all apparent contradictions to his predictions.

The combined assumptions of maximizing behavior, market equilibrium, and stable preferences, used relentlessly and unflinchingly, form the heart of the economic approach as I see it. They are responsible for the many theorems associated with this approach. For example, that (1) a rise in price reduces quantity demanded,[7] be it a rise in the market price of eggs reducing the demand for eggs, a rise in the "shadow" price of children

---

[6] An excellent statement of structural analysis can be found in Merton (1975).

[7] That maximizing behavior is not necessary to reach this conclusion is shown below in chapter 8.

reducing the demand for children, or a rise in the office waiting time for physicians, which is one component of the full price of physician services, reducing the demand for their services; (2) a rise in price increases the quantity supplied, be it a rise in the market price of beef increasing the number of cattle raised and slaughtered, a rise in the wage rate offered to married women increasing their labor force participation, or a reduction in "cruising" time raising the effective price received by taxicab drivers and thereby increasing the supply of taxicabs; (3) competitive markets satisfy consumer preferences more effectively than monopolistic markets, be it the market for aluminum or the market for ideas (see Director 1964, Coase 1974); or (4) a tax on the output of a market reduces that output, be it an excise tax on gasoline that reduces the use of gasoline, punishment of criminals (which is a "tax" on crime) that reduces the amount of crime, or a tax on wages that reduces the labor supplied to the market sector.

The economic approach is clearly not restricted to material goods and wants, nor even to the market sector. Prices, be they the money prices of the market sector or the "shadow" imputed prices of the nonmarket sector, measure the opportunity cost of using scarce resources, and the economic approach predicts the same kind of response to shadow prices as to market prices. Consider, for example, a person whose only scarce resource is his limited amount of time. This time is used to produce various commodities that enter his preference function, the aim being to maximize utility. Even without a market sector, either directly or indirectly, each commodity has a relevant marginal "shadow" price, namely, the time required to produce a unit change in that commodity; in equilibrium, the ratio of these prices must equal the ratio of the marginal utilities.[8] Most importantly, an increase in the relative price of any commodity—i.e., an increase in the time required to produce a unit of that commodity—would tend to reduce the consumption of that commodity.

The economic approach does not assume that all participants in any market necessarily have complete information or engage in costless transactions. Incomplete information or costly transactions should not, however, be confused with irrational or volatile behavior.[9] The economic approach has developed a theory of the optimal or rational accumulation

---

[8] He maximizes $U = U(Z_i \ldots Z_m)$ subject to

$$Z_i = f_i(t_i),$$

and

$$\sum t_i = t,$$

where Z_i is the ith commodity, f_i the production function for Z_i, and t_i is the time input into Z_i. The well-known first-order equilibrium conditions for the allocation of his scarce resource, time, are:

$$\frac{\partial U}{\partial Z_i} = \lambda \frac{\partial t_i}{\partial Z_i} = \frac{\lambda}{\partial Z_i/\partial t_i} = \frac{\lambda}{MP_{t_i}},$$

where λ is his marginal utility of time.

[9] Schumpeter appears to confuse them, although with considerable modification (1950, chap. 21, section "Human Nature in Politics").

of costly information[10] that implies, for example, greater investment in information when undertaking major than minor decisions—the purchase of a house or entrance into marriage versus the purchase of a sofa or bread. The assumption that information is often seriously incomplete because it is costly to acquire is used in the economic approach to explain the same kind of behavior that is explained by irrational and volatile behavior, or traditional behavior, or "nonrational" behavior in other discussions.

When an apparently profitable opportunity to a firm, worker, or household is not exploited, the economic approach does not take refuge in assertions about irrationality, contentment with wealth already acquired, or convenient ad hoc shifts in values (i.e., preferences). Rather it postulates the existence of costs, monetary or psychic, of taking advantage of these opportunities that eliminate their profitability—costs that may not be easily "seen" by outside observers. Of course, postulating the existence of costs closes or "completes" the economic approach in the same, almost tautological, way that postulating the existence of (sometimes unobserved) uses of energy completes the energy system, and preserves the law of the conservation of energy. Systems of analysis in chemistry, genetics, and other fields are completed in a related manner. The critical question is whether a system is completed in a useful way; the important theorems derived from the economic approach indicate that it has been completed in a way that yields much more than a bundle of empty tautologies in good part because, as I indicated earlier, the assumption of stable preferences provides a foundation for predicting the responses to various changes.

Moreover, the economic approach does not assume that decisions units are necessarily conscious of their efforts to maximize or can verbalize or otherwise describe in an informative way reasons for the systematic patterns in their behavior.[11] Thus it is consistent with the emphasis on the subconscious in modern psychology and with the distinction between manifest and latent functions in sociology (Merton 1968). In addition, the economic approach does not draw conceptual distinctions between major and minor decisions, such as those involving life and death[12] in contrast to the choice of a brand of coffee; or between decisions said to involve strong emotions and those with little emotional involvement,[13]

---

[10] The pioneering paper is Stigler's "The Economics of Information" (1961).

[11] This point is stressed in Milton Friedman's seminal article, "The Methodology of Positive Economics" (1953).

[12] The length of life itself is a decision variable in the important study by Grossman (1972).

[13] Jeremy Bentham said "As to the proposition that passion does not calculate, this, like most of these very general and oracular propositions is not true . . . . I would not say that even a madman does not calculate. Passion calculates, more or less, in every man" (1963). He does add, however, that "of all passions, the most given to calculation . . . [is] the motive of pecuniary interest."

such as in choosing a mate or the number of children in contrast to buying paint; or between decisions by persons with different incomes, education, or family backgrounds.

Indeed, I have come to the position that the economic approach is a comprehensive one that is applicable to all human behavior, be it behavior involving money prices or imputed shadow prices, repeated or infrequent decisions, large or minor decisions, emotional or mechanical ends, rich or poor persons, men or women, adults or children, brilliant or stupid persons, patients or therapists, businessmen or politicians, teachers or students. The applications of the economic approach so conceived are as extensive as the scope of economics in the definition given earlier that emphasizes scarce means and competing ends. It is an appropriate approach to go with such a broad and unqualified definition, and with the statement by Shaw that begins this essay.

For whatever its worth in evaluating this conclusion, let me indicate that I did not arrive at it quickly. In college I was attracted by the problems studied by sociologists and the analytical techniques used by economists. These interests began to merge in my doctoral study,[14] which used economic analysis to understand racial discrimination (see chapter 2 and Becker 1971). Subsequently, I applied the economic approach to fertility, education, the uses of time, crime, marriage, social interactions, and other "sociological," "legal," and "political" problems. Only after long reflection on this work and the rapidly growing body of related work by others did I conclude that the economic approach was applicable to all human behavior.

The economic approach to human behavior is not new, even outside the market sector. Adam Smith often (but not always!) used this approach to understand political behavior. Jeremy Bentham was explicit about his belief that the pleasure-pain calculus is applicable to all human behavior: "Nature has placed mankind under the governance of two sovereign masters, *pain and pleasure.* It is for them alone to point out what we ought to do, as well as to determine what we shall do . . . . They govern us in all we do, in all we say, in all we think" (1963). The pleasure-pain calculus is said to be applicable to *all* we do, say, and think, without restriction to monetary decisions, repetitive choices, unimportant decisions, etc. Bentham did apply his calculus to an extremely wide range of human behavior, including criminal sanctions, prison reform, legislation, usury laws, and jurisprudence as well as the markets for goods and services. Although Bentham explicitly states that the pleasure-pain calculus is applicable to what we "shall" do as well as to what we "ought" to do, he was primarily interested in "ought"—he was first and foremost a reformer —and did not develop a theory of actual human behavior with many

[14] Actually, a little earlier in an essay that applied economic analysis to political behavior.

testable implications. He often became bogged down in tautologies because he did not maintain the assumption of stable preferences, and because he was more concerned about making his calculus consistent with all behavior than about deriving the restrictions it imposed on behavior.

Marx and his followers have applied what is usually called an "economic" approach to politics, marriage, and other nonmarket behavior as well as to market behavior. But to the Marxist, the economic approach means that the organization of production is decisive in determining social and political structure, and he places much emphasis upon material goods, processes, and ends, conflict between capitalists and workers, and general subjugation of one class by another. What I have called the "economic approach" has little in common with this view. Moreover, the Marxist, like the Benthamite, has concentrated on what ought to be, and has often emptied his approach of much predictive content in the effort to make it consistent with all events.

Needless to say, the economic approach has not provided equal insight into and understanding of all kinds of behavior: for example, the determinants of war and of many other political decisions have not yet been much illuminated by this approach (or by any other approach). I believe, however, that the limited success is mainly the result of limited effort and not lack of relevance. For, on the one hand, the economic approach has not been systematically applied to war, and its application to other kinds of political behavior is quite recent; on the other hand, much apparently equally intractable behavior—such as fertility, child-rearing, labor force participation, and other decisions of families—has been greatly illuminated in recent years by the systematic application of the economic approach.

The following essays, through the variety of subjects covered, and (I hope) the insights yielded, provide some support for the wide applicability of the economic approach. Greater support is provided by the extensive literature developed in the last twenty years that uses the economic approach to analyze an almost endlessly varied set of problems, including the evolution of language (Marschak 1965), church attendance (Azzi and Ehrenberg 1975), capital punishment (Ehrlich 1975), the legal system (Posner 1973, Becker and Landes 1974), the extinction of animals (Smith 1975), and the incidence of suicide (Hammermesh and Soss 1974). To convey dramatically the flavor of the economic approach, I discuss briefly three of the more unusual and controversial applications.

Good health and a long life are important aims of most persons, but surely no more than a moment's reflection is necessary to convince anyone that they are not the only aims: somewhat better health or a longer life may be sacrificed because they conflict with other aims. The economic approach implies that there is an "optimal" expected length of life, where the value in utility of an additional year is less than the utility foregone by using time and other resources to obtain that year. Therefore, a person may be a heavy smoker or so committed to work as to omit all exercise, not necessarily because he is ignorant of the consequences or "incapable" of using the information he possesses, but because the life-span forfeited is not worth the cost to him of quitting smoking or work-ing less intensively. These would be unwise decisions if a long life were the only aim, but as long as other aims exist, they could be informed and in this sense "wise."

According to the economic approach, therefore, *most* (if not all!) deaths are to some extent "suicides" in the sense that they could have been postponed if more resources had been invested in prolonging life. This not only has implications for the analysis of what are ordinarily called suicides,[15] but also calls into question the common distinction between suicides and "natural" deaths. Once again the economic approach and modern psychology come to similar conclusions since the latter emphasizes that a "death wish" lies behind many "accidental" deaths and others allegedly due to "natural" causes.

The economic approach does not merely restate in language familiar to economists different behavior with regard to health, removing all possi-bility of error by a series of tautologies. The approach implies, for example, that both health and medical care would rise as a person's wage rate rose, that aging would bring declining health although expenditures on medical care would rise, and that more education would induce an increase in health even though expenditures on medical care would fall. None of these or other implications are necessarily true, but all appear to be consistent with the available evidence.[16]

According to the economic approach, a person decides to marry when the utility expected from marriage exceeds that expected from remaining single or from additional search for a more suitable mate (see chapter 11). Similarly, a married person terminates his (or her) marriage when the utility anticipated from becoming single or marrying someone else exceeds the loss in utility from separation, including losses due to physical separa-tion from one's children, division of joint assets, legal fees, and so forth. Since many persons are looking for mates, a *market* in marriages can be said to exist: each person tries to do the best he can, given that everyone else in the market is trying to do the best they can. A sorting of persons into different marriages is said to be an equilibrium sorting if persons not married to each other in this sorting could not marry and make each better off.

Again, the economic approach has numerous implications about behavior that could be falsified. For example, it implies that "likes" tend to marry each other, when measured by intelligence, education, race, family background, height, and many other variables, and that "unlikes" marry when measured by wage rates and some other variables. The

---

[15] Some of these implications are developed in Hammermesh and Soss (1974).

[16] These implications are derived, and the evidence is examined, in Grossman (1971).

implication that men with relatively high wage rates marry women with relatively low wage rates (other variables being held constant) surprises many, but appears consistent with the available data when they are adjusted for the large fraction of married women who do not work (see chapter 11). The economic approach also implies that higher-income persons marry younger and divorce less frequently than others, implications consistent with the available evidence (see Keeley 1974) but not with common beliefs. Still another implication is that an increase in the relative earnings of wives increases the likelihood of marital dissolution, which partly explains the greater dissolution rate among black than white families.

According to the Heisenberg indeterminary principle, the phenomena analyzed by physical scientists cannot be observed in a "natural" state because their observations change these phenomena. An even stronger principle has been suggested for social scientists since they are participants as well as analysts and, therefore, are supposed to be incapable of objective observation. The economic approach makes a very different but distantly related point: namely that persons only choose to follow scholarly or other intellectual or artistic pursuits if they expect the benefits, both monetary and psychic, to exceed those available in alternative occupations. Since the criterion is the same as in the choice of more commonplace occupations, there is no obvious reason why intellectuals would be less concerned with personal rewards, more concerned with social well-being, or more intrinsically honest than others.[17]

It then follows from the economic approach that an increased demand by different interest groups or constituencies for particular intellectual arguments and conclusions would stimulate an increased supply of these arguments, by the theorem cited earlier on the effect of a rise in "price" on quantity supplied. Similarly, a flow of foundation or government funds into particular research topics, even "ill-advised" topics, would have no difficulty generating proposals for research on those topics. What the economic approach calls normal responses of supply to changes in demand, others may call intellectual or artistic "prostitution" when applied to intellectual or artistic pursuits. Perhaps, but attempts to distinguish sharply the market for intellectual and artistic services from the market for "ordinary" goods have been the source of confusion and inconsistency (see Director 1964, Coase 1974).

I am not suggesting that the economic approach is used by all economists for all human behavior or even by most economists for most. Indeed, many economists are openly hostile to all but the traditional applications. Moreover, economists cannot resist the temptation to hide their own lack of understanding behind allegations of irrational behavior, unnecessary

[17] This example is taken from Stigler (1976). Also see the discussion of the reward system in science and of related issues in Merton (1973, esp. part 4).

ignorance, folly, ad hoc shifts in values, and the like, which is simply acknowledging defeat in the guise of considered judgment. For example, if some Broadway theater owners charge prices that result in long delays before seats are available, the owners are alleged to be ignorant of the profit-maximizing price structure rather than the analyst ignorant of why actual prices do maximize profits. When only a portion of the variation in earnings among individuals is explained, the unexplained portion is attributed to luck or chance,[18] not to ignorance of or inability to measure additional systematic components. The coal industry is called inefficient because certain cost and output calculations point in that direction (see Henderson 1958), although an attractive alternative hypothesis is that the calculations are seriously in error.

War is said to be caused by madmen, and political behavior, more generally, dominated by folly and ignorance. Recall Keynes's remark about "madmen in authority, who hear voices in the air" (1962, p. 383), and although Adam Smith, the principal founder of the economic approach, interpreted some laws and legislation in the same way that he interpreted market behavior, even he, without much discussion, lamely dismissed others as a result of folly and ignorance.[19]

Examples abound in the economic literature of changes in preferences conveniently introduced ad hoc to explain puzzling behavior. Education is said to change preferences—about different goods and services, political candidates, or family size—rather than real income or the relative cost of different choices.[20] Businessmen talk about the social responsibilities of business because their attitudes are said to be influenced by public discussions of this question rather than because such talk is necessary to maximize their profits, given the climate of public intervention. Or advertisers are alleged to take advantage of the fragility of consumer preferences, with little explanation of why, for example, advertising is heavier in some industries than others, changes in importance in a given industry over time, and occurs in quite competitive industries as well as in monopolistic ones.[21]

Naturally, what is tempting to economists nominally committed to the economic approach becomes irresistible to others without this commitment,

[18] An extreme example is Jencks (1972). Jencks even grossly understates the portion that can be explained because he neglects the important work by Mincer and others (see especially Mincer [1974]).

[19] See Stigler (1971). Smith does not indicate why ignorance is dominant in the passage of certain laws and not others.

[20] For an interpretation of the effects of education on consumption entirely in terms of income and price effects, Michael (1972).

[21] For an analysis of advertising that is consistent with stable preferences, and implies that advertising might even be more important in competitive than monopolistic industries, see Stigler and Becker (1974). For a good discussion of advertising that also does not rely on shifts in preferences, see Nelson (1975).

and without a commitment to the scientific study of sociology, psychology, or anthropology. With an ingenuity worthy of admiration if put to better use, almost any conceivable behavior is alleged to be dominated by ignorance and irrationality, values and their frequent unexplained shifts, custom and tradition, the compliance somehow induced by social norms, or the ego and the id.

I do not mean to suggest that concepts like the ego and the id, or social norms, are without any scientific content. Only that they are tempting materials, as are concepts in the economic literature, for ad hoc and useless explanations of behavior. There is no apparent embarrassment in arguing, for example, both that the sharp rise in fertility during the late 1940s and early 1950s resulted from a renewed desire for large families, and that the prolonged decline starting just a few years later resulted from a reluctance to be tied down with many children. Or developing countries are supposed simply to copy the American's "compulsiveness" about time, whereas the growing value of their own time is a more fruitful explanation of their increased effort to economize in their use of time (see chapter 5). More generally, custom and tradition are said to be abandoned in developing countries because their young people are seduced by Western ways; it is not recognized that while custom and tradition are quite useful in a relatively stationary environment, they are often a hindrance in a dynamic world, especially for young people (see Stigler and Becker 1974).

Even those believing that the economic approach is applicable to all human behavior recognize that many noneconomic variables also significantly affect human behavior. Obviously, the laws of mathematics, chemistry, physics, and biology have a tremendous influence on behavior through their influence on preferences and productions possibilities. That the human body ages, that the rate of population growth equals the birth rate plus the migration rate minus the death rate, that children of more intelligent parents tend to be more intelligent than children of less intelligent parents, that people need to breathe to live, that a hybrid plant has a particular yield under one set of environmental conditions and a very different yield under another set, that gold and oil are located only in certain parts of the world and cannot be made from wood, or that an assembly line operates according to certain physical laws—all these and more influence choices, the production of people and goods, and the evolution of societies.

To say this, however, is not the same as saying that, for example, the rate of population growth is itself "noneconomic" in the sense that birth, migration, and death rates cannot be illuminated by the economic approach, or that the rate of adoption of new hybrids is "noneconomic" because it cannot be explained by the economic approach. Indeed, useful implications about the number of children in different families have been obtained by assuming that families maximize their utility from stable preferences subject to a constraint on their resources and prices, with resources and prices partly determined by the gestation period for pregnancies, the abilities of children, and other noneconomic variables (see chapters 9 and 10; see also Schultz 1975). Similarly, the rate of adoption of hybrid corn in different parts of the United States has been neatly explained by assuming that farmers maximize profits: new hybrids were more profitable, and thus adopted earlier, in some parts because weather, soil, and other physical conditions were more favorable (Griliches 1957).

Just as many noneconomic variables are necessary for understanding human behavior, so too are the contributions of sociologists, psychologists, sociobiologists, historians, anthropologists, political scientists, lawyers, and others. Although I am arguing that the economic approach provides a useful framework for understanding all human behavior, I am not trying to downgrade the contributions of other social scientists, nor even to suggest that the economist's are more important. For example, the preferences that are given and stable in the economic approach, and that determine the predictions from this approach, are analyzed by the sociologist, psychologist, and probably most successfully by the sociobiologist (see Wilson 1975). How preferences have become what they are, and their perhaps slow evolution over time, are obviously relevant in predicting and understanding behavior. The value of other social sciences is not diminished even by an enthusiastic and complete acceptance of the economic approach.

At the same time, however, I do not want to soften the impact of what I am saying in the interest of increasing its acceptability in the short run. I am saying that the economic approach provides a valuable unified framework for understanding *all* human behavior, although I recognize, of course, that much behavior is not yet understood, and that noneconomic variables and the techniques and findings from other fields contribute significantly to the understanding of human behavior. That is, although a comprehensive *framework* is provided by the economic approach, many of the important concepts and techniques are provided and will continue to be provided by other disciplines.

The heart of my argument is that human behavior is not compartmentalized, sometimes based on maximizing, sometimes not, sometimes motivated by stable preferences, sometimes by volatile ones, sometimes resulting in an optimal accumulation of information, sometimes not. Rather, all human behavior can be viewed as involving participants who maximize their utility from a stable set of preferences and accumulate an optimal amount of information and other inputs in a variety of markets.

If this argument is correct, the economic approach provides a unified framework for understanding behavior that has long been sought by and eluded Bentham, Comte, Marx, and others. The reader of the following essays will judge for himself the power of the economic approach.

Part 2   Price and Prejudice

The essay in this section is taken from my book *The Economics of Discrimination*, first published in 1957, which was a greatly revised version of a 1955 Ph.D. dissertation with the more attractive title "Discrimination in the Market Place." It was my first published effort to apply the economic approach to a problem outside of conventional fields of economics, and was greeted with indifference or hostility by the overwhelming majority of the economics profession. (In 1956 a prominent young economist expressed surprise at learning that I was working on racial discrimination, saying that I was supposed to be a neo-classical type economist. My attempt to explain why my study was an application of neo-classical economics was greeted very skeptically.) The reception among some sociologists and other social scientists was, on the other hand, surprisingly (to me!) favorable, at least to judge by their book reviews.

In the mid-sixties, stimulated by the civil rights movement, economists began seriously to study racial discrimination and, a few years later, discrimination against women. Numerous studies since then have applied the economic approach to different minorities, and "minority economics" is a thriving field today.

2   Effective Discrimination

An MDC between any two groups can be defined for a particular labor or capital market or for all markets combined; in the latter, interest would center on the effect of discrimination on the total incomes of these groups. For example, discrimination by whites presumably reduces the income of Negroes, but how does it affect their own incomes? Many writers have asserted that discrimination in the market place by whites is in their own self-interest; i.e., it is supposed to raise their incomes. If this were correct, it would be in the self-interest of Negroes to "retaliate" against whites by discriminating against them, since this should raise Negro incomes. If, on the other hand, discrimination by whites reduces their own incomes as well, is the percentage reduction in their incomes greater or less than that in Negro incomes? It is an implicit assumption of most discussions that minority groups like Negroes usually suffer more from market discrimination than do majority groups like whites, but no one has isolated the fundamental structural reasons why this is so. It is shown in the following that discrimination by any group W reduces their own incomes as well as N's, and thus retaliation by N makes it worse for N rather than better. It is also shown why minorities suffer much more from discrimination than do majorities.

1. The Model

New insights are gained and the analysis made simpler if the discussion is phrased in terms of trade between two "societies," one inhabited solely by N, the other by W. Government and monopolies are ignored for the

Adapted from *The Economics of Discrimination*, 2d ed. (University of Chicago Press, 1971). © 1957, 1971, by The University of Chicago.

present, as the analysis is confined to perfectly competitive societies. Since our emphasis here is on the over-all incomes of W and N, the multiplicity of factors of production will also be ignored, and the discussion will be confined to two homogeneous factors in each society—labor and capital— with each unit of labor and capital in N being a perfect substitute in *production* for each unit of labor and capital in W. These societies do not "trade" commodities but factors of production used in producing commodities. Each society finds it advantageous to "export" its relatively abundant factors: W exports capital, and N labor. The amount of labor exported by N at a given rate of exchange of labor for capital is the difference between the total amount of labor in N and the amount used "domestically"; the amount of capital exported by W is derived in a similar manner.

The following conditions would be satisfied in a full equilibrium with no discrimination: (*a*) payment to each factor would be independent of whether it was employed with N or W; (*b*) the price of each product would be independent of whether it was produced by N or W; and (*c*) the unit payment to each factor would equal its marginal value product. If members of W develop a desire to discriminate against labor and capital owned by N, they become willing to forfeit money income in order to avoid working with N. This taste for discrimination reduces the net return[1] that W capital can receive by combining with N labor, and this leads to a reduction in the amount of W capital exported. Since this, in turn, reduces the income that N labor can receive by combining with W capital, less N labor is also exported. In the new equilibrium, then, less labor and capital are exported by N and W, respectively. It can be shown that this change in resource allocation reduces the equilibrium net incomes of both N and W.[2] Since discrimination by W hurts W as well as N, it cannot be a subtle means by which W augments its net command of economic goods.[3]

---

[1] If W wants to discriminate, exported capital must receive a higher equilibrium money return than domestically used capital, to compensate for working with N labor. However, if all W has the same taste for discrimination, the equilibrium net return must be the same for all W capital. Net and money returns to domestic capital are identical, since there are no psychic costs to working with W labor; therefore, the equilibrium money return to domestic capital can be used as the equilibrium net return to all W capital. The money and net returns to all W labor are the same, since it works only with W capital.

[2] See the appendix to this chapter.

[3] If we compare discrimination with tariffs, we find that, although some of their effects are similar, other effects are quite different. Discrimination always decreases both societies' net incomes, while a tariff of the appropriate size can, as Bickerdike long ago pointed out, increase the levying society's net income. A tariff operates by driving a wedge between the price a society pays for imported goods and the price each individual member pays; it does not create any distinction between net income and total command over goods. Discrimination does create such a distinction and does not drive a wedge between private and social prices. Discrimination has more in common with transportation costs than with tariffs.

2. Discrimination and Capitalists

Although the aggregate net incomes of W and N are reduced by discrimination, all factors are not affected in the same way: the return to W capital and N labor decreases, but the return to W labor and N capital actually increases. There is a remarkable agreement in the literature on the proposition that capitalists from the dominant group are the major beneficiaries of prejudice and discrimination in a competitive capitalistic economic system.[4] If W is considered to represent whites or some other dominant group, the fallacious nature of this proposition becomes clear, since discrimination *harms* W capitalists and benefits W workers. The most serious non sequitur in the mistaken analyses is the (explicit or implicit) conclusion that, if tastes for discrimination cause N laborers to receive a lower wage rate than W laborers, the difference between these wage rates must accrue as "profits" to W capitalists.[5] These profits would exist only if this wage differential resulted from price discrimination (due to monopsony power), rather than from a taste for discrimination.

3. Discrimination and Segregation

Trade between two societies is maximized when there is no discrimination, and it decreases with all increases in discrimination. Tastes for discrimination might become so large that it would no longer pay to trade; each society would be in economic isolation and would have to get along with its own resources. Since members of each society would be working only with each other, complete economic isolation would also involve *complete* economic *segregation*. More generally, since an increase in discrimination decreases trade and since a decrease in trade means an increase in economic segregation, an increase in discrimination must be accompanied by an increase in segregation.

The total MDC against N is defined as the difference between the actual

---

[4] Saenger, a psychologist, said: "Discriminatory practices appear to be of definite advantage for the representatives of management in a competitive economic system" (1953, p. 96). Allport, another psychologist, likewise said: "We conclude, therefore, that the Marxist theory of prejudice is far too simple, even though it points a sure finger at *one* of the factors involved in prejudice, viz., rationalized self-interest of the upper classes" (1955, p. 210). Similar statements can be found in Rose (1951), p. 7; and throughout Cox (1948), Dollard (1937), McWilliams (1948), Aptheker (1946); and many other books as well.

[5] D. A. Wilkerson, in his Introduction to Aptheker's book, said: "Precisely this same relationship between material interests and Negro oppression exists today. . . . The per capita annual income of southern Negro tenant farmers and day laborers in 1930 was about $71, as compared with $97 for similar white workers. Multiply this difference of $26 by the 1,205,000 Negro tenants and day laborers on southern farms in 1930, and it is seen that planters 'saved' approximately $31,000,000 by the simple device of paying Negro workers less than they paid white workers" (Aptheker 1946, p. 10).

ratio of the incomes of W and N and this ratio without discrimination.[6]
There is "effective discrimination" against N whenever this MDC is
positive. If effective discrimination occurs against N at all levels of discrimination by W, the income of N relative to W must be less when completely isolated from W than when freely trading with W; under these
circumstances, N gains more from trade than W does.

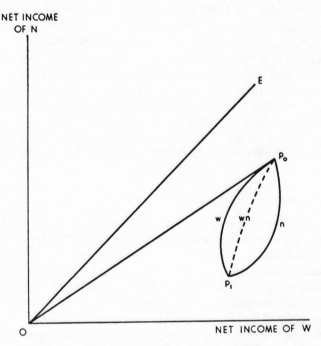

FIG. 1.—The effect of discrimination on incomes

It is proved in the appendix to this chapter that if effective discrimination occurs against N at all levels of discrimination by W, the absolute and
relative income of N declines continuously as discrimination increases.
This is shown in figure 1, in which the horizontal axis measures W's and
the vertical axis N's net income; p_0 represents their incomes when there
is no discrimination, p_1 when there is complete segregation, and the curve
$p_0 w p_1$ when there are different amounts of discrimination by W. We
have assumed that effective discrimination always occurs against N;
therefore, $p_0 w p_1$ is never above the line $o p_0$. The total MDC against N
increases as discrimination increases; incomes reach a *minimum* and the

[6] Let $\dot{Y}(N)$ and $Y(W)$ represent the actual incomes of N and W, and $Y_0(N)$ and
$Y_0(W)$ their incomes without discrimination. The total MDC is defined as

$$\text{MDC} = \frac{Y(W)}{Y(N)} - \frac{Y_0(W)}{Y_0(N)}.$$

total MDC a *maximum* when tastes for discrimination become sufficiently large to preclude any trade between W and N. This conclusion is very relevant to a proposal that has stimulated considerable discussion in the past, namely, that minority groups should avoid discrimination from the majority by completely segregating themselves, economically and otherwise.[7] If the minority is identified with N and the majority with W, this analysis demonstrates that complete segregation reduces the absolute and relative income of the minority and therefore increases, rather than decreases, the market discrimination against it. Effective discrimination occurs against a minority partly because it gains so much by "trading" with the majority; accordingly, complete segregation does not avoid the bad economic effects of discrimination but only multiplies them.

4. Discrimination and Economic Minorities

I have shown that a necessary and sufficient condition for effective discrimination to occur against N at all levels of discrimination by W is[8]

$$\frac{Y_0(W)}{Y_0(N)} > \frac{l_n}{l_w}, \tag{1}$$

where l_n and l_w represent the amount of labor supplied by N and W, and $Y_0(W)$ and $Y_0(N)$ represent the aggregate incomes of W and N in the absence of discrimination. If N is a numerical minority, $l_n < l_w$[9] and $c_n < c_w$,[10] where c_n and c_w represent the amount of capital supplied by N and W. Therefore

$$\frac{Y_0(W)}{Y_0(N)} > 1, \tag{2}$$

and a fortiori that inequality (1) holds. Inequality (2) states that N's income is less than W's and hence that N is an economic minority. Therefore, if N is a numerical minority, it is also an economic minority, and effective discrimination must occur against it. If N is not a numerical minority, inequalities (1) and (2) no longer necessarily hold; they hold only if N is more of an economic minority than W is a numerical minority.[11]

---

[7] In the 1920s there was a large movement, under the leadership of Marcus Garvey, to take Negroes in America back to Africa to "escape from" discrimination. This conclusion is also helpful in understanding some effects of "Apartheid."

[8] See the appendix to this chapter.

[9] If N is a numerical minority, the amount of labor owned by $N(l'_n)$ is less than that owned by $W(l'_w)$. The amount supplied to the market is $l_n = a_n l'_n$ and $l_w = a_w l'_w$. If $a_n = a_w$, $l'_n < l'_w$ implies $l_n < l_w$. More generally, $l'_n < l'_w$ implies $l_n < l_w$ if, and only if, $a_n/a_w < l'_w/l'_n$. This seems like a plausible restriction and is implicit in the inferences drawn in the text.

[10] N exports labor if, and only if, $l_n/l_w > c_n/c_w$. If $l_n < l_w$, then $c_n < c_w$.

[11] This statement is completely rigorous only if $a_n = a_w$.

It turns out, then, that a necessary condition for effective discrimination against N is that N be an economic minority; a sufficient condition is that N be a numerical minority; a necessary *and* sufficient condition is that N be more of an economic minority than a numerical majority. It has long been recognized that discrimination is closely connected with the minorities question, the emphasis being put on the inadequate political representation of numerical minorities. This analysis of discrimination in competitive free-enterprise societies also uses a minority-majority framework, but the concept of economic minorities is somewhat more important here than that of numerical ones. It seems reasonable that economic discrimination in competitive societies be related to economic minorities, and political discrimination to political minorities.

5. Discrimination in the Real World

(a) Negroes in the United States

Only about 10 percent of the total population of the United States is Negro; hence the amount of labor they supply is substantially less than the amount supplied by whites. Moreover, Negroes must be a net "exporter" of labor, since they clearly have more labor relative to capital than do the whites. These two conditions imply (by n. 10 and inequality [1]) that tastes for discrimination would produce—via the workings of a competitive economic system—effective discrimination against Negroes. There is evidence not only that effective discrimination occurs against Negroes but also that the total MDC is quite large. Negroes in the United States have owned an extremely small amount of capital, while whites have had a more balanced distribution of resources;[12] a substantial decline in the amount of white capital available to Negroes would greatly reduce the absolute and relative incomes of Negroes.

Estimates could be made of the economic loss to various groups resulting from discrimination in the market place if there were knowledge of the actual quantity of discrimination, the nature of production functions, and the amount of labor and capital supplied. A general technique for making these estimates will be illustrated by an example that also roughly indicates the magnitude of the economic loss to Negroes and whites in the United States resulting from discrimination in the market place by whites.

The production function is assumed to be of the following (Cobb-Douglas) form

$$X = kl^r c^{1-r},$$

---

[12] Some mutual interaction may have occurred here, since poverty is a cause, as well as a result, of an unbalanced distribution of resources. For example, poor individuals often find it very difficult to obtain funds for investments in themselves.

with $r = \frac{2}{3}$. The amount of labor supplied by whites is taken as 9 times that supplied by Negroes, and of capital as 150 times.[13] Since units of measurement can be chosen at will, Negroes are assumed to have one unit of both labor and capital; these assumptions state that $l_n = 1$, $c_n = 1$, $l_w = 9$, and $c_w = 150$. If there were no discrimination, the incomes of Negroes and whites would be $Y_0(N) = 1.7$ and $Y_0(W) = 23.5$, and whites would export 14 units of capital; if discrimination were sufficiently large to cause complete segregation, their incomes would be $Y_1(N) = 1.0$ and $Y_1(W) = 23.2$ (see section 4 above). The maximum reduction in the income of Negroes is about 40 percent; the income of whites would be reduced by an almost imperceptible amount. With no discrimination, Negro per capita incomes would be about 66 percent of those of whites, and, with complete segregation, about 39 percent of those of whites.

The actual equilibrium position falls somewhere between these two extremes. If discrimination reduces the amount of capital exported by whites by about 40 percent, they would actually export 8 rather than 14 units of capital; Negro and white incomes would be 1.5 and 23.3, and thus per capita Negro incomes would be 57 percent of per capita white incomes. An MDC against Negro labor can be defined as the percentage difference between actual white and Negro net wage rates; an MDC against Negro capital as the percentage difference between actual white and Negro net rents on capital. These MDC's would be $+0.21$ and -0.31, respectively; hence the return to labor would be greater for whites, and the return to capital would be greater for Negroes. White labor and Negro capital gain from discrimination, and white capital and Negro labor lose from it; but, since the net loss of Negroes is greater than that of whites, total market discrimination occurs against Negroes. Discrimination in the market place by whites reduces Negro incomes by 13 percent, or, to put this in other words, Negro incomes would increase 16 percent if market discrimination ceased. Discrimination reduces the incomes of whites by a negligible amount because they gain very little from trading with Negroes.

The estimated economic loss to Negroes would be greater if the production function was more capital-intensive, if white capital was larger

---

[13] This considers capital invested in humans as capital and not labor. If it were considered as labor, the assumption that Negro and white labor were perfect substitutes in production would be untenable, since whites have more capital invested in themselves than Negroes have. Since the number of Negroes in the labor force is about one-ninth the number of whites, the assumption that white labor is nine times that of Negro is reasonable if the innate capacities of whites and Negroes are roughly the same. The ratio of white to Negro capital was arrived at essentially by a guess. Our model implies that Negroes in the United States "export" unskilled labor to whites and that whites "export" capital—including skilled labor—to Negroes.

relative to Negro capital, or if discrimination reduced the amount of capital exported by more than 40 percent. Likewise, the estimated loss would be smaller if the opposite conditions were assumed. Inadequate knowledge of these variables makes it impossible to estimate this loss precisely, and 16 percent is an extremely rough estimate. The economic loss to Negroes seems substantial and important, although a far cry from the loss assumed in some discussions.[14]

It is often explicitly or implicitly assumed that the total MDC against Negroes is very large (to use the terms of this study); explanations have emphasized political discrimination, class warfare, monopolies, and market imperfections. My analysis shows that none of these influences is necessary, since substantial market discrimination against Negroes in the United States could easily result from the manner in which individual tastes for discrimination allocate resources within a competitive free-enterprise framework. The United States is often considered the best example of a country using competition to determine economic values. This implies that monopolies, political discrimination, and the like, are, at most, secondary determinants of market discrimination and that individual tastes for discrimination operating within a competitive framework constitute the primary determinant.

(b) Nonwhites in South Africa

In South Africa, nonwhites are about 80 percent of the total population; this is taken to mean that l_n is roughly four times l_w (see inequality [1]). Since nonwhites are a numerical majority, effective discrimination does not *necessarily* occur against them; it would occur if aggregate white net

---

[14] I have come across only one clear and explicit attempt to estimate the economic costs of discrimination. The technique used is clearly stated in the following paragraph:

"The results of these calculations represent a shocking reminder of the real costs of discrimination to our country in production, expressed in dollars and cents terms. We found that the average annual income of the Negro family is $1043. The average income for Whites is $3062, or roughly three times that of Negroes. And, when the difference in income is multiplied by the number of Negro family units which could add to the productive wealth of the nation, we discovered the appalling loss of four billion dollars of real wealth annually because of discrimination against Negroes alone" (Roper 1948, p. 18).

Roper's implicit assumption that Negroes and whites would receive the same income without discrimination is a mistake: whites would receive larger incomes than Negroes because they have much more capital per capita. In the example used here, eliminating all discrimination would raise per capita Negro incomes to only 66 percent of per capita white incomes. This mistake partly explains why Roper assumed that Negro incomes would increase by 200 percent, this being about ten times my estimated increase. On the other hand, his implicit assumption that whites suffer a negligible economic loss is correct.

incomes were at least four times aggregate nonwhite net incomes.[15] The very crude available evidence suggests that aggregate white net incomes are much more than four times those of nonwhites.[16] Therefore, tastes for discrimination in the private economic sector alone seems to have produced effective discrimination against nonwhites. The South African government has been active in regulating the economic activities of nonwhites. For this reason the market discrimination produced by the competitive economic sector *may* be less important than that produced by other sources; but it need not be, since it alone could be quite large.

6. Discrimination by Minorities

N may discriminate, in our model, by distinguishing between W and N capital; the money return for working with W capital must be sufficient to offset the psychic costs of doing so. A general analysis incorporating discrimination by both W and N could be developed, but there is no point in going into the details of this beyond stressing one important relationship. W's net income is uniquely determined by the amount of capital exported; discrimination determines this amount, and the latter alone determines W's income. N's net income depends on the amount of capital imported and its own taste for discrimination. For a given amount imported, N's net income is maximized if it is indifferent between indigenous and imported capital; the greater the preference for indigenous capital, the smaller the net income. Hence, given W's net income and thus the amount of capital exported, N's net income is smaller, the greater the discrimination. Therefore, if both N and W discriminate, inequality (1) is sufficient but not necessary for effective discrimination always to occur against N; any necessary and sufficient condition would depend on the relative amount of discrimination by N. Consider figure 1 again. The curve p_0np_1 represents

---

[15] Inequality (1) refers to white and nonwhite incomes in equilibrium without discrimination; yet the condition stated above is in terms of actual net income with discrimination. However, there is no contradiction between these statements, since this condition implies inequality (1). If there were effective discrimination against *whites*, their relative net income would be less with discrimination than without it; so that, if their actual net incomes were at least four times those of nonwhites, their incomes without discrimination would also be at least four times those of nonwhites. But, by inequality (1), this implies that there must be effective discrimination against nonwhites rather than against whites. Consequently, if white net incomes were at least four times those of nonwhites, there must be effective discrimination against nonwhites.

[16] See the study of native income by Houghton and Philcox (1950, pp. 418–38) and the data giving the national income of South Africa in the report of the United Nations Statistical Office (1950). These income figures overestimate the net incomes of whites and nonwhites, since the nonmonetary costs of working with each other have not been netted out of the gross production figures. It is unlikely, although not impossible, that the true net incomes of whites are less than four times those of nonwhites.

the incomes of N and W for different levels of discrimination by N, and it must be below $p_0 w p_1$ at all points except p_0 and p_1. If both W and N discriminate, the point representing their incomes would be in the area bounded by $p_0 n p_1 w$; the curve $p_0 w n p_1$ summarizes a set of situations in which W discriminates more than N does.

Minority groups are often tempted to "retaliate" against discrimination from others by returning the discrimination. This is a mistake, since effective economic discrimination occurs against them, not because of the distribution of tastes but because of the distribution of resources. That is, majorities have a more balanced distribution of labor and capital than they do. Figure 1 clearly shows that, although N is hurt by W's discrimination, it is hurt even more by its own discrimination.

7. Mathematical Appendix

Call the net (=money) return to domestic labor and capital in W, $\pi_l(W)$ and $\pi_c(W)$. In a competitive equilibrium position the return to each factor equals its marginal productivity: hence

$$\pi_c(W) = \frac{\partial f}{\partial c}(c = c_w - c_t; l = l_w) = \frac{\partial f}{\partial c}(c_w - c_t; l_w),$$

$$\pi_l(W) = \frac{\partial f}{\partial l}(c = c_w - c_t; l = l_w) = \frac{\partial f}{\partial l}(c_w - c_t; l_w),$$

where f is the production function in W; c_w and l_w are the total amount of labor and capital supplied by W; and c_t is the amount of capital exported. By footnote 1 of this chapter the equilibrium net income of W is

$$Y(W) = c_w \pi_c(W) + l_w \pi_l(W)$$

$$= c_w \frac{\partial f}{\partial c}(c_w - c_t; l_w) + l_w \frac{\partial f}{\partial l}(c_w - c_t; l_w).$$

N allocates its labor between W and N capital, with the intent of equalizing its marginal physical product in both uses. The equilibrium net income of N is

$$Y(N) = c_n \pi_c(N) + l_n \pi_l(N)$$

$$= c_n \frac{\partial f'}{\partial c}(c_n + c_t; l_n) + l_n \frac{\partial f'}{\partial l}(c_n + c_t; l_n),$$

where f' is the production function in N, and c_n and l_n are the total amount of labor and capital supplied by N. The impact of discrimination on $Y(W)$ and $Y(N)$ could be determined by explicitly introducing tastes for discrimination; however, the analysis is simpler with another approach.

An increase in discrimination by W decreases the quantity of capital exported, and therefore the latter is a monotonic function of W's taste for discrimination.

It can be shown that if f and f' are homogeneous of the first degree,

$$\frac{\partial Y(W)}{\partial c_t} > 0, \tag{A1}$$

$$\frac{\partial Y(N)}{\partial c_t} > 0, \tag{A1'}$$

and thus discrimination by W reduces the net incomes of both N and W. Inequality (A1) can be proved thus: If a function is homogeneous of the first degree, all first-order partial derivatives are homogeneous of zero degree; in particular, $\partial f/\partial c$ is homogeneous of zero degree. By Euler's theorem for homogeneous functions,

$$c\frac{\partial(\partial f/\partial c)}{\partial c} + l\frac{\partial(\partial f/\partial c)}{\partial l} \equiv 0,$$

or

$$c\frac{\partial^2 f}{\partial c^2} + l\frac{\partial^2 f}{\partial l \partial c} \equiv 0. \tag{A2}$$

According to a well-known theorem on the derivative of a function of a function,

$$\frac{\partial f}{\partial c_t} \equiv \frac{\partial f}{\partial c}\frac{\partial c}{\partial c_t}.$$

Since $c = c_w - c_t$, then $\partial c/\partial c_t = -1$, and

$$\frac{\partial f}{\partial c_t} \equiv -\frac{\partial f}{\partial c}. \tag{A3}$$

It follows from identity (A3) that

$$\frac{\partial Y(W)}{\partial c_t} \equiv l\frac{\partial^2 f}{\partial l \partial c_t} - c_w\frac{\partial^2 f}{\partial c_t^2}, \tag{A4}$$

and from identities (A2) and (A3) that

$$c\frac{\partial^2 f}{\partial c_t^2} \equiv l\frac{\partial^2 f}{\partial l \partial c_t}. \tag{A5}$$

By substituting identity (A5) in identity (A4), one obtains

$$\frac{\partial Y(W)}{\partial c_t} \equiv -c_t\frac{\partial^2 f}{\partial c_t^2}. \tag{A6}$$

If there is diminishing marginal productivity, $\partial^2 f / \partial c_t^2 < 0$. Since $c_t \geq 0$, it must follow that

$$\frac{\partial Y(W)}{\partial c_t} \geq 0. \qquad \text{Q.E.D.}$$

Inequality (A1′) can be proved in the same way.

By looking at the problem in a slightly different way, it is possible to acquire an intuitive understanding of this result. Suppose labor enters the United States from abroad and that some United States capital (c_t) is employed with this labor. A well-known economic theorem states that United States citizens must (economically) benefit from immigration as long as there is diminishing marginal productivity of labor, since intra-marginal immigrants raise the productivity of American capital. The net income of United States citizens is an increasing function of the amount of immigration, which can be measured by c_t, the amount of capital employed with immigrants. This discussion shows that treating discrimination as a problem in trade and migration is far from artificial, since they are closely and profoundly related.

Let us define

$$R = \frac{Y(N)}{Y(W)}.$$

Then

$$\frac{\partial R}{\partial c_t} = \frac{Y(W)[\partial Y(N)/\partial c_t] - Y(N)[\partial Y(W)/\partial c_t]}{[Y(W)]^2},$$

or, from identity (A6),

$$\frac{\partial R}{\partial c_t} = \frac{Y(W)[-c_t(\partial^2 f'/\partial c_t^2)] - Y(N)[-c_t(\partial^2 f/\partial c_t^2)]}{[Y(W)]^2}.$$

Hence

$$\frac{\partial R}{\partial c_t} \gtreqless 0 \qquad \text{as} \qquad Y(N) \frac{\partial^2 f}{\partial c_t^2} \gtreqless Y(W) \frac{\partial^2 f'}{\partial c_t^2}. \tag{A7}$$

If f were identical with f' and if there were no discrimination, the amount of capital exported would be just sufficient to equalize the equilibrium relative supply of factors "abroad" with the relative supply at "home." That is to say,

$$\frac{c_n + \hat{c}_t}{l_n} = \frac{c_w - \hat{c}_t}{l_w},$$

or

$$l_n = bl_w,$$

and

$$c_n + \hat{c}_t = b(c_w - \hat{c}_t).$$

Since $\partial f/\partial c_t$ is homogeneous of zero degree in c and l, $\partial^2 f/\partial c_t^2$ must be homogeneous of -1 degree in c and l,

$$\frac{\partial^2 f}{\partial c_t^2}\,(ac, al) = \frac{1}{a}\frac{\partial^2 f}{\partial c_t^2}\,(c, l),$$

where a is any number. If $c = c_w - \hat{c}_t$, $l = l_w$, and $a = b$, it follows that

$$\frac{\partial^2 f}{\partial c_t^2}\,(c_n + \hat{c}_t, l_n) = \frac{l_w}{l_n}\frac{\partial^2 f}{\partial c_t^2}\,(c_w - \hat{c}_t, l_w).$$

Substituting this in inequality (A7) and using the assumption of diminishing marginal productivity, we get the following simple condition:

$$\frac{\partial R}{\partial c_t/c_t = \hat{c}_t} \gtreqqless 0 \quad\text{as}\quad \frac{Y(N)}{Y(W)} \lesseqqgtr \frac{l_w}{l_n}, \tag{A8}$$

or

$$\frac{Y(W)}{Y(N)} \gtreqqless \frac{l_n}{l_w}.$$

If, in the absence of discrimination, N's relative income were less than W's relative supply of labor, a slight taste for discrimination by W would reduce N's income by a greater percentage than it would W's.

If $\partial R/(\partial c_t/c_t = \hat{c}_t) > 0$, $\partial R/\partial c_t$ would probably be greater than zero for all admissible values of c_t. For example, if

$$\frac{\partial R}{\partial c_t/c_t = \hat{c}_t} > 0 \quad\text{and}\quad \frac{\partial^3 f}{\partial c_t^3} > 0,$$

it would follow that

$$\frac{R}{c_t = \hat{c}_t - \varepsilon} < \frac{R}{c_t = \hat{c}_t},$$

where ε is a small positive number, and

$$\frac{\partial^2 f/(\partial c_t^2/c_t = \hat{c}_t - \varepsilon)}{\partial^2 f'/(\partial c_t^2/c_t = \hat{c}_t - \varepsilon)} < \frac{\partial^2 f/(\partial c_t^2/c_t = \hat{c}_t)}{\partial^2 f'/(\partial c_t^2/c_t = \hat{c}_t)} = 1.$$

Accordingly, if

$$R < \frac{\partial^2 f'/\partial c_t^2}{\partial^2 f/\partial c_t^2},$$

when $c_t = \hat{c}_t$, it must a fortiori be true when $c_t = \hat{c}_t - \varepsilon$. By continuing to reason along these lines, one would readily show that it must be true for all c_t.[17] This analysis is the basis for the assumption in this chapter and the rest of the appendix that an increase in discrimination by W must reduce N's net income relative to W's, if and only if

$$\frac{1}{R} = \frac{Y(W)}{Y(N)/c_t = \hat{c}_t} > \frac{l_n}{l_w}. \tag{A9}$$

If there are different tastes for discrimination among W (or N), some new problems enter the analysis; a few are mentioned now, and more are discussed in succeeding chapters. The unit money price of domestic W capital would not equal the unit net price of exported capital: capital on the margin between working with labor supplied by N and W would, of course, receive the same net return "abroad" and "domestically"; capital with smaller tastes for discrimination would find it advantageous to work with N. All capital working with W labor would receive the same net return, but capital with relatively small tastes for discrimination would receive a larger net return for working with N labor. It follows that net income as defined here would underestimate true net income, since it assumes that the net return to all capital is the same as the net return to marginal capital. The curve representing the net incomes of W and N for various levels of discrimination by W would touch $p_0 w p_1$ at p_0 and p_1 (in fig. 1) and would be to its right at intermediate positions.

Clearly, if inequality (A9) were satisfied, there still would be effective discrimination against N; but would it be a necessary condition even if W alone discriminates? Assume that the level of discrimination by W varies by proportionate changes in the average taste for discrimination and in the dispersion around the average. In a small neighborhood around the point p_0 the average would be of the same order of smalls as the dispersion. It is conjectured that in this neighborhood the difference between the net income of marginal and intra-marginal capital would be of a higher order of smalls. If this were true, the curve representing net incomes of W and N for various levels of discrimination by W would be tangent to $p_0 w p_1$ at p_0, and inequality (A9) would be necessary, as well as sufficient.

---

[17] Although production functions that are homogeneous of the first degree do not necessarily have positive third-order partial derivatives, a wide and important class of them does, e.g., all homogeneous Cobb-Douglas functions. In general, if f is homogeneous of the first degree, Euler's theorem states that

$$l\frac{\partial f}{\partial l} + c\frac{\partial f}{\partial c} \equiv X.$$

After twice differentiating this identity with respect to c, one gets

$$\frac{c\partial^3 f}{\partial c^3} + \frac{\partial^2 f}{\partial c^2} + \frac{l\partial^3 f}{\partial l\partial c^2} \equiv 0.$$

Since $\partial^2 f/\partial c^2 < 0$, $\partial^3 f/\partial c^3$ *must* be > 0 if $l\partial^3 f/\partial l\partial c^2 \leq 0$, and it *may* be > 0 if $\partial^3 f/\partial l\partial c^2 > 0$. It seems plausible that $\partial^3 f/\partial l\partial c^2 \leq 0$. In any case, the assumption that $\partial^3 f/\partial c^3 > 0$ is sufficient but not necessary for the conclusions reached above; it is necessary merely that $Y(W)/Y(N)$ increase at a faster rate than $(\partial^2 f/\partial c_t^2)/(\partial^2 f'/\partial c_t^2)$ as c_t decreases.

Part 3   Law and Politics

Stimulated mainly by Schumpeter's *Capitalism, Socialism and Democracy*, I wrote a paper in 1952 applying the economic approach to the political behavior of democracies, and submitted it to the *Journal of Political Economy*. After initial encouragement from the editor it was rejected because of an adverse referee report. Discouraged, I did nothing with this topic until I published in 1958 the much shorter and, in some ways, less satisfactory version that is included here. In the meantime, Anthony Downs (1957*a*) had published a much more comprehensive study that took a similar approach to political behavior. Downs's study has greatly influenced the work of political scientists as well as economists.

The paper on crime and punishment applies the economic approach to criminal behavior and public policy toward crime. It questions the prevailing intellectual view that imprisonment and other punishments are not effective in deterring crime, and discusses the trade-off between punishment and more effective apprehension of criminals, the relative merits of fines, imprisonments, and other kinds of punishment, and the goals of public policy toward crime. These issues are being vigorously debated currently as a result of the rapid growth in crime during the last two decades and the resulting dissatisfaction with many traditional answers about deterrence and criminal procedure.

3　Competition and Democracy

Economists have often argued that if an industry acts as a monopolist it would be desirable government policy either to break up the monopoly or, if this is undesirable because of increasing returns, to regulate and perhaps even nationalize it.[1] This proposition, although extremely well known and often accepted as obvious, turns out upon close examination to be far from obvious, and to involve several assumptions of doubtful validity. The argument supporting this proposition goes something as follows: Monopolies cause a maldistribution of resources, since the price charged by a monopolist exceeds marginal costs and an optimal distribution requires price equal to marginal cost. An optimal allocation would occur if the industry were made competitive, since price equals marginal costs in competitive industries. If the industry were a "natural" monopoly, price could be made equal to marginal cost either indirectly by government regulation or directly by government administration. Therefore, the recommendation is an anti-trust law to prevent or break up contrived monopolies and government regulation or government administration of natural monopolies.

The non-sequitur in this argument is the sentence beginning with "therefore"; the recommendation of government intervention does not follow from the demonstration that government intervention could improve matters. Demonstrating that a set of government decisions would improve matters is not the same as demonstrating that actual government decisions would do so. This kind of inference is logically equivalent to identifying the actual workings of the market sector with its ideal workings.

Reprinted from the *Journal of Law and Economics* 1 (1958): 105–9, © 1958 by The University of Chicago Law School, with an addendum.
[1] Simons (1948) vigorously argued that all "natural" monopolies (i.e., monopolies caused by increasing returns) should be nationalized by the state.

In section 1 a theory of the workings of a political democracy under ideal conditions is developed. It is shown that an ideal democracy is very similar to an ideal free enterprise system in the market place. That is, political decisions would be determined by the values of the electorate and the political sector would be run very efficiently. Section 2 tries to determine why actual democracies differ significantly from the ideal, and whether government regulation of private monopolies in actual democracies would improve matters.

1. Competition in Ideal Democracies

An ideal political democracy is defined as: *an institutional arrangement for arriving at political decisions in which individuals endeavor to acquire political office through perfectly free competition for the votes of a broadly based electorate.*[2] Three aspects of this definition warrant some discussion. No country could legitimately be called a political democracy unless a large fraction of its population could vote. Although "large" is a matter of degree, it is clear that countries have differed greatly; for example, 17th century England had much too narrow a franchise to qualify as a political democracy.

It is often said that the transfer of activities from the market place to the political sector would reduce the role of competition in organizing activities. In a political democracy individuals (or parties) do compete for political office—in, say, periodic elections—by offering platforms to the electorate. In an ideal political democracy competition is free in the sense that no appreciable costs or artificial barriers prevent an individual from running for office, and from putting a platform before the electorate. The transfer of activities from the market to the state in a political democracy does not necessarily reduce the amount of competition, but does change its form from competition by enterprises to competition by parties. Indeed, perfect competition is as necessary to an ideal political democracy as it is to an ideal free enterprise system. This suggests that the analysis of the workings of a free enterprise economy can be used to understand the workings of a political democracy.

The immediate aim of any political party is to be chosen by the electorate, just as the immediate aim of any firm is to be chosen by consumers. This immediate aim of the firm is consistent with a wide range of ultimate aims, such as the desire to help consumers (altruism) or the desire for economic power; the one most consistent with available data and most frequently used is the desire to maximize income or "profits." Likewise this immediate aim of the political party is consistent with many ultimate aims, such as the desire to help one's country (altruism) or the desire for prestige and

[2] For a similar definition, see Schumpeter (1942).

income; the one most frequently used[3] is the desire for power, which can be defined as the ability to influence behavior of others. Most of this paper requires only an assumption about the immediate aim of parties; at several points, however, the analysis is also related to some ultimate aims.

This definition has several important implications. First, it is easy to show that there must be freedom of speech and expression in ideal democracies. If an individual is free to offer a platform to the electorate, he is free to criticize the platform of others. Unless all possessed at least as much freedom as candidates they could increase their freedom merely by running for office. Since this situation is unstable they would ultimately have to possess as much freedom as candidates do.

Another important implication of this definition can be shown most simply by assuming that all voters have the same preferences. If the party in office did not adopt the policies preferred by the electorate, another party could gain more popular support by offering a platform closer to these preferences. Consequently, the only equilibrium platform would be one that perfectly satisfied these preferences. An ideal political democracy would be perfectly responsive to the "will" of the people.

Under certain assumptions, even if voters had different preferences, an ideal democracy would still be perfectly responsive to the "will" of the people. Assume that the political decision is to choose a value of a continuous numerical variable (a minimum wage rate, a utility's permitted rate of return, a discrimination coefficient, etc.). Each voter's preference is measured by one value of this variable: the closer the political choice is to this value, the better off he is. A frequency distribution of values would then completely describe the distribution of preferences among the electorate. It seems plausible to call the median the electorate's "will" since this is a "democratic" compromise between the preferences of different voters.[4]

It is easy to show, at least with only two political parties and majority rule, that the equilibrium political choice equals the electorate's "will" so defined.[5] If, for example, party a were promising the value at the 25th percentile and b the value at the 45th percentile, b would win because it would receive at least 55 percent of the votes (all those with values exceeding the 45th percentile). The same argument shows that the median

---

[3] See, for example, Kaplan and Lasswell (1950), p. 75.

[4] Clearly, each voter would like to minimize $|W - X|$, where W is the political choice, and X is his own preference. A democratic society might want to minimize

$$\int_{-\infty}^{+\infty} |W - X| f(X)\, dX,$$

where $f(X)$ is the frequency distribution among the voters. This expression is minimized only when W equals the median of $f(X)$.

[5] This analysis is applied to political discrimination against minorities in my *The Economics of Discrimination* (1971).

could defeat any other promise since the median would attract at least 50 percent of the votes. Therefore, the median would be the equilibrium political choice.[6]

The ultimate aim of each party may be to acquire political power, but in equlibrium no one, including those "in power," has any political power.[7] There is no room for choice by political officials because political decisions are completely determined by electorate preferences. This theorem casts light on the controversy of whether a representative should vote according to his own dictates or according to the will of his constituents.[8] In an ideal democracy unless he follows the "will" of his constituents, he does not remain in office very long.

Third, in an ideally competitive free enterprise system, only the most efficient firms survive; for example, if the level of a firm's costs were independent of output and varied from firm to firm, only the firm with the lowest costs would survive. Similarly, in an ideal democracy only the most efficient parties survive; if the costs incurred by the state in operating an industry were independent of output and dependent on the party in office, only the party with the lowest costs could remain in office. An industry would be operated equally efficiently by the state and by the market place if the most efficient party had the same costs as the most efficient firm. This does not merely state—as the analysis by Lange of socialism does—that the political sector conceptually *could* reproduce the free enterprise equilibrium, but that it would do so. The costs of the most efficient party and most efficient firm may differ if different individuals are drawn into political and market activity. Private enterprise would operate an industry more efficiently than the state only if the most efficient firm had lower costs than the most efficient party, and vice versa.

2. Competition in Actual Democracies

There is relatively little to choose between an ideal free enterprise system and an ideal political democracy; both are efficient and responsive to preferences of the "electorate." Those advocating a shift of activities from the market place to the state must argue that the actual enterprise system is far from ideal because it contains numerous monopolies and other imperfections. Those advocating a minimum number of state activities must argue that the actual political system is even further from the ideal. Imperfections in the market place have elsewhere been

[6] The aforegoing two paragraphs are reproduced with minor changes from the 1952 draft referred to in the introduction to part 3.

[7] Similarly, in a full market equilibrium no firm makes any "profits" although each may be motivated by a desire for profits.

[8] The classic statement of one viewpoint is contained in Burke's speech to the electors of Bristol in 1774.

discussed extensively, so we can concentrate on some important political imperfections.

Since each person has a fixed number of votes—either 1 or 0—regardless of the amount of information he has and the intelligence used in acting on this information, and since minorities are usually given no representation, it does not "pay" to be well-informed and thoughtful on political issues, or even to vote. An efficient party may be unable to convince enough voters that it is more efficient than other parties. In the market place minorities have "representation" and the number of "votes" a person has is related to his "proportioned productivity," so the incentives to act wisely are greater here than in the political sector. Therefore, it is relatively easy for an efficient firm to survive since it need only gain the support of creditors and consumers who have a direct personal interest in making wise decisions.

Political competition is reduced by the large scale required for political organizations. Candidates for many offices, such as the presidency and state governorships, must have enough resources to reach millions of voters. Many groups that would like to compete for these offices do not have sufficient resources to reach large numbers of voters. Although it is sometimes necessary for a firm to organize on a national or state basis, this is clearly less important in the market sector than in the political sector. The scale of political activity is large, also, because many offices tie together numerous activities. A candidate who knows how to run the Post Office efficiently must convince voters that he knows something about immigration policy, public utility regulations and a host of other problems in addition to post-office administration. This tie-in of activities may prevent persons who are efficient at one activity only from running for office. Tie-ins are also found in the market place, but since they cover relatively few activities, a firm can usually specialize in the product or process at which it is most efficient. Since an ideal democracy as well as an ideal enterprise system has an optimal separation of activities, it is somewhat puzzling that tie-ins are much more important in the political sector. I suspect that an electorate with a limited amount of political information finds it easier to place one person in charge of many activities than to choose one person for each activity.

Although ignorance and the large scale required of political organizations are perhaps the two most potent forces producing monopoly and other imperfections in democracies, periodic rather than continuous elections, and different preferences among members of the electorate also do so.[9] I am inclined to believe that monopoly and other imperfections are at least as important, and perhaps substantially more so, in the political sector as in the market place. If this belief is even approximately correct,

[9] For relation between political tie-ins and different preferences among the electorate see Becker (1957, pp. 64–66).

it has important implications for the query which opened this essay; namely, does the existence of market imperfections justify government intervention? The answer would be "no" if the imperfections in government behavior were greater than those in the market. It may be preferable not to regulate economic monopolies and to suffer their bad effects, rather than to regulate them and suffer the effects of political imperfections.

4 Crime and Punishment: An Economic Approach

I. Introduction

Since the turn of the century, legislation in Western countries has expanded rapidly to reverse the brief dominance of laissez faire during the nineteenth century. The state no longer merely protects against violations of person and property through murder, rape, or burglary but also restricts "discrimination" against certain minorities, collusive business arrangements, "jaywalking," travel, the materials used in construction, and thousands of other activities. The activities restricted not only are numerous but also range widely, affecting persons in very different pursuits and of diverse social backgrounds, education levels, ages, races, etc. Moreover, the likelihood that an offender will be discovered and convicted and the nature and extent of punishments differ greatly from person to person and activity to activity. Yet, in spite of such diversity, some common properties are shared by practically all legislation, and these properties form the subject matter of this essay.

In the first place, obedience to law is not taken for granted, and public and private resources are generally spent in order both to prevent offenses and to apprehend offenders. In the second place, conviction is not generally considered sufficient punishment in itself; additional and sometimes severe punishments are meted out to those convicted. What determines the amount and type of resources and punishments used to enforce a piece of legislation? In particular, why does enforcement differ so greatly among different kinds of legislation?

Reprinted from the *Journal of Political Economy* 76, no. 2 (March/April 1968): 169–217. © 1968 by The University of Chicago.

The main purpose of this essay is to answer normative versions of these questions, namely, how many resources and how much punishment *should* be used to enforce different kinds of legislation? Put equivalently, although more strangely, how many offenses *should* be permitted and how many offenders *should* go unpunished? The method used formulates a measure of the social loss from offenses and finds those expenditures of resources and punishments that minimize this loss. The general criterion of social loss is shown to incorporate as special cases, valid under special assumptions, the criteria of vengeance, deterrence, compensation, and rehabilitation that historically have figured so prominently in practice and criminological literature.

The optimal amount of enforcement is shown to depend on, among other things, the cost of catching and convicting offenders, the nature of punishments—for example, whether they are fines or prison terms—and the responses of offenders to changes in enforcement. The discussion, therefore, inevitably enters into issues in penology and theories of criminal behavior. A second, although because of lack of space subsidiary, aim of this essay is to see what insights into these questions are provided by our "economic" approach. It is suggested, for example, that a useful theory of criminal behavior can dispense with special theories of anomie, psychological inadequacies, or inheritance of special traits and simply extend the economist's usual analysis of choice.

II. Basic Analysis

A. The Cost of Crime

Although the word "crime" is used in the title to minimize terminological innovations, the analysis is intended to be sufficiently general to cover all violations, not just felonies—like murder, robbery, and assault, which receive so much newspaper coverage—but also tax evasion, the so-called white-collar crimes, and traffic and other violations. Looked at this broadly, "crime" is an economically important activity or "industry," notwithstanding the almost total neglect by economists.[1] Some relevant evidence recently put together by the President's Commission on Law

---

[1] This neglect probably resulted from an attitude that illegal activity is too immoral to merit any systematic scientific attention. The influence of moral attitudes on a scientific analysis is seen most clearly in a discussion by Alfred Marshall. After arguing that even fair gambling is an "economic blunder" because of diminishing marginal utility, he says, "It is true that this loss of probable happiness need not be greater than the pleasure derived from the excitement of gambling, and we are then thrown back upon the induction [*sic*] that pleasures of gambling are in Bentham's phrase 'impure'; since experience shows that they are likely to engender a restless, feverish character, unsuited for steady work as well as for the higher and more solid pleasures of life" (Marshall, 1961, Note X, Mathematical Appendix).

Enforcement and Administration of Justice (the "Crime Commission") is reproduced in Table 1. Public expenditures in 1965 at the federal, state, and local levels on police, criminal courts and counsel, and "corrections" amounted to over $4 billion, while private outlays on burglar alarms, guards, counsel, and some other forms of protection were about $2 billion. Unquestionably, public and especially private expenditures are significantly understated, since expenditures by many public agencies in the course of enforcing particular pieces of legislation, such as state fair-employment laws,[2] are not included, and a myriad of private precautions against crime, ranging from suburban living to taxis, are also excluded.

TABLE 1
ECONOMIC COSTS OF CRIMES

Type	Costs (Millions of Dollars)
Crimes against persons	815
Crimes against property	3,932
Illegal goods and services	8,075
Some other crimes	2,036
Total	14,858
Public expenditures on police, prosecution, and courts	3,178
Corrections	1,034
Some private costs of combatting crime	1,910
Over-all total	20,980

Source: President's Commission, (1967*d*, p. 44).

Table 1 also lists the Crime Commission's estimates of the direct costs of various crimes. The gross income from expenditures on various kinds of illegal consumption, including narcotics, prostitution, and mainly gambling, amounted to over $8 billion. The value of crimes against property, including fraud, vandalism, and theft, amounted to almost $4 billion,[3] while about $3 billion worth resulted from the loss of earnings due to homicide, assault, or other crimes. All the costs listed in the table total about $21 billion, which is almost 4 per cent of reported national

[2] Expenditures by the thirteen states with such legislation in 1959 totaled almost $2 million (see Landes, 1966).

[3] Superficially, frauds, thefts, etc., do not involve true social costs but are simply transfers, with the loss to victims being compensated by equal gains to criminals. While these are transfers, their market value is, nevertheless, a first approximation to the direct social cost. If the theft or fraud industry is "competitive," the sum of the value of the criminals' time input—including the time of "fences" and prospective time in prison—plus the value of capital input, compensation for risk, etc., would approximately equal the market value of the loss to victims. Consequently, aside from the input of intermediate products, losses can be taken as a measure of the value of the labor and capital input into these crimes, which are true social costs.

income in 1965. If the sizeable omissions were included, the percentage might be considerably higher.

Crime has probably become more important during the last forty years. The Crime Commission presents no evidence on trends in costs but does present evidence suggesting that the number of major felonies per capita has grown since the early thirties (President's Commission, 1967a, pp. 22–31). Moreover, with the large growth of tax and other legislation, tax evasion and other kinds of white-collar crime have presumably grown much more rapidly than felonies. One piece of indirect evidence on the growth of crime is the large increase in the amount of currency in circulation since 1929. For sixty years prior to that date, the ratio of currency either to all money or to consumer expenditures had declined very substantially. Since then, in spite of further urbanization and income growth and the spread of credit cards and other kinds of credit,[4] both ratios have increased sizeably.[5] This reversal can be explained by an unusual increase in illegal activity, since currency has obvious advantages over checks in illegal transactions (the opposite is true for legal transactions) because no record of a transaction remains.[6]

B. The Model

It is useful in determining how to combat crime in an optimal fashion to develop a model to incorporate the behavioral relations behind the costs listed in Table 1. These can be divided into five categories: the relations between (1) the number of crimes, called "offenses" in this essay, and the cost of offenses, (2) the number of offenses and the punishments meted out, (3) the number of offenses, arrests, and convictions and the public expenditures on police and courts, (4) the number of convictions and the costs of imprisonments or other kinds of punishments, and (5) the number of offenses and the private expenditures on protection and apprehension. The first four are discussed in turn, while the fifth is postponed until a later section.

1. Damages

Usually a belief that other members of society are harmed is the motivation behind outlawing or otherwise restricting an activity. The amount of harm

[4] For an analysis of the secular decline to 1929 that stresses urbanization and the growth in incomes, see Cagan (1965, chap. iv).

[5] In 1965, the ratio of currency outstanding to consumer expenditures was 0.08, compared to only 0.05 in 1929. In 1965, currency outstanding per family was a whopping $738.

[6] Cagan (1965, chap. iv) attributes much of the increase in currency holdings between 1929 and 1960 to increased tax evasion resulting from the increase in tax rates.

would tend to increase with the activity level, as in the relation

$$H_i = H_i(O_i),$$

with   (1)

$$H_i' = \frac{dH_i}{dO_i} > 0,$$

where H_i is the harm from the ith activity and O_i is the activity level.[7] The concept of harm and the function relating its amount to the activity level are familiar to economists from their many discussions of activities causing external diseconomies. From this perspective, criminal activities are an important subset of the class of activities that cause diseconomies, with the level of criminal activities measured by the number of offenses.

The social value of the gain to offenders presumably also tends to increase with the number of offenses, as in

$$G = G(O),$$

with   (2)

$$G' = \frac{dG}{dO} > 0.$$

The net cost or damage to society is simply the difference between the harm and gain and can be written as

$$D(O) = H(O) - G(O). \tag{3}$$

If, as seems plausible, offenders usually eventually receive diminishing marginal gains and cause increasing marginal harm from additional offenses, $G'' < 0$, $H'' > 0$, and

$$D'' = H'' - G'' > 0, \tag{4}$$

which is an important condition used later in the analysis of optimality positions (see, for example, the Mathematical Appendix). Since both H' and $G' > 0$, the sign of D' depends on their relative magnitudes. It follows from (4), however, that

$$D'(O) > 0 \text{ for all } O > O_a \text{ if } D'(O_a) \geq 0. \tag{5}$$

Until Section V the discussion is restricted to the region where $D' > 0$, the region providing the strongest justification for outlawing an activity. In that section the general problem of external diseconomies is reconsidered from our viewpoint, and there $D' < 0$ is also permitted.

The top part of Table 1 lists costs of various crimes, which have been interpreted by us as estimates of the value of resources used up in these

---

[7] The ith subscript will be suppressed whenever it is to be understood that only one activity is being discussed.

crimes. These values are important components of, but are not identical to, the net damages to society. For example, the cost of murder is measured by the loss in earnings of victims and excludes, among other things, the value placed by society on life itself; the cost of gambling excludes both the utility to those gambling and the "external" disutility to some clergy and others; the cost of "transfers" like burglary and embezzlement excludes social attitudes toward forced wealth redistributions and also the effects on capital accumulation of the possibility of theft. Consequently, the $15 billion estimate for the cost of crime in Table 1 may be a significant understatement of the net damages to society, not only because the costs of many white-collar crimes are omitted, but also because much of the damage is omitted even for the crimes covered.

2. The Cost of Apprehension and Conviction

The more that is spent on policemen, court personnel, and specialized equipment, the easier it is to discover offenses and convict offenders. One can postulate a relation between the output of police and court "activity" and various inputs of manpower, materials, and capital, as in $A = f(m, r, c)$, where f is a production function summarizing the "state of the arts." Given f and input prices, increased "activity" would be more costly, as summarized by the relation

$$C = C(A)$$

and   (6)

$$C' = \frac{dC}{dA} > 0.$$

It would be cheaper to achieve any given level of activity the cheaper were policemen,[8] judges, counsel, and juries and the more highly developed the state of the arts, as determined by technologies like fingerprinting, wire-tapping, computer control, and lie-detecting.[9]

One approximation to an empirical measure of "activity" is the number of offenses cleared by conviction. It can be written as

$$A \cong pO,$$ (7)

where p, the ratio of offenses cleared by convictions to all offenses, is the over-all probability that an offense is cleared by conviction. By substituting

---

[8] According to the Crime Commission, 85–90 per cent of all police costs consist of wages and salaries (President's Commission, 1967a, p. 35).

[9] A task-force report by the Crime Commission deals with suggestions for greater and more efficient usage of advanced technologies (President's Commission, 1967e).

(7) into (6) and differentiating, one has

$$C_p = \frac{\partial C(pO)}{\partial p} = C'O > 0$$

and   (8)

$$C_o = C'p > 0$$

if $pO \neq 0$. An increase in either the probability of conviction or the number of offenses would increase total costs. If the marginal cost of increased "activity" were rising, further implications would be that

$$C_{pp} = C''O^2 > 0,$$
$$C_{oo} = C''p^2 > 0,$$ (9)

and

$$C_{po} = C_{op} = C''pO + C' > 0.$$

A more sophisticated and realistic approach drops the implication of (7) that convictions alone measure "activity," or even that p and O have identical elasticities, and introduces the more general relation

$$A = h(p, O, a).$$ (10)

The variable a stands for arrests and other determinants of "activity," and there is no presumption that the elasticity of h with respect to p equals that with respect to O. Substitution yields the cost function $C = C(p, O, a)$. If, as is extremely likely, h_p, h_o, and h_a are all greater than zero, then clearly C_p, C_o, and C_a are all greater than zero.

In order to insure that optimality positions do not lie at "corners," it is necessary to place some restrictions on the second derivatives of the cost function. Combined with some other assumptions, it is *sufficient* that

$$C_{pp} \geq 0,$$
$$C_{oo} \geq 0,$$ (11)

and

$$C_{po} \cong 0$$

(see the Mathematical Appendix). The first two restrictions are rather plausible, the third much less so.[10]

Table 1 indicates that in 1965 public expenditures in the United States on police and courts totaled more than \$3 billion, by no means a minor

---

[10] Differentiating the cost function yields $C_{pp} = C''(h_p)^2 + C'h_{pp}$; $C_{oo} = C''(h_o)^2 + C'h_{oo}$; $C_{po} = C''h_o h_p + C'h_{po}$. If marginal costs were rising, C_{pp} or C_{oo} could be negative only if h_{pp} or h_{oo} were sufficiently negative, which is not very likely. However, C_{po} would be approximately zero only if h_{po} were sufficiently negative, which is also unlikely. Note that if "activity" is measured by convictions alone, $h_{pp} = h_{oo} = 0$, and $h_{po} > 0$.

item. Separate estimates were prepared for each of seven major felonies.[11] Expenditures on them averaged about \$500 per offense (reported) and about \$2,000 per person arrested, with almost \$1,000 being spent per murder (President's Commission, 1967a, pp. 264–65); \$500 is an estimate of the average cost

$$AC = \frac{C(p, O, a)}{O}$$

of these felonies and would presumably be a larger figure if the number of either arrests or convictions were greater. Marginal costs (C_o) would be at least \$500 if condition (11), $C_{oo} \geq 0$, were assumed to hold throughout.

3. The Supply of Offenses

Theories about the determinants of the number of offenses differ greatly, from emphasis on skull types and biological inheritance to family upbringing and disenchantment with society. Practically all the diverse theories agree, however, that when other variables are held constant, an increase in a person's probability of conviction or punishment if convicted would generally decrease, perhaps substantially, perhaps negligibly, the number of offenses he commits. In addition, a common generalization by persons with judicial experience is that a change in the probability has a greater effect on the number of offenses than a change in the punishment,[12] although, as far as I can tell, none of the prominent theories shed any light on this relation.

The approach taken here follows the economists' usual analysis of choice and assumes that a person commits an offense if the expected utility to him exceeds the utility he could get by using his time and other resources at other activities. Some persons become "criminals," therefore, not because their basic motivation differs from that of other persons, but because their benefits and costs differ. I cannot pause to discuss the many general implications of this approach,[13] except to remark that criminal behavior becomes part of a much more general theory and does not require ad hoc concepts of differential association, anomie, and the like,[14] nor does it assume perfect knowledge, lightening-fast calculation, or any of the other caricatures of economic theory.

[11] They are willful homicide, forcible rape, robbery, aggravated assault, burglary, larceny, and auto theft.

[12] For example, Lord Shawness (1965) said, "Some judges preoccupy themselves with methods of punishment. This is their job. But in preventing crime it is of less significance than they like to think. Certainty of detection is far more important than severity of punishment." Also see the discussion of the ideas of C. B. Beccaria, an insightful eighteenth-century Italian economist and criminologist, in Radzinowicz (1948, I, 282).

[13] See, however, the discussions in Smigel (1965) and Ehrlich (1967).

[14] For a discussion of these concepts, see Sutherland (1960).

This approach implies that there is a function relating the number of offenses by any person to his probability of conviction, to his punishment if convicted, and to other variables, such as the income available to him in legal and other illegal activities, the frequency of nuisance arrests, and his willingness to commit an illegal act. This can be represented as

$$O_j = O_j(p_j, f_j, u_j), \tag{12}$$

where O_j is the number of offenses he would commit during a particular period, p_j his probability of conviction per offense, f_j his punishment per offense, and u_j a portmanteau variable representing all these other influences.[15]

Since only convicted offenders are punished, in effect there is "price discrimination" and uncertainty: if convicted, he pays f_j per convicted offense, while otherwise he does not. An increase in either p_j or f_j would reduce the utility expected from an offense and thus would tend to reduce the number of offenses because either the probability of "paying" the higher "price" or the "price" itself would increase.[16] That is,

$$O_{p_j} = \frac{\partial O_j}{\partial p_j} < 0$$

and (13)

$$O_{f_j} = \frac{\partial O_j}{\partial f_j} < 0,$$

which are the generally accepted restrictions mentioned above. The effect of changes in some components of u_j could also be anticipated. For example, a rise in the income available in legal activities or an increase in law-abidingness due, say, to "education" would reduce the incentive to enter illegal activities and thus would reduce the number of offenses. Or a shift in the form of the punishment, say, from a fine to imprisonment,

---

[15] Both p_j and f_j might be considered distributions that depend on the judge, jury, prosecutor, etc., that j happens to receive. Among other things, u_j depends on the p's and f's meted out for other competing offenses. For evidence indicating that offenders do substitute among offenses, see Smigel (1965).

[16] The utility expected from committing an offense is defined as

$$EU_j = p_j U_j(Y_j - f_j) + (1 - p_j)U_j(Y_j),$$

where Y_j is his income, monetary plus psychic, from an offense; U_j is his utility function; and f_j is to be interpreted as the monetary equivalent of the punishment. Then

$$\frac{\partial EU_j}{\partial p_j} = U_j(Y_j - f_j) - U_j(Y_j) < 0$$

and

$$\frac{\partial EU_j}{\partial f_j} = -p_j U_j'(Y_j - f_j) < 0$$

as long as the marginal utility of income is positive. One could expand the analysis by incorporating the costs and probabilities of arrests, detentions, and trials that do not result in conviction.

would tend to reduce the number of offenses, at least temporarily, because they cannot be committed while in prison.

This approach also has an interesting interpretation of the presumed greater response to a change in the probability than in the punishment. An increase in p_j "compensated" by an equal percentage reduction in f_j would not change the expected income from an offense[17] but could change the expected utility, because the amount of risk would change. It is easily shown that an increase in p_j would reduce the expected utility, and thus the number of offenses, more than an equal percentage increase in f_j[18] if j has preference for risk; the increase in f_j would have the greater effect if he has aversion to risk; and they would have the same effect if he is risk neutral.[19] The widespread generalization that offenders are more deterred by the probability of conviction than by the punishment when convicted turns out to imply in the expected-utility approach that offenders are risk preferrers, at least in the relevant region of punishments.

The total number of offenses is the sum of all the O_j and would depend on the set of p_j, f_j, and u_j. Although these variables are likely to differ significantly between persons because of differences in intelligence, age, education, previous offense history, wealth, family upbringing, etc., for simplicity I now consider only their average values, p, f, and u,[20] and write the market offense function as

$$O = O(p, f, u). \tag{14}$$

This function is assumed to have the same kinds of properties as the individual functions, in particular, to be negatively related to p and f and to be more responsive to the former than the latter if, and only if, offenders on balance have risk preference. Smigel (1965) and Ehrlich (1967) estimate

[17] $EY_j = p_j(Y_j - f_j) + (1 - p_j)Y_j = Y_j - p_jf_j.$

[18] This means that an increase in p_j "compensated" by a reduction in f_j would reduce utility and offenses.

[19] From n. 16

$$-\frac{\partial EU_j}{\partial p_j}\frac{p_j}{U_j} = [U_j(Y_j) - U_j(Y_j - f_j)]\frac{p_j}{U_j} \gtreqless -\frac{\partial EU_j}{\partial f_j}\frac{f_j}{U_j} = p_jU_j'(Y_j - f_j)\frac{f_j}{U_j}$$

as

$$\frac{U_j(Y_j) - U_j(Y_j - f_j)}{f_j} \gtreqless U_j'(Y_j - f_j).$$

The term on the left is the average change in utility between $Y_j - f_j$ and Y_j. It would be greater than, equal to, or less than $U_j'(Y_j - f_j)$ as $U_j'' \gtreqless 0$. But risk preference is defined by $U_j'' > 0$, neutrality by $U_j'' = 0$, and aversion by $U_j'' < 0$.

[20] p can be defined as a weighted average of the p_j, as

$$p = \sum_{j=1}^{n} \frac{O_jp_j}{\sum_{i=1}^{n} O_i},$$

and similar definitions hold for f and u.

functions like (14) for seven felonies reported by the Federal Bureau of Investigation using state data as the basic unit of observation. They find that the relations are quite stable, as evidenced by high correlation coefficients; that there are significant negative effects on O of p and f; and that usually the effect of p exceeds that of f, indicating preference for risk in the region of observation.

A well-known result states that, in equilibrium, the real incomes of persons in risky activities are, at the margin, relatively high or low as persons are generally risk avoiders or preferrers. If offenders were risk preferrers, this implies that the real income of offenders would be lower, at the margin, than the incomes they could receive in less risky legal activities, and conversely if they were risk avoiders. Whether "crime pays" is then an implication of the attitudes offenders have toward risk and is not directly related to the efficiency of the police or the amount spent on combatting crime. If, however, risk were preferred at some values of p and f and disliked at others, public policy could influence whether "crime pays" by its choice of p and f. Indeed, it is shown later that the social loss from illegal activities is usually minimized by selecting p and f in regions where risk is preferred, that is, in regions where "crime does not pay."

4. Punishments

Mankind has invented a variety of ingenious punishments to inflict on convicted offenders: death, torture, branding, fines, imprisonment, banishment, restrictions on movement and occupation, and loss of citizenship are just the more common ones. In the United States, less serious offenses are punished primarily by fines, supplemented occasionally by probation, petty restrictions like temporary suspension of one's driver's license, and imprisonment. The more serious offenses are punished by a combination of probation, imprisonment, parole, fines, and various restrictions on choice of occupation. A recent survey estimated for an average day in 1965 the number of persons who were either on probation, parole, or institutionalized in a jail or juvenile home (President's Commission 1967*b*). The total number of persons in one of these categories came to about 1,300,000, which is about 2 per cent of the labor force. About one-half were on probation, one-third were institutionalized, and the remaining one-sixth were on parole.

The cost of different punishments to an offender can be made comparable by converting them into their monetary equivalent or worth, which, of course, is directly measured only for fines. For example, the cost of an imprisonment is the discounted sum of the earnings foregone and the value placed on the restrictions in consumption and freedom. Since the earnings foregone and the value placed on prison restrictions vary from person to person, the cost even of a prison sentence of given duration is not a unique quantity but is generally greater, for example, to offenders who could earn more outside of prison.[21] The cost to each offender would be greater the longer the prison sentence, since both foregone earnings and foregone consumption are positively related to the length of sentences.

Punishments affect not only offenders but also other members of society. Aside from collection costs, fines paid by offenders are received as revenue by others. Most punishments, however, hurt other members as well as offenders: for example, imprisonment requires expenditures on guards, supervisory personnel, buildings, food, etc. Currently about $1 billion is being spent each year in the United States on probation, parole, and institutionalization alone, with the daily cost per case varying tremendously from a low of $0.38 for adults on probation to a high of $11.00 for juveniles in detention institutions (President's Commission, 1967b, pp. 193–94).

The total social cost of punishments is the cost to offenders plus the cost or minus the gain to others. Fines produce a gain to the latter that equals the cost to offenders, aside from collection costs, and so the social cost of fines is about zero, as befits a transfer payment. The social cost of probation, imprisonment, and other punishments, however, generally exceeds that to offenders, because others are also hurt. The derivation of optimality conditions in the next section is made more convenient if social costs are written in terms of offender costs as

$$f' \equiv bf, \tag{15}$$

where f' is the social cost and b is a coefficient that transforms f into f'. The size of b varies greatly between different kinds of punishments: $b \cong 0$ for fines, while $b > 1$ for torture, probation, parole, imprisonment, and most other punishments. It is especially large for juveniles in detention homes or for adults in prisons and is rather close to unity for torture or for adults on parole.

III. Optimality Conditions

The relevant parameters and behavioral functions have been introduced, and the stage is set for a discussion of social policy. If the aim simply were deterrence, the probability of conviction, p, could be raised close to 1, and punishments, f, could be made to exceed the gain: in this way the number of offenses, O, could be reduced almost at will. However, an increase in p increases the social cost of offenses through its effect on the cost of combatting offenses, C, as does an increase in f if $b > 0$ through the effect on the cost of punishments, bf. At relatively modest values of p and f, these effects might outweigh the social gain from increased deterrence. Similarly,

[21] In this respect, imprisonment is a special case of "waiting time" pricing that is also exemplified by queuing (see Becker, 1965, esp. pp. 515–16, and Kleinman, 1967).

if the aim simply were to make "the punishment fit the crime," p could be set close to 1, and f could be equated to the harm imposed on the rest of society. Again, however, such a policy ignores the social cost of increases in p and f.

What is needed is a criterion that goes beyond catchy phrases and gives due weight to the damages from offenses, the costs of apprehending and convicting offenders, and the social cost of punishments. The social-welfare function of modern welfare economics is such a criterion, and one might assume that society has a function that measures the social loss from offenses. If

$$L = L(D, C, bf, O) \tag{16}$$

is the function measuring social loss, with presumably

$$\frac{\partial L}{\partial D} > 0, \qquad \frac{\partial L}{\partial C} > 0, \qquad \frac{\partial L}{\partial bf} > 0, \tag{17}$$

the aim would be to select values of f, C, and possibly b that minimize L.

It is more convenient and transparent, however, to develop the discussion at this point in terms of a less general formulation, namely, to assume that the loss function is identical with the total social loss in real income from offenses, convictions, and punishments, as in

$$L = D(O) + C(p, O) + bpfO. \tag{18}$$

The term $bpfO$ is the total social loss from punishments, since bf is the loss per offense punished and pO is the number of offenses punished (if there are a fairly large number of independent offenses). The variables directly subject to social control are the amounts spent in combatting offenses, C; the punishment per offense for those convicted, f; and the form of punishments, summarized by b. Once chosen, these variables, via the D, C, and O functions, indirectly determine p, O, D, and ultimately the loss L.

Analytical convenience suggests that p rather than C be considered a decision variable. Also, the coefficient b is assumed in this section to be a given constant greater than zero. Then p and f are the only decision variables, and their optimal values are found by differentiating L to find the two first-order optimality conditions,[22]

$$\frac{\partial L}{\partial f} = D'O_f + C'O_f + bpfO_f + bpO = 0 \tag{19}$$

and

$$\frac{\partial L}{\partial p} = D'O_p + C'O_p + C_p + bpfO_p + bfO = 0. \tag{20}$$

[22] The Mathematical Appendix discusses second-order conditions.

Law and Politics

If O_f and O_p are not equal to zero, one can divide through by them, and recombine terms, to get the more interesting expressions

$$D' + C' = -bpf\left(1 - \frac{1}{\varepsilon_f}\right) \tag{21}$$

and

$$D' + C' + C_p \frac{1}{O_p} = -bpf\left(1 - \frac{1}{\varepsilon_p}\right), \tag{22}$$

where

$$\varepsilon_f = -\frac{f}{O} O_f$$

and

$$\varepsilon_p = -\frac{p}{O} O_p. \tag{23}$$

The term on the left side of each equation gives the marginal cost of increasing the number of offenses, O: in equation (21) through a reduction in f and in (22) through a reduction in p. Since $C' > 0$ and O is assumed to be in a region where $D' > 0$, the marginal cost of increasing O through f must be positive. A reduction in p partly reduces the cost of combatting offenses, and, therefore, the marginal cost of increasing O must be less when p rather than when f is reduced (see Fig. 1); the former could even be negative if C_p were sufficiently large. Average "revenue," given by $-bpf$, is negative, but marginal revenue, given by the right-hand side of

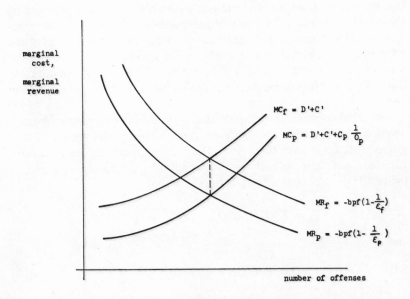

FIG. 1

equations (21) and (22), is not necessarily negative and would be positive if the elasticities ε_p and ε_f were less than unity. Since the loss is minimized when marginal revenue equals marginal cost (see Fig. 1), the optimal value of ε_f must be less than unity, and that of ε_p could only exceed unity if C_p were sufficiently large. This is a reversal of the usual equilibrium condition for an income-maximizing firm, which is that the elasticity of demand must exceed unity, because in the usual case average revenue is assumed to be positive.[23]

Since the marginal cost of changing O through a change in p is less than that of changing O through f, the equilibrium marginal revenue from p must also be less than that from f. But equations (21) and (22) indicate that the marginal revenue from p can be less if, and only if, $\varepsilon_p > \varepsilon_f$. As pointed out earlier, however, this is precisely the condition indicating that offenders have preference for risk and thus that "crime does not pay." Consequently, the loss from offenses is minimized if p and f are selected from those regions where offenders are, on balance, risk preferrers. Although only the attitudes offenders have toward risk can directly determine whether "crime pays," rational public policy indirectly insures that "crime does not pay" through its choice of p and f.[24]

I indicated earlier that the actual p's and f's for major felonies in the United States generally seem to be in regions where the effect (measured by elasticity) of p on offenses exceeds that of f, that is, where offenders are risk preferrers and "crime does not pay" (Smigel, 1965; Ehrlich, 1967). Moreover, both elasticities are generally less than unity. In both respects, therefore, actual public policy is consistent with the implications of the optimality analysis.

If the supply of offenses depended only on pf—offenders were risk neutral—a reduction in p "compensated" by an equal percentage increase in f would leave unchanged pf, O, $D(O)$, and $bpfO$ but would reduce the loss, because the costs of apprehension and conviction would be lowered by the reduction in p. The loss would be minimized, therefore, by lowering p arbitrarily close to zero and raising f sufficiently high so that the product pf would induce the optimal number of offenses.[25] A fortiori, if offenders

[23] Thus if $b < 0$, average revenue would be positive and the optimal value of ε_f would be greater than 1, and that of ε_p could be less than 1 only if C_p were sufficiently large.

[24] If $b < 0$, the optimality condition is that $\varepsilon_p < \varepsilon_f$, or that offenders are risk avoiders. Optimal social policy would then be to select p and f in regions where "crime does pay."

[25] Since $\varepsilon_f = \varepsilon_p = \varepsilon$ if O depends only on pf, and $C = 0$ if $p = 0$, the two equilibrium conditions given by eqs. (21) and (22) reduce to the single condition

$$D' = -bpf\left(1 - \frac{1}{\varepsilon}\right).$$

From this condition and the relation $O = O(pf)$, the equilibrium values of O and pf could be determined.

were risk avoiders, the loss would be minimized by setting p arbitrarily close to zero, for a "compensated" reduction in p reduces not only C but also O and thus D and $bpfO$.[26]

There was a tendency during the eighteenth and nineteenth centuries in Anglo-Saxon countries, and even today in many Communist and under-developed countries, to punish those convicted of criminal offenses rather severely, at the same time that the probability of capture and conviction was set at rather low values.[27] A promising explanation of this tendency is that an increased probability of conviction obviously absorbs public and private resources in the form of more policemen, judges, juries, and so forth. Consequently, a "compensated" reduction in this probability obviously reduces expenditures on combatting crime, and, since the expected punishment is unchanged, there is no "obvious" offsetting increase in either the amount of damages or the cost of punishments. The result can easily be continuous political pressure to keep police and other expenditures relatively low and to compensate by meting out strong punishments to those convicted.

Of course, if offenders are risk preferrers, the loss in income from offenses is generally minimized by selecting positive and finite values of p and f, even though there is no "obvious" offset to a compensated reduction in p. One possible offset already hinted at in footnote 27 is that judges or juries may be unwilling to convict offenders if punishments are set very high. Formally, this means that the cost of apprehension and conviction, C, would depend not only on p and O but also on f.[28] If C were more responsive to f than p, at least in some regions,[29] the loss in income could be minimized at finite values of p and f even if offenders were risk avoiders. For then a compensated reduction in p could raise, rather than lower, C and thus contribute to an increase in the loss.

Risk avoidance might also be consistent with optimal behavior if the loss function were not simply equal to the reduction in income. For example, suppose that the loss were increased by an increase in the ex post "price discrimination" between offenses that are not and those that are cleared by punishment. Then a "compensated" reduction in p would

---

[26] If $b < 0$, the optimal solution is p about zero and f arbitrarily high if offenders are either risk neutral or risk preferrers.

[27] For a discussion of English criminal law in the eighteenth and nineteenth centuries, see Radzinowicz (1948, Vol. I). Punishments were severe then, even though the death penalty, while legislated, was seldom implemented for less serious criminal offenses.

Recently South Vietnam executed a prominent businessman allegedly for "speculative" dealings in rice, while in recent years a number of persons in the Soviet Union have either been executed or given severe prison sentences for economic crimes.

[28] I owe the emphasis on this point to Evsey Domar.

[29] This is probably more likely for higher values of f and lower values of p.

increase the "price discrimination," and the increased loss from this could more than offset the reductions in C, D, and $bpfO$.[30]

IV. Shifts in the Behavioral Relations

This section analyzes the effects of shifts in the basic behavioral relations—the damage, cost, and supply-of-offenses functions—on the optimal values of p and f. Since rigorous proofs can be found in the Mathematical Appendix, here the implications are stressed, and only intuitive proofs are given. The results are used to explain, among other things, why more damaging offenses are punished more severely and more impulsive offenders less severely.

An increase in the marginal damages from a given number of offenses, D', increases the marginal cost of changing offenses by a change in either p or f (see Fig. 2a and b). The optimal number of offenses would necessarily decrease, because the optimal values of both p and f would increase. In this case (and, as shortly seen, in several others), the optimal values of p and f move in the same, rather than in opposite, directions.[31]

An interesting application of these conclusions is to different kinds of offenses. Although there are few objective measures of the damages done

---

[30] If p is the probability that an offense would be cleared with the punishment f, then $1 - p$ is the probability of no punishment. The expected punishment would be $\mu = pf$, the variance $\sigma^2 = p(1 - p)f^2$, and the coefficient of variation

$$v = \frac{\sigma}{\mu} = \sqrt{\frac{1 - p}{p}};$$

v increases monotonically from a low of zero when $p = 1$ to an infinitely high value when $p = 0$.
If the loss function equaled

$$L' = L + \psi(v), \qquad \psi' > 0,$$

the optimality conditions would become

$$D' + C' = -bpf\left(1 - \frac{1}{\varepsilon_f}\right) \tag{21}$$

and

$$D' + C' + C_p\frac{1}{O_p} + \psi'\frac{dv}{dp}\frac{1}{O_p} = -bpf\left(1 - \frac{1}{\varepsilon_p}\right). \tag{22}$$

Since the term $\psi'(dv/dp)(1/O_p)$ is positive, it could more than offset the negative term $C_p(1/O_p)$.

[31] I stress this primarily because of Bentham's famous and seemingly plausible dictum that "the more deficient in certainty a punishment is, the severer it should be" (1931b, chap. ii of section entitled "Of Punishment," second rule). The dictum would be correct if p (or f) were exogenously determined and if L were minimized with respect to f (or p) alone, for then the optimal value of f (or p) would be inversely related to the given value of p (or f) (see the Mathematical Appendix). If, however, L is minimized with respect to both, then frequently they move in the same direction.

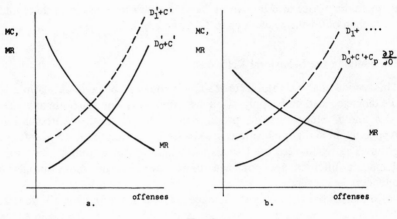

FIG. 2

by most offenses, it does not take much imagination to conclude that offenses like murder or rape generally do more damage than petty larceny or auto theft. If the other components of the loss in income were the same, the optimal probability of apprehension and conviction and the punishment when convicted would be greater for the more serious offenses.

Table 2 presents some evidence on the actual probabilities and punishments in the United States for seven felonies. The punishments are simply the average prison sentences served, while the probabilities are ratios of the estimated number of convictions to the estimated number of offenses and unquestionably contain a large error (see the discussions in Smigel, 1965, and Ehrlich, 1967). If other components of the loss function are ignored, and if actual and optimal probabilities and punishments are positively related, one should find that the more serious felonies have higher probabilities and longer prison terms. And one does: in the table, which lists the felonies in decreasing order of presumed seriousness, both the actual probabilities and the prison terms are positively related to seriousness.

Since an increase in the marginal cost of apprehension and conviction for a given number of offenses, C', has identical effects as an increase in marginal damages, it must also reduce the optimal number of offenses and increase the optimal values of p and f. On the other hand, an increase in the other component of the cost of apprehension and conviction, C_p, has no direct effect on the marginal cost of changing offenses with f and *reduces* the cost of changing offenses with p (see Fig. 3). It therefore reduces the optimal value of p and only partially compensates with an increase in f, so that the optimal number of offenses increases. Accordingly, an increase in both C' and C_p must increase the optimal f but can

TABLE 2

PROBABILITY OF CONVICTION AND AVERAGE PRISON TERM FOR SEVERAL MAJOR FELONIES, 1960

	Murder and Non-negligent Manslaughter	Forcible Rape	Robbery	Aggravated Assault	Burglary	Larceny	Auto Theft	All These Felonies Combined
1. Average time served (months) before first release:								
a) Federal civil institutions	111.0	63.6	56.1	27.1	26.2	16.2	20.6	18.8
b) State institutions	121.4	44.8	42.4	25.0	24.6	19.8	21.3	28.4
2. Probabilities of apprehension and conviction (per cent):								
a) Those found guilty of offenses known	57.9	37.7	25.1	27.3	13.0	10.7	13.7	15.1
b) Those found guilty of offenses charged	40.7	26.9	17.8	16.1	10.2	9.8	11.5	15.0
c) Those entering federal and state prisons (excludes many juveniles)	39.8	22.7	8.4	3.0	2.4	2.2	2.1	2.8

Source: 1, Bureau of Prisons (1960, Table 3); 2 (a) and (b), Federal Bureau of Investigation (1960, Table 10); 2 (c), Federal Bureau of Investigation (1961, Table 2), Bureau of Prisons (n.d., Table A1; 1961, Table 8).

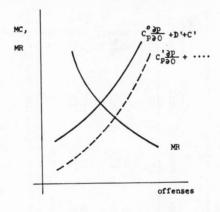

FIG. 3

either increase or decrease the optimal p and optimal number of offenses, depending on the relative importance of the changes in C' and C_p.

The cost of apprehending and convicting offenders is affected by a variety of forces. An increase in the salaries of policemen increases both C' and C_p, while improved police technology in the form of fingerprinting, ballistic techniques, computer control, and chemical analysis, or police and court "reform" with an emphasis on professionalism and merit, would tend to reduce both, not necessarily by the same extent. Our analysis implies, therefore, that although an improvement in technology and reform may or may not increase the optimal p and reduce the optimal number of offenses, it does reduce the optimal f and thus the need to rely on severe punishments for those convicted. Possibly this explains why the secular improvement in police technology and reform has gone hand in hand with a secular decline in punishments.

C_p, and to a lesser extent C', differ significantly between different kinds of offenses. It is easier, for example, to solve a rape or armed robbery than a burglary or auto theft, because the evidence of personal identification is often available in the former and not in the latter offenses.[32] This might tempt one to argue that the p's decline significantly as one moves across Table 2 (left to right) primarily because the C_p's are significantly lower for the "personal" felonies listed to the left than for the "impersonal" felonies listed to the right. But this implies that the f's would increase as one moved across the table, which is patently false. Consequently, the positive correlation between p, f, and the severity of offenses observed in

[32] "If a suspect is neither known to the victim nor arrested at the scene of the crime, the chances of ever arresting him are very slim" (President's Commission, 1967*e*, p. 8). This conclusion is based on a study of crimes in parts of Los Angeles during January, 1966.

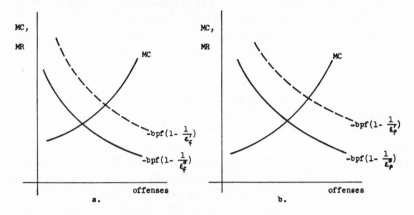

FIG. 4

the table cannot be explained by a negative correlation between C_p (or C') and severity.

If $b > 0$, a reduction in the elasticity of offenses with respect to f increases the marginal revenue of changing offenses by changing f (see Fig. 4a). The result is an increase in the optimal number of offenses and a decrease in the optimal f that is partially compensated by an increase in the optimal p. Similarly, a reduction in the elasticity of offenses with respect to p also increases the optimal number of offenses (see Fig. 4b), decreases the optimal p, and partially compensates by an increase in f. An equal percentage reduction in both elasticities a fortiori increases the optimal number of offenses and also tends to reduce both p and f. If $b = 0$, both marginal revenue functions lie along the horizontal axis, and changes in these elasticities have no effect on the optimal values of p and f.

The income of a firm would usually be larger if it could separate, at little cost, its total market into submarkets that have substantially different elasticities of demand: higher prices would be charged in the submarkets having lower elasticities. Similarly, if the total "market" for offenses could be separated into submarkets that differ significantly in the elasticities of supply of offenses, the results above imply that if $b > 0$ the total loss would be reduced by "charging" *lower* "prices"—that is, lower p's and f's—in markets with *lower* elasticities.

Sometimes it is possible to separate persons committing the same offense into groups that have different responses to punishments. For example, unpremeditated murderers or robbers are supposed to act impulsively and, therefore, to be relatively unresponsive to the size of punishments; likewise, the insane or the young are probably less affected than other offenders by future consequences and, therefore,[33] probably less deterred by increases in the probability of conviction or in the punishment when convicted. The trend during the twentieth century toward relatively smaller prison terms and greater use of probation and therapy for such groups and, more generally, the trend away from the doctrine of "a given punishment for a given crime" is apparently at least broadly consistent with the implications of the optimality analysis.

An increase in b increases the marginal revenue from changing the number of offenses by changing p or f and thereby increases the optimal number of offenses, reduces the optimal value of f, and increases the optimal value of p. Some evidence presented in Section II indicates that b is especially large for juveniles in detention homes or adults in prison and is small for fines or adults on parole. The analysis implies, therefore, that other things the same, the optimal f's would be smaller and the optimal p's larger if punishment were by one of the former rather than one of the latter methods.

V. Fines

A. Welfare Theorems and Transferable Pricing

The usual optimality conditions in welfare economics depend only on the levels and not on the slopes of marginal cost and average revenue functions, as in the well-known condition that marginal costs equal prices. The social loss from offenses was explicitly introduced as an application of the approach used in welfare economics, and yet slopes as incorporated into elasticities of supply do significantly affect the optimality conditions. Why this difference? The primary explanation would appear to be that it is almost always implicitly assumed that prices paid by consumers are fully transferred to firms and governments, so that there is no social loss from payment.

If there were no social loss from punishments, as with fines, b would equal zero, and the elasticity of supply would drop out of the optimality condition given by equation (21).[34] If $b > 0$, as with imprisonment, some of the payment "by" offenders would not be received by the rest of society, and a net social loss would result. The elasticity of the supply of offenses then becomes an important determinant of the optimality conditions, because it determines the change in social costs caused by a change in punishments.

---

[33] But see Becker (1962) for an analysis indicating that impulsive and other "irrational" persons may be as deterred from purchasing a commodity whose price has risen as more "rational" persons.

[34] It remains in eq. (22), through the slope O_p, because ordinarily prices do not affect marginal costs, while they do here through the influence of p on C.

Although transferable monetary pricing is the most common kind today, the other is not unimportant, especially in underdeveloped and Communist countries. Examples in addition to imprisonment and many other punishments are the draft, payments in kind, and queues and other waiting-time forms of rationing that result from legal restrictions on pricing (see Becker, 1965) and from random variations in demand and supply conditions. It is interesting, and deserves further exploration, that the optimality conditions are so significantly affected by a change in the assumptions about the transferability of pricing.

B. Optimality Conditions

If $b = 0$, say, because punishment was by fine, and if the cost of apprehending and convicting offenders were also zero, the two optimality conditions (21) and (22) would reduce to the same simple condition

$$D'(O) = 0. \tag{24}$$

Economists generally conclude that activities causing "external" harm, such as factories that pollute the air or lumber operations that strip the land, should be taxed or otherwise restricted in level until the marginal external harm equalled the marginal private gain, that is, until marginal net damages equalled zero, which is what equation (24) says. If marginal harm always exceeded marginal gain, the optimum level would be presumed to be zero, and that would also be the implication of (24) when suitable inequality conditions were brought in. In other words, if the costs of apprehending, convicting, and punishing offenders were nil and if each offense caused more external harm than private gain, the social loss from offenses would be minimized by setting punishments high enough to eliminate all offenses. Minimizing the social loss would become identical with the criterion of minimizing crime by setting penalties sufficiently high.[35]

Equation (24) determines the optimal number of offenses, $\hat{O}$, and the fine and probability of conviction must be set at levels that induce offenders to commit just $\hat{O}$ offenses. If the economists' usual theory of choice is applied to illegal activities (see Sec. II), the marginal value of these penalties has to equal the marginal private gain:

$$V = G'(\hat{O}), \tag{25}$$

where $G'(\hat{O})$ is the marginal private gain at $\hat{O}$ and V is the monetary value of the marginal penalties. Since by equations (3) and (24), $D'(\hat{O}) = H'(\hat{O}) - G'(\hat{O}) = 0$, one has by substitution in (25)

$$V = H'(\hat{O}). \tag{26}$$

---

[35] "The evil of the punishment must be made to exceed the advantage of the offense" (Bentham, 1931b, first rule).

The monetary value of the penalties would equal the marginal harm caused by offenses.

Since the cost of apprehension and conviction is assumed equal to zero, the probability of apprehension and conviction could be set equal to unity without cost. The monetary value of penalties would then simply equal the fines imposed, and equation (26) would become

$$f = H'(\hat{O}). \tag{27}$$

Since fines are paid by offenders to the rest of society, a fine determined by (27) would exactly compensate the latter for the marginal harm suffered, and the criterion of minimizing the social loss would be identical, at the margin, with the criterion of compensating "victims."[36] If the harm to victims always exceeded the gain to offenders, both criteria would reduce in turn to eliminating all offenses.

If the cost of apprehension and conviction were not zero, the optimality condition would have to incorporate marginal costs as well as marginal damages and would become, if the probability of conviction were still assumed to equal unity,

$$D'(\hat{O}) + C'(\hat{O}, 1) = 0. \tag{28}$$

Since $C' > 0$, (28) requires that $D' < 0$ or that the marginal private gain exceed the marginal external harm, which generally means a smaller number of offenses than when $D' = 0$.[37] It is easy to show that equation (28) would be satisfied if the fine equalled the sum of marginal harm and marginal costs:

$$f = H'(\hat{O}) + C'(\hat{O}, 1).^{38} \tag{29}$$

In other words, offenders have to compensate for the cost of catching them as well as for the harm they directly do, which is a natural generalization of the usual externality analysis.

The optimality condition

$$D'(\hat{O}) + C'(\hat{O}, \hat{p}) + C_p(\hat{O}, \hat{p}) \frac{1}{O_p} = 0 \tag{30}$$

would replace equation (28) if the fine rather than the probability of

[36] By "victims" is meant the rest of society and not just the persons actually harmed.

[37] This result can also be derived as a special case of the results in the Mathematical Appendix on the effects of increases in C'.

[38] Since equilibrium requires that $f = G'(\hat{O})$, and since from (28)

$$D'(\hat{O}) = H'(\hat{O}) - G'(\hat{O}) = -C'(\hat{O}, 1),$$

then (29) follows directly by substitution.

conviction were fixed. Equation (30) would usually imply that $D'(\hat{O}) > 0$,[39] and thus that the number of offenses would exceed the optimal number when costs were zero. Whether costs of apprehension and conviction increase or decrease the optimal number of offenses largely depends, therefore, on whether penalties are changed by a change in the fine or in the probability of conviction. Of course, if both are subject to control, the optimal probability of conviction would be arbitrarily close to zero, unless the social loss function differed from equation (18) (see the discussion in Sec. III).

C. The Case for Fines

Just as the probability of conviction and the severity of punishment are subject to control by society, so too is the form of punishment: legislation usually specifies whether an offense is punishable by fines, probation, institutionalization, or some combination. Is it merely an accident, or have optimality considerations determined that today, in most countries, fines are the predominant form of punishment, with institutionalization reserved for the more serious offenses? This section presents several arguments which imply that social welfare is increased if fines are used *whenever feasible*.

In the first place, probation and institutionalization use up social resources, and fines do not, since the latter are basically just transfer payments, while the former use resources in the form of guards, supervisory personnel, probation officers, and the offenders' own time.[40] Table 1 indicates that the cost is not minor either: in the United States in 1965, about $1 billion was spent on "correction," and this estimate excludes, of course, the value of the loss in offenders' time.[41]

---

[39] That is, if, as seems plausible,

$$\frac{dC}{dp} = C' \frac{\partial O}{\partial p} + C_p > 0,$$

then

$$C' + C_p \frac{1}{\partial O/\partial p} < 0,$$

and

$$D'(\hat{O}) = -\left(C' + C_p \frac{1}{\partial O/\partial p}\right) > 0.$$

[40] Several early writers on criminology recognized this advantage of fines. For example, "Pecuniary punishments are highly economical, since all the evil felt by him who pays turns into an advantage for him who receives" (Bentham, 1931*b*, chap. vi), and "Imprisonment would have been regarded in these old times [*ca.* tenth century] as a useless punishment; it does not satisfy revenge, it keeps the criminal idle, and do what we may, *it is costly*" (Pollock and Maitland, 1952, p. 516; my italics).

[41] On the other hand, some transfer payments in the form of food, clothing, and shelter are included.

Moreover, the determination of the optimal number of offenses and severity of punishments is somewhat simplified by the use of fines. A wise use of fines requires knowledge of marginal gains and harm and of marginal apprehension and conviction costs; admittedly, such knowledge is not easily acquired. A wise use of imprisonment and other punishments must know this too, however, and, in addition, must know about the elasticities of response of offenses to changes in punishments. As the bitter controversies over the abolition of capital punishment suggest, it has been difficult to learn about these elasticities.

I suggested earlier that premeditation, sanity, and age can enter into the determination of punishments as proxies for the elasticities of response. These characteristics may not have to be considered in levying fines, because the optimal fines, as determined, say, by equations (27) or (29), do not depend on elasticities. Perhaps this partly explains why economists discussing externalities almost never mention motivation or intent, while sociologists and lawyers discussing criminal behavior invariably do. The former assume that punishment is by a monetary tax or fine, while the latter assume that non-monetary punishments are used.

Fines provide compensation to victims, and optimal fines at the margin fully compensate victims and restore the status quo ante, so that they are no worse off than if offenses were not committed.[42] Not only do other punishments fail to compensate, but they also require "victims" to spend additional resources in carrying out the punishment. It is not surprising, therefore, that the anger and fear felt toward ex-convicts who in fact have *not* "paid their debt to society" have resulted in additional punishments,[43] including legal restrictions on their political and economic opportunities[44] and informal restrictions on their social acceptance. Moreover, the absence of compensation encourages efforts to change and otherwise "rehabilitate" offenders through psychiatric counseling, therapy, and other programs. Since fines do compensate and do not create much additional cost, anger toward and fear of appropriately fined persons do not easily develop. As a result, additional punishments are not usually levied against "ex-finees," nor are strong efforts made to "rehabilitate" them.

One argument made against fines is that they are immoral because, in effect, they permit offenses to be bought for a price in the same way that

[42] Bentham recognized this and said, "To furnish an indemnity to the injured party is another useful quality in a punishment. It is a means of accomplishing two objects at once—punishing an offense and repairing it: removing the evil of the first order, and putting a stop to alarm. This is a characteristic advantage of pecuniary punishments" (1931, chap. vi).

[43] In the same way, the guilt felt by society in using the draft, a forced transfer *to* society, has led to additional payments to veterans in the form of education benefits, bonuses, hospitalization rights, etc.

[44] See Sutherland (1960, pp. 267–68) for a list of some of these.

bread or other goods are bought for a price.[45] A fine *can* be considered the price of an offense, but so too can any other form of punishment; for example, the "price" of stealing a car might be six months in jail. The only difference is in the units of measurement: fines are prices measured in monetary units, imprisonments are prices measured in time units, etc. If anything, monetary units are to be preferred here as they are generally preferred in pricing and accounting.

Optimal fines determined from equation (29) depend only on the marginal harm and cost and not at all on the economic positions of offenders. This has been criticized as unfair, and fines proportional to the incomes of offenders have been suggested.[46] If the goal is to minimize the social loss in income from offenses, and not to take vengeance or to inflict harm on offenders, then fines should depend on the total harm done by offenders, and not directly on their income, race, sex, etc. In the same way, the monetary value of optimal prison sentences and other punishments depends on the harm, costs, and elasticities of response, but not directly on an offender's income. Indeed, if the monetary value of the punishment by, say, imprisonment were independent of income, the length of the sentence would be *inversely* related to income, because the value placed on a given sentence is positively related to income.

We might detour briefly to point out some interesting implications for the probability of conviction of the fact that the monetary value of a given fine is obviously the same for all offenders, while the monetary equivalent or "value" of a given prison sentence or probation period is generally positively related to an offender's income. The discussion in Section II suggested that actual probabilities of conviction are not fixed to all offenders but usually vary with their age, sex, race, and, in particular, income. Offenders with higher earnings have an incentive to spend more on planning their offenses, on good lawyers, on legal appeals, and even on bribery to reduce the probability of apprehension and conviction for offenses punishable by, say, a given prison term, because the cost to them of conviction is relatively large compared to the cost of these expenditures.

[45] The very early English law relied heavily on monetary fines, even for murder, and it has been said that "every kind of blow or wound given to every kind of person had its price, and much of the jurisprudence of the time must have consisted of a knowledge of these preappointed prices" (Pollock and Maitland, 1952, p. 451).

The same idea was put amusingly in a recent *Mutt and Jeff* cartoon which showed a police car carrying a sign that read: "Speed limit 30 M per H—$5 fine every mile over speed limit—pick out speed you can afford."

[46] For example, Bentham said, "A pecuniary punishment, if the sum is fixed, is in the highest degree unequal. ... Fines have been determined without regard to the profit of the offense, to its evil, or to the wealth of the offender. ... Pecuniary punishments should always be regulated by the fortune of the offender. The relative amount of the fine should be fixed, not its absolute amount; for such an offense, such a part of the offender's fortune" (1931b, chap. ix). Note that optimal fines, as determined by eq. (29), do depend on "the profit of the offense" and on "its evil."

Similarly, however, poorer offenders have an incentive to use more of their time in planning their offenses, in court appearances, and the like to reduce the probability of conviction for offenses punishable by a given fine, because the cost to them of conviction is relatively large compared to the value of their time.[47] The implication is that the probability of conviction would be systematically related to the earnings of offenders: negatively for offenses punishable by imprisonment and positively for those punishable by fines. Although a negative relation for felonies and other offenses punishable by imprisonment has been frequently observed and deplored (see President's Commission, 1967c, pp. 139–53), I do not know of any studies of the relation for fines or of any recognition that the observed negative relation may be more a consequence of the nature of the punishment than of the influence of wealth.

Another argument made against fines is that certain crimes, like murder or rape, are so heinous that no amount of money could compensate for the harm inflicted. This argument has obvious merit and is a special case of the more general principle that fines cannot be relied on exclusively whenever the harm exceeds the resources of offenders. For then victims could not be fully compensated by offenders, and fines would have to be supplemented with prison terms or other punishments in order to discourage offenses optimally. This explains why imprisonments, probation, and parole are major punishments for the more serious felonies; considerable harm is inflicted, and felonious offenders lack sufficient resources to compensate. Since fines are preferable, it also suggests the need for a flexible system of instalment fines to enable offenders to pay fines more readily and thus avoid other punishments.

This analysis implies that if some offenders could pay the fine for a given offense and others could not,[48] the former should be punished solely by fine and the latter partly by other methods. In essence, therefore, these methods become a vehicle for punishing "debtors" to society. Before the cry is raised that the system is unfair, especially to poor offenders, consider the following.

Those punished would be debtors in "transactions" that were never agreed to by their "creditors," not in voluntary transactions, such as loans,[49] for which suitable precautions could be taken in advance by creditors. Moreover, punishment in any economic system based on

---

[47] Note that the incentive to use time to reduce the probability of a given prison sentence is unrelated to earnings, because the punishment is fixed in time, not monetary, units; likewise, the incentive to use money to reduce the probability of a given fine is also unrelated to earnings, because the punishment is fixed in monetary, not time, units.

[48] In one study, about half of those convicted of misdemeanors could not pay the fines (see President's Commission, 1967c, p. 148).

[49] The "debtor prisons" of earlier centuries generally housed persons who could not repay loans.

voluntary market transactions inevitably must distinguish between such "debtors" and others. If a rich man purchases a car and a poor man steals one, the former is congratulated, while the latter is often sent to prison when apprehended. Yet the rich man's purchase is equivalent to a "theft" subsequently compensated by a "fine" equal to the price of the car, while the poor man, in effect, goes to prison because he cannot pay this "fine."

Whether a punishment like imprisonment in lieu of a full fine for offenders lacking sufficient resources is "fair" depends, of course, on the length of the prison term compared to the fine.[50] For example, a prison term of one week in lieu of a $10,000 fine would, if anything, be "unfair" to wealthy offenders paying the fine. Since imprisonment is a more costly punishment to society than fines, the loss from offenses would be reduced by a policy of leniency toward persons who are imprisoned because they cannot pay fines. Consequently, optimal prison terms for "debtors" would not be "unfair" to them in the sense that the monetary equivalent to them of the prison terms would be less than the value of optimal fines, which in turn would equal the harm caused or the "debt."[51]

It appears, however, that "debtors" are often imprisoned at rates of exchange with fines that place a low value on time in prison. Although I have not seen systematic evidence on the different punishments actually offered convicted offenders, and the choices they made, many statutes in

[50] Yet without any discussion of the actual alternatives offered, the statement is made that "the money judgment assessed the punitive damages defendant hardly seems comparable in effect to the criminal sanctions of death, imprisonment, and stigmatization" ("Criminal Safeguards...," 1967).

[51] A formal proof is straightforward if for simplicity the probability of conviction is taken as equal to unity. For then the sole optimality condition is

$$D' + C' = -bf\left(1 - \frac{1}{\varepsilon_f}\right). \tag{1'}$$

Since $D' = H' - G'$, by substitution one has

$$G' = H' + C' + bf\left(1 - \frac{1}{\varepsilon_f}\right), \tag{2'}$$

and since equilibrium requires that $G' = f$,

$$f = H' + C' + bf\left(1 - \frac{1}{\varepsilon_f}\right), \tag{3'}$$

or

$$f = \frac{H' + C'}{1 - b(1 - 1/\varepsilon_f)}. \tag{4'}$$

If $b > 0$, $\varepsilon_f < 1$ (see Sec. III), and hence by eq. (4'),

$$f < H' + C', \tag{5'}$$

where the term on the right is the full marginal harm. If p as well as f is free to vary, the analysis becomes more complicated, but the conclusion about the relative monetary values of optimal imprisonments and fines remains the same (see the Mathematical Appendix).

the United States do permit fines and imprisonment that place a low value on time in prison. For example, in New York State, Class A Misdemeanors cán be punished by a prison term as long as one year or a fine no larger than $1,000 and Class B Misdemeanors, by a term as long as three months or a fine no larger than $500 (*Laws of New York*, 1965, chap. 1030, Arts. 70 and 80).[52] According to my analysis, these statutes permit excessive prison sentences relative to the fines, which may explain why imprisonment in lieu of fines is considered unfair to poor offenders, who often must "choose" the prison alternative.

D. Compensation and the Criminal Law

Actual criminal proceedings in the United States appear to seek a mixture of deterrence, compensation, and vengeance. I have already indicated that these goals are somewhat contradictory and cannot generally be simultaneously achieved; for example, if punishment were by fine, minimizing the social loss from offenses would be equivalent to compensating "victims" fully, and deterrence or vengeance could only be partially pursued. Therefore, if the case for fines were accepted, and punishment by optimal fines became the norm, the traditional approach to criminal law would have to be significantly modified.

First and foremost, the primary aim of all legal proceedings would become the same: not punishment or deterrence, but simply the assessment of the "harm" done by defendants. Much of traditional criminal law would become a branch of the law of torts,[53] say "social torts," in which the public would collectively sue for "public" harm. A "criminal" action would be defined fundamentally not by the nature of the action[54] but by the inability of a person to compensate for the "harm" that he caused. Thus an action would be "criminal" precisely because it results in uncompensated "harm" to others. Criminal law would cover all such actions, while tort law would cover all other (civil) actions.

As a practical example of the fundamental changes that would be wrought, consider the antitrust field. Inspired in part by the economist's classic demonstration that monopolies distort the allocation of resources and reduce economic welfare, the United States has outlawed conspiracies

---

[52] "Violations," however, can only be punished by prison terms as long as fifteen days or fines no larger than $250. Since these are maximum punishments, the actual ones imposed by the courts can, and often are, considerably less. Note, too, that the courts can punish by imprisonment, by fine, or by *both* (*Laws of New York*, 1965, chap. 1030, Art. 60).

[53] "The cardinal principle of damages in Anglo-American law [of torts] is that of *compensation* for the injury caused to plaintiff by defendant's breach of duty" (Harper and James, 1956, p. 1299).

[54] Of course, many traditional criminal actions like murder or rape would still usually be criminal under this approach too.

and other constraints of trade. In practice, defendants are often simply required to cease the objectionable activity, although sometimes they are also fined, become subject to damage suits, or are jailed.

If compensation were stressed, the main purpose of legal proceedings would be to levy fines equal to [55] the harm inflicted on society by constraints of trade. There would be no point to cease and desist orders, imprisonment, ridicule, or dissolution of companies. If the economist's theory about monopoly is correct, and if optimal fines were levied, firms would automatically cease any constraints of trade, because the gain to them would be less than the harm they cause and thus less than the fines expected. On the other hand, if Schumpeter and other critics are correct, and certain constraints of trade raise the level of economic welfare, fines could fully compensate society for the harm done, and yet some constraints would not cease, because the gain to participants would exceed the harm to others.[56]

One unexpected advantage, therefore, from stressing compensation and fines rather than punishment and deterrence is that the validity of the classical position need not be judged a priori. If valid, compensating fines would discourage all constraints of trade and would achieve the classical aims. If not, such fines would permit the socially desirable constraints to continue and, at the same time, would compensate society for the harm done.

Of course, as participants in triple-damage suits are well aware, the harm done is not easily measured, and serious mistakes would be inevitable. However, it is also extremely difficult to measure the harm in many civil suits,[57] yet these continue to function, probably reasonably well on the whole. Moreover, as experience accumulated, the margin of error would decline, and rules of thumb would develop. Finally, one must realize that difficult judgments are also required by the present antitrust policy, such as deciding that certain industries are "workably" competitive or that certain mergers reduce competition. An emphasis on fines and compensation would at least help avoid irrelevant issues by focusing attention on the information most needed for intelligent social policy.

[55] Actually, fines should exceed the harm done if the probability of conviction were less than unity. The possibility of avoiding conviction is the intellectual justification for punitive, such as triple, damages against those convicted.

[56] The classical view is that $D'(M)$ always is greater than zero, where M measures the different constraints of trade and D' measures the marginal damage; the critic's view is that for some M, $D'(M) < 0$. It has been shown above that if D' always is greater than zero, compensating fines would discourage all offenses, in this case constraints of trade, while if D' sometimes is less than zero, some offenses would remain (unless $C'[M]$, the marginal cost of detecting and convicting offenders, were sufficiently large relative to D').

[57] Harper and James said, "Sometimes [compensation] can be accomplished with a fair degree of accuracy. But obviously it cannot be done in anything but a figurative and essentially speculative way for many of the consequences of personal injury. Yet it is the aim of the law to attain at least a rough correspondence between the amount awarded as damages and the extent of the suffering" (1956, p. 1301).

VI. Private Expenditures against Crime

A variety of private as well as public actions also attempt to reduce the number and incidence of crimes: guards, doormen, and accountants are employed, locks and alarms installed, insurance coverage extended, parks and neighborhoods avoided, taxis used in place of walking or subways, and so on. Table 1 lists close to $2 billion of such expenditures in 1965, and this undoubtedly is a gross underestimate of the total. The need for private action is especially great in highly interdependent modern economies, where frequently a person must trust his resources, including his person, to the "care" of employees, employers, customers, or sellers.

If each person tries to minimize his expected loss in income from crimes, optimal private decisions can be easily derived from the previous discussion of optimal public ones. For each person there is a loss function similar to that given by equation (18):

$$L_j = H_j(O_j) + C_j(p_j, O_j, C, C_k) + b_j p_j f_j O_j. \tag{31}$$

The term H_j represents the harm to j from the O_j offenses committed against j, while C_j represents his cost of achieving a probability of conviction of p_j for offenses committed against him. Note that C_j not only is positively related to O_j but also is negatively related to C, public expenditures on crime, and to C_k, the set of private expenditures by other persons.[58]

The term $b_j p_j f_j O_j$ measures the expected[59] loss to j from punishment of offenders committing any of the O_j. Whereas most punishments result in a net loss to society as a whole, they often produce a gain for the actual victims. For example, punishment by fines given to the actual victims is just a transfer payment for society but is a clear gain to victims; similarly, punishment by imprisonment is a net loss to society but is a negligible loss to victims, since they usually pay a negligible part of imprisonment costs. This is why b_j is often less than or equal to zero, at the same time that b, the coefficient of social loss, is greater than or equal to zero.

Since b_j and f_j are determined primarily by public policy on punishments, the main decision variable directly controlled by j is p_j. If he chooses a p_j that minimizes L_j, the optimality condition analogous to

[58] An increase in C_k—O_j and C held constant—presumably helps solve offenses against j, because more of those against k would be solved.

[59] The expected private loss, unlike the expected social loss, is apt to have considerable variance because of the small number of independent offenses committed against any single person. If j were not risk neutral, therefore, L would have to be modified to include a term that depended on the distribution of $b_j p_j f_j O_j$.

equation (22) is

$$H'_j + C'_j + C_{jp_j} \frac{\partial p_j}{\partial O_j} = -b_j p_j f_j \left(1 - \frac{1}{\varepsilon_{jp_j}}\right).^{60} \tag{32}$$

The elasticity ε_{jp_j} measures the effect of a change in p_j on the number of offenses committed against j. If $b_j < 0$, and if the left-hand side of equation (32), the marginal cost of changing O_j, were greater than zero, then (32) implies that $\varepsilon_{jp_j} > 1$. Since offenders can substitute among victims, ε_{jp_j} is probably much larger than ε_p, the response of the total number of offenses to a change in the average probability, p. There is no inconsistency, therefore, between a requirement from the optimality condition given by (22) that $\varepsilon_p < 1$ and a requirement from (32) that $\varepsilon_{jp_j} > 1$.

VII. Some Applications

A. Optimal Benefits

Our analysis of crime is a generalization of the economist's analysis of external harm or diseconomies. Analytically, the generalization consists in introducing costs of apprehension and conviction, which make the probability of apprehension and conviction an important decision variable, and in treating punishment by imprisonment and other methods as well as by monetary payments. A crime is apparently not so different analytically from any other activity that produces external harm and when crimes are punishable by fines, the analytical differences virtually vanish.

Discussions of external economies or advantages are usually perfectly symmetrical to those of diseconomies, yet one searches in vain for analogues to the law of torts and criminality. Generally, compensation cannot be collected for the external advantages as opposed to harm caused, and no public officials comparable to policemen and district attorneys apprehend and "convict" benefactors rather than offenders. Of course, there is

---

[60] I have assumed that

$$\frac{\partial C}{\partial p_j} = \frac{\partial C_k}{\partial p_j} = 0,$$

in other words, that j is too "unimportant" to influence other expenditures. Although usually reasonable, this does suggest a modification to the optimality conditions given by eqs. (21) and (22). Since the effects of public expenditures depend on the level of private ones, and since the public is sufficiently "important" to influence private actions, eq. (22) has to be modified to

$$D' + C' + C_p \frac{\partial p}{\partial O} + \sum_{i=1}^{n} \frac{dC}{dC_i} \frac{dC_i}{dp} \frac{\partial p}{\partial O} = -bpf \left(1 + \frac{1}{\varepsilon_p}\right), \tag{22'}$$

and similarly for eq. (21). "The" probability p is, of course, a weighted average of the p_j. Eq. (22') incorporates the presumption that an increase in public expenditures would be partially thwarted by an induced decrease in private ones.

public interest in benefactors: medals, prizes, titles, and other privileges have been awarded to military heroes, government officials, scientists, scholars, artists, and businessmen by public and private bodies. Among the most famous are Nobel Prizes, Lenin Prizes, the Congressional Medal of Honor, knighthood, and patent rights. But these are piecemeal efforts that touch a tiny fraction of the population and lack the guidance of any body of law that codifies and analyzes different kinds of advantages.

Possibly the explanation for this lacuna is that criminal and tort law developed at the time when external harm was more common than advantages, or possibly the latter have been difficult to measure and thus considered too prone to favoritism. In any case, it is clear that the asymmetry in the law does not result from any analytical asymmetry, for a formal analysis of advantages, benefits, and benefactors can be developed that is quite symmetrical to the analysis of damages, offenses, and offenders. A function $A(B)$, for example, can give the net social advantages from B benefits in the same way that $D(O)$ gives the net damages from O offenses. Likewise, $K(B, p_1)$ can give the cost of apprehending and rewarding benefactors, where p_1 is the probability of so doing, with K' and $K_p > 0$; $B(p_1, a, v)$ can give the supply of benefits, where a is the award per benefit and v represents other determinants, with $\partial B/\partial p_1$ and $\partial B/\partial a > 0$; and b_1 can be the fraction of a that is a net loss to society. Instead of a loss function showing the decrease in social income from offenses, there can be a profit function showing the increase in income from benefits:

$$\Pi = A(B) - K(B, p_1) - b_1 p_1 a B. \tag{33}$$

If Π is maximized by choosing appropriate values of p_1 and a, the optimality conditions analogous to equations (21) and (22) are

$$A' - K' = b_1 p_1 a \left(1 + \frac{1}{e_a}\right) \tag{34}$$

and

$$A' - K' - K_p \frac{\partial p_1}{\partial B} = b_1 p_1 a \left(1 + \frac{1}{e_p}\right), \tag{35}$$

where

$$e_a = \frac{\partial B}{\partial a} \frac{a}{B}$$

and

$$e_p = \frac{\partial B}{\partial p_1} \frac{p_1}{B}$$

are both greater than zero. The implications of these equations are related to and yet differ in some important respects from those discussed earlier for (21) and (22).

For example, if $b_1 > 0$, which means that a is not a pure transfer but costs society resources, clearly (34) and (35) imply that $e_p > e_a$, since both $K_p > 0$ and $\partial p_1/\partial B > 0$. This is analogous to the implication of (21) and

(22) that $\varepsilon_p > \varepsilon_f$, but, while the latter implies that, at the margin, offenders are risk *preferrers*, the former implies that, at the margin, benefactors are risk *avoiders*.[61] Thus, while the optimal values of p and f would be in a region where "crime does not pay"—in the sense that the marginal income of criminals would be less than that available to them in less risky legal activities—the optimal values of p_1 and a would be where "benefits do pay"—in the same sense that the marginal income of benefactors would exceed that available to them in less risky activities. In this sense it "pays" to do "good" and does not "pay" to do "bad."

As an illustration of the analysis, consider the problem of rewarding inventors for their inventions. The function $A(B)$ gives the total social value of B inventions, and A' gives the marginal value of an additional one. The function $K(B, p_1)$ gives the cost of finding and rewarding inventors; if a patent system is used, it measures the cost of a patent office, of preparing applications, and of the lawyers, judges, and others involved in patent litigation.[62] The elasticities e_p and e_a measure the response of inventors to changes in the probability and magnitude of awards, while b_1 measures the social cost of the method used to award inventors. With a patent system, the cost consists in a less extensive use of an invention than would otherwise occur, and in any monopoly power so created.

Equations (34) and (35) imply that with any system having $b_1 > 0$, the smaller the elasticities of response of inventors, the smaller should be the probability and magnitude of awards. (The value of a patent can be changed, for example, by changing its life.) This shows the relevance of the controversy between those who maintain that most inventions stem from a basic desire "to know" and those who maintain that most stem from the prospects of financial awards, especially today with the emphasis on systematic investment in research and development. The former quite consistently usually advocate a weak patent system, while the latter equally consistently advocate its strengthening.

[61] The relation $e_p > e_a$ holds if, and only if,

$$\frac{\partial EU}{\partial p_1}\frac{p_1}{U} > \frac{\partial EU}{\partial a}\frac{a}{U}, \tag{1'}$$

where

$$EU = p_1 U(Y + a) + (1 - p_1)U(Y) \tag{2'}$$

(see the discussion on pp. 177–78). By differentiating eq. (2'), one can write (1') as

$$p_1[U(Y + a) - U(Y)] > p_1 a U'(Y + a), \tag{3'}$$

or

$$\frac{U(Y + a) - U(Y)}{a} > U'(Y + a). \tag{4'}$$

But (4') holds if everywhere $U'' < 0$ and does not hold if everywhere $U'' \geq 0$, which was to be proved.

[62] These costs are not entirely trivial: for example, in 1966 the U.S. Patent Office alone spent $34 million (see Bureau of the Budget, 1967), and much more was probably spent in preparing applications and in litigation.

Even if A', the marginal value of an invention, were "sizeable," the optimal decision would be to abolish property rights in an invention, that is, to set $p_1 = 0$, if b_1 and K[63] were sufficiently large and/or the elasticities e_p and e_a sufficiently small. Indeed, practically all arguments to eliminate or greatly alter the patent system have been based either on its alleged costliness, large K or b_1, or lack of effectiveness, low e_p or e_a (see, for example, Plant, 1934, or Arrow, 1962).

If a patent system were replaced by a system of cash prizes, the elasticities of response would become irrelevant for the determination of optimal policies, because b_1 would then be approximately zero.[64] A system of prizes would, moreover, have many of the same other advantages that fines have in punishing offenders (see the discussion in Sec. V). One significant advantage of a patent system, however, is that it automatically "meters" A', that is, provides an award that is automatically positively related to A', while a system of prizes (or of fines and imprisonment) has to estimate A' (or D') independently and often somewhat arbitrarily.

B. The Effectiveness of Public Policy

The anticipation of conviction and punishment reduces the loss from offenses and thus increases social welfare by discouraging some offenders. What determines the increase in welfare, that is "effectiveness," of public efforts to discourage offenses? The model developed in Section III can be used to answer this question if social welfare is measured by income and if "effectiveness" is defined as a ratio of the maximum feasible increase in income to the increase if all offenses causing net damages were abolished by fiat. The maximum feasible increase is achieved by choosing optimal values of the probability of apprehension and conviction, p, and the size of punishments, f (assuming that the coefficient of social loss from punishment, b, is given).[65]

---

[63] Presumably one reason patents are not permitted on basic research is the difficulty (that is, cost) of discovering the ownership of new concepts and theorems.

[64] The right side of both (34) and (35) would vanish, and the optimality conditions would be

$$A' - K' = 0 \tag{34'}$$

and

$$A' - K' - K_p \frac{\partial p_1}{\partial B} = 0. \tag{35'}$$

Since these equations are not satisfied by any finite values of p_1 and a, there is a difficulty in allocating the incentives between p_1 and a (see the similar discussion for fines in Sec. V).

[65] In symbols, effectiveness is defined as

$$E = \frac{D(O_1) - [D(\hat{O}) + C(\hat{p}, \hat{O}) + b\hat{p}\hat{f}\hat{O}]}{D(O_1) - D(O_2)},$$

where $\hat{p}$, $\hat{f}$, and $\hat{O}$ are optimal values, O_1 offenses would occur if $p = f = 0$, and O_2 is the value of O that minimizes D.

Effectiveness so defined can vary between zero and unity and depends essentially on two behavioral relations: the costs of apprehension and conviction and the elasticities of response of offenses to changes in p and f. The smaller these costs or the greater these elasticities, the smaller the cost of achieving any given reduction in offenses and thus the greater the effectiveness. The elasticities may well differ considerably among different kinds of offenses. For example, crimes of passion, like murder or rape, or crimes of youth, like auto theft, are often said to be less responsive to changes in p and f than are more calculating crimes by adults, like embezzlement, antitrust violation, or bank robbery. The elasticities estimated by Smigel (1965) and Ehrlich (1967) for seven major felonies do differ considerably but are not clearly smaller for murder, rape, auto theft, and assault than for robbery, burglary, and larceny.[66]

Probably effectiveness differs among offenses more because of differences in the costs of apprehension and conviction than in the elasticities of response. An important determinant of these costs, and one that varies greatly, is the time between commission and detection of an offense.[67] For the earlier an offense is detected, the earlier the police can be brought in and the more likely that the victim is able personally to identify the offender. This suggests that effectiveness is greater for robbery than for a related felony like burglary, or for minimum-wage and fair-employment legislation than for other white-collar legislation like antitrust and public-utility regulation.[68]

C. A Theory of Collusion

The theory developed in this essay can be applied to any effort to preclude certain kinds of behavior, regardless of whether the behavior is "unlawful." As an example, consider efforts by competing firms to collude in order to obtain monopoly profits. Economists lack a satisfactory theory of the determinants of price and output policies by firms in an industry, a theory that could predict under what conditions perfectly competitive, monopolistic, or various intermediate kinds of behavior would emerge. One by-product of our approach to crime and punishment is a theory of collusion that appears to fill a good part of this lacuna.[69]

[66] A theoretical argument that also casts doubt on the assertion that less "calculating" offenders are less responsive to changes in p and f can be found in Becker (1962).

[67] A study of crimes in parts of Los Angeles during January, 1966, found that "more than half the arrests were made within 8 hours of the crime, and almost two-thirds were made within the first week" (President's Commission 1967e, p. 8).

[68] Evidence relating to the effectiveness of actual, which are not necessarily optimal, penalties for these white-collar crimes can be found in Stigler (1962, 1966), Landes (1966), and Johnson (1967).

[69] Jacob Mincer first suggested this application to me.

The gain to firms from colluding is positively related to the elasticity of their marginal cost curves and is inversely related to the elasticity of their collective demand curve. A firm that violates a collusive arrangement by pricing below or producing more than is specified can be said to commit an "offense" against the collusion. The resulting harm to the collusion would depend on the number of violations and on the elasticities of demand and marginal cost curves, since the gain from colluding depends on these elasticities.

If violations could be eliminated without cost, the optimal solution would obviously be to eliminate all of them and to engage in pure monopoly pricing. In general, however, as with other kinds of offenses, there are two costs of eliminating violations. There is first of all the cost of discovering violations and of "apprehending" violators. This cost is greater the greater the desired probability of detection and the greater the number of violations. Other things the same, the latter is usually positively related to the number of firms in an industry, which partly explains why economists typically relate monopoly power to concentration. The cost of achieving a given probability of detection also depends on the number of firms, on the number of customers, on the stability of customer buying patterns, and on government policies toward collusive arrangements (see Stigler, 1964).

Second, there is the cost to the collusion of punishing violators. The most favorable situation is one in which fines could be levied against violators and collected by the collusion. If fines and other legal recourse are ruled out, methods like predatory price-cutting or violence have to be used, and they hurt the collusion as well as violators.

Firms in a collusion are assumed to choose probabilities of detection, punishments to violators, and prices and outputs that minimize their loss from violations, which would at the same time maximize their gain from colluding. Optimal prices and outputs would be closer to the competitive position the more elastic demand curves were, the greater the number of sellers and buyers, the less transferable punishments were, and the more hostile to collusion governments were. Note that misallocation of resources could not be measured simply by the deviation of actual from competitive outputs but would depend also on the cost of enforcing collusions. Note further, and more importantly, that this theory, unlike most theories of pricing, provides for continuous variation, from purely competitive through intermediate situations to purely monopolistic pricing. These situations differ primarily because of differences in the "optimal" number of violations, which in turn are related to differences in the elasticities. concentrations, legislation, etc., already mentioned.

These ideas appear to be helpful in understanding the relative success of collusions in illegal industries themselves! Just as firms in legal industries have an incentive to collude to raise prices and profits, so too do firms producing illegal products, such as narcotics, gambling, prostitution, and abortion. The "syndicate" is an example of a presumably highly successful collusion that covers several illegal products.[70] In a country like the United States that prohibits collusions, those in illegal industries would seem to have an advantage, because force and other illegal methods could be used against violators without the latter having much legal recourse. On the other hand, in countries like prewar Germany that legalized collusions, those in legal industries would have an advantage, because violators could often be legally prosecuted. One would predict, therefore, from this consideration alone, relatively more successful collusions in illegal industries in the United States, and in legal ones in prewar Germany.

VIII. Summary and Concluding Remarks

This essay uses economic analysis to develop optimal public and private policies to combat illegal behavior. The public's decision variables are its expenditures on police, courts, etc., which help determine the probability (p) that an offense is discovered and the offender apprehended and convicted, the size of the punishment for those convicted (f), and the form of the punishment: imprisonment, probation, fine, etc. Optimal values of these variables can be chosen subject to, among other things, the constraints imposed by three behavioral relations. One shows the damages caused by a given number of illegal actions, called offenses (O), another the cost of achieving a given p, and the third the effect of changes in p and f on O.

"Optimal" decisions are interpreted to mean decisions that minimize the social loss in income from offenses. This loss is the sum of damages, costs of apprehension and conviction, and costs of carrying out the punishments imposed, and can be minimized simultaneously with respect to p, f, and the form of f unless one or more of these variables is constrained by "outside" considerations. The optimality conditions derived from the minimization have numerous interesting implications that can be illustrated by a few examples.

If carrying out the punishment were costly, as it is with probation, imprisonment, or parole, the elasticity of response of offenses with respect to a change in p would generally, in equilibrium, have to exceed its response to a change in f. This implies, if entry into illegal activities can be explained by the same model of choice that economists use to explain entry into legal activities, that offenders are (at the margin) "risk preferrers." Consequently, illegal activities "would not pay" (at the margin)

---

[70] An interpretation of the syndicate along these lines is also found in Schilling (1967).

in the sense that the real income received would be less than what could be received in less risky legal activities. The conclusion that "crime would not pay" is an optimality condition and not an implication about the efficiency of the police or courts; indeed, it holds for any level of efficiency, as long as optimal values of p and f appropriate to each level are chosen.

If costs were the same, the optimal values of both p and f would be greater, the greater the damage caused by an offense. Therefore, offenses like murder and rape should be solved more frequently and punished more severely than milder offenses like auto theft and petty larceny. Evidence on actual probabilities and punishments in the United States is strongly consistent with this implication of the optimality analysis.

Fines have several advantages over other punishments: for example, they conserve resources, compensate society as well as punish offenders, and simplify the determination of optimal p's and f's. Not surprisingly, fines are the most common punishment and have grown in importance over time. Offenders who cannot pay fines have to be punished in other ways, but the optimality analysis implies that the monetary value to them of these punishments should generally be less than the fines.

Vengeance, deterrence, safety, rehabilitation, and compensation are perhaps the most important of the many desiderata proposed throughout history. Next to these, minimizing the social loss in income may seem narrow, bland, and even quaint. Unquestionably, the income criterion can be usefully generalized in several directions, and a few have already been suggested in the essay. Yet one should not lose sight of the fact that it is more general and powerful than it may seem and actually includes more dramatic desiderata as special cases. For example, if punishment were by an optimal fine, minimizing the loss in income would be equivalent to compensating "victims" fully and would eliminate the "alarm" that so worried Bentham; or it would be equivalent to deterring all offenses causing great damage if the cost of apprehending, convicting, and punishing these offenders were relatively small. Since the same could also be demonstrated for vengeance or rehabilitation, the moral should be clear: minimizing the loss in income is actually very general and thus is *more useful* than these catchy and dramatic but inflexible desiderata.

This essay concentrates almost entirely on determining optimal policies to combat illegal behavior and pays little attention to actual policies. The small amount of evidence on actual policies that I have examined certainly suggests a positive correspondence with optimal policies. For example, it is found for seven major felonies in the United States that more damaging ones are penalized more severely, that the elasticity of response of offenses to changes in p exceeds the response to f, and that both are usually less than unity, all as predicted by the optimality analysis. There are, however, some discrepancies too: for example, the actual tradeoff between imprisonment and fines in different statutes is frequently less, rather than the predicted more, favorable to those imprisoned. Although many more studies of actual policies are needed, they are seriously hampered on the empirical side by grave limitations in the quantity and quality of data on offenses, convictions, costs, etc., and on the analytical side by the absence of a reliable theory of political decision-making.

Reasonable men will often differ on the amount of damages or benefits caused by different activities. To some, any wage rates set by competitive labor markets are permissible, while to others, rates below a certain minimum are violations of basic rights; to some, gambling, prostitution, and even abortion should be freely available to anyone willing to pay the market price, while to others, gambling is sinful and abortion is murder. These differences are basic to the development and implementation of public policy but have been excluded from my inquiry. I assume consensus on damages and benefits and simply try to work out rules for an optimal implementation of this consensus.

The main contribution of this essay, as I see it, is to demonstrate that optimal policies to combat illegal behavior are part of an optimal allocation of resources. Since economics has been developed to handle resource allocation, an "economic" framework becomes applicable to, and helps enrich, the analysis of illegal behavior. At the same time, certain unique aspects of the latter enrich economic analysis: some punishments, such as imprisonments, are necessarily non-monetary and are a cost to society as well as to offenders; the degree of uncertainty is a decision variable that enters both the revenue and cost functions; etc.

Lest the reader be repelled by the apparent novelty of an "economic" framework for illegal behavior, let him recall that two important contributors to criminology during the eighteenth and nineteenth centuries, Beccaria and Bentham, explicitly applied an economic calculus. Unfortunately, such an approach has lost favor during the last hundred years, and my efforts can be viewed as a resurrection, modernization, and thereby I hope improvement on these much earlier pioneering studies.

Mathematical Appendix

This Appendix derives the effects of changes in various parameters on the optimal values of p and f. It is assumed throughout that $b > 0$ and that equilibrium occurs where

$$\frac{\partial D}{\partial O} + \frac{\partial C}{\partial O} + \frac{\partial C}{\partial p}\frac{\partial p}{\partial O} = D' + C' + C_p\frac{\partial p}{\partial O} > 0;$$

the analysis could easily be extended to cover negative values of b and of this marginal cost term. The conclusion in the text (Sec. II) that $D'' + C'' > 0$ is relied on here. I take it to be a reasonable first approximation that the elasticities of O with respect to p or f are constant. At several places a sufficient condition for the conclusions reached is that

$$C_{pO} = C_{Op} = \frac{\partial^2 C}{\partial p \partial O} = \frac{\partial^2 C}{\partial O \partial p}$$

is "small" relative to some other terms. This condition is utilized in the form of a strong assumption that $C_{pO} = 0$, although I cannot claim any supporting intuitive or other evidence.

The social loss in income from offenses has been defined as

$$L = D(O) + C(O, p) + bpfO. \tag{A1}$$

If b and p were fixed, the value of f that minimized L would be found from the necessary condition

$$\frac{\partial L}{\partial f} = 0 = (D' + C')\frac{\partial O}{\partial f} + bpf(1 - E_f)\frac{\partial O}{\partial f}, \tag{A2}$$

or

$$0 = D' + C' + bpf(1 - E_f), \tag{A3}$$

if

$$\frac{\partial O}{\partial f} = O_f \neq 0,$$

where

$$E_f = \frac{-\partial f}{\partial O}\frac{O}{f}.$$

The sufficient condition would be that $\partial^2 L/\partial f^2 > 0$; using $\partial L/\partial f = 0$ and E_f is constant, this condition becomes

$$\frac{\partial^2 L}{\partial f^2} = (D'' + C'')O_f^2 + bp(1 - E_f)O_f > 0, \tag{A4}$$

or

$$\Delta \equiv D'' + C'' + bp(1 - E_f)\frac{1}{O_f} > 0. \tag{A5}$$

Since $D' + C' > 0$, and b is not less than zero, equation (A3) implies that $E_f > 1$. Therefore Δ would be greater than zero, since we are assuming that $D'' + C'' > 0$; and $\hat{f}$, the value of f satisfying (A3), would minimize (locally) the loss L.

Suppose that D' is positively related to an exogenous variable α. The effect of a change in α on $\hat{f}$ can be found by differentiating equation (A3):

$$D'_\alpha + (D'' + C'')O_f\frac{d\hat{f}}{d\alpha} + bp(1 - E_f)\frac{d\hat{f}}{d\alpha} = 0,$$

or

$$\frac{d\hat{f}}{d\alpha} = \frac{-D'_\alpha(1/O_f)}{\Delta}. \tag{A6}$$

Since $\Delta > 0$, $O_f < 0$, and by assumption $D'_\alpha > 0$, then

$$\frac{d\hat{f}}{d\alpha} = \frac{+}{+} > 0. \tag{A7}$$

In a similar way it can be shown that, if C' is positively related to an exogenous variable β,

$$\frac{d\hat{f}}{d\beta} = \frac{-C'_\beta(1/O_f)}{\Delta} = \frac{+}{+} > 0. \tag{A8}$$

If b is positively related to γ, then

$$(D'' + C'')O_f \frac{df}{d\gamma} + bp(1 - E_f) \frac{df}{d\gamma} + pf(1 - E_f)b\gamma = 0,$$

or

$$\frac{df}{d\gamma} = \frac{-b_\gamma pf(1 - E_f)(1/O_f)}{\Delta}. \tag{A9}$$

Since $1 - E_f < 0$, and by assumption $b_\gamma > 0$,

$$\frac{df}{d\gamma} = \frac{-}{+} < 0. \tag{A10}$$

Note that since $1/E_f < 1$,

$$\frac{d(pfO)}{d\gamma} < 0. \tag{A11}$$

If E_f is positively related to δ, then

$$\frac{df}{d\delta} = \frac{E_{f\delta} bpf(1/O_f)}{\Delta} = \frac{-}{+} < 0. \tag{A12}$$

Since the elasticity of O with respect to f equals

$$\epsilon_f = -O_f \frac{f}{O} = \frac{1}{E_f},$$

by (A12), a reduction in ϵ_f would reduce f.

Suppose that p is related to the exogenous variable r. Then the effect of a shift in r on f can be found from

$$(D'' + C'')O_f \frac{df}{dr} + (D'' + C'')O_p p_r + C_{pO} p_r$$
$$+ bp(1 - E_f) \frac{\partial f}{\partial r} + bf(1 - E_f)p_r = 0,$$

or

$$\frac{df}{dr} = \frac{-(D'' + C'')O_p(1/O_f)p_r - bf(1 - E_f)p_r(1/O_f)}{\Delta}, \tag{A13}$$

since by assumption $C_{pO} = 0$. Since $O_p < 0$, and $(D'' + C'') > 0$,

$$\frac{df}{dr} = \frac{(-) + (-)}{+} = \frac{-}{+} < 0. \tag{A14}$$

If f rather than p were fixed, the value of p that minimizes L, $\hat{p}$, could be found from

$$\frac{\partial L}{\partial p} = \left[D' + C' + C_p \frac{1}{O_p} + bpf(1 - E_p) \right] O_p = 0, \tag{A15}$$

as long as

$$\frac{\partial^2 L}{\partial p^2} = \left[(D'' + C'')O_p + C_p' + C_{pp} \frac{1}{O_p} + C_{pO} + C_p \frac{\partial^2 p}{\partial O \partial p} \right.$$
$$\left. + bf(1 - E_p) \right] O_p > 0. \tag{A16}$$

Since $C'_p = C_{pO} = 0$, (A16) would hold if

$$\Delta' \equiv D'' + C'' + C_{pp}\frac{1}{O_p^2} + C_p\frac{1}{O_p}\frac{\partial^2 p}{\partial O \partial p} + bf(1 - E_p)\frac{1}{O_p} > 0. \tag{A17}$$

It is suggested in Section II that C_{pp} is generally greater than zero. If, as assumed,

$$D' + C' + C_p\frac{1}{O_p} > 0,$$

equation (A15) implies that $E_p > 1$ and thus that

$$bf(1 - E_p)\frac{1}{O_p} > 0.$$

If E_p were constant, $\partial^2 p/\partial O \partial p$ would be negative,[71] and, therefore, $C_p(1/O_p)(\partial^2 p/\partial O \partial p)$ would be positive. Hence, none of the terms of (A17) are negative, and a value of p satisfying equation (A15) would be a local minimum.

The effects of changes in different parameters on $\hat{p}$ are similar to those already derived for $\hat{f}$ and can be written without comment:

$$\frac{d\hat{p}}{d\alpha} = \frac{-D'_\alpha(1/O_p)}{\Delta'} > 0, \tag{A18}$$

$$\frac{d\hat{p}}{d\beta} = \frac{-C'_\beta(1/O_p)}{\Delta'} > 0, \tag{A19}$$

and

$$\frac{d\hat{p}}{d\gamma} = \frac{-b_\gamma pf(1 - E_p)(1/O_p)}{\Delta'} < 0. \tag{A20}$$

If E_p is positively related to δ',

$$\frac{d\hat{p}}{d\delta'} = \frac{E_{p\delta'}bpf(1/O_p)}{\Delta'} < 0. \tag{A21}$$

If C_p were positively related to the parameter s, the effect of a change in s on $\hat{p}$ would equal

$$\frac{d\hat{p}}{ds} = \frac{-C_{ps}(1/O_p^2)}{\Delta'} < 0. \tag{A22}$$

If f were related to the exogenous parameter t, the effect of a change in t on $\hat{p}$ would be given by

$$\frac{d\hat{p}}{dt} = \frac{-(D'' + C'')O_pf_t(1/O_p) - bf(1 - E_p)f_t(1/O_p) - C_p(\partial^2 p/\partial O \partial f)f_t(1/O_p)}{\Delta'} < 0 \tag{A23}$$

(with $C_{pO} = 0$), since all the terms in the numerator are negative.

If both p and f were subject to control, L would be minimized by choosing optimal values of both variables simultaneously. These would be given by the

[71] If E_p and E_f are constants, $O = kp^{-a}f^{-b}$, where $a = 1/E_p$ and $b = 1/E_f$.

Then

$$\frac{\partial p}{\partial O} = -\frac{1}{ka}p^{a+1}f^b,$$

and

$$\frac{\partial^2 p}{\partial O \partial p} = \frac{-(a + 1)}{ka}p^af^b < 0.$$

solutions to the two first-order conditions, equations (A2) and (A15), assuming that certain more general second-order conditions were satisfied. The effects of changes in various parameters on these optimal values can be found by differentiating both first-order conditions and incorporating the restrictions of the second-order conditions.

The values of p and f satisfying (A2) and (A15), $\hat{p}$ and $\hat{f}$, minimize L if

$$L_{pp} > 0, \; L_{ff} > 0, \tag{A24}$$

and

$$L_{pp}L_{ff} > L_{fp}^2 = L_{pf}^2. \tag{A25}$$

But $L_{pp} = O_p^2 \Delta'$, and $L_{ff} = O_f^2 \Delta$, and since both Δ' and Δ have been shown to be greater than zero, (A24) is proved already, and only (A25) remains. By differentiating L_f with respect to p and utilizing the first-order condition that $L_f = 0$, one has

$$L_{fp} = O_f O_p [D'' + C'' + bf(1 - E_f)p_0] = O_f O_p \Sigma, \tag{A26}$$

where Σ equals the term in brackets. Clearly $\Sigma > 0$.

By substitution, (A25) becomes

$$\Delta \Delta' > \Sigma^2, \tag{A27}$$

and (A27) holds if Δ and Δ' are both greater than Σ. $\Delta > \Sigma$ means that

$$D'' + C'' + bp(1 - E_f)f_0 > D'' + C'' + bf(1 - E_f)p_0, \tag{A28}$$

or

$$\frac{bfp}{O}(1 - E_f)E_f < \frac{bpf}{O}(1 - E_f)E_p. \tag{A29}$$

Since $1 - E_f < 0$, (A29) implies that

$$E_f > E_p, \tag{A30}$$

which necessarily holds given the assumption that $b > 0$; prove this by combining the two first-order conditions (A2) and (A15). $\Delta' > \Sigma$ means that

$$D'' + C'' + C_{pp}p_0^2 + C_p p_0 o_{p} + bf(1 - E_p)p_0 > D'' + C'' + bf(1 - E_f)p_0. \tag{A31}$$

Since $C_{pp}p_0^2 > 0$, and $p_0 < 0$, this necessarily holds if

$$C_p p o_p + bpf(1 - E_p) < bpf(1 - E_f). \tag{A32}$$

By eliminating $D' + C'$ from the first-order conditions (A2) and (A15) and by combining terms, one has

$$C_p p_0 - bpf(E_p - E_f) = 0. \tag{A33}$$

By combining (A32) and (A33), one gets the condition

$$C_p p o_p < C_p p_0, \tag{A34}$$

or

$$E_{p_O,p} = \frac{p}{p_0}\frac{\partial p_0}{\partial p} > 1. \tag{A35}$$

It can be shown that

$$E_{p_O,p} = 1 + \frac{1}{E_p} > 1, \tag{A36}$$

and, therefore, (A35) is proven.

It has now been proved that the values of p and f that satisfy the first-order conditions (A2) and (A15) do indeed minimize (locally) L. Changes in different parameters change these optimal values, and the direction and magnitude can be found from the two linear equations

$$O_f \Delta \frac{\partial \tilde{f}}{\partial z} + O_p \Sigma \frac{\partial \tilde{p}}{\partial z} = C_1$$

and   (A37)

$$O_f \Sigma \frac{\partial \tilde{f}}{\partial z} + O_p \Delta' \frac{\partial \tilde{p}}{\partial z} = C_2.$$

By Cramer's rule,

$$\frac{\partial \tilde{f}}{\partial z} = \frac{C_1 O_p \Delta' - C_2 O_p \Sigma}{O_p O_f (\Delta \Delta' - \Sigma^2)} = \frac{O_p (C_1 \Delta' - C_2 \Sigma)}{+}, \qquad (A38)$$

$$\frac{\partial \tilde{p}}{\partial z} = \frac{C_2 O_f \Delta - C_1 O_f \Sigma}{O_p O_f (\Delta \Delta' - \Sigma^2)} = \frac{O_f (C_2 \Delta - C_1 \Sigma)}{+}, \qquad (A39)$$

and the signs of both derivatives are the same as the signs of the numerators.

Consider the effect of a change in D' resulting from a change in the parameter α. It is apparent that $C_1 = C_2 = -D'_\alpha$, and by substitution

$$\frac{\partial \tilde{f}}{\partial \alpha} = \frac{-O_p D'_\alpha (\Delta' - \Sigma)}{+} = \frac{+}{+} > 0 \qquad (A40)$$

and

$$\frac{\partial \tilde{p}}{\partial \alpha} = \frac{-O_p D'_\alpha (\Delta - \Sigma)}{+} = \frac{+}{+} > 0, \qquad (A41)$$

since O_f and $O_p < 0$, $D'_\alpha > 0$, and Δ and $\Delta' > \Sigma$.

Similarly, if C' is changed by a change in β, $C_1 = C_2 = -C'_\beta$,

$$\frac{\partial \tilde{f}}{\partial \beta} = \frac{-O_p C'_\beta (\Delta' - \Sigma)}{+} = \frac{+}{+} > 0, \qquad (A42)$$

and

$$\frac{\partial \tilde{p}}{\partial \beta} = \frac{-O_f C'_\beta (\Delta - \Sigma)}{+} = \frac{+}{+} > 0. \qquad (A43)$$

If E_f is changed by a change in δ, $C_1 = E_{f\delta} bpf$, $C_2 = 0$,

$$\frac{\partial \tilde{f}}{\partial \delta} = \frac{O_p E_f bpf \Delta'}{+} = \frac{-}{+} < 0, \qquad (A44)$$

and

$$\frac{\partial \tilde{p}}{\partial \delta} = \frac{-O_f E_f bpf \Sigma}{+} = \frac{+}{+} > 0. \qquad (A45)$$

Similarly, if E_p is changed by a change in δ', $C_1 = 0$, $C_2 = E_{p\delta'} bpf$,

$$\frac{\partial \tilde{f}}{\partial \delta'} = -\frac{O_p E_{p\delta'} bpf \Sigma}{+} = \frac{+}{+} > 0, \qquad (A46)$$

and

$$\frac{\partial \tilde{p}}{\partial \delta'} = \frac{O_f E_{p\delta'} bpf \Delta}{+} = \frac{-}{+} < 0. \qquad (A47)$$

If b is changed by a change in γ, $C_1 = -b_\gamma pf(1 - E_f)$, $C_2 = -b_\gamma pf(1 - E_p)$, and

$$\frac{\partial \tilde{f}}{\partial \gamma} = \frac{-O_p b_\gamma pf[(1 - E_f)\Delta' - (1 - E_p)\Sigma]}{+} = \frac{-}{+} < 0, \qquad (A48)$$

since $E_f > E_p > 1$ and $\Delta' > \Sigma$; also,

$$\frac{\partial \tilde{p}}{\partial \gamma} = \frac{-O_f b_\gamma pf[(1 - E_p)\Delta - (1 - E_f)\Sigma]}{+} = \frac{+}{+} > 0, \qquad (A49)$$

for it can be shown that $(1 - E_p)\Delta > (1 - E_f)\Sigma$.[72] Note that when f is held constant the optimal value of p is decreased, not increased, by an increase in γ.

If C_p is changed by a change in s, $C_2 = -p_O C_{ps}$, $C_1 = 0$,

$$\frac{\partial \tilde{f}}{\partial s} = \frac{O_p p_O C_{ps}\Sigma}{+} = \frac{C_{ps}\Sigma}{+} = \frac{+}{+} > 0, \qquad (A50)$$

and

$$\frac{\partial \tilde{p}}{\partial s} = \frac{-O_f p_O C_{ps}\Delta}{+} = \frac{-}{+} < 0. \qquad (A51)$$

[72] The term $(1 - E_p)\Delta$ would be greater than $(1 - E_f)\Sigma$ if

$$(D'' + C'')(1 - E_p) + bp(1 - E_f)(1 - E_p)f_O > (D'' + C'')(1 - E_f) + bf(1 - E_f)^2 p_O,$$

or

$$(D'' + C'')(E_f - E_p) > -\frac{bpf}{O}(1 - E_f)\left[(1 - E_p)\frac{f_O O}{f} - (1 - E_f)\frac{p_O O}{p}\right],$$

$$(D'' + C'')(E_f - E_p) > -\frac{bpf}{O}(1 - E_f)[(1 - E_p)(E_f) - (1 - E_f)E_p],$$

$$(D'' + C'')(E_f - E_p) > -\frac{bpf}{O}(1 - E_f)(E_f - E_p).$$

Since the left-hand side is greater than zero, and the right-hand side is less than zero, the inequality must hold.

Part 4   Time and Household Production

The paper on the allocation of time (chapter 5) applies the
economic approach not only to the allocation of time
between the market and nonmarket sectors, but also within
the nonmarket sector. Much apparently disparate behavior
is given a unified interpretation as responses simply to
differences in the value of time. In contrast to the book on
discrimination, this paper was enthusiastically received
immediately, largely because applications were so apparent.
This analysis of the allocation of time is applied in chapter 6
to life cycle decisions.

    The paper on the allocation of time also reformulates the
theory of the household so that households are no longer
simply passive consumers of goods and services purchased
in the market sector, but active producers of nonmarketable
commodities, such as health or prestige. These commodities
are produced by combining market goods and services, the
own time of household members, education, ability, and
other "environmental" variables. The household production
function approach is exposited in chapter 7.

5 A Theory of the Allocation of Time

I. Introduction

THROUGHOUT history the amount of time spent at work has never consistently been much greater than that spent at other activities. Even a work week of fourteen hours a day for six days still leaves half the total time for sleeping, eating and other activities. Economic development has led to a large secular decline in the work week, so that whatever may have been true of the past, to-day it is below fifty hours in most countries, less than a third of the total time available. Consequently the allocation and efficiency of non-working time may now be more important to economic welfare than that of working time; yet the attention paid by economists to the latter dwarfs any paid to the former.

Fortunately, there is a movement under way to redress the balance. The time spent at work declined secularly, partly because young persons increasingly delayed entering the labour market by lengthening their period of schooling. In recent years many economists have stressed that the time of students is one of the inputs into the educational process, that this time could be used to participate more fully in the labour market and therefore that one of the costs of education is the forgone earnings of students. Indeed, various estimates clearly indicate that forgone earnings is the dominant private and an important social cost of both high-school and college education in the United States.[1] The increased awareness of the importance of forgone earnings has resulted in several attempts to economise on students' time, as manifested, say, by the spread of the quarterly and tri-mester systems.[2]

Most economists have now fully grasped the importance of forgone earnings in the educational process and, more generally, in all investments in human capital, and criticise educationalists and others for neglecting them. In the light of this it is perhaps surprising that economists have not been

[1] See T. W. Schultz, " The Formation of Human Capital by Education," *Journal of Political Economy* (December 1960), and my *Human Capital* (Columbia University Press for the N.B.E.R., 1964), Chapter IV. I argue there that the importance of forgone earnings can be directly seen, *e.g.*, from the failure of free tuition to eliminate impediments to college attendance or the increased enrolments that sometimes occur in depressed areas or time periods.

[2] On the cause of the secular trend towards an increased school year see my comments, *ibid.*, p. 103.

Reprinted from the *Economic Journal* 75, no. 299 (September 1965): 493–517.

equally sophisticated about other non-working uses of time. For example, the cost of a service like the theatre or a good like meat is generally simply said to equal their market prices, yet everyone would agree that the theatre and even dining take time, just as schooling does, time that often could have been used productively. If so, the full costs of these activities would equal the sum of market prices and the forgone value of the time used up. In other words, indirect costs should be treated on the same footing when discussing all non-work uses of time, as they are now in discussions of schooling.

In the last few years a group of us at Columbia University have been occupied, perhaps initially independently but then increasingly less so, with introducing the cost of time systematically into decisions about non-work activities. J. Mincer has shown with several empirical examples how estimates of the income elasticity of demand for different commodities are biased when the cost of time is ignored;[1] J. Owen has analysed how the demand for leisure can be affected;[2] E. Dean has considered the allocation of time between subsistence work and market participation in some African economies;[3] while, as already mentioned, I have been concerned with the use of time in education, training and other kinds of human capital. Here I attempt to develop a general treatment of the allocation of time in all other non-work activities. Although under my name alone, much of any credit it merits belongs to the stimulus received from Mincer, Owen, Dean and other past and present participants in the Labor Workshop at Columbia.[4]

The plan of the discussion is as follows. The first section sets out a basic theoretical analysis of choice that includes the cost of time on the same footing as the cost of market goods, while the remaining sections treat various empirical implications of the theory. These include a new approach to changes in hours of work and " leisure," the full integration of so-called " productive " consumption into economic analysis, a new analysis of the effect of income on the quantity and " quality " of commodities consumed, some suggestions on the measurement of productivity, an economic analysis of queues and a few others as well. Although I refer to relevant empirical

[1] See his " Market Prices, Opportunity Costs, and Income Effects," in *Measurement in Economics: Studies in Mathematical Economics and Econometrics in Memory of Yehuda Grunfeld* (Stanford University Press, 1963). In his well-known earlier study Mincer considered the allocation of married women between " housework " and labour force participation. (See his " Labor Force Participation of Married Women," in *Aspects of Labor Economics* (Princeton University Press, 1962).)

[2] See his *The Supply of Labor and the Demand for Recreation* (unpublished Ph.D. dissertation, Columbia University, 1964).

[3] See his *Economic Analysis and African Response to Price* (unpublished Ph.D. dissertation, Columbia University, 1963).

[4] Let me emphasise, however, that I alone am responsible for any errors.

I would also like to express my appreciation for the comments received when presenting these ideas to seminars at the Universities of California (Los Angeles), Chicago, Pittsburgh, Rochester and Yale, and to a session at the 1963 Meetings of the Econometric Society. Extremely helpful comments on an earlier draft were provided by Milton Friedman and by Gregory C. Chow; the latter also assisted in the mathematical formulation. Linda Kee provided useful research assistance. My research was partially supported by the IBM Corporation.

work that has come to my attention, little systematic testing of the theory has been attempted.

II. A Revised Theory of Choice

According to traditional theory, households maximise utility functions of the form

$$U = U(y_1, y_2, \ldots, y_n) \quad \cdot \quad \cdot \quad \cdot \quad \cdot \quad \cdot \quad (1)$$

subject to the resource constraint

$$\sum p_i' y_i = I = W + V \quad \cdot \quad \cdot \quad \cdot \quad \cdot \quad (2)$$

where y_i are goods purchased on the market, p'_i are their prices, I is money income, W is earnings and V is other income. As the introduction suggests, the point of departure here is the systematic incorporation of non-working time. Households will be assumed to combine time and market goods to produce more basic commodities that directly enter their utility functions. One such commodity is the seeing of a play, which depends on the input of actors, script, theatre and the playgoer's time; another is sleeping, which depends on the input of a bed, house (pills?) and time. These commodities will be called Z_i and written as

$$Z_i = f_i(x_i, T_i) \quad \cdot \quad \cdot \quad \cdot \quad \cdot \quad \cdot \quad (3)$$

where x_i is a vector of market goods and T_i a vector of time inputs used in producing the ith commodity.[1] Note that, when capital goods such as refrigerators or automobiles are used, x refers to the services yielded by the goods. Also note that T_i is a vector because, *e.g.*, the hours used during the day or on weekdays may be distinguished from those used at night or on week-ends. Each dimension of T_i refers to a different aspect of time. Generally, the partial derivatives of Z_i with respect to both x_i and T_i are non-negative.[2]

In this formulation households are both producing units and utility maximisers. They combine time and market goods via the " production functions " f_i to produce the basic commodities Z_i, and they choose the best combination of these commodities in the conventional way by maximising a utility function

$$U = U(Z_i, \ldots Z_m) \equiv U(f_1, \ldots f_m) \equiv U(x_1, \ldots x_m; \ T_1, \ldots T_m) \quad (4)$$

---

[1] There are several empirical as well as conceptual advantages in assuming that households combine goods and time to produce commodities instead of simply assuming that the amount of time used at an activity is a direct function of the amount of goods consumed. For example, a change in the cost of goods relative to time could cause a significant substitution away from the one rising in relative cost. This, as well as other applications, are treated in the following sections.

[2] If a good or time period was used in producing several commodities I assume that these " joint costs " could be fully and uniquely allocated among the commodities. The problems here are no different from those usually arising in the analysis of multi-product firms.

subject to a budget constraint

$$g(Z_i, \ldots Z_m) = Z \qquad \ldots \ldots \quad (5)$$

where g is an expenditure function of Z_i' and Z is the bound on resources. The integration of production and consumption is at odds with the tendency for economists to separate them sharply, production occurring in firms and consumption in households. It should be pointed out, however, that in recent years economists increasingly recognise that a household is truly a " small factory ":[1] it combines capital goods, raw materials and labour to clean, feed, procreate and otherwise produce useful commodities. Undoubtedly the fundamental reason for the traditional separation is that firms are usually given control over working time in exchange for market goods, while " discretionary " control over market goods and consumption time is retained by households as they create their own utility. If (presumably different) firms were also given control over market goods and consumption time in exchange for providing utility the separation would quickly fade away in analysis as well as in fact.

The basic goal of the analysis is to find measures of g and Z which facilitate the development of empirical implications. The most direct approach is to assume that the utility function in equation (4) is maximised subject to separate constraints on the expenditure of market goods and time, and to the production functions in equation (3). The goods constraint can be written as

$$\sum_1^m p_i x_i = I = V + T_w \bar{w} \qquad \ldots \ldots \quad (6)$$

where p_i is a vector giving the unit prices of x_i, T_w is a vector giving the hours spent at work and $\bar{w}$ is a vector giving the earnings per unit of T_w. The time constraints can be written as

$$\sum_1^m T_i = T_c = T - T_w \qquad \ldots \ldots \quad (7)$$

where T_c is a vector giving the total time spent at consumption and T is a vector giving the total time available. The production functions (3) can be written in the equivalent form

$$\left. \begin{array}{c} T_i \equiv t_i Z_i \\ x_i \equiv b_i Z_i \end{array} \right\} \qquad \ldots \ldots \quad (8)$$

where t_i is a vector giving the input of time per unit of Z_i and b_i is a similar vector for market goods.

The problem would appear to be to maximise the utility function (4) subject to the multiple constraints (6) and (7) and to the production relations (8). There is, however, really only one basic constraint: (6) is not independent of (7) because time can be converted into goods by using less time

---

[1] See, *e.g.*, A. K. Cairncross, " Economic Schizophrenia," *Scottish Journal of Political Economy* (February 1958).

at consumption and more at work. Thus, substituting for T_w in (6) its equivalent in (7) gives the single constraint [1]

$$\sum p_i x_i + \sum T_i \bar{w} = V + T\bar{w} \quad . \quad . \quad . \quad . \quad (9)$$

By using (8), (9) can be written as

$$\sum (p_i b_i + t_i \bar{w}) Z_i = V + T\bar{w} \quad . \quad . \quad . \quad (10)$$

with
$$\begin{aligned} \pi_i &\equiv p_i b_i + t_i \bar{w} \\ S' &\equiv V + T\bar{w} \end{aligned} \Bigg\} \quad . \quad . \quad . \quad . \quad (11)$$

The full price of a unit of Z_i (π_i) is the sum of the prices of the goods and of the time used per unit of Z_i. That is, the full price of consumption is the sum of direct and indirect prices in the same way that the full cost of investing in human capital is the sum of direct and indirect costs.[2] These direct and indirect prices are symmetrical determinants of total price, and there is no analytical reason to stress one rather than the other.

The resource constraint on the right side of equation (10), S', is easy to interpret if $\bar{w}$ were a constant, independent of the Z_i. For then S' gives the money income achieved if all the time available were devoted to work. This achievable income is " spent " on the commodities Z_i either directly through expenditures on goods, $\sum p_i b_i Z_i$, or indirectly through the forgoing of income, $\sum t_i \bar{w} Z_i$, i.e., by using time at consumption rather than at work. As long as $\bar{w}$ were constant, and if there were constant returns in producing Z_i so that b_i and t_i were fixed for given p_i and $\bar{w}$ the equilibrium condition resulting from maximising (4) subject to (10) takes a very simple form:

$$U_i = \frac{\partial U}{\partial Z_i} = \lambda \pi_i \qquad i = 1, \ldots m \quad . \quad . \quad . \quad (12)$$

where λ is the marginal utility of money income. If $\bar{w}$ were not constant the resource constraint in equation (10) would not have any particularly useful interpretation: $S' = V + T\bar{w}$ would overstate the money income achievable as long as marginal wage-rates were below average ones. Moreover, the equilibrium conditions would become more complicated than (12) because marginal would have to replace average prices.

The total resource constraint could be given the sensible interpretation of the maximum money income achievable only in the special and unlikely case when average earnings were constant. This suggests dropping the approach based on explicitly considering separate goods and time constraints and substituting one in which the total resource constraint necessarily equalled the maximum money income achievable, which will be simply called " full income." [3] This income could in general be obtained by devoting all the

---

[1] The dependency among constraints distinguishes this problem from many other multiple-constraint situations in economic analysis, such as those arising in the usual theory of rationing (see J. Tobin, " A Survey of the Theory of Rationing," *Econometrica* (October, 1952)). Rationing would reduce to a formally identical single-constraint situation if rations were saleable and fully convertible into money income.

[2] See my *Human Capital, op. cit.*

[3] This term emerged from a conversation with Milton Friedman.

time and other resources of a household to earning income, with no regard for consumption. Of course, all the time would not usually be spent " at " a job: sleep, food, even leisure are required for efficiency, and some time (and other resources) would have to be spent on these activities in order to maximise money income. The amount spent would, however, be determined solely by the effect on income and not by any effect on utility. Slaves, for example, might be permitted time " off " from work only in so far as that maximised their output, or free persons in poor environments might have to maximise money income simply to survive.[1]

Households in richer countries do, however, forfeit money income in order to obtain additional utility, *i.e.*, they exchange money income for a greater amount of psychic income. For example, they might increase their leisure time, take a pleasant job in preference to a better-paying unpleasant one, employ unproductive nephews or eat more than is warranted by considerations of productivity. In these and other situations the amount of money income forfeited measures the cost of obtaining additional utility.

Thus the full income approach provides a meaningful resource constraint and one firmly based on the fact that goods and time can be combined into a single overall constraint because time can be converted into goods through money income. It also incorporates a unified treatment of all substitutions of non-pecuniary for pecuniary income, regardless of their nature or whether they occur on the job or in the household. The advantages of this will become clear as the analysis proceeds.

If full income is denoted by S, and if the total earnings forgone or " lost " by the interest in utility is denoted by L, the identity relating L to S and I is simply

$$L(Z_1, \ldots, Z_m) \equiv S - I(Z_1, \ldots, Z_m) \quad . \quad . \quad . \quad (13)$$

I and L are functions of the Z_i because how much is earned or forgone depends on the consumption set chosen; for example, up to a point, the less leisure chosen the larger the money income and the smaller the amount forgone.[2] Using equations (6) and (8), equation (13) can be written as

$$\sum p_i b_i Z_i + L(Z_1, \ldots, Z_m) \equiv S \quad . \quad . \quad . \quad . \quad (14)$$

[1] Any utility received would only be an incidental by-product of the pursuit of money income. Perhaps this explains why utility analysis was not clearly formulated and accepted until economic development had raised incomes well above the subsistence level.

[2] Full income is achieved by maximising the earnings function

$$W = W(Z_1, \ldots Z_m) \quad . \quad . \quad . \quad . \quad . \quad . \quad . \quad (1)$$

subject to the expenditure constraint in equation (6), to the inequality

$$\sum_1^m T_1 \leq T \quad . \quad . \quad . \quad . \quad . \quad . \quad . \quad . \quad . \quad (2')$$

and to the restrictions in (8). I assume for simplicity that the amount of each dimension of time used in producing commodities is less than the total available, so that (2') can be ignored; it is not

This basic resource constraint states that full income is spent either directly on market goods or indirectly through the forgoing of money income. Unfortunately, there is no simple expression for the average price of Z_i as there is in equation (10). However, marginal, not average, prices are relevant for behaviour, and these would be identical for the constraint in (10) only when average earnings, $\bar{w}$, was constant. But, if so, the expression for the loss function simplifies to

$$L = \bar{w}T_c = \bar{w}\sum t_i Z_i \quad . \quad . \quad . \quad . \quad . \quad (15)$$

and (14) reduces to (10). Moreover, even in the general case the total marginal prices resulting from (14) can always be divided into direct and indirect components: the equilibrium conditions resulting from maximising the utility function subject to (14) [1] are

$$U_i = T(p_i b_i + L_i), \qquad i = 1, \ldots, m \quad . \quad . \quad . \quad (16)$$

where $p_i b_i$ is the direct and L_i the indirect component of the total marginal price $p_i b_i + L_i$.[2]

Behind the division into direct and indirect costs is the allocation of time and goods between work-orientated and consumption-orientated activities. This suggests an alternative division of costs; namely, into those resulting from the allocation of goods and those resulting from the allocation of time. Write $L_i = \partial L/\partial Z_i$ as

$$L_i = \frac{\partial L}{\partial T_i}\frac{\partial T_i}{\partial Z_i} + \frac{\partial L}{\partial x_i}\frac{\partial x_i}{\partial Z_i} \quad . \quad . \quad . \quad . \quad (17)$$

$$= l_i t_i + c_i b_i \quad . \quad . \quad . \quad . \quad . \quad . \quad . \quad (18)$$

where $l_i = \dfrac{\partial L}{\partial T_i}$ and $c_i = \dfrac{\partial L}{\partial x_i}$ are the marginal forgone earnings of using more time and goods respectively on Z_i. Equation (16) can then be written as

$$U_i = T[b_i(p_i + c_i) + t_i l_i] \quad . \quad . \quad . \quad (19)$$

The total marginal cost of Z_i is the sum of $b_i(p_i + c_i)$, the marginal cost of using goods in producing Z_i, and $t_i l_i$, the marginal cost of using time. This division would be equivalent to that between direct and indirect costs only if $c_i = 0$ or if there were no indirect costs of using goods.

---

difficult to incorporate this constraint. Maximising (1′) subject to (6) and (8) yields the following conditions

$$\frac{\partial W}{\partial Z_i} = \frac{p_i b_i \sigma}{1 + \sigma} \quad . \quad . \quad . \quad . \quad . \quad . \quad . \quad . \quad (3′)$$

where σ is the marginal productivity of money income. Since the loss function $L = (S - V) - W$, the equilibrium conditions to minimise the loss is the same as (3′) except for a change in sign.

[1] Households maximise their utility subject only to the single total resource constraint given by (14), for once the full income constraint is satisfied, there is no other restriction on the set of Z_i that can be chosen. By introducing the concept of full income the problem of maximising utility subject to the time and goods constraints is solved in two stages: first, full income is determined from the goods and time constraints, and then utility is maximised subject only to the constraint imposed by full income.

[2] It can easily be shown that the equilibrium conditions of (16) are in fact precisely the same as those following in general from equation (10).

The accompanying figure shows the equilibrium given by equation (16) for a two-commodity world. In equilibrium the slope of the full income

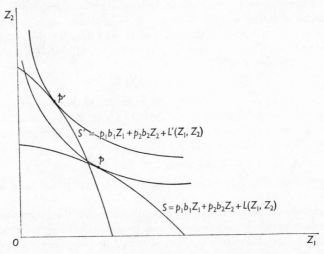

opportunity curve, which equals the ratio of marginal prices, would equal the slope of an indifference curve, which equals the ratio of marginal utilities. Equilibrium occurs at p and p' for the opportunity curves S and S' respectively.

The rest of the paper is concerned with developing numerous empirical implications of this theory, starting with determinants of hours worked and concluding with an economic interpretation of various queueing systems. To simplify the presentation, it is assumed that the distinction between direct and indirect costs is equivalent to that between goods and time costs; in other words, the marginal forgone cost of the use of goods, c_i, is set equal to zero. The discussion would not be much changed, but would be more cumbersome were this not assumed.[1] Finally, until Section IV goods and time are assumed to be used in fixed proportions in producing commodities; that is, the coefficients b_i and t_i in equation (8) are treated as constants.

III. APPLICATIONS

(a) *Hours of Work*

If the effects of various changes on the time used on consumption, T_c, could be determined their effects on hours worked, T_w, could be found residually from equation (7). This section considers, among other things, the effects of changes in income, earnings and market prices on T_c, and thus on T_w,

---

[1] Elsewhere I have discussed some effects of the allocation of goods on productivity (see my "Investment in Human Capital: A Theoretical Analysis," *Journal of Political Economy*, special supplement (October 1962), Section 2); essentially the same discussion can be found in *Human Capital, op. cit.*, Chapter II.

using as the major tool of analysis differences among commodities in the importance of forgone earnings.

The relative marginal importance of forgone earnings is defined as

$$\alpha_i = \frac{l_i t_i}{p_i b_i + l_i t_i} \quad \cdot \quad \cdot \quad \cdot \quad \cdot \quad \cdot \quad (20)$$

The importance of forgone earnings would be greater the larger l_i and t_i, the forgone earnings per hour of time and the number of hours used per unit of Z_i respectively, while it would be smaller the larger p_i and b_i, the market price of goods and the number of goods used per unit of Z_i respectively. Similarly, the relative marginal importance of time is defined as

$$\gamma_i = \frac{t_i}{p_i b_i + l_i t_i} \quad \cdot \quad \cdot \quad \cdot \quad \cdot \quad \cdot \quad (21)$$

If full income increased solely because of an increase in V (other money income) there would simply be a parallel shift of the opportunity curve to the right with no change in relative commodity prices. The consumption of most commodities would have to increase; if all did, hours worked would decrease, for the total time spent on consumption must increase if the output of all commodities did, and by equation (7) the time spent at work is inversely related to that spent on consumption. Hours worked could increase only if relatively time intensive commodities, those with large γ, were sufficiently inferior.[1]

A uniform percentage increase in earnings for all allocations of time would increase the cost per hour used in consumption by the same percentage for all commodities.[2] The relative prices of different commodities would, however, change as long as forgone earnings were not equally important for all; in particular, the prices of commodities having relatively important forgone earnings would rise more. Now the fundamental theorem of

---

[1] The problem is: under what conditions would

$$\frac{-\partial T_w}{\partial V} = \frac{\partial T_c}{\partial V} = \Sigma t_i \frac{\partial Z_i}{\partial V} < 0 \quad \cdot \quad \cdot \quad \cdot \quad \cdot \quad \cdot \quad \cdot \quad (1')$$

when

$$\Sigma(p_i b_i + l_i t_i) \frac{\partial Z_i}{\partial V} = 1 \quad \cdot \quad \cdot \quad \cdot \quad \cdot \quad \cdot \quad \cdot \quad \cdot \quad (2')$$

If the analysis were limited to a two-commodity world where Z_1 was more time intensive, then it can easily be shown that (1') would hold if, and only if,

$$\frac{\partial Z_1}{\partial V} < \frac{-\gamma_2}{(\gamma_1 - \gamma_2)(p_1 b_1 + l_1 t_1)} < 0 \quad \cdot \quad \cdot \quad \cdot \quad \cdot \quad \cdot \quad (3')$$

[2] By a uniform change of β is meant

$$W_1 = (1 + \beta) W_0(Z_1, \ldots Z_n)$$

where W_0 represents the earnings function before the change and W_1 represents it afterwards. Since the loss function is defined as

$$L = S - W - V$$
$$= W(\hat{Z}) - W(Z),$$

then

$$L_1 = W_1(\hat{Z}) - W_1(Z)$$
$$= (1 + \beta)[W_0(\hat{Z}) - W_0(Z)] = (1 + \beta)L_0$$

Consequently, all opportunities costs also change by β.

demand theory states that a compensated change in relative prices would induce households to consume less of commodities rising in price. The figure shows the effect of a rise in earnings fully compensated by a decline in other income: the opportunity curve would be rotated clockwise through the initial position p if Z_1 were the more earnings-intensive commodity. In the figure the new equilibrium p' must be to the left and above p, or less Z_1 and more Z_2 would be consumed.

Therefore a compensated uniform rise in earnings would lead to a shift away from earnings-intensive commodities and towards goods-intensive ones. Since earnings and time intensiveness tend to be positively correlated,[1] consumption would be shifted from time-intensive commodities. A shift away from such commodities would, however, result in a reduction in the total time spent in consumption, and thus an increase in the time spent at work.[2]

The effect of an uncompensated increase in earnings on hours worked would depend on the relative strength of the substitution and income effects. The former would increase hours, the latter reduce them; which dominates cannot be determined *a priori*.

The conclusion that a pure rise in earnings increases and a pure rise in income reduces hours of work must sound very familiar, for they are traditional results of the well-known labour–leisure analysis. What, then, is the relation between our analysis, which treats all commodities symmetrically and stresses only their differences in relative time and earning intensities, and the usual analysis, which distinguishes a commodity having special properties called " leisure " from other more commonplace commodities? It is easily shown that the usual labour–leisure analysis can be looked upon as a special case of ours in which the cost of the commodity called leisure consists entirely of forgone earnings and the cost of other commodities entirely of goods.[3]

---

[1] According to the definitions of earning and time intensity in equations (20) and (21), they would be positively correlated unless l_i and t_i were sufficiently negatively correlated. See the further discussion later on.

[2] Let it be stressed that this conclusion usually holds, even when households are irrational; sophisticated calculations about the value of time at work or in consumption, or substantial knowledge about the amount of time used by different commodities is not required. Changes in the hours of work, even of non-maximising, impulsive, habitual, etc., households would tend to be positively related to compensated changes in earnings because demand curves tend to be negatively inclined even for such households (see G. S. Becker, " Irrational Behavior and Economic Theory," *Journal of Political Economy* (February 1962)).

[3] Suppose there were two commodities Z_1 and Z_2, where the cost of Z_1 depended only on the cost of market goods, while the cost of Z_2 depended only on the cost of time. The goods-budget constraint would then simply be

$$p_1 b_1 Z_1 = I = V + T_w \bar{w}$$

and the constraint on time would be

$$t_2 Z_2 = T - T_w$$

This is essentially the algebra of the analysis presented by Henderson and Quandt, and their treatment is representative. They call Z_2 " leisure," and Z_1 an average of different commodities. Their

As a description of reality such an approach, of course, is not tenable, since virtually all activities use both time and goods. Perhaps it would be defended either as an analytically necessary or extremely insightful approximation to reality. Yet the usual substitution and income effects of a change in resources on hours worked have easily been derived from a more general analysis which stresses only that the relative importance of time varies among commodities. The rest of the paper tries to go further and demonstrate that the traditional approach, with its stress on the demand for " leisure," apparently has seriously impeded the development of insights about the economy, since the more direct and general approach presented here naturally leads to a variety of implications never yet obtained.

The two determinants of the importance of forgone earnings are the amount of time used per dollar of goods and the cost per unit of time. Reading a book, taking a haircut or commuting use more time per dollar of goods than eating dinner, frequenting a night-club or sending children to private summer camps. Other things the same, forgone earnings would be more important for the former set of commodities than the latter.

The importance of forgone earnings would be determined solely by time intensity only if the cost of time was the same for all commodities. Presumably, however, it varies considerably among commodities and at different periods. For example, the cost of time is often less on week-ends and in the evenings because many firms are closed then,[1] which explains why a famous liner intentionally includes a week-end in each voyage between the United States and Europe.[2] The cost of time would also tend to be less for commodities that contribute to productive effort, traditionally called " productive consumption." A considerable amount of sleep, food and even " play " fall under this heading. The opportunity cost of the time is less because these commodities indirectly contribute to earnings. Productive consumption has had a long but bandit-like existence in economic thought; our analysis does systematically incorporate it into household decision-making.

Although the formal specification of leisure in economic models has ignored expenditures on goods, cannot one argue that a more correct specification would simply associate leisure with relatively important forgone earnings? Most conceptions of leisure do imply that it is time intensive and does not indirectly contribute to earnings,[3] two of the important

---

equilibrium condition that the rate of substitution between goods and leisure equals the real wage-rate is just a special case of our equation (19) (see *Microeconomic Theory* (McGraw-Hill, 1958), p. 23).

[1] For workers receiving premium pay on the week-ends and in the evenings, however, the cost of time may be considerably greater then.

[2] See the advertisement by United States Lines in various issues of the *New Yorker* magazine: " The S.S. *United States* regularly includes a week-end in its 5 days to Europe, saving [economic] time for businessmen " (my insertion).

[3] For example, *Webster's Collegiate Dictionary* defines leisurely as " characterized by leisure, taking *abundant time* " (my italics); or S. de Grazia, in his recent *Of Time, Work and Leisure*, says, " Leisure is a state of being in which activity is performed for its own sake or as its own end " (New York: The Twentieth Century Fund, 1962, p. 15).

characteristics of earnings-intensive commodities. On the other hand, not all of what are usually considered leisure activities do have relatively important forgone earnings: night-clubbing is generally considered leisure, and yet, at least in its more expensive forms, has a large expenditure component. Conversely, some activities have relatively large forgone earnings and are not considered leisure: haircuts or child care are examples. Consequently, the distinction between earnings-intensive and other commodities corresponds only partly to the usual distinction between leisure and other commodities. Since it has been shown that the relative importance of forgone earnings rather than any concept of leisure is more relevant for economic analysis, less attention should be paid to the latter. Indeed, although the social philosopher might have to define precisely the concept of leisure,[1] the economist can reach all his traditional results as well as many more without introducing it at all!

Not only is it difficult to distinguish leisure from other non-work [2] but also even work from non-work. Is commuting work, non-work or both? How about a business lunch, a good diet or relaxation? Indeed, the notion of productive consumption was introduced precisely to cover those commodities that contribute to work as well as to consumption. Cannot pure work then be considered simply as a limiting commodity of such joint commodities in which the contribution to consumption was nil? Similarly, pure consumption would be a limiting commodity in the opposite direction in which the contribution to work was nil, and intermediate commodities would contribute to both consumption and work. The more important the contribution to work relative to consumption, the smaller would tend to be the relative importance of forgone earnings. Consequently, the effects of changes in earnings, other income, etc., on hours worked then become assimiliated to and essentially a special case of their effects on the consumption of less earnings-intensive commodities. For example, a pure rise in earnings would reduce the relative price, and thus increase the time spent on these commodities, *including the time spent at work*; similarly, for changes in income and other variables. The generalisation wrought by our approach is even greater than may have appeared at first.

Before concluding this section a few other relevant implications of our

[1] S. de Grazia has recently entertainingly shown the many difficulties in even reaching a reliable definition, and *a fortiori*, in quantitatively estimating the amount of leisure. See *ibid.*, Chapters III and IV; also see W. Moore, *Man, Time and Society* (New York: Wiley, 1963), Chapter II; J. N. Morgan, M. H. David, W. J. Cohen and H. E. Brazer, *Income and Welfare in the United States* (New York: McGraw-Hill, 1962), p. 322, and Owen, *op. cit.*, Chapter II.

[2] Sometimes true leisure is defined as the amount of discretionary time available (see Moore, *op. cit.*, p. 18). It is always difficult to attach a rigorous meaning to the word " discretionary " when referring to economic resources. One might say that in the short run consumption time is and working time is not discretionary, because the latter is partially subject to the authoritarian control of employers. (Even this distinction would vanish if households gave certain firms authoritarian control over their consumption time; see the discussion in Section II.) In the long run this definition of discretionary time is suspect too because the availability of alternative sources of employment would make working time also discretionary.

theory might be briefly mentioned.   Just as a (compensated) rise in earnings would increase the prices of commodities with relatively large forgone earnings, induce a substitution away from them and increase the hours worked, so a (compensated) fall in market prices would also induce a substitution away from them and increase the hours worked: the effects of changes in direct and indirect costs are symmetrical.   Indeed, Owen presents some evidence indicating that hours of work in the United States fell somewhat more in the first thirty years of this century than in the second thirty years, not because wages rose more during the first period, but because the market prices of recreation commodities fell more then.[1]

A well-known result of the traditional labour–leisure approach is that a rise in the income tax induces at least a substitution effect away from work and towards " leisure."   Our approach reaches the same result only via a substitution towards time-intensive consumption rather than leisure.   A simple additional implication of our approach, however, is that if a rise in the income tax were combined with an appropriate excise on the goods used in time-intensive commodities or subsidy to the goods used in other commodities there need be no change in full relative prices, and thus no substitution away from work.   The traditional approach has recently reached the same conclusion, although in a much more involved way.[2]

There is no exception in the traditional approach to the rule that a pure rise in earnings would not induce a decrease in hours worked.   An exception does occur in ours, for if the time and earnings intensities (*i.e.*, $l_i t_i$ and t_i) were negatively correlated a pure rise in earnings would induce a substitution towards time-intensive commodities, and thus away from work.[3]   Although this exception does illustrate the greater power of our approach, there is no reason to believe that it is any more important empirically than the exception to the rule on income effects.

(b) *The Productivity of Time*

Most of the large secular increase in earnings, which stimulated the development of the labour–leisure analysis, resulted from an increase in the productivity of working time due to the growth in human and physical capital, technological progress and other factors.   Since a rise in earnings resulting from an increase in productivity has both income and substitution

[1] See *op. cit.*, Chapter VIII.   Recreation commodities presumably have relatively large forgone earnings.

[2] See W. J. Corbett and D. C. Hague, " Complementarity and the Excess Burden of Taxation," *Review of Economic Studies*, Vol. XXI (1953–54); also A. C. Harberger, " Taxation, Resource Allocation and Welfare," in the *Role of Direct and Indirect Taxes in the Federal Revenue System* (Princeton University Press, 1964).

[3] The effect on earnings is more difficult to determine because, by assumption, time intensive commodities have smaller costs per unit time than other commodities.   A shift towards the former would, therefore, raise hourly earnings, which would partially and perhaps more than entirely offset the reduction in hours worked.   Incidentally, this illustrates how the productivity of hours worked is influenced by the consumption set chosen.

effects, the secular decline in hours worked appeared to be evidence that the income effect was sufficiently strong to swamp the substitution effect.

The secular growth in capital and technology also improved the productivity of consumption time: supermarkets, automobiles, sleeping pills, safety and electric razors, and telephones are a few familiar and important examples of such developments. An improvement in the productivity of consumption time would change relative commodity prices and increase full income, which in turn would produce substitution and income effects. The interesting point is that a very different interpretation of the observed decline in hours of work is suggested because these effects are precisely the opposite of those produced by improvements in the productivity of working time.

Assume a uniform increase only in the productivity of consumption time, which is taken to mean a decline in all t_i, time required to produce a unit of Z_i, by a common percentage. The relative prices of commodities with large forgone earnings would fall, and substitution would be induced towards these and away from other commodities, causing hours of work also to fall. Since the increase in productivity would also produce an income effect,[1] the demand for commodities would increase, which, in turn, would induce an increased demand for goods. But since the productivity of working time is assumed not to change, more goods could be obtained only by an increase in work. That is, the higher real income resulting from an advance in the productivity of consumption time would cause hours of work to *increase*.

Consequently, an emphasis on the secular increase in the productivity of consumption time would lead to a very different interpretation of the secular decline in hours worked. Instead of claiming that a powerful income effect swamped a weaker substitution effect, the claim would have to be that a powerful substitution effect swamped a weaker income effect.

Of course, the productivity of both working and consumption time increased secularly, and the true interpretation is somewhere between these extremes. If both increased at the same rate there would be no change in relative prices, and thus no substitution effect, because the rise in l_i induced by one would exactly offset the decline in t_i induced by the other, marginal forgone earnings $(i_i t_i)$ remaining unchanged. Although the income effects would tend to offset each other too, they would do so completely only if the income elasticity of demand for time-intensive commodities was equal to unity. Hours worked would decline if it was above and increase if it was below unity.[2] Since these commodities have probably on

---

[1] Full money income would be unaffected if it were achieved by using all time at pure work activities. If other uses of time were also required it would tend to increase. Even if full money income were unaffected, however, full real income would increase because prices of the Z_i would fall.

[2] So the " Knight " view that an increase in income would increase " leisure " is not necessarily true, even if leisure were a superior good and even aside from Robbins' emphasis on the substitution effect (see L. Robbins, " On the Elasticity of Demand for Income in Terms of Effort," *Economica* (June 1930)).

the whole been luxuries, such an increase in income would tend to reduce hours worked.

The productivity of working time has probably advanced more than that of consumption time, if only because of familiar reasons associated with the division of labour and economies of scale.[1] Consequently, there probably has been the traditional substitution effect towards and income effect away from work, as well as an income effect away from work because time-intensive commodities were luxuries. The secular decline in hours worked would only imply therefore that the combined income effects swamped the substitution effect, not that the income effect of an advance in the productivity of working time alone swamped its substitution effect.

Cross-sectionally, the hours worked of males have generally declined less as incomes increased than they have over time. Some of the difference between these relations is explained by the distinction between relevant and reported incomes, or by interdependencies among the hours worked by different employees;[2] some is probably also explained by the distinction between working and consumption productivity. There is a presumption that persons distinguished cross-sectionally by money incomes or earnings differ more in working than consumption productivity because they are essentially distinguished by the former. This argument does not apply to time series because persons are distinguished there by calendar time, which in principle is neutral between these productivities. Consequently, the traditional substitution effect towards work is apt to be greater cross-sectionally, which would help to explain why the relation between the income and hours worked of men is less negatively sloped there, and be additional evidence that the substitution effect for men is not weak.[3]

Productivity in the service sector in the United States appears to have advanced more slowly, at least since 1929, than productivity in the goods sector.[4] Service industries like retailing, transportation, education and health, use a good deal of the time of households that never enter into input, output and price series, or therefore into measures of productivity. Incorporation of such time into the series and consideration of changes in its productivity would contribute, I believe, to an understanding of the apparent differences in productivity advance between these sectors.

An excellent example can be found in a recent study of productivity

---

[1] Wesley Mitchell's justly famous essay " The Backward Art of Spending Money " spells out some of these reasons (see the first essay in the collection, *The Backward Art of Spending Money and Other Essays* (New York: McGraw-Hill, 1932)).

[2] A. Finnegan does find steeper cross-sectional relations when the average incomes and hours of different occupations are used (*see* his " A Cross-Sectional Analysis of Hours of Work," *Journal of Political Economy* (October, 1962)).

[3] Note that Mincer has found a very strong substitution effect for women (see his " Labor Force Participation of Married Women," *op. cit.*).

[4] See the essay by Victor Fuchs, " Productivity Trends in the Goods and Service Sectors, 1929–61: A Preliminary Survey," N.B.E.R. Occasional Paper, October 1964.

trends in the barbering industry in the United States.[1] Conventional productivity measures show relatively little advance in barbers' shops since
1929, yet a revolution has occurred in the activities performed by these shops.
In the 1920s shaves still accounted for an important part of their sales, but
declined to a negligible part by the 1950s because of the spread of home safety
and electric razors. Instead of travelling to a shop, waiting in line, receiving
a shave and continuing to another destination, men now shave themselves at
home, saving travelling, waiting and even some shaving time. This considerable advance in the productivity of shaving nowhere enters measures
for barbers' shops. If, however, a productivity measure for general
barbering activities, including shaving, was constructed, I suspect that it
would show an advance since 1929 comparable to most goods.[2]

(c) *Income Elasticities*

Income elasticities of demand are often estimated cross-sectionally from
the behaviour of families or other units with different incomes. When these
units buy in the same market-place it is natural to assume that they face the
same prices of goods. If, however, incomes differ because earnings do,
and cross-sectional income differences are usually dominated by earnings
differences, commodities prices would differ systematically. All commodities prices would be higher to higher-income units because their forgone
earnings would be higher (which means, incidentally, that differences in real
income would be less than those in money income), and the prices of earnings-
intensive commodities would be unusually so.

Cross-sectional relations between consumption and income would not
therefore measure the effect of income alone, because they would be affected
by differences in relative prices as well as in incomes.[3] The effect of income
would be underestimated for earnings-intensive and overestimated for other
commodities, because the higher relative prices of the former would cause a
substitution away from them and towards the latter. Accordingly, the
income elasticities of demand for " leisure," unproductive and time-intensive
commodities would be under-stated, and for " work," productive and other
goods-intensive commodities over-stated by cross-sectional estimates. Low
apparent income elasticities of earnings-intensive commodities and high
apparent elasticities of other commodities may simply be illusions resulting
from substitution effects.[4]

---

[1] See J. Wilburn, " Productivity Trends in Barber and Beauty Shops," mimeographed report,
N.B.E.R., September 1964.
[2] The movement of shaving from barbers' shops to households illustrates how and why even in
urban areas households have become " small factories." Under the impetus of a general growth
in the value of time they have been encouraged to find ways of saving on travelling and waiting time
by performing more activities themselves.
[3] More appropriate income elasticities for several commodities are estimated in Mincer,
" Market Prices . . .," *op. cit.*
[4] In this connection note that cross-sectional data are often preferred to time-series data in
estimating income elasticities precisely because they are supposed to be largely free of co-linearity

Moreover, according to our theory demand depends also on the importance of earnings as a source of income. For if total income were held constant an increase in earnings would create only substitution effects: away from earnings-intensive and towards goods-intensive commodities. So one unusual implication of the analysis that can and should be tested with available budget data is that the source of income may have a significant effect on consumption patterns. An important special case is found in comparisons of the consumption of employed and unemployed workers. Unemployed workers not only have lower incomes but also lower forgone costs, and thus lower relative prices of time and other earnings-intensive commodities. The propensity of unemployed workers to go fishing, watch television, attend school and so on are simply vivid illustrations of the incentives they have to substitute such commodities for others.

One interesting application of the analysis is to the relation between family size and income.[1] The traditional view, based usually on simple correlations, has been that an increase in income leads to a reduction in the number of children per family. If, however, birth-control knowledge and other variables were held constant economic theory suggests a positive relation between family size and income, and therefore that the traditional negative correlation resulted from positive correlations between income, knowledge and some other variables. The data I put together supported this interpretation, as did those found in several subsequent studies.[2]

Although positive, the elasticity of family size with respect to income is apparently quite low, even when birth-control knowledge is held constant. Some persons have interpreted this (and other evidence) to indicate that family-size formation cannot usefully be fitted into traditional economic analysis.[3] It was pointed out, however, that the small elasticity found for children is not so inconsistent with what is found for goods as soon as quantity and quality income elasticities are distinguished.[4] Increased expenditures on many goods largely take the form of increased quality–expenditure per pound, per car, etc.—and the increase in quantity is modest. Similarly, increased expenditures on children largely take the form of increased expenditures per child, while the increase in number of children is very modest.

---

between prices and incomes (see, *e.g.*, J. Tobin, " A Statistical Demand Function for Food in the U.S.A.," *Journal of the Royal Statistical Society*, Series A (1950)).

[1] Biases in cross-sectional estimates of the demand for work and leisure were considered in the last section.

[2] See G. S. Becker, "An Economic Analysis of Fertility," *Demographic and Economic Change in Developed Countries* (N.B.E.R. Conference Volume, 1960); R. A. Easterlin, " The American Baby Boom in Historical Perspective," *American Economic Review* (December 1961); I. Adelman, " An Econometric Analysis of Population Growth," *American Economic Review* (June 1963); R. Weintraub, " The Birth Rate and Economic Development: An Empirical Study," *Econometrica* (October 1962); Morris Silver, *Birth Rates, Marriages, and Business Cycles* (unpublished Ph.D. dissertation, Columbia University, 1964); and several other studies; for an apparent exception, see the note by D. Freedman, " The Relation of Economic Status to Fertility," *American Economic Review* (June 1963).

[3] See, for example, Duesenberry's comment on Becker, *op. cit.*   [4] See Becker, *op. cit.*

Nevertheless, the elasticity of demand for number of children does seem somewhat smaller than the quantity elasticities found for many goods. Perhaps the explanation is simply the shape of indifference curves; one other factor that may be more important, however, is the increase in forgone costs with income.[1]   Child care would seem to be a time-intensive activity that is not " productive " (in terms of earnings) and uses many hours that could be used at work.   Consequently, it would be an earnings-intensive activity, and our analysis predicts that its relative price would be higher to higher-income families.[2]   There is already some evidence suggesting that the positive relation between forgone costs and income explains why the apparent quantity income elasticity of demand for children is relatively small.   Mincer found that cross-sectional differences in the forgone price of children have an important effect on the number of children.[3]

(d) *Transportation*

Transportation is one of the few activities where the cost of time has been explicitly incorporated into economic discussions.   In most benefit-cost evaluations of new transportation networks the value of the savings in transportation time has tended to overshadow other benefits.[4]   The importance of the value placed on time has encouraged experiment with different methods of determination: from the simple view that the value of an hour equals average hourly earnings to sophisticated considerations of the distinction between standard and overtime hours, the internal and external margins, etc.

The transport field offers considerable opportunity to estimate the marginal productivity or value of time from actual behaviour.   One could, for example, relate the ratio of the number of persons travelling by aeroplane to those travelling by slower mediums to the distance travelled (and, of course, also to market prices and incomes).   Since relatively more people use faster mediums for longer distances, presumably largely because of the greater importance of the saving in time, one should be able to estimate a marginal value of time from the relation between medium and distance travelled.[5]

[1] In *Ibid.*, p. 214 fn. 8, the relation between forgone costs and income was mentioned but not elaborated.

[2] Other arguments suggesting that higher-income families face a higher price of children have generally confused price with quality (see *ibid.*, pp. 214–15).

[3] See Mincer, " Market Prices . . .," *op. cit.*   He measures the price of children by the wife's potential wage-rate, and fits regressions to various cross-sectional data, where number of children is the dependent variable, and family income and the wife's potential wage-rate are among the independent variables.

[4] See, for example, H. Mohring, " Land Values and the Measurement of Highway Benefits," *Journal of Political Economy* (June 1961).

[5] The only quantitative estimate of the marginal value of time that I am familiar with uses the relation between the value of land and its commuting distance from employment (see *ibid.*).   With many assumptions I have estimated the marginal value of time of those commuting at about 40% of their average hourly earnings.   It is not clear whether this value is so low because of errors in these assumptions or because of severe kinks in the supply and demand functions for hours of work.

Another transportation problem extensively studied is the length and mode of commuting to work.[1] It is usually assumed that direct commuting costs, such as train fare, vary positively and that living costs, such as space, vary negatively with the distance commuted. These assumptions alone would imply that a rise in incomes would result in longer commutes as long as space ("housing") were a superior good.[2]

A rise in income resulting at least in part from a rise in earnings would, however, increase the cost of commuting a given distance because the forgone value of the time involved would increase. This increase in commuting costs would discourage commuting in the same way that the increased demand for space would encourage it. The outcome depends on the relative strengths of these conflicting forces: one can show with a few assumptions that the distance commuted would increase as income increased if, and only if, space had an income elasticity greater than unity.

For let Z_1 refer to the commuting commodity, Z_2 to other commodities, and let

$$Z_1 = f_1(x, t) \quad . \quad . \quad . \quad . \quad . \quad (22)$$

where t is the time spent commuting and x is the quantity of space used. Commuting costs are assumed to have the simple form $a + l_1 t$, where a is a constant and l_1 is the marginal forgone cost per hour spent commuting. In other words, the cost of time is the only variable commuting cost. The cost per unit of space is $p(t)$, where by assumption $p' < 0$. The problem is to maximise the utility function

$$U = U(x, t, Z_2) \quad . \quad . \quad . \quad . \quad . \quad (23)$$

subject to the resource constraint

$$a + l_1 t + px + h(Z_2) = S \quad . \quad . \quad . \quad . \quad . \quad (24)$$

If it were assumed that $U_t = 0$—commuting was neither enjoyable nor irksome—the main equilibrium condition would reduce to

$$l_1 + p'x = 0 \quad [3] \quad . \quad . \quad . \quad . \quad . \quad (25)$$

which would be the equilibrium condition if households simply attempt to minimise the sum of transportation and space costs.[4] If $l_1 = kS$, where k

---

[1] See L. N. Moses and H. F. Williamson, "Value of Time, Choice of Mode, and the Subsidy Issue in Urban Transportation," *Journal of Political Economy* (June 1963), R. Muth, "Economic Change and Rural–Urban Conversion," *Econometrica* (January 1961), and J. F. Kain, *Commuting and the Residential Decisions of Chicago and Detroit Central Business District Workers* (April 1963).

[2] See Muth, *op. cit.*

[3] If $U_t \neq 0$, the main equilibrium condition would be

$$\frac{U_t}{U_x} = \frac{l_1 + p'x}{p}$$

Probably the most plausible assumption is that $U_t < 0$, which would imply that $l_1 + p'x < 0$.

[4] See Kain, *op. cit.*, pp. 6–12.

is a constant, the effect of a change in full income on the time spent commuting can be found by differentiating equation (25) to be

$$\frac{\partial t}{\partial S} = \frac{k(\epsilon_x - 1)}{p''x} \quad \cdots \cdots \quad (26)$$

where ϵ_x is the income elasticity of demand for space. Since stability requires that $p'' > 0$, an increase in income increases the time spent commuting if, and only if, $\epsilon_x > 1$.

In metropolitan areas of the United States higher-income families tend to live further from the central city,[1] which contradicts our analysis if one accepts the traditional view that the income elasticity of demand for housing is less than unity. In a definitive study of the demand for housing in the United States, however, Margaret Reid found income elasticities greater than unity.[2] Moreover, the analysis of distance commuted incorporates only a few dimensions of the demand for housing; principally the demand for outdoor space. The evidence on distances commuted would then only imply that outdoor space is a " luxury," which is rather plausible [3] and not even inconsistent with the traditional view about the total elasticity of demand for housing.

(e) *The Division of Labour Within Families*

Space is too limited to do more than summarise the main implications of the theory concerning the division of labour among members of the same household. Instead of simply allocating time efficiently among commodities, multi-person households also allocate the time of different members. Members who are relatively more efficient at market activities would use less of their time at consumption activities than would other members. Moreover, an increase in the relative market efficiency of any member would effect a reallocation of the time of all other members towards consumption activities in order to permit the former to spend more time at market activities. In short, the allocation of the time of any member is greatly influenced by the opportunities open to other members.

IV. SUBSTITUTION BETWEEN TIME AND GOODS

Although time and goods have been assumed to be used in fixed proportions in producing commodities, substitution could take place because different commodities used them in different proportions. The assumption of fixed proportions is now dropped in order to include many additional implications of the theory.

It is well known from the theory of variable proportions that households

[1] For a discussion, including many qualifications, of this proposition see L. F. Schnore, " The Socio-Economic Status of Cities and Suburbs," *American Sociological Review* (February 1963).

[2] See her *Housing and Income* (University of Chicago Press, 1962), p. 6 and *passim*.

[3] According to Reid, the elasticity of demand for indoor space is less than unity (*ibid.*, Chapter 12). If her total elasticity is accepted this suggests that outdoor space has an elasticity exceeding unity.

would minimise costs by setting the ratio of the marginal product of goods to that of time equal to the ratio of their marginal costs.[1] A rise in the cost of time relative to goods would induce a reduction in the amount of time and an increase in the amount of goods used per unit of each commodity. Thus, not only would a rise in earnings induce a substitution away from earnings-intensive commodities but also a substitution away from time and towards goods in the production of each commodity. Only the first is (implicitly) recognised in the labour–leisure analysis, although the second may well be of considerable importance. It increases one's confidence that the substitution effect of a rise in earnings is more important than is commonly believed.

The change in the input coefficients of time and goods resulting from a change in their relative costs is defined by the elasticity of substitution between them, which presumably varies from commodity to commodity. The only empirical study of this elasticity assumes that recreation goods and " leisure " time are used to produce a recreation commodity.[2] Definite evidence of substitution is found, since the ratio of leisure time to recreation goods is negatively related to the ratio of their prices. The elasticity of substitution appears to be less than unity, however, since the share of leisure in total factor costs is apparently positively related to its relative price.

The incentive to economise on time as its relative cost increases goes a long way towards explaining certain broad aspects of behaviour that have puzzled and often disturbed observers of contemporary life. Since hours worked have declined secularly in most advanced countries, and so-called " leisure " has presumably increased, a natural expectation has been that " free " time would become more abundant, and be used more " leisurely " and " luxuriously." Yet, if anything, time is used more carefully to-day than a century ago.[3] If there was a secular increase in the productivity of working time relative to consumption time (see Section III (*b*)) there would be an increasing incentive to economise on the latter because of its greater expense (our theory emphatically cautions against calling such time " free "). Not surprisingly, therefore, it is now kept track of and used more carefully than in the past.

Americans are supposed to be much more wasteful of food and other

---

[1] The cost of producing a given amount of commodity Z_i would be minimised if

$$\frac{\partial f_i/\partial x_i}{\partial f_i/\partial T_i} = \frac{P_i}{\partial L/\partial T_i}$$

If utility were considered an indirect function of goods and time rather than simply a direct function of commodities the following conditions, among others, would be required to maximise utility:

$$\frac{\partial U/\partial x_i}{\partial U/\partial T_i} \equiv \frac{\partial Z_i/\partial x_i}{\partial Z_i/\partial T_i} = \frac{p_i}{\partial L/\partial T}$$

which are exactly the same conditions as above. The ratio of the marginal utility of x_i to that of T_i depends only on f_i, x_i and T_i, and is thus independent of other production functions, goods and time. In other words, the indirect utility function is what has been called " weakly separable " (see R. Muth, " Household Production and Consumer Demand Functions," unpublished manuscript).

[2] See Owen, *op. cit.*, Chapter X.   [3] See, for example, de Grazia, *op. cit.*, Chapter IV.

goods than persons in poorer countries, and much more conscious of time: they keep track of it continuously, make (and keep) appointments for specific minutes, rush about more, cook steaks and chops rather than time-consuming stews and so forth.[1] They are simultaneously supposed to be wasteful—of material goods—and overly economical—of immaterial time. Yet both allegations may be correct and not simply indicative of a strange American temperament because the market value of time is higher relative to the price of goods there than elsewhere. That is, the tendency to be economical about time and lavish about goods may be no paradox, but in part simply a reaction to a difference in relative costs.

The substitution towards goods induced by an increase in the relative cost of time would often include a substitution towards more expensive goods. For example, an increase in the value of a mother's time may induce her to enter the labour force and spend less time cooking by using pre-cooked foods and less time on child-care by using nurseries, camps or baby-sitters. Or barbers' shops in wealthier sections of town charge more and provide quicker service than those in poorer sections, because waiting by barbers is substituted for waiting by customers. These examples illustrate that a change in the quality of goods [2] resulting from a change in the relative cost of goods may simply reflect a change in the methods used to produce given commodities, and not any corresponding change in *their* quality.

Consequently, a rise in income due to a rise in earnings would increase the quality of goods purchased not only because of the effect of income on quality but also because of a substitution of goods for time; a rise in income due to a rise in property income would not cause any substitution, and should have less effect on the quality of goods. Put more dramatically, with total income held constant, a rise in earnings should increase while a rise in property income should decrease the quality chosen. Once again, the composition of income is important and provides testable implications of the theory.

One analytically interesting application of these conclusions is to the recent study by Margaret Reid of the substitution between store-bought and home-delivered milk.[3] According to our approach, the cost of inputs into the commodity " milk consumption at home " is either the sum of the price of milk in the store and the forgone value of the time used to carry it home or simply the price of delivered milk. A reduction in the price of store relative to delivered milk, the value of time remaining constant, would reduce the cost of the first method relatively to the second, and shift production towards the first. For the same reason a reduction in the value of time, market prices

---

[1] For a comparison of the American concept of time with others see Edward T. Hall, *The Silent Language* (New York: Doubleday, 1959), Chapter 9.

[2] Quality is usually defined empirically by the amount spent per physical unit, such as pound of food, car or child. See especially S. J. Prais and H. Houthakker, *The Analysis of Family Budgets* (Cambridge, 1955); also my " An Economic Analysis of Fertility," *op. cit.*

[3] See her " Consumer Response to the Relative Price of Store versus Delivered Milk," *Journal of Political Economy* (April 1963).

of milk remaining constant, would also shift production towards the first method.

Reid's finding of a very large negative relation between the ratio of store to delivered milk and the ratio of their prices, income and some other variables held constant, would be evidence both that milk costs are a large part of total production costs and that there is easy substitution between these alternative methods of production. The large, but not quite as large, negative relation with income simply confirms the easy substitution between methods, and indicates that the cost of time is less important than the cost of milk. In other words, instead of conveying separate information, her price and income elasticities both measure substitution between the two methods of producing the same commoditity, and are consistent and plausible.

The importance of forgone earnings and the substitution between time and goods may be quite relevant in interpreting observed price elasticities. A given percentage increase in the price of goods would be less of an increase in commodity prices the more important forgone earnings are. Consequently, even if all commodities had the same true price elasticity, those having relatively important forgone earnings would show lower apparent elasticities in the typical analysis that relates quantities and prices of goods alone.

The importance of forgone earnings differs not only among commodities but also among households for a given commodity because of differences in income. Its importance would change in the same or opposite direction as income, depending on whether the elasticity of substitution between time and goods was less or greater than unity. Thus, even when the true price elasticity of a commodity did not vary with income, the observed price elasticity of goods would be negatively or positively related to income as the elasticity of substitution was less or greater than unity.

The importance of substitution between time and goods can be illustrated in a still different way. Suppose, for simplicity, that only good x and no time was initially required to produce commodity Z. A price ceiling is placed on x, it nominally becomes a free good, and the production of x is subsidised sufficiently to maintain the same output. The increased quantity of x and Z demanded due to the decline in the price of x has to be rationed because the output of x has not increased. Suppose that the system of rationing made the quantity obtained a positive function of the time and effort expended. For example, the quantity of price-controlled bread or medical attention obtained might depend on the time spent in a queue outside a bakery or in a physician's office. Or if an appointment system were used a literal queue would be replaced by a figurative one, in which the waiting was done at "home," as in the Broadway theatre, admissions to hospitals or air travel during peak seasons. Again, even in depressed times the likelihood of obtaining a job is positively related to the time put into job hunting.

Although x became nominally a free good, Z would not be free, because the time now required as an input into Z is not free. The demand for Z would be greater than the supply (fixed by assumption) if the cost of this time was less than the equilibrium price of Z before the price control. The scrambling by households for the limited supply would increase the time required to get a unit of Z, and thus its cost. Both would continue to increase until the average cost of time tended to the equilibrium price before price control. At that point equilibrium would be achieved because the supply and demand for Z would be equal.

Equilibrium would take different forms depending on the method of rationing. With a literal " first come first served " system the size of the queue (say outside the bakery or in the doctor's office) would grow until the expected cost of standing in line discouraged any excess demand;[1] with the figurative queues of appointment systems, the " waiting " time (say to see a play) would grow until demand was sufficiently curtailed. If the system of rationing was less formal, as in the labour market during recessions, the expected time required to ferret out a scarce job would grow until the demand for jobs was curtailed to the limited supply.

Therefore, price control of x combined with a subsidy that kept its amount constant would not change the average private equilibrium price of Z,[2] but would substitute indirect time costs for direct goods costs.[3] Since, however, indirect costs are positively related to income, the price of Z would be raised to higher-income persons and reduced to lower-income ones, thereby redistributing consumption from the former to the latter. That is, women, the poor, children, the unemployed, etc., would be more willing to spend their time in a queue or otherwise ferreting out rationed goods than would high-earning males.

V. Summary and Conclusions

This paper has presented a theory of the allocation of time between different activities. At the heart of the theory is an assumption that households are producers as well as consumers; they produce commodities by combining inputs of goods and time according to the cost-minimisation rules of the traditional theory of the firm. Commodities are produced in quantities determined by maximising a utility function of the commodity set subject to

[1] In queueing language the cost of waiting in line is a " discouragement " factor that stabilises the queueing scheme (see, for example, D. R. Cox and W. L. Smith, *Queues* (New York: Wiley 1961)).

[2] The social price, on the other hand, would double, for it is the sum of private indirect costs and subsidised direct costs.

[3] Time costs can be criticised from a Pareto optimality point of view because they often result in external diseconomies: *e.g.*, a person joining a queue would impose costs on subsequent joiners. The diseconomies are real, not simply pecuniary, because time is a cost to demanders, but is not revenue to suppliers.

prices and a constraint on resources. Resources are measured by what is called full income, which is the sum of money income and that forgone or " lost " by the use of time and goods to obtain utility, while commodity prices are measured by the sum of the costs of their goods and time inputs.

The effect of changes in earnings, other income, goods prices and the productivity of working and consumption time on the allocation of time and the commodity set produced has been analysed. For example, a rise in earnings, compensated by a decline in other income so that full income would be unchanged, would induce a decline in the amount of time used at consumption activities, because time would become more expensive. Partly goods would be substituted for the more expensive time in the production of each commodity, and partly goods-intensive commodities would be substituted for the more expensive time-intensive ones. Both substitutions require less time to be used at consumption, and permit more to be used at work. Since the reallocation of time involves simultaneously a reallocation of goods and commodities, all three decisions become intimately related.

The theory has many interesting and even novel interpretations of, and implications about, empirical phenomena. A few will be summarised here.

A traditional " economic " interpretation of the secular decline in hours worked has stressed the growth in productivity of working time and the resulting income and substitution effects, with the former supposedly dominating. Ours stresses that the substitution effects of the growth in productivity of working and consumption time tended to offset each other, and that hours worked declined secularly primarily because time-intensive commodities have been luxuries. A contributing influence has been the secular decline in the relative prices of goods used in time-intensive commodities.

Since an increase in income partly due to an increase in earnings would raise the relative cost of time and of time-intensive commodities, traditional cross-sectional estimates of income elasticities do not hold either factor or commodity prices constant. Consequently, they would, among other things, be biased downward for time-intensive commodities, and give a misleading impression of the effect of income on the quality of commodities consumed. The composition of income also affects demand, for an increase in earnings, total income held constant, would shift demand away from time-intensive commodities and input combinations.

Rough estimates suggest that forgone earnings are quantitatively important and therefore that full income is substantially above money income. Since forgone earnings are primarily determined by the use of time, considerably more attention should be paid to its efficiency and allocation. In particular, agencies that collect information on the expenditure of money income might simultaneously collect information on the " expenditure " of time.   The resulting time budgets, which have not been seriously investigated in most countries, including the United States and Great Britain, should be integrated with the money budgets in order to give a more accurate picture of the size and allocation of full income.

6   The Allocation of
Time and Goods over Time

Basic Model

This section discusses the allocation of time and goods over a lifetime
among three main sectors: consumption, investment in human capital,
and labor force participation. It uses the framework developed in my
"A Theory of the Allocation of Time," *Economic Journal*, September
1965. That paper, however, considered the allocation only at a moment of time among various kinds of consumption and time utiliza-
tions; this discussion generalizes the analysis to decisions over time and
to investment in human capital.

Reprinted from Gary S. Becker, *Human Capital: A Theoretical and Empirical Analysis*,
with Special Reference to Education, second edition (New York: Columbia University
Press for the National Bureau of Economic Research, 1975), pp. 56–71. © 1975 by the
National Bureau of Economic Research, Inc. Originally written in 1967, this paper was
first published, with slight revisions, in the 1975 edition of *Human Capital* as an addendum to chapter 3, "Investment in Human Capital: Rates of Return." Since it is reproduced here from that printed version, the numbering of the equations, footnotes, and
charts has been retained unchanged.

Assume that a person is certain that he will live n periods. His economic welfare depends on his consumption over time of objects of choice called commodities, as in

$$U = U(C_i, \ldots C_n), \tag{32}$$

where C_i is the amount of the commodity consumed during period i. As assumed in the paper cited above, C_i is in turn produced "at home" with inputs of his market goods and his own time. Let the (composite) market goods used in period i be x_i, and the (composite) amount of time combined with x_i be t_{c_i}. Then

$$C_i = {}_if(x_i, t_{c_i}), \quad i = 1, \ldots n \tag{33}$$

where ${}_if$ is the production function in period i. If initially it is assumed that time can be allocated only between consumption and labor force participation (called "work"), the following identity holds in each period

$$t_{c_i} + t_{w_i} = t, \quad i = 1, \ldots n \tag{34}$$

where t_{w_i} is the amount of work in i, and t, the total time available during i, is independent of i if all periods are equally long.

The "endowment" in each period is not simply a fixed amount of "income" since that is affected by the hours spent at work, which is a decision variable. Instead it is the vector (w_i, v_i), where v_i is the amount of property income and w_i is the wage rate available in the ith period.

Suppose that there is a perfect capital market with an interest rate, r, the same in each period. Then a constraint on goods that complements the constraints on time given by (34) is that the present value of expenditures on goods must equal the present value of incomes:[18]

$$\sum_{i=1}^{n} \frac{p_i x_i}{(1+r)^{i-1}} = \sum_{i=1}^{n} \frac{w_i t_{w_i} + v_i}{(1+r)^{i-1}}. \tag{35}$$

[18] Savings in period i is defined as

$$S_i = w_i t_{w_i} + v_i - p_i x_i.$$

Our formulation is implicitly assuming that the savings process itself takes no time; a somewhat weaker assumption, say that savings is less time-intensive than consumption, would not result in greatly different conclusions. I. Ehrlich and U. Ben-Zion have since analyzed the effect of time on savings in "A Theory of Productive Savings," University of Chicago, 1972.

Substitution for t_{w_i} from equation (34) into (35) gives the set of constraints

$$\sum_{i=1}^{n} \frac{p_i x_i + w_i t_{c_i}}{(1+r)^{i-1}} = \sum_{i=1}^{n} \frac{w_i t + v_i}{(1+r)^{i-1}}, \qquad (36)$$

and

$$0 \leq t_{c_i} \leq t, \quad x_i \geq 0. \qquad i = 1, \ldots n \quad (37)$$

The term on the right equals "full wealth," which is an extension of the definition of "full income" given in my earlier article. The term on the left shows how this full wealth is "spent": either on goods or on the foregone earnings associated with the use of time in consumption. Each person (or family) is assumed to maximize his utility function given by equation (32) subject to the constraints given by (36) and (37), and the production functions given by (33). The decision variables are the t_{c_i} and x_i, $2n$ variables. If the optimal values of these variables are assumed to be in the interior of the regions given by (37), and if the wage rates w_i are independent of x_i and t_{c_i}, the first order optimality conditions are simply

$$U_i \, {}_i f_x = \frac{\lambda p_i}{(1+r)^{i-1}} \qquad i = 1, \ldots n \quad (38)$$

$$U_i \, {}_i f_t = \frac{\lambda w_i}{(1+r)^{i-1}} \qquad i = 1, \ldots n \quad (39)$$

where

$$_i f_x = \frac{\partial_i f}{\partial x_i}, \quad _i f_t = \frac{\partial_i f}{\partial t_{c_i}}, \quad U_i = \frac{\partial U}{\partial C_i}$$

and λ is a Lagrangian multiplier equal to the marginal utility of wealth.

Dividing equation (39) by (38) gives

$$\frac{_i f_t}{_i f_x} = \frac{w_i}{p_i}, \qquad i = 1, \ldots n \quad (40)$$

or in each period the marginal product of consumption time relative to goods equals the real wage rate in the same period, and is independent of the interest rate. In other words, consumption time should have a relatively high marginal product when the real wage rate is relatively high.

To understand the implications of equation (40) somewhat better, assume that all f are homogeneous of the first degree, which is a fairly innocuous assumption in the present context. Let us also temporarily assume that the productivity of goods and consumption time do not vary with age, so that f's are the same. Since the marginal productivities of linear homogeneous production functions depend only on factor proportions, equation (40) implies, if marginal products are declining, with these additional assumptions that the production of commodities is relatively time-intensive when real wages are relatively low, and relatively goods-intensive when real wages are relatively high.

Note that this last result is a "substitution" effect and is unambiguous: it is not offset by any "income" effect that operates in the opposite direction. There is no offsetting income or wealth effect because "full" wealth is *fixed,* by the right-hand side of equation (36), and is *completely* independent of the allocation of time and goods over time or at a moment in time. Note, however, that this "substitution" effect is in terms of the *relative* time or goods intensities in different periods, and *not* in terms of the *absolute* amount of consumption time (sometimes called "leisure") in different periods. The latter cannot be determined from equation (40) alone, and depends on the allocation of commodities over time. Only if the consumption of commodities were the same at all periods would relative and absolute intensities necessarily move in the same direction.

To see what happens to commodity consumption over time, consider an alternative form of equation (38):

$$\frac{U_i}{U_j} = \frac{p_i f_{x_i}}{p_j f_{x_i}} (1 + r)^{(j-i)}. \qquad i, j = 1, \ldots n \quad (41)$$

If prices are assumed to be stable, $p_i = p_j = 1$ and equation (41) becomes

$$\frac{U_i}{U_j} = \frac{f_{x_i}}{f_{x_i}} (1 + r)^{(j-i)}. \qquad (42)$$

It has been shown that $t_{c_i}/x_i > t_{c_j}/x_j$ if $w_j > w_i$. It follows from the assumptions of homogeneity and diminishing returns that $f_{x_i} > f_{x_j}$. Hence from (42)

$$\frac{U_i}{U_j} \lesseqgtr (1 + r)^{(j-i)} \quad \text{as} \quad w_i \lesseqgtr w_j. \qquad (43)$$

Note that equality of the left- and right-hand sides, which is undoubtedly the most famous equilibrium condition in the allocation of consumption over time,[19] holds if, and only if, the wage rates are the same in the ith and jth periods.

Consider the implications of (43) for the optimal consumption path over time. I assume neutral time preference in the weak sense that all the U_i would be the same if all the C_i were the same. Then if equality held in (43), all the C_i would be the same if $r = 0$, and would tend to rise over time (ignoring differential wealth effects) if $r > 0$. Equality holds, however, only if the w_i were the same in all periods. But actual wage rates tend to rise with age until the mid-forties, fifties, or sixties, and then begin to decline. With that pattern for the w_i, (43) implies that if $r = 0$, the C_i would not be stationary, but would tend to decline with age until the peak w_i was reached, and then would tend to rise as the w_i fell (see Chart 2).[20]

The rate of fall and then rise of the C_i depends, of course, on the elasticities of substitution in consumption. In addition, the initial decline in C_i would be shorter and less steep and the subsequent rise would be longer, the larger r was (see Chart 2); for sufficiently large r, C_i might rise throughout.

Since $\frac{t_c}{x}$, the ratio of consumption time to goods, would fall as the wage rate rose, and rise as it fell (see Chart 3), if C_i were constant, the absolute value of t_c would have the same pattern as this ratio. A fortiori, if $r = 0$, and if C_i declined as w_i rose and rose as w_i fell (see Chart 2), t_c would fall as w_i rose and rise as it fell (see Chart 3). If $r > 0$, C_i declines more briefly and less rapidly than when $r = 0$, and consequently, so would t_c; in particular, t_c would reach a minimum before w_i reached a maximum. Put differently, hours of work, t_w, would reach a maximum before the wage rate did. The difference between the peaks in t_w and w would be positively related to the size of r, and the elasticities of substitution between different C_i and C_j. Households faced with high interest rates, for example, should hit their peak hours of work earlier than otherwise similar households with low interest rates.

[19] Its derivation is presumably due to I. Fisher (see *The Theory of Interest,* New York, 1965, Chapters XII and XIII); it is also used in countless other studies: see, for example, J. Henderson and R. Quandt, *Microeconomics: A Mathematical Approach,* New York, 1971.

[20] I say "tend to" because of possible differential degrees of substitution between consumption in different periods. For example, high consumption in period l might so raise the marginal utility of consumption in period k as to cause the equilibrium value of C_k to exceed C_j, even though $w_j < w_k$. If the utility function is fully separable, this cannot occur.

CHART 2

Relations between Age, Wage Rates, and Commodity Consumption
Indexes

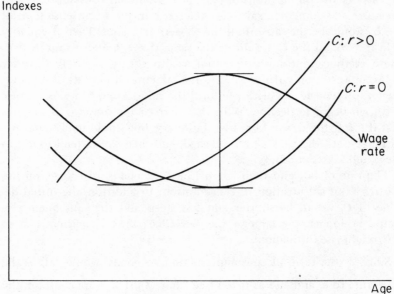

It may appear that the Fisherian equality has simply been hidden
and not replaced by the concentration on C instead of x. Indeed, equation (42) does imply a kind of Fisherian equality if the f terms are
transposed to the left side to yield

$$\frac{MU_{x_j}}{MU_{x_i}} = \frac{U_i f_{x_i}}{U_j f_{x_j}} = (1+r)^{j-i}. \tag{44}$$

The term $U_i f_{x_i}$ is the marginal utility of an additional unit of x_i,
and similarly for the j term. Equation (44) would seem to imply a horizontal path of the x_i if $r = 0$ and if time preference were neutral, the
Fisherian result.

However plausible, this conclusion does not follow, and the Fisherian
result cannot be saved. This is partly because the utility function depends directly on C and only indirectly on x, and partly because the
path of x is also dependent on the production function f. If $r = 0$ and
U implied neutral time preference with respect to the C, then the
movement in C would tend to be inversely, and that in x/t_c directly,

CHART 3

Relations between Age, Wage Rates, and Time Spent in Consumption

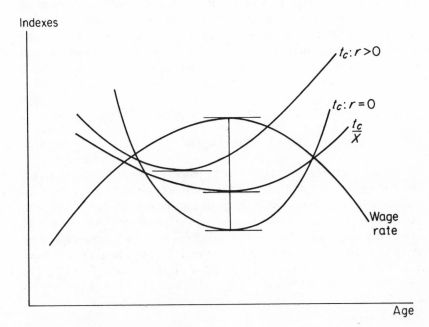

Indexes

$t_c: r > 0$

$t_c: r = 0$

$\dfrac{t_c}{x}$

Wage
rate

Age

related to the movement in w. The size of these respective movements depends on the elasticities of substitution between the C in U, and between x and t_c in f. The movement in C tends to make x inversely related to the movement in w, whereas that in x/t_c makes it directly related.

The actual movement in x, therefore, is determined by the relative strength of these opposing forces, that is, by the relative size of the elasticities of substitution in consumption and in production. The larger the latter elasticity, the more likely that x is directly related to w. Only if the elasticities were identical would the two substitutions offset each other, and would x be stationary with $r = 0$.[21] Of course, x (and C) are more likely to rise over time the higher r is.

Note that a rise in the consumption of goods with age, which is

[21] For further developments, see G. Ghez, *A Theory of Life Cycle Consumption,* Ph.D. dissertation, Columbia University, 1970, and G. Ghez and G. Becker, *The Allocation of Time and Goods over the Life Cycle,* New York, NBER, 1975.

frequently observed at least until age forty-five, can be explained without recourse to assumptions about time preference for the future, elastic responses to interest rate changes, or underestimation of future incomes. Neutral time preference, negligible interest rate responses, and perfect anticipation of the future could all be assumed if there were sufficiently easy substitution between time and goods in the production of commodities. The time path of goods consumption is not, however, a reliable guide to the path of true consumption (that is, of commodities) since the latter could well be inversely correlated with the former.

Investment in Human Capital

Instead of assuming that time can be allocated only between market labor force activity and nonmarket consumption activity, I now introduce a third category, investment in human capital. For the present an increased amount of human capital, measured by E, is assumed to affect only wage rates. Each person produces his own human capital by using some of his time and goods to attend "school," receive on-the-job training, etc. The rate of change in his capital equals the difference between his rate of production and the rate of depreciation on his stock.[22]

In symbols,

$$\phi_i = \psi_i(t_{e_i}, x_{e_i}),\tag{45}$$

where ϕ_i is the output of human capital in the ith period, and t_{e_i} and x_{e_i} are the time and goods inputs, respectively. Then

$$E_{i+1} = E_i + \phi_i - dE_i,\tag{46}$$

where E_{i+1} is the stock at the beginning of the $i+1$ period, and d is the rate of depreciation during a period. Each household maximizes the utility function in (32), subject to the production constraints in

[22] This model of human capital accumulation is very similar to and much influenced by that found in Y. Ben-Porath, "The Production of Human Capital and the Life Cycle of Earnings," *Journal of Political Economy*, August 1967, or in the addendum to this volume "Human Capital and the Personal Distribution of Income: An Analytical Approach," pp. 94–144.

(33), (45), and (46), and to the following time and goods "budget" constraints

$$t_{c_i} + t_{w_i} + t_{e_i} = t, \qquad i = 1, \ldots n \quad (47)$$

$$\sum_{i=1}^{n} \frac{x_i + x_{e_i}}{(1 + r)^i} = \sum_{i=1}^{n} \frac{\alpha_i E_i t_{w_i} + v_i}{(1 + r)^i}, \qquad (48)$$

where $w_i = \alpha_i E_i$ and α_i is the payment per unit of human capital in period i. If, for simplicity, one assumes that ϕ_i depends only on t_{e_i} and that ψ_i is the same in all periods, and if the optimal solution has nonzero values of x_i, t_{c_i}, t_{w_i}, and t_{e_i}, the first order optimality conditions are

$$U_i f_{x_i} = \lambda \frac{1}{(1 + r)^i} \qquad i = 1, \ldots n \quad (49)$$

$$U_i f_{t_i} = \lambda \frac{\alpha_i E_i}{(1 + r)^i} \qquad i = 1, \ldots n \quad (50)$$

$$0 = \lambda \left[\frac{\alpha_i E_i}{(1 + r)^i} - \sum_{j=i+1}^{n} \frac{\alpha_j t_{w_j}}{(1 + r)^j} \frac{\partial E_j}{\partial t_{e_i}} \right]. \qquad (51)$$

Equations (49) and (50) are essentially the same as (38) and (39). Therefore, investment in human capital, under the present assumptions, does not basically change the implications derived so far. For example, the time spent in consuming, t_c, would still tend to decline with age, reach a trough before the peak wage rate age, and then increase, and the time path of goods would still depend on the interest rate, and the elasticities of substitution in consumption and production. Two significant differences are, first, that the path of the wage rate is no longer given, but is determined by the path of the endogenous variable E_i. The wage rate would reach a peak before, at, or after the peak in α_i as E_i peaked before, at, or after α_i. Second, the behavior of t_w is no longer simply the complement of the behavior of t_c, since t_w also depends on t_e, which is determined by equation (51).

Equation (51) expresses the well-known equilibrium condition that the present value of the marginal cost of investing in human capital equals the present value of future returns. This equation clearly shows that the amount of time spent investing in human capital would tend to decline with age for two reasons. One is that the number of remaining periods, and thus the present value of future returns, would decline with age. The other is that the cost of investment would tend to rise with age as E_i rose because foregone earnings would rise.

Several interesting consequences follow from the tendency for t_{e_i} to fall as i increases. One is that hours of work, t_w, would be lower at younger ages and rise more rapidly than if there were no investment in human capital. Consequently, as long as t_{e_i} was positive, the peak in t_w would tend to come after the trough in t_c, and might even also come after the peak in w_i. However, since t_e declines with age, if it became sufficiently small by some age p before n, then for $i > p$, the behavior of t_w would be approximately the complement of the behavior of t_c.

If so much time at younger ages were put into investment in human capital that no time remained to allocate to work ($t_w = 0$), t_c and t_e would be complements at these ages. Marginal investment costs would not be measured by foregone earnings, but by the marginal value of time used in consumption, which would exceed foregone earnings (otherwise $t_w > 0$).

If $t_{w_i} = 0$, $i = 1, \ldots q$, instead of equations (49) to (51), the first order optimality condition for $i = 1, \ldots q$ would be

$$U_i f_{x_i} = \lambda \frac{1}{(1 + r)^i} \qquad\qquad i = 1, \ldots q \quad (52)$$

$$U_i f_{t_i} = s_i \qquad\qquad i = 1, \ldots q \quad (53)$$

$$s_i = \lambda \sum_{j=i+1}^{n} \frac{\alpha_j t_{w_j}}{(1 + r)^j} \frac{\partial E_j}{\partial t_{e_i}} \qquad\qquad i = 1, \ldots q \quad (54)$$

where s_i is the marginal utility of an additional hour of time spent at consumption in the ith period. If $U_i f_{t_i}$ is substituted for s_i in equation (54),

$$\frac{U_i f_{t_i}}{\lambda} = \sum_{j=i+1}^{n} \frac{\alpha_j t_{w_j}}{(1 + r)^i} \frac{\partial E_j}{\partial t_{e_i}}, \qquad i = 1 \ldots q \quad (55)$$

or the present value of the returns from an additional hour spent investing would equal not foregone earnings but the money equivalent of the marginal utility from an additional hour spent in consumption.

When equation (53) is divided by (52), and a substitution for s_i is made from (54), one has

$$\frac{f_{t_i}}{f_{x_i}} = \sum_{j=i+1}^{n} \frac{\alpha_j t_{w_j}}{(1 + r)^{i-i}} \frac{\partial E_j}{\partial t_{e_i}}; \qquad i = 1 \ldots q \quad (56)$$

the ratio of the marginal products of time and goods is not equated to the wage rate since no time is spent working, but to the monetary value of the marginal productivity of time used in investing. Even if w_i for $i < q$ were small, therefore, the production of commodities would be goods-intensive if the return to investment time were high.

Age and the Production Functions

By assuming that the production functions for commodities and human capital are the same at all ages, I have been able to analyze the different time and goods combinations at different ages in terms of differences in real wage rates and returns alone. Yet presumably as a person gains (or loses) experience, knowledge, and strength with age, the production possibilities available to him also change. This section analyzes the consequences of such changes for the optimal allocation of goods and time.

Let us concentrate on changes in the production functions for commodities, and assume that productive efficiency rises with age until a peak efficiency is reached, and then declines until age n. If the changes in efficiency were factor neutral, the production functions could be written as

$$_if = g_i f(t_{c_i}, x_i), \tag{57}$$

where the g_j are coefficients that rise at first and then decline. Equation (49) would become

$$U_i \, _if_{x_i} \equiv g_i U_i f_{x_i} = \lambda \frac{1}{(1+r)^i}, \tag{58}$$

equation (50) would become

$$U_i \, _if_{t_i} = g_i U_i f_{t_i} = \lambda \frac{\alpha_i E_i}{(1+r)^i}, \tag{59}$$

while equation (51) would be unaffected.

If equation (58) is divided by (59), the efficiency coefficients g_i drop out, and the optimal combination of time and goods depends, as before, only on the shape of f and $\alpha_i E_i$. Therefore, goods intensity rises until a peak is reached at the peak wage age, and then falls, and does not at all depend on the path of the s_i.

If $r = 0$ and w were rising with age, the decline in C with age would be greater than when production functions did not change if productive efficiency (measured by g) were falling with age because the marginal cost of producing C would rise faster with age; conversely if g were rising with age. The effect on the x and t_c is less definite and depends also on the elasticity of substitution in consumption because changes in the efficiency of producing C—the use of x and t_c per unit of C—can offset the change in C. If this elasticity exceeded unity, changes in efficiency would change x and t_c in the same direction as it changes C.

If changes in efficiency were not factor neutral but, say, changed the marginal product of consumption time more than that of goods ("goods-saving" change), there would be less incentive to substitute goods for time as wages rose if efficiency also rose. Therefore, production would not become as goods-intensive when wages and efficiency were rising, or as time-intensive when they were both falling. The converse would hold, of course, if changes in efficiency changed the marginal product of goods more than time.

Human Capital and Consumption

So far I have assumed that an increase in human capital directly only changes the productivity of time in the marketplace. Human capital might, however, also change the productivity of time and goods used in producing household consumption or in producing additional human capital itself.

Studies of investment in education and other human capital have been repeatedly criticized for ignoring the consumption aspects, although critics have been no more successful than others in treating these aspects in a meaningful way. One approach is to permit human capital to enter utility functions, but given the difficulties in measuring, quantifying, and comparing utilities, this does not seem too promising. An alternative is to assume that human capital "shifts" household production functions,[23] as in

$$C_i = {}_if(x_i, t_{c_i}; E_i). \tag{60}$$

The marginal effect of human capital on consumption in the ith period can be defined as the marginal product or "shift" of C_i with respect to E_i:

$$MP_{e_i} = \frac{\partial C_i}{\partial E_i} = \frac{\partial_i f}{\partial E_i} = {}_if_{e_i}. \tag{61}$$

[23] This approach is treated in considerable detail, both theoretically and empirically, by R. Michael, *The Effect of Education on Efficiency in Consumption*, New York, NBER, 1972, an outgrowth of a 1969 Ph.D. dissertation at Columbia.

The optimal allocation of time and goods can still be found by differentiating the utility function subject to the production functions and budget constraints. Equilibrium conditions (49) and (50) or (52) and (53) would be formally unaffected by the inclusion of E in the production of commodities. The equilibrium conditions with respect to t_e, the time spent investing in human capital, would, however, change from equation (51) to

$$\sum_{j=i+1}^{n} U_j f_{e_i} \frac{\partial E_j}{\partial t_{e_i}} = \lambda \left(\frac{\alpha_i E_i}{(1+r)^i} - \sum_{j=i+1}^{n} \frac{\alpha_j t_{w_i}}{(1+r)^i} \frac{\partial E_j}{\partial t_{e_i}} \right) \qquad (62)$$

or

$$\frac{\alpha_i E_i}{(1+r)^i} = \sum_{j=i+1}^{n} \frac{U_j}{\lambda} f_{e_i} \frac{\partial E_j}{\partial t_{e_i}} + \sum_{j=i+1}^{n} \frac{\alpha_j t_{w_i}}{(1+r)^i} \frac{\partial E_j}{\partial t_{e_i}}. \qquad (63)$$

A similar change would be produced in equation (54).

The term on the left-hand side of equation (63) is the present value of foregone earnings in period i—the cost of using more time in period i to produce human capital—and the terms on the right give the present value of the benefits. The second term on the right is the familiar present value of monetary returns, and gives the increase in wealth resulting from an additional investment in human capital in period i. The first term on the right is less familiar and measures the effect of additional investment on consumption. It essentially measures the present value of the reduction in goods and time required to produce a given basket of commodities resulting from increased investment in period i.[24]

24 Since f is homogeneous of the first degree in x and t_c,

$$C_i \equiv f_{x_i} x_i + f_{t_i} t_{c_i}, \qquad (1')$$

then

$$\frac{\partial C_i}{\partial E_i} \equiv f_{e_i} \equiv \frac{\partial f_{x_i}}{\partial E_i} x_i + \frac{\partial f_{t_i}}{\partial E_i} t_{c_i}. \qquad (2')$$

Define

$$\widetilde{f}_{x_i} \equiv \frac{\partial f_{x_e}}{\partial E_i} \bigg/ f_{x_i} \quad \text{and} \quad \widetilde{f}_{t_i} \equiv \frac{\partial f_{t_i}}{\partial E_i} \bigg/ f_{t_i}. \qquad (3')$$

Then

$$f_{e_i} \equiv \widetilde{f}_{x_i}(f_{x_i} x_i) + \widetilde{f}_{t_i}(f_{t_i} t_{c_i}). \qquad (4')$$

Substituting from the equilibrium conditions (49) and (50) for f_{x_i} and f_{t_i} yields

$$f_{e_i} = \frac{\lambda}{U_i} \left(\widetilde{f}_{x_i} \frac{x_i}{(1+r)^i} + \widetilde{f}_{t_i} \frac{\alpha_i E_i t_{c_i}}{(1+r)^i} \right), \qquad (5')$$

Treated in this way, the effect of human capital on consumption becomes symmetrical to its effect on investment: the latter gives the monetary value of the stream of increased incomes, whereas the former gives the monetary value of the stream of reduced costs.

A few implications of the inclusion of the consumption effects of human capital can be noted briefly. Since they clearly raise the total benefits from investment, more time at each age would be spent investing than if these effects were nil. This in turn implies a greater likelihood of "corner" solutions, especially at younger ages, with the equilibrium conditions given by equations (52), (53), and an extension of (54)[25] being relevant. Moreover, there would now be justification for an assumption that efficiency in consumption and wage rates rise and fall together, because they would be the joint results of changes in the stock of human capital.

Some Extensions of the Analysis

It is neither realistic nor necessary to assume that wage rates are given, aside from the effects of human capital. The average wage rate and the number of hours a person works are generally related because of fatigue, differences between part-time and full-time opportunities,

---

and thus

$$\frac{U_i}{\lambda} f_{e_i} = \widetilde{f}_{x_i} \frac{x_i}{(1+r)^i} + \widetilde{f}_{t_i} \frac{\alpha_i E_i t_{c_i}}{(1+r)^i}. \tag{6'}$$

The terms $\widetilde{f}_{x_i}$ and $\widetilde{f}_{t_i}$ equal the percentage reductions in goods and time respectively in period i required to produce a given C_i resulting from the "shift" in f caused by a unit increase in E_i. Hence, the full term on the right-hand side of (6') gives the present value of the savings in goods and time in period i required to achieve a given amount of C_i. Consequently,

$$\sum_{j=i+1}^{n} \frac{U_j}{\lambda} f_{e_j} \frac{\partial E_j}{\partial t_{e_i}} = \sum_{j=i+1}^{n} \frac{\widetilde{f}_{x_j} x_j}{(1+r)^j} + \frac{\widetilde{f}_{t_j} \alpha_j E_j t_{c_j}}{(1+r)^j} \frac{\partial E_j}{\partial t_{e_i}} \tag{7'}$$

gives the full present value of the savings in goods and time resulting from additional investment in human capital in period i.

25 With consumption effects, equation (54) is replaced by

$$\sum_{j=i+1}^{n} U_j \frac{\partial E_j}{\partial t_{e_i}} - s_i + \lambda \sum_{j=i+1}^{n} \frac{\alpha_j t_{w_j}}{(1+r)^j} \frac{\partial E_j}{\partial t_{e_i}} = 0,$$

or

$$\frac{s_i}{\lambda} = \sum_{j=i+1}^{n} \frac{U_j}{\lambda} f_{e_j} \frac{\partial E_j}{\partial t_{e_i}} + \sum_{j=i+1}^{n} \frac{\alpha_j t_{w_j}}{(1+r)^j} \frac{\partial E_j}{\partial t_{e_i}}. \tag{54'}$$

fixed costs of working, overtime provisions, and so forth. Our analysis can easily incorporate an effect of t_w on w, as in

$$w_i = w_i(t_{w_i}), \qquad (64)$$

or even more generally in

$$w_i = w_i(t_{w_i}, t_{w_{i-1}}, \ldots t_{w_1}) \qquad (65)$$

if on-the-job learning is to be analyzed separately from other human capital. Marginal, not average, wage rates are the relevant measures of the cost of time and would enter the equilibrium conditions.[26]

It would also be more realistic to consider several commodities at any moment in time, each having its own production function and goods and time inputs. This could easily be done by introducing the utility function

$$U = U(C_{1l}, \ldots C_{1n}, C_{2l}, \ldots C_{2n}, \ldots C_{ml}, \ldots C_{mn}), \qquad (66)$$

where C_j is the amount of the jth commodity consumed in the ith period. This function would be maximized subject to separate production functions for each commodity (and perhaps in each period) and to the budget constraints. One of the main implications is that when wage rates are relatively high, not only is the production of each commodity relatively goods-intensive, but consumption shifts toward relatively goods-intensive commodities and away from time-intensive commodities. The latter (such as children or grandchildren) would be consumed more at younger and older ages if wage rates or more generally the cost of time rose at younger ages and fell eventually; conversely, goods-intensive commodities would be consumed more at middle ages. These age patterns in the consumption of time and goods-intensive commodities strengthen the tendency for consumption time to fall initially and for goods to rise initially with age.

The accumulation of human capital might also "shift" the production function used to produce human capital itself since investors with much human capital might well be more productive than those with little. This has been discussed elsewhere,[27] and I only mention here

[26] For example, if equation (64) is the wage rate function, equation (65) would be replaced by

$$U_i f_{t_i} = \lambda \left(\frac{\alpha_i E_i}{(1+r)^i} + \frac{\partial \alpha_i}{\partial t_{w_i}} \frac{t_{w_i} E_i}{(1+r)^i} \right). \qquad (65')$$

[27] See Ben-Porath, *op. cit.*, and addendum to this volume "Human Capital and the Personal Distribution of Income: An Analytical Approach," pp. 94–144.

one implication. The tendency for the amount invested to decline with age would be somewhat retarded because investment would be encouraged as capital was accumulated, since time would become more productive and this would offset the effect of its becoming more costly.

The allocation over a lifetime should be put in a family context, with the decisions of husbands, wives, and possibly also children interacting with each other. For example, if wives' wage rates are more stationary than their husbands', the analysis in this paper predicts that the labor force participation of married women would be relatively high at younger and older ages, and relatively low at middle ages, precisely what is observed. A similar result would follow if the productivity in consumption of married women's time is higher at middle ages because child rearing is time-intensive. The analysis developed here seems capable of throwing considerable light on the differential labor force participation patterns by age of husbands and wives.[28]

Empirical Analysis

Some implications of this model have been tested by the author with data from the 1960 Census 1/1000 sample giving earnings, hours, and weeks worked, cross-classified by age, sex, race, and education.[29]

[28] This has been confirmed in several studies since this was written; see A. Leibowitz, "Women's Allocation of Time to Market and Non-Market Activities," Ph.D. dissertation, Columbia University, 1972; or H. Ofek, "Allocation of Goods and Time in a Family Context," Ph.D. dissertation, Columbia University, 1971; or J. Smith, "A Life Cycle Family Model, NBER Working Paper 5, 1973.

[29] The results are published in Ghez and Becker, *op. cit.*, Chapter 3.

7

On the New Theory of Consumer Behavior

Summary

This essay advocates a reformulation of the theory of consumer behavior, based on the household production function approach suggested in Becker's "A Theory of the Allocation of Time" [1]. The case for the reformulation rests, in part, on inadequacies of the traditional theory of choice, and more importantly, on the new approach's capacity to generate a wide range of cogent testable hypotheses and to provide the social scientist with tools relevant for understanding a broad spectrum of observed human behavior.

> Much that is of chief interest in the science of wants, is borrowed from the science of efforts and activities.
>
> Alfred Marshall

I. The Traditional Theory of Choice

Exposition of the Traditional Theory

The received theory of consumer behavior rests on the view that the consumer unit, say the household, attempts to maximize utility, U, which it obtains directly from the services of goods, x_i, purchased in the marketplace:

$$U = u(x_1, x_2, ..., x_n),[1] \tag{1}$$

Reprinted from the *Swedish Journal of Economics*, vol. 75 (1973): 378–95. Becker's principal contribution is an earlier unpublished paper, "Consumption Theory: Some Criticisms and a Suggested Approach" (May 1968). Robert T. Michael elaborated on this paper and was primarily responsible for writing the present paper.

[1] For expositional simplicity we assume proportionality between the quantity of goods and their service-flow, thus x_i can refer to either the good or the service-flow.

subject to a constraint on its purchases of the goods. In a single period frame-work

$$I = \sum_{i=1}^{n} x_i p_i \tag{2}$$

where I is money income, p_i is the money price of the good x_i, with the goods inclusively defined. The effects of changes in real income and relative prices on the demand for x_1 are summarized by the demand function

$$x_1 = d_1 \left(\frac{I}{p}, \frac{p_l}{p}, \frac{p_i}{p}, T \right) \tag{3}$$

where p is a price index. Variations in demand which are not related to changes in real income and relative prices are attributed to changes in tastes, T. To-gether these three factors—income, prices and tastes—fully explain consumption behavior.

The single important behavioral "law" which emerges from this approach is that income-compensated (i.e., "pure") changes in the relative price of any good lead to changes in the opposite direction in the quantity demanded of that good,[1] although a few other implications can also be derived. Economists have frequently modified the theory of consumer choice in an attempt to broaden its range of applicability.[2] But these and other modifications leave the basic analytical framework of consumer choice—as expressed in equations (1) through (3)—essentially unaltered. Rather than consider these modifica-tions, we wish to take that basic framework seriously and to point out some of its fundamental weaknesses. While recent modifications in the theory suc-cessfully circumvent some of these weaknesses, we will argue that a more fundamental reformulation of the basic model—as suggested below in Part II —does so more effectively and in a less piecemeal fashion.

Weaknesses in the Traditional Theory

Survey data are typically grouped into a relatively small number of cells cross-classified by some set of variables, with cell averages used as observa-tions in analyses. The use of grouped data involves no bias in estimation of regression coefficients (see Cramer [9]) and is frequently used as a way of re-ducing errors of measurement and other problems with the independent vari-ables, and because economists are frequently interested in aggregate responses rather than the responses of individual consumer units. An additional motiva-tion for using grouped data, however, is that even with sophisticated operational

---

[1] Even this "law" of human behavior can be viewed under fairly general assumptions as a nonvolitional response resulting simply from the constraint on resources. See Becker [3].
[2] For example, the analyses of searching for information about prices, qualities or varie-ties and of formulating expectations about the future behavior of prices and income in-corporates aspects of decision-making under uncertainty.

definitions of income and prices, these explanatory variables alone appear to "explain" only a small part of the variations in demand for specific goods and services in individual household data. Grouping observations by the independent variables considerably increases the "explanatory power" of the estimating equation (see Cramer [9] or Rockwell [39]).

To whatever extent income and prices do not explain observed behavior, the explanation rests with variations in tastes since they are the portmanteau in the demand curve (see equation (3)). Moreover, even grouped data do not eliminate the need to rely on variations in tastes as an explanation for observed behavior. Indeed, aggregate data exhibit systematic effects on behavior of such factors as family size, family age-structure, education, housing tenure, occupation, race, socio-economic status or other proxies for tastes. For economists to rest a large part of their theory of choice on differences in tastes is disturbing since they admittedly have no useful theory of the formation of tastes, nor can they rely on a well-developed theory of tastes from any other discipline in the social sciences, since none exists. Put differently, the theory which the empirical researcher utilizes is unable to assist him in choosing the appropriate taste proxies on a priori grounds or in formulating predictions about the effects of these variables on behavior. The weakness in the received theory of choice, then, is the extent to which it relies on differences in tastes to "explain" behavior when it can neither explain how tastes are formed nor predict their effects.

To illustrate the reliance on "changes in tastes" in interpreting observed behavior, consider the following examples. If a household's utility function has heating fuel as an argument then its tastes must change seasonally to explain why it purchases more fuel in the winter (when the price of fuel is usually higher). Or, couples must experience a shift in preferences toward snow removal services and medical care services and away from sporting goods equipment and high-cholesterol foods as they age since the market prices of these items are not related to age and yet expenditure patterns appear to change with the couple's age.[1] Of course, by incorporating an intuitively appealing explanation in each case, economists usually interpret these observations in reasonable ways. The important point, however, is that the received theory of choice itself is of modest use in that undertaking.

Furthermore, by implying that utility is derived from goods and services purchased in the market place, the received theory has generally been formulated in terms of monetary prices and monetary income. Hence, its application has tended to be restricted to the market sector where transactions are most easily quantified by the "measuring rod of money".[2] Many other be-

---

[1] These effects of age are not, as a first approximation at least, a response to the durability of the item.

[2] However, "shadow" prices are increasingly being introduced in discussing the non-monetary sector.

havioral decisions involving choices made with limited resources among competing ends—a common definition of economics—have been avoided. Decisions about the allocation of a consumer's nonmarket time and decisions about his choice of a religion, a marriage mate, a family size, a divorce, a political party, or a "life style" all involve the allocation of scarce resources among competing ends. Yet, these choices are related to non-monetary factors and have often been ignored by economists.

This concentration on analyzing responses to monetary phenomena has considerably limited the theory's appeal to other social scientists. The political scientist, sociologist, or anthropologist is typically concerned with behavior where monetary phenomena are not pervasive. Hence these other disciplines seldom borrow the economist's theory of choice. Small wonder when that theory relies so heavily on money prices and attributes so much of observed behavior to unexplained variations in tastes.

Indeed, one may wonder why such a theory has survived as a fundamental part of standard economics. But "inefficient" firms may survive in the absence of more efficient ones, particularly when the inefficiency is defined in some absolute sense; so too with theories.

The main point of our paper is that the theory of choice, as formulated, does not make adequate use of its relatively powerful implications. By reformulating the theory of choice, we believe it is capable of explaining a wide range of important phenomena with which the traditional formulation does not cope.

II. The Household Production Function Approach: An Exposition

A fundamental break with the standard approach to the theory of choice has recently been suggested.[1] In broad outline, this approach views as the primary objects of consumer choice various entities, called commodities, from which utility is directly obtained. These commodities are produced by the consumer unit itself through the productive activity of combining purchased market goods and services with some of the household's own time. In this framework all market goods are inputs used in production processes of the nonmarket sector. The consumer's demand for these market goods is a derived demand analogous to the derived demand by a firm for any factor of production.

Formally, let the household's utility function be

$$U = u(Z_1, Z_2, ..., Z_n) \tag{4}$$

where Z_i stands for both the services from and the quantity of the commodity Z_i. The commodity is produced by the household using a vector of market goods x_i and a vector of quantities of its own time, t_i:

[1] See Becker [1], Lancaster [22] and [23] and his more extended exposition of the "characteristics analysis" in [24] and Muth [35].

$$Z_i = z_i(x_i, t_i; E) \tag{5}$$

where E is a vector of variables which represents the environment in which the production takes place.[1] These "environmental variables" reflect the state of the art of production, or the level of technology of the production process. The utility function is maximized subject to the production function constraints (equation (5)) and a constraint on the household's available time:

$$T = t_w + \sum_{i=1}^{n} t_i \tag{6}$$

as well as the usual income constraint:

$$I = \sum_{i=1}^{n} p_i x_i, \tag{7}$$

where t_w and t_i are the household's time spent in the labor market and in producing Z_i, respectively,[2] and p_i and x_i are the price and quantity of the market-good input used in producing Z_i.

The time and money income constraints can be collapsed into a single resource constraint on the household's "full income", S.[3]

$$S = wT + V = \sum_i (wt_i + p_i x_i) \tag{8}$$

where w is the wage rate, assumed to be constant, and V is the household's nonwage income. The importance of this concept of full income is that it embodies both the time and money income constraints and its magnitude is independent of the fraction of time the household chooses to allocate to income-earning activities.[4]

The utility function (4) is maximized subject to the constraints of the production functions (5) and full income (8). The Lagrangian may be expressed as

$$L = u(Z_1, Z_2, ..., Z_n) - \lambda(\sum_i (wt_i + p_i x_i) - S) \tag{9}$$

---

[1] For most of the exposition which follows the x_i, t_i and E will be treated as scalars although it should be kept in mind that x_i is actually a set of market goods, $x_{i1}, x_{i2}, ..., x_{im}$ used in producing Z_i, and similarly for t_i and E.

[2] For expositional simplicity, no distinction will be made between the time of various members of the household, although in principle the time constraint should be applied to each member separately.

[3] By substitution of (6) into the definition of money income

$$I = \sum_j w_j t_{w_j} + V = \sum_j w_j (T_j - \sum_i t_{ji}) + V$$

or

$$I + \sum_j w_j \sum_i t_{ji} = \sum_j w_j T_j + V \equiv S$$

where w_j is the wage rate of the jth family member. Again, the distinction between family members will not be made in the text of this essay.

[4] For a full discussion of its derivation and application see Becker [1].

where the first order conditions for maximization with respect to the commodities imply:

$$\frac{MU_i}{MU_j} = \frac{w\,\dfrac{dt_i}{dZ_i} + p_i\,\dfrac{dx_i}{dZ_i}}{w\,\dfrac{dt_j}{dZ_j} + p_j\,\dfrac{dx_j}{dZ_j}} \equiv \frac{\pi_i}{\pi_j}. \tag{10}$$

The ratio of the marginal utilities of any two commodities Z_i and Z_j, MU_i/MU_j, must equal the ratio of their marginal costs, π_i/π_j, where the derivatives in (10) are marginal input–output coefficients. These marginal costs are the shadow prices of the Z_i that are determined by the prices of market goods and time, and by the productivity of each in producing Z_i.

Similarly, equation (9) can be differentiated with respect to all factors of production to determine their optimal use:

$$\frac{\dfrac{\partial U}{\partial Z_i}\dfrac{\partial Z_i}{\partial f_{ik}}}{\dfrac{\partial U}{\partial Z_j}\dfrac{\partial Z_j}{\partial f_{jl}}} = \frac{MU_i}{MU_j}\frac{MP_{ik}}{MP_{jl}} = \frac{p_{f_{ik}}}{p_{f_{jl}}}, \tag{11}$$

where f_{ik} is the factor k (either goods or time) used in producing Z_i and f_{jl} is the factor l (either goods or time) used in producing Z_j. When both factors are used in the same production function $(i=j)$, the condition reduces to a familiar one—equality of the ratio of marginal products to the ratio of the factor prices. Or, alternatively, if $k=l$ (i.e., if the same factor input is used in several production functions) equation (11) implies that the factor will be allocated among commodities to equalize the utility value of its marginal product in the production of different commodities.[1]

Changes in environment, E, may affect factor prices and the input coefficients and thereby alter a commodity's relative price π_i/π, where π is an index of all commodity prices. It may also affect the price level, π, itself by raising or lowering the average π_i as a whole. A change in the average price of all commodities is comparable to a change in the household's cost of living,

---

[1] The existence of joint products (the use of a factor in more than one production process *at the same time*) can be handled in an analogous manner with the value of the marginal product of factor f_k being

$$\sum_i \frac{\partial U}{\partial Z_i}\frac{\partial Z_i}{\partial f_{ik}}$$

with i an index over the commodities which jointly use the factor f_k. In general, the price of any commodity is then affected by the level of output of the other commodities which use f_k. For an analysis of joint production, see Grossman [16].

Notice that the possibility of using different units of a single input in producing different commodities is not a case of joint production and the commodities' prices are unaffected by the level of production of each other so long as the factor's price remains constant.

or to a change in its opportunity set. So full money income, S, can be converted into full "real" income, S/π, by dividing full money income by the commodity price level.[1] The single constraint on the household's full real income indicates the limitation on its achievable basket of commodities. Forces which affect the market prices households pay and the productivity of the inputs they use alter their π and thus change their full real income. Every household's π may differ just as its full money income may; more efficient household managers have larger real opportunity sets than less efficient ones with the same full money income, S.[2]

Its Antecedents

Although the household production function approach represents a fundamental reformulation of the theory of consumer demand, it is less of a break with the historical development of the theory of choice than it may seem. Jeremy Bentham's *Principles of Legislation* in 1789 set out a list of fifteen "simple pleasures" which he argued was "the inventory of our sensations". These pleasures, which were supposed to exhaust the list of basic arguments in one's pleasure (i.e., utility) function are of senses, riches, address, friendship, good reputation, power, piety, benevolence, malevolence, knowledge, memory, imagination, hope, association and relief of pain.[3] Presumably these pleasures are "produced" partly by the goods purchased in the market sector.

Alfred Marshall suggested an even smaller set of arguments for the utility function when he stated that the basic sources of satisfaction are but two: distinction and excellence.[4] Neither Marshall nor later theoreticians explored the implications of a utility function with so few desiderata, but the household production functions are an attempt to develop a theory of consumer choice consistent with Marshall's contention quoted at the outset of this paper.

Many discussions of the notion that goods are desired not for their own sake but for some specific service which they perform can be found throughout the literature. In discussing the concept of consumption, Nassau Senior

---

[1] For a more extensive discussion of full real income, see Michael [29].

[2] If the environmental variable E were endogenous, its equilibrium quantity would be determined by introducing E into the budget constraint with some price p_E, and differentiating the Lagrangian. The equilibrium condition is:

$$\sum_{i=1}^{n} \frac{\partial U}{\partial Z_i} \frac{\partial Z_i}{\partial E} = \lambda p_E,$$

if the effects of E last only one period; that is, if E is a nondurable.

If the effects of E persist over several periods then its optimal level is determined by the conventional tools of investment theory by comparing the present worth of the stream of its value-marginal-product to the present worth of its costs. (See Ghez–Becker [12].)

[3] The obverse of these pleasures constituted "simple pains". For his discussion of each separately, see Bentham [8], pp. 20–27.

[4] See Marshall's chapter on this point for further bibliography on the analysis of wants and desires. Marshall [28], Book III, Chapter II.

notes that "the word consumption has been applied universally as expressing the making use of anything", and hence he suggests that, "it would be an improvement in the language of Political Economy if the expression 'to use' could be substituted for that 'to consume'."[1] Indeed, the interpretation of consumption as both the exchange of money for market goods and services and, concomitantly, the acquisition of utility from these goods and services, has little intuitive appeal. This interpretation of consumption sheds no light on whether the utility is derived from the acquisition, possession, or utilization of the purchased item. By emphasizing that the consumption of the market good involves its use in the production of a more basic commodity, insight is provided into the nature of the usefulness of the good.

Recent literature abounds with studies in which the demand for a product is considered to be derived from a desire for some more basic aims that are produced using characteristics of the product. Keynes' discussion of the demand for money being derived from speculative, precautionary, and other "motives"; Stigler's essay on food consumption to satisfy nutritional requirements; Griliches and others' use of hedonic price indices in relating, say, the demand for automobiles to an implicit demand for such characteristics as horsepower, wheelbase, power steering, automatic transmission, and so forth suggest the pervasiveness of this general view.[2]

Another antecedent is the effort to analyze and quantify the extent of production of goods and services within the home. Reid's 1934 volume *Economics of Household Production* [38] exemplifies this effort. Reid discusses changes over time in the nature and methods of household production (defined as unpaid activities carried on by and for household members but which could be replaced by market goods and services). Both Reid and Mitchell [34] emphasize the importance of good decision making in the managerial role in household production and both point out the difficulty in wide-spread application of "scientific management" in the household.[3] The household production function approach to consumer behavior adopts the notion of production in the home but extends it to incorporate all nonmarket activities and places greater emphasis on technical aspects of multi-commodity production.

Finally, the property of separability of the utility function which has received much attention in recent years is related to the concept of the household production function. Not only does Leontief's early essay on separability

---

[1] Senior [42], p. 54.
[2] See Keynes [20], Chapter 15; Stigler [44]; and Griliches [13].
[3] Likening wives to managers in industry, Reid suggests that "scientific management" such as "extensive experimentation often does not appear worthwhile since household production is small scale and unspecialized" ([38] pp. 180–181). In his essay "The Backward Art of Spending Money," Mitchell argues that "The trained intelligence and the conquering capacity of the highly efficient housewife cannot be applied to the congenial task of setting to rights the disordered households of her inefficient neighbors .... What ability in spending money is developed among scattered individuals, we dam up within the walls of the single household" ([34] p. 10).

use essentially the same mathematical notation as equations (4) and (5) above, he argues for its adoption in the analysis of consumer behavior:

> The lack of a precise, operational device for dealing with well-defined groups of individual commodities reduced, however, an important part of the theory of consumers' behavior to hardly more than a collection of isolated, arbitrary definitions.
>
> It is true that practical economists assisted by practicing statisticians, speak of and deal in food, clothing, or cultural needs in general, even measuring the aggregative quantities of these fictitious entities. This, however, only serves to emphasize the limited usefulness of the conceptual apparatus offered to them by the theoretician. The analysis of the internal structure of functions of many variables, ... and the concept of functional separability in particular might help to close that particular gap between pure and applied economics.[1]

The household production function interpretation of functional separability is an important application and one discussed in the following section.

III. Applications of the Household Production Function Approach

By incorporating production concepts into the theory of consumption, the household production function approach implies that households respond to changes in the prices and productivities of factors, to changes in the relative shadow prices of commodities and to changes in their full real income as they attempt to minimize their costs of production and to maximize their utility. A reduction in the price of some factor of production will shift the production process toward techniques that are more intensive in the use of that factor and toward commodities that use the factor relatively intensely. The theory of derived demand implies, for example, that the relative increase in the use of the factor will be larger the greater the elasticities of substitution in production and in consumption.

Likewise, if factor prices remain constant, an increase in the marginal productivity of some input induces several responses. To minimize costs of production, the factor's relative use in the production process will increase. Since the relative price of the commodity using this factor most intensively is reduced, the relative consumption of this commodity will increase. Since the rise in productivity raises full real income, the demand for all "normal" commodities (those with positive income elasticities) will increase. The absolute demand for the factor whose productivity rose will rise (or fall) if the combined effects of substitution in production and consumption and of expansion through the change in income outweigh (or are outweighed by) the productivity effect itself.

The theory of household production functions abounds with empirical applications. Some stem from the resulting structure of consumer demand theory

---

[1] See Leontief [26] (p. 164 in *Essays in Economics*).

and include an implication regarding relative magnitudes of cross-price elasticities, an interpretation of functional separability, a rationalization of the often-made assumption of diminishing marginal utility of income, and a justification for the use of the household as a basic unit of observation. In addition, the model has proven useful in analyzing behavior related to travel, fertility, marriage, the influence of education, migration and health, and cross-sectional and life cycle patterns of consumption expenditure and time allocation. We will indicate several of these applications briefly.

For any change in the price of one factor, the effect will be greater upon relative *factor* prices than upon relative commodity prices. Hence, in the absence of a much stronger degree of substitutability in consumption than production, the model suggests that factors used in producing the same commodity will have greater cross-price elasticities than factors used in producing different commodities.[1] Thus, the demand for beef and chicken, which are used in producing nutrition, will be more closely related than will the demand for beef and, say, pianos. This intuitively evident implication about substitution, as Lancaster [22] emphasized, cannot be derived from the traditional theory of consumer choice since that theory has nothing to say about which products are close substitutes.

The household production function approach yields a simple interpretation of weakly separable functions.[2] If the utility function is written indirectly with all market goods and nonmarket time as arguments, then

$$\frac{\partial U}{\partial x_i} = \frac{\partial U}{\partial Z_i} \frac{\partial Z_i}{\partial x_i},$$
(12)

therefore, for any two factor inputs f_1 and f_2 of the m factors used in the same production process,

$$\frac{MU_{f_1}}{MU_{f_2}} = \frac{MP_{i_1}}{MP_{i_2}} = \phi_i \, (f_1, \, f_2, \, ..., \, f_m)$$
(13)

where MP_{i1} is the marginal product of f_1 in producing Z_i. Thus, the ratio of the marginal utilizes depends only on the factors used in that single production process.[3]

---

[1] If, for example, p_{xi}, the price of factor x in the production of z_i rises by one percent, the impact on the relative factor price p_{xi}/p_{ti} is also one percent. But the effect on π_i/π_j depends upon x_i's share in the total cost of Z_i. So long as the share is less than one, π_i/π_j changes by less than p_{xi}/p_{ti} and unless the substitution in consumption (between commodities) is sufficiently greater than the substitution in production (between factors in one production process), the effect of a change in p_{xi} on the demand for t_i will be greater than its effect on the demand for, say, x_i or t_j. The argument easily generalizes to the less restrictive case of many different goods and time inputs used in each production function.
[2] Richard Muth explores the separability issue in some depth in [35].
[3] The existence of joint production as discussed above, undermines the separability of the production processes. Some studies related to the use of time in many production activities simultaneously are now underway.

From the usual assumptions of homogeneity of the production function, the marginal product of market goods relative to the marginal product of time declines as the ratio of goods to time rises. From equation (13), the relative marginal utility of market goods or money income also declines. At first glance this proposition may appear to imply diminishing marginal utility of income, but equation (13) pertains to the *ratio* of marginal utilities. As money income rises, the relative decline in its marginal utility (or marginal product) induces households to behave in ways which conserve time and use money relatively intensively. It has been alleged that wealthy households reveal their relatively low evaluation of their money by "frivolous" expenditures on "inessential" convenience items, but these expenditures may also be interpreted as an efficient substitution away from their relatively scarce resource, time, and toward timesaving, more expensive (in money) convenience items. Such behavior indicates nothing about the absolute direction of change in the marginal utility of money income.

The household production function framework emphasizes the parallel services performed by firms and households as organizational units. Similar to the typical firm analyzed in standard production theory, the household invests in capital assets (savings), capital equipment (durable goods) and capital embodied in its "labor force" (human capital of family members). As an organizational entity, the household, like the firm, engages in production using this labor and capital.[1] Each is viewed as maximizing its objective function subject to resource and technological constraints. The production model not only emphasizes that the household is the appropriate basic unit of analysis in consumption theory, it also brings out the interdependence of several household decisions: decisions about family labor supply and time and goods expenditures in a single time-period analysis, and decisions about marriage, family size, labor force attachment and expenditures on goods and human capital investments in a life cycle analysis.

The recognition of the importance of time as a scarce resource in the household has played an integral role in the development of empirical applications of the household production function approach. The essential nature of the time constraint has been stressed in Mincer's analyses of estimated income effects [32] and the division of time between housework and market work [33] as well as in Becker's general treatment of the time constraint [1]. The subsequent empirical work in the past few years may be characterized as falling into three categories.

The first category pertains to activities in which the use of nonmarket time is an essential or relatively large component. Examples include Gronau's [14] study of the demand for modes of passenger transportation in the production

---

[1] This includes the production of market-earnings potential. See the discussion of the influence of the characteristics of one family member on the earnings of another family member in Benham [6].

of intercity visits, and Owen's [37] study of the demand for leisure time and recreational facilities. Additionally, it has long been recognized not only that consumers sell time in labor markets, but also that they buy time in the form of certain consumer goods and services: the tax consultant, medical advisor, professor, and auto mechanic, as well as the cookbook, frozen foods, vacuum cleaner and television set are all in some measure time-savers. The demand for such items would be quite different if time were not a scarce resource.

Furthermore, the satisfaction obtained from many market goods depends upon the amount of time with which they are consumed. A boat moored to the dock all season, the daily newspaper tossed out without being unfolded, or a quick lunch gulped down between appointments contributes less produce and hence less utility than would a leisurely (time consuming) use of each of these items. So an understanding of the use of time seems necessary for an understanding of the consumption of most market goods and services.[1]

The value of time changes for an individual at various stages in his life and these changes induce substitution toward relatively cheaper means of production as well. The student's life is probably one with a relatively low value of time or high value of goods; hence fraternity bull sessions, hitchhiking and the contemplative life are simply time-intensive modes of producing certain commodities. (Of course, during examination periods time becomes relatively scarce and poor eating and sleeping habits are attempts to conserve this temporarily scarce resource.) During the prime working years, say from age 30 to 55, the value of time is relatively high and one observes the individual working more hours and taking less leisure time. At later stages in the life cycle, when the value of time is again relatively lower, the decline in hours worked, long hours at gardening and viewing television, and other types of leisure activities are evidence of a shift back toward less time-saving behavior.[2]

The second category of applications stems from the close relationship between this framework and the growing human capital literature.[3] With the consumer's own time introduced into the analysis of consumption behavior, the productivity of this time—and hence the human capital embodied in the individual consumer—becomes an important object of analysis. Not only does the productivity of nonmarket time affect consumer behavior, but also the effect of human capital on nonmarket production is one source of the yield on investments in human capital. That is, the analysis of the incentive to invest in education, health, migration, search and so forth should, in principle, incorporate the 'consumption returns" or the nonmarket benefits accruing to the investment. Human capital can raise full real income, S/π (see the discus-

---

[1] Becker [1] indicates several broad applications and Linder [27] presents an enjoyable and stimulating discussion of some of the ways in which an effective time constraint affects modern society.

[2] For a rigorous analysis of substitution over the life cycle in the allocation of goods and time, see Ghez–Becker [12] and Heckman [17].

[3] For a recent discussion of this literature see T. W. Schultz [40].

sion on p. 384), not only by raising the market value of time (and thereby raising S) but also by raising the productivity of nonmarket consumption activities (and thereby lowering the commodity price index π).

Michael [29] develops this argument empirically and, by studying shifts in detailed expenditure patterns related to increases in the level of schooling, obtains a rough empirical estimate of the magnitude of the consumption return to investments in schooling. Grossman [15] analyzes the household's production of health capital and its derived demand for medical services. He shows, among other thing, how the length of life itself is partly endogenously related to decisions about the optimal investment path in health capital.

This line of development of the model offers a promising approach to estimating the nonmarket returns to human capital investments. Furthermore, it emphasizes the importance of the environment in which nonmarket production takes place. Within this framework the effects of climate (meteorological, political or social), the ability of household members, as well as differences in family size, age, sex, etc. may be analyzed. Fortuitously, the recent popular interest in the nonmonetary "quality" of life and the environment coincides with these developments in the approach to consumer behavior.[1]

Another area in which human capital research is complemented by the household production function approach is in the analysis of labor supply. The new approach not only reproduces the implications of the traditional work-leisure model, but also facilitates analysis of more complicated labor supply decisions. Recent studies by Heckman [17], Ofek [36], and Smith [43] have used this framework to investigate the interaction between the labor force decisions of husbands and wives, as related to their wage rates, age, number of children, wealth, and other variables. Ehrlich [10] has likewise employed the household production function model as part of his analysis of the response of criminal activities to the probabilities of apprehension, punishment, and other variables, while Komasar [21] has studied criminal victimization rates using a similar model. Furthermore, the approach has facilitated the analysis of the supply of parental time to pre-school investments in young children (see Leibowitz [25]).

A third category of applications or behavioral implications of this framework concerns marriage and fertility. By emphasizing the importance of the household as the appropriate unit of analysis, the model is a natural framework in which to analyze decisions about marriage. Becker [4] analyzes the incentives to marry and the optimal sorting of marriage mates by I.Q., education, and other characteristics and applications such as the interaction between marital and fertility behavior. Freidan [11] adopts this framework in empirically ana-

---

[1] For example, the National Bureau of Economic Research, with the financial support of the National Science Foundation, has recently undertaken a large-scale research program designed to measure social performance and the rate of output in the nonmarket sector (see Juster [19]).

lyzing differences in marriage propensities. Across states in the U.S. this type of analysis also yields implications about the timing of marriage and divorce, and the nature of other other organizational forms of nonmarket production (e.g., polygamous marriage units, extended families, communes, single-member households). (See Becker [5] for a discussion of polygamy.)

In the analysis of fertility, Willis [45] has utilized the household production function framework to develop an extensive model of the demand for children, and is using this model to test the form and stability of the completed-fertility demand function in the United States. Ben-Porath [7] has tested a comparable model with Israeli data; Michael [31] has analyzed the role of education in affecting fertility behavior, especially contraceptive efficiency. These studies and others presented at a recent fertility conference exemplify the considerable progress made in the past decade in the analysis of economic aspects of human fertility (see Schultz [41]).

IV. An Evaluation

Although the approach is relatively new and many of its implications are unexplored as yet, the applications indicated above suggest the diverse uses of the household production function approach to consumption theory. The new approach is not in conflict with the traditional implications regarding household responses to changes in relative prices or real income. On the contrary, an important advantage of the new approach is its greater emphasis on income and price effects and, correspondingly, its reduced emphasis on the role of "tastes" in interpreting behavior.

This shift in emphasis toward changes in prices and income and away from changes in tastes may appear to be simply one of semantics—of hiding an inability to explain tastes behind the camouflage of a production function. But if behavioral responses are attributed to differences in tastes, not much more can be said since there is no useful theory of the formation of tastes. If, however, they are attributed to differences in production processes, these in turn imply differences in prices and income, and some guidance about these effects can be obtained. This distinction seems crucial. Since factors associated with the formation of tastes have been outside the purview of their discipline, economists have conveniently "grouped" their data to reduce the influence of differences in tastes and then proceeded to ignore or analyze in an ad hoc fashion the remaining taste differences. But economists profess to know something about factors associated with production efficiency and have successfully studied such factors. The household production function approach provides new insights into the consumption process; what was previously outside the domain of economic research now appears amenable to economic analysis. Even if most economists continue to focus on more traditional topics, the household production function approach offers a means by which a wider variety of family behavior can be analyzed.

Consider a logical extension of the view that behavior differences previously attributed to differences in tastes are in fact due to differences in productive efficiency. One might argue that indeed all households have precisely the *same* utility function and that all observed behavioral differences result from differences in relative prices and access to real resources.[1] In the standard theory all consumers behave similarly in the sense that they all maximize the same thing—utility or satisfaction. It is only a further extension then to argue that they all derive that utility from the same "basic pleasures" or preference function, and differ only in their ability to produce these "pleasures". From this point of view, the Latin expression *de gustibus non est disputandum* suggests not so much that it is impossible to resolve disputes arising from differences in tastes but rather than in fact no such disputes arise![2]

The household production function approach incorporates into the theory of choice at a fundamental level the constraints of time, consumer knowledge and inter-household differences in consumption efficiency. While studies have in the past brought in these additional constraints to explain observed behavior, the new approach gives the technology of consumption a principal role in the analysis and treats the money, time and productivity constraints symmetrically. Although the objection by many non-economists that the theory of choice assumes rationality is not well founded,[3] it is difficult to distinguish operationally between irrational choices and poorly informed ones, and the new approach to the theory of choice does give appropriate recognition to the investment in and costly accumulation of information.

If observed differences in behavior are assumed to result from differences in tastes, and if the satisfaction of each person's tastes is used as a guide to normative statements, then differences in behavior cannot be judged normatively. If, however, the observed behavior is assumed to result from different efficiencies with the same set of tastes, these can be judged by the level of full real income which they produce: i.e., by their level of productivity. For example, if education is said to alter tastes, one cannot speak of the effects of education on the level of utility: what is preferable to the college graduate may

---

[1] Such a view is not a theory of economic determinism except in the tautological sense that the behavior which results from making choices must be a response to the relative scarcities confronted in making those choices.

[2] To venture one further step, if genetical natural selection and rational behavior reinforce each other in producing speedier and more efficient responses to changes in the environment, perhaps that common preference function has evolved over time by natural selection and rational choice as that preference function best adopted to human society. That is, in the short run the preference function is fixed and households attempt to maximize the objective function subject to their resource and technology constraints. But in the very long run, perhaps those preferences survive which are most suited to satisfaction given the broad technological constraints of human society (e.g., physical size, mental ability, et cetera).

[3] See Becker [3].

not be so to the grade school dropout and the two cannot, even in principle, reach an agreement on which set of tastes is "better". But these judgments can be made if education affects the efficiency of household production functions. Whatever yields greater commodity output is preferable and can be considered as such by both individuals. The school-dropout's behavior differs if his efficiency is less for the same reason it differs if he faces higher market prices— both restrict his opportunity set. The difference in the opportunity set is a measure of the "consumption return" to education and this return should be added to the "market return" in determining the benefit from additional education.[1]

If households can affect the environment in which they live, they will substitute toward those aspects which enhance productivity. They can "produce" higher education, better health, more favorable weather or greater political stability by attending school, exercising, moving, voting, et cetera. If education and age increase one's capacity to evaluate correctly the long-run effects of behavior, the uneducated and the young might be expected to consume more "irrationally". From such reasoning, which is included here as only illustrative, welfare implications about the desirability of various policies might be obtained.

One can substitute the household production functions (equation (5)) into the utility function (equation (4)) to get the "derived" utility function in terms of goods, time and environmental variables:

$$U = u\ (x_1, ..., x_n, t_1, ..., t_n;\ E_1, ..., E_p). \tag{14}$$

Why then do we use the more complicated and less familiar two-stage formulation given by equations (4) and (5) instead of simply maximizing the derived utility function given by equation (14) subject to the full income constraint? Would this not be more in tune with current theory and just as useful as the alternative approach advocated in this paper? We feel strongly that this is not as useful, even though every statement about the production functions can be translated into an equivalent statement about the derived utility function. The several advantages of the household production function approach are these:

(1) The utility function should pertain exclusively to preferences; it should deal with the final objects of choice by the consumer unit. The derived utility function does not separate preferences from resources and is instead a hodgepodge of some arguments which yield satisfaction, some quantities of time and goods which are directly distasteful, and several arguments—e.g., age, education—which may have little direct utility associated with them. The household production functions effectively separate objects of choice from the means used to produce them.

---

[1] For some rough estimates see Michael [30].

(2) The two-stage formulation implies a major restriction on the derived utility function, namely, that it is separable in the goods and time used to produce a given commodity. This restriction is extremely important in partitioning goods and time-uses into natural divisions of complements and substitutes (see the discussion on p. 387). The derived utility approach per se says nothing about which goods and time-uses are substitutes and which are complements.

(3) The two-stage formulation permits all the concepts and tools of production theory to be used directly in analyzing consumption: these include factor-neutral or factor-augmenting productivity changes, returns to scale, substitution elasticities, "entrepreneurial" efficiency, and the like.

(4) Put more generally, the household production function approach seems to provide useful parameters for the analysis of consumption, even though all statements are translatable into statements about the derived utility function. (Similarly, although all statements about the quantity theory approach to the demand for money and income determination are translatable into statements about the savings and investment approach, this does not mean they are equally useful approaches. The heated controversies for the last thirty years have been based on different allegations about which approach provides the more useful and stable parameters.)

V. Conclusion

This essay suggests that the household production function approach to consumption theory is a powerful tool of analysis. It systematically and symmetrically incorporates numerous constraints on the household's behavior, strengthens the reliance on changes in income and prices as explanations of observed behavior, and correspondingly reduces the reliance on differences in tastes or preferences. These alterations are desirable primarily because they yield a variety of additional behavioral predictions without heroic ingenuity or ad hoc theorizing by the researcher. By reducing the role of tastes, which have defied effective theoretical analysis, the new approach expands the applicability of the economist's theory of choice into the nonmarket sector and hence makes the theory more useful in analyzing household behavior in its many dimensions.

Of course, the final evaluation of any approach depends on its usefulness. Studies discussed in the previous section dealing with the production of commodities such as "good health", children, marriage, or "intercity visits" are indicative of the kinds of research stimulated by this approach. Still wider application has been inhibited by limited data, and the theory is helpful in indicating some of the kinds of new data which would be of use to researchers. The new variables are more global in nature than the goods and resources traditionally considered. They encompass concepts such as envy, prestige, physical and psychological health, "circumspectness", and so on—notions often grappled with by sociologists and psychologists. The renewed interest in "social accounting", as distinct from "national income accounting", is consistent with the directions for new research indicated by the household production function view of consumer behavior.

Consumption theory at the hands of practitioners of the household production function approach has been transformed from one of the more sterile areas of economics into one of the most exciting. This, ultimately, is the most convincing evidence of its analytical power and practical advantage.

References

1. Becker, G. S.: A theory of the allocation of time. *The Economic Journal* 75, 493–517, 1965.
2. Becker, G. S.: Consumption theory: Some criticisms and a suggested approach (mimeo), May 1968.
3. Becker, G S.: Irrational behavior and economic theory. *Journal of Political Economy 70*, 1–13, 1962.
4. Becker, G. S.: A theory of marriage: Part I. *Journal of Political Economy*, July/August 1973.
5. Becker, G. S.: A theory of marriage: Part II. *Journal of Political Economy*, March/April 1974, Part II, forthcoming.
6. Benham, L.: Benefits of women's education within marriage. *Journal of Political Economy*, March/April 1974, Part II, forthcoming.
7. Ben-Porath, Y.: Economic analysis of fertility in Israel: point and counterpoint. *Journal of Political Economy*, March/April 1973, Supplement, S202–S233.
8. Bentham, J.: *Principles of Legislation.* Harcourt, Brace and Co., New York, 1931.
9. Cramer, J. S.: Efficient grouping, regression and correlation in Engel curve analysis. *Journal of the American Statistical Association 59*, 233–50, 1964.
10. Ehrlich, I.: Participation in illegal activities: an economic analysis. *Journal of Political Economy*, May/June 1973, 521–565.
11. Freidan, A.: The U.S. marriage market.

Journal of Political Economy, March/April 1974, Part II, forthcoming.
12. Ghez, G. R. & Becker, G. S.: The allocation of time and goods over the life cycle. National Bureau of Economic Research (mimeo), May 1972.
13. Griliches, Z.: Hedonic price indexes for automobiles: an econometric analysis of quality change. In *The Price Statistics of the Federal Government*, National Bureau of Economic Research (General Series no. 73), 1961.
14. Gronau, R.: *The Value of Time in Passenger Transportation: The Demand for Air Travel*, National Bureau of Economic Research, 1970.
15. Grossman, M.: *The Demand for Health: A Theoretical and Empirical Investigation*, National Bureau of Economic Research, 1972.
16. Grossman, M.: The economics of joint production in the household, Center for Mathematical Studies in Business and Economics, Report 7145, University of Chicago, September 1971.
17. Heckman, J.: Three essays on household labor supply and the demand for market goods. Ph.D. Dissertation, Princeton University, 1971.
18. Houthakker, H. S.: The present state of consumption theory. *Econometrica 29*, 704–740, 1961.
19. Juster, F. T.: A framework for the measurement of economic and social performance. National Bureau of Economic Research (mimeo draft), November 1971.

20. Keynes, J. M.: *The General Theory of Employment, Interest, and Money*, Harcourt, Brace & World, Inc., 1962.

21. Komasar, N. K.: Economic analysis of criminal victimization. *Journal of Legal Studies*, June 1973.

22. Lancaster, K. J.: A new approach to consumer theory. *The Journal of Political Economy 74*, 132–57, 1966.

23. Lancaster, K. J.: Change and innovation in the technology of consumption. *American Economic Review 56*, 14–23, 1966.

24. Lancaster, K. J.: *Consumer Demand.* Columbia University Press, 1971.

25. Leibowitz, A. S.: Women's allocation of time to market and non-market activities: differences by education. Ph.D. Dissertation, Columbia University, 1972.

26. Leontief, W.: Introduction to a theory of the internal structure of functional relationships. *Econometrica 15*, No. 4 (reprinted in his *Essays in Economics*, 1947, Oxford University Press, New York, 1966).

27. Linder, S.: *The Harried Leisure Class.* Columbia University Press, New York, 1970.

28. Marshall, A.: *Principles of Economics.* Macmillan, New York, 1961.

29. Michael, R. T.: *The Effect of Education on Efficiency in Consumption.* National Bureau of Economic Research, 1972.

30. Michael, R. T.: Education in nonmarket production. *Journal of Political Economy*, March/April 1973, 306–327.

31. Michael, R. T.: Education and the derived demand for children. *Journal of Political Economy*, March/April 1973, Part II, S128–S164.

32. Mincer, J.: Market prices, opportunity costs and income effects. In *Measurement in Economics* (ed. Carl Christ). Stanford University Press, 1963.

33. Mincer, J.: Labor force participation of married women. In *Aspects of Labor Economics*. National Bureau of Economic Research, 1963.

34. Mitchell, W. C.: *The Backward Art of Spending Money and Other Essays.* McGraw-Hill, New York, 1937.

35. Muth, R. F.: Household production and consumer demand functions. *Econometrica 34*, 699–708, 1966.

36. Ofek, H.: Allocation of goods and time in a family context. Ph.D. Dissertation, Columbia University, 1971.

37. Owen, J. D.: *The Price of Leisure*, Rotterdam University Press and McGill-Queens University Press, 1969.

38. Reid, M. G.: *Economics of Household Production.* Wiley, New York, 1934.

39. Rockwell, G. R.: *Income and Household Composition: Their Effects on Food Consumption* (Marketing Research Report no. 340), U.S. Department of Agriculture, Washington, D.C., 1959.

40. Schultz, T. W.: Human capital: policy issues and research opportunities. *Human Resources*, National Bureau of Economic Research—Colloquium VI, 1972.

41. Schultz, T. W. (ed.): New economic approaches to fertility. *Journal of Political Economy*, March/April 1973, Part II.

42. Senior, N. W.: *An Outline of the Science of Political Economy.* Sentry Press, New York, 1965.

43. Smith, J. P.: Life cycle allocation of time in a family context. Ph.D. Dissertation, Chicago University 1972.

44. Stigler, G. J.: The cost of subsistence. *Journal of Farm Economics 27*, 303–314, 1945.

45. Willis, R. J.: A new approach to the economic theory of fertility behavior. *Journal of Political Economy*, March/April 1973, Part II, S14–S64.

Part 5   Irrational Behavior

The sole essay in this part shows that the basic theorem in the traditional theory of consumer demand, namely, that demand curves are negatively inclined, does not require maximization or stable preferences but essentially follows from the scarcity of resources. This result provides a useful antidote to many reckless criticisms of the economic approach, and suggests a probabilistic approach to behavior that may be worth following up.

Nevertheless, I have continued to rely on maximization and stable preferences in subsequent discussions of the household as well as other behavior units. This is mainly because the new theory of the household is much richer and more extensive than the traditional theory, involving nonmarketable commodities, household production, the joint allocation of the time of many household members, shadow prices, investment in human capital, and the like. The approach using maximization and stable preferences has provided a more insightful guide to the influence of these different variables than have the models of "irrational" behavior used in this essay.

8 Irrational Behavior and Economic Theory

1. Introduction

Although it has long been agreed that traditional economic theory "assumes" rational behavior, at one time there was considerable disagreement over the meaning of the word "rational." To many, the word suggested an outdated psychology, lightning-fast calculation, hedonistic motivation, and other presumably unrealistic behavior. As economic theory became more clearly and precisely formulated, controversy over the meaning of the assumptions diminished greatly, and now everyone more or less agrees that rational behavior simply implies consistent maximization of a well-ordered function, such as a utility or profit function.

Strong and even violent differences developed, however, at a different level. Critics claim that households and firms do not maximize, at least not consistently, that preferences are not well ordered, and that the theory is not useful in explaining behavior. Some theorists have replied that economic theory is valid only as a broad tendency, not in each specific instance; some noted that the "proof of the pudding is in the eating," and argued that this theory gives useful predictions even though decisions do not "seem" to be rational; still others claimed that only rational behavior has much chance of surviving a very harsh competitive world.

The purpose of this paper is not to contribute still another defense of economic rationality. Rather it is to show how the important theorems of modern economics result from a general principle which not only includes rational behavior and survivor arguments as special cases, but also much irrational behavior. No matter what the intent, some readers might believe that the effect of this demonstration is to provide another and more powerful

Reprinted from the *Journal of Political Economy* 70, no. 1 (February 1962). © 1962 by The University of Chicago.

defense of economic rationality. I believe it does provide an important defense of the *theorems* of modern economics, although, of course, the only ultimate defense is an empirical one, and no new empirical materials are introduced. Since, however, these theorems are shown to be consistent also with an extremely wide class of irrational behavior, a defense of them is not necessarily a defense of individual rational behavior. Indeed, perhaps the main conclusion of this study is that economic theory is much more compatible with irrational behavior than had been previously suspected.

Although economists have typically been interested in the reactions of large markets to changes in different variables, economic theory has been developed for the individual firm and household with market responses obtained simply by blowing up, so to speak, the response of a typical unit. Confusion resulted because comment and analysis were directed away from the market and toward the individual, or away from the economist's main interests. Those arguing that rationality is only a broad tendency, or that only a few units need behave rationally in order for markets to do so, were well aware of the difference between market and individual levels of analysis. Unfortunately, however, one can equally well argue that irrationality is only a broad tendency, or that only a few units need behave irrationally in order for markets to do so. An argument supporting rationality at the market level must imply that rational unit responses would tend to outweigh irrational ones. This paper clearly distinguishes between the market and individual levels and produces such an argument implying rationality at the market level. Perhaps it will help shift the analytical interests of economists toward the same level as their substantive interests.

Section 2 first presents the traditional theory of household choices and then shows why its main implication—that market demand curves are negatively inclined—can also be derived from a wide variety of irrational behavior. Section 3 develops similar arguments for firms, and 4 summarizes the discussion and adds a few additional implications.

2. Households

Traditional Theory

Traditional theory assumes that households choose the best collection of commodities consistent with the limited resources available to them. To determine which collection is "best" a preference or utility function is introduced with the properties that any collection A always gives more, less, or the same utility as any other collection B (the consistency assumption), and that if A is preferred to B, and B to C, A must be preferred to C (the transitivity assumption). The best collection produces more utility than any feasible alternative. This theory is usually illustrated geometrically by the diagram shown in figure 1: commodity X is plotted along the horizontal axis, the "other" commodity Y along the vertical axis, AB is the budget line and OAB defines the feasible collections, and preferences are represented by the set of equal utility or indifference curves. The best collection must be on AB at the point p where AB is tangent to an indifference curve.

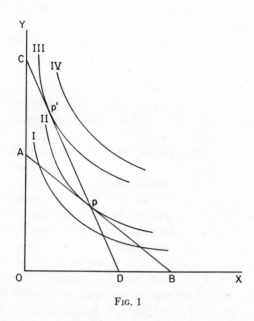

Fɪɢ. 1

A change in relative prices or real income would change the location of the best collection, and the fundamental theorem of this theory is that the demand curve for any commodity, real income held constant, must be negatively inclined. In figure 1 a change in the budget line from AB to CD increases the relative price of X and reduces that of Y, and attempts to hold real income constant by holding the ratio of money income to a Laspeyres price index constant.[1] This is the method most commonly used in empirical demand studies to separate relative price from real income effects. The best collection is changed from p to p', and the fundamental theorem states that p' is to the left and above p, or less X and more Y is chosen. Since the demand curve of a market with many households is usually obtained by horizontal summation of the individual demand curves, it would simply be a blown-up or macroscopic reproduction of the individual micro curves and, consequently, would also be negatively inclined.[2]

---

[1] It is well known that real income would be approximately held constant in the sense that households would tend to remain on the same indifference curve.

[2] Even if household demand curves were interdependent the market curve would tend to be negatively inclined, but more or less elastic than the average micro curve, depending on whether "bandwagon" or "snob" effects predominated.

Market demand curves of many commodities have been extensively investigated empirically and almost invariably are found to be negatively inclined,[3] as predicted by traditional theory, while household demand curves, on the other hand, have seldom been investigated and little is known about them. Other implications of utility theory[4] have almost never been empirically investigated at either the market or the household level and are of little practical use.

The utility approach to household decisions has been extensively criticized ever since its conception, although both formulation and criticism have changed drastically over time. Today, critics either deny that households maximize any function or that the function maximized is consistent and transitive. In effect, they deny that households act "rationally" since rational behavior is now taken to signify maximization of a consistent and transitive function.[5]

How can these extensive criticisms be reconciled with the fact that the main implication of utility theory—that market demand curves would be negatively inclined—has been consistently verified empirically and found extremely useful in practical problems? Perhaps one explanation is that the assumptions of a theory are often "tested" individually rather than as a whole, or what amounts to the same thing, rather than by their implications. Surely another is that many criticisms are really aimed only at the normative implications of utility theory. In this paper I suggest a reconciliation along very different lines; principally, by showing that negatively inclined market demand curves result not so much from rational behavior per se as from a general principle which includes a wide class of irrational behavior as well. Therefore, households can be said to behave not only "as if" they were rational but also "as if" they were irrational: the major piece of empirical evidence justifying the first statement can equally well justify the second.

A General Approach

Economists have long been aware that some changes in the feasible or opportunity sets of households would lead to the same response *regardless of the decision rule used*. For example, a decrease in real income necessarily decreases the amount spent on at least one commodity, and the average percentage change in expenditures on all commodities must equal the percentage decrease in income. These theorems, although "obvious" and "arithmetic," have been extremely useful in practical problems. It has

---

[3] Widespread confidence in the universality of negative market curves has, however, resulted in some "cheating." Other findings are often simply not published or altered until more "reasonable" findings emerge.

[4] The whole set of implications can be summarized in the negative semidefiniteness of a certain quadratic form. See, e.g., Samuelson, (1947, p. 114).

[5] See e.g., Edwards (1954).

seldom been realized, however, that the change in opportunities resulting from a change in relative prices also tends to produce a systematic response, regardless of the decision rule. In particular, the fundamental theorem of traditional theory—that demand curves are negatively inclined—largely results from the change in opportunities alone and is largely independent of the decision rule.

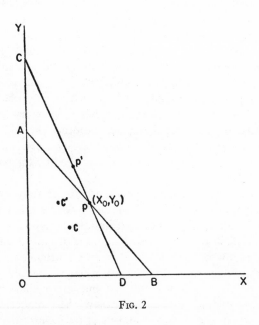

FIG. 2

Since the budget line CD in figure 2 has a higher relative price for commodity X and a lower price for Y than does AB, the set OCD inclosed by CD offers more opportunity to consume Y and less opportunity to consume X than does the set OAB. If point p represents the amounts of X and $Y(X_0, Y_0)$ that would be chosen from OAB by a particular decision rule, OCD can be said to offer smaller opportunity to consume more than X_0 of X and greater opportunity to consume more than Y_0 of Y than OAB does. *If the amount of any commodity chosen by a decision rule were positively related to its availability,* less X than X_0 and more Y than Y_0 would necessarily be chosen from OCD. Demand would be negatively related to price for all such decision rules, no matter how they differed in other respects.

The traditional theory of rational behavior is easily shown to be a rule that depends on the effect of a change in relative prices on the distribution of opportunities. In equilibrium a rational household would gain the same utility from spending an additional dollar on any commodity. A change in relative prices would shift marginal as well as average consumption opportunities toward relatively cheaper and away from more expensive commodities because a dollar now buys more of the former and less of the latter. Consequently an additional dollar at the old equilibrium position would add more utility if it were spent on the former than the latter. Hence rational households would have an incentive to change their consumption, along with the opportunity set, toward relatively cheaper and away from more expensive commodities.

Not only utility maximization but also many other decision rules, incorporating a wide variety of irrational behavior,[6] lead to negatively inclined demand curves because of the effect of a change in prices on opportunities. This will be demonstrated with two models of irrational behavior that encompass both a wide and an allegedly "realistic" class of behavior. On the one hand, households are often said to be impulsive, erratic, and subject to never-ending whim, and on the other hand, inert, habitual, and sluggish. One view alleges that momentary impulses beget a confusing array of undirected change, the other that the past permits little current change or choice. Between these two extremes lies a wide spectrum of irrational behavior, partly determined by the past and partly by current impulses.

If the implications of such behavior are to be fully developed, the attributes of "impulsiveness" and "inertia" must be given a precise and quantitative formulation. To that end, impulsive behavior will be represented by a probabilistic model in which decisions are determined, so to speak, by the throw of a multisided die; inert behavior by a model in which decisions are determined by the past whenever possible (the meaning of this clause is fully developed shortly); and intermediate behavior by a weighted average of these extremes. I believe these models do effectively capture the spirit of the strongest and most frequent criticisms of utility theory, although this cannot be rigorously shown. In any case, they vividly illustrate how irrational choices can also be systematically affected by a change in the distribution of opportunities.

Impulsive households are assumed to act "as if" they only consulted a probability mechanism: no preference system or utility function is consulted. Indeed, to eliminate any vestige of utility maximization, it is assumed that every opportunity has an equal chance of being selected.[7] Although the consumption of a single household could not be determined in advance, the average consumption of a large number of independent households would almost certainly be at the middle of the opportunity set, which is also the (mathematically) expected consumption of a single household. If opportunities were initially restricted to the budget line AB

---

[6] Any deviation from utility maximization is considered "irrational" in this paper: a more precise or philosophical definition is not required for our purposes and is not attempted.

[7] Zvi Griliches pointed out to me that this model was also presented in a very brief appendix to the article by R. L. Marris (1957). The appendix is said to be based on a conversation with Harry Johnson.

in figure 2, the average consumption of many households would be close to p, the midpoint of AB, with different households uniformly distributed around p.

A change in relative prices which held a market-weighted Laspeyres price index constant would rotate the budget line through p, the point representing market consumption.[8] The line CD represents a compensated increase in the price of X, and points would now be chosen at random along CD instead of AB. Each household could be anywhere on CD, but again the average location of many independent households would almost certainly be at the middle, represented by p' in the figure. It should be clear geometrically and is easily shown algebraically that p' is not to the left and above p by accident: a compensated increase in the price of X always shifts the midpoint of the budget line upward and to the left, while a compensated decrease shifts it downward and to the right.[9]

The fundamental theorem of rational behavior, that market demand curves are negatively inclined, is, therefore, also implied by impulsive behavior, at least in markets with large numbers of households. The expected demand curve of each household must also be negatively inclined, although many actual individual curves would not be.[10] Both expected individual and actual market demand curves are negatively inclined because of the effect of a change in prices on the distribution of opportunities. An increase in the relative price of X shifts opportunities away from X, increases the fraction of those with less X than in the initial position, and thereby increases the probability that an impulsive household would reduce its consumption of X. And what is simply more probable for a particular household becomes a certainty for a large number of independent ones.

Consider now a model of inertia: wherever possible, households consume exactly what they did in the past. Point p can again represent the average consumption of a large group of households faced with the budget line AB, and CD the line resulting from a compensated increase in the price of X. Households initially in the region Ap could remain there indefinitely after the price change, although they would no longer be on the budget line. Some, however, would also have to be initially in the

---

[8] Since utility maximization is not assumed, a compensated price change could no longer be said to hold the level of utility (approximately) constant. The important point for our purposes, however, is that empirical studies usually separate price from income effects in this way, and the negative slope of empirical demand curves is a valid and important regularity, regardless of whether utility "really" has been held constant.

[9] Since the midpoint of any budget line is given by $(I/2P_x, I/2P_y)$, where I is money income and P_x and P_y are unit prices, a compensated change in the price of X must change the midpoint of X in the opposite and that of Y in the same direction.

[10] An individual demand curve is more likely to be negatively inclined the greater the number of price observations and the longer the time period covered by each one. Averaging over prices or time is as effective in canceling out erratic behavior here as averaging over households is in a market.

half-open region pB, unless all were at p, and they could not remain there indefinitely after prices changed, no matter how much they wanted to, because pB would be outside the new opportunity set OCD. Obviously, households forced to adjust are not by accident precisely those with an above average consumption of X, for an increase in X's price shifts opportunities away from X.

If the average household in pB had been consuming more than OD of X, the average amount of X consumed by all households would necessarily decline. Those in Ap would not change, and those in pB would have to reduce their X since OD is the maximum X permitted by the budget line CD. In general, the larger the change in relative prices and the larger the dispersion among households,[11] the more likely is it that the maximum X permitted by the new budget line would be smaller than the average in pB. Although the adjustments made by households in pB cannot be determined precisely until a decision rule is specified, their consumption of X would probably decline even when not arithmetically necessary: a wide variety of decision rules would do this because they were consuming relatively large amounts of X, and the opportunity set shifted away from X. The conclusion is warranted, therefore, that a group of inert consumers, along with rational and impulsive ones, would tend to have negatively inclined demand curves.

A broad class of irrational behavior, including inert and impulsive behavior as extreme cases, would be encompassed by a model in which current choices were partly determined by past ones and partly by a probability mechanism.[12] In other words, these choices are a weighted average of those made by impulsive and inert households. Since market demand curves at both these extremes would tend to be negatively inclined, the market curves of any weighted average would also tend to be. So all behavior in this class would reproduce the fundamental theorem of rational behavior.

A utility-maximizing household would necessarily have negatively inclined compensated demand curves and a consistent and transitive "revealed" preference system. A compensated change in prices to an irrational household, on the other hand, would have very different effects. For example, a compensated change to a single inert household, rather than to a group of them, would not cause any change in consumption; and although an impulsive household would tend to have negatively inclined demand curves and consistent and transitive revealed preferences, there would be many exceptions. The market demand curve in markets with many irrational households would, however, be negatively inclined, and the market's revealed preference system could be said to be rational

---

[11] Average consumption in pB is positively related to the dispersion around the overall average represented by p.

[12] Mathematically this model is a first-order Markov process.

(consistent and transitive) in the sense that a compensated change in prices would push the market outside its initial opportunity set.

Hence the market would act as if "it" were rational not only when households were rational, but also when they were inert, impulsive, or otherwise irrational. This analytical statement must be distinguished from the frequently encountered arithmetical statement that a market would behave rationally even if only a few households did, assuming always that the average consumption of other households did not move perversely. The same arithmetic demonstrates that a market would behave irrationally even if only a few households did, again assuming that the average consumption of others did not move "perversely." Our statement goes beyond arithmetic and stems from an analysis of the responses of rational and irrational households.

A "representative" household would act rationally even when actual ones did not if "representative" simply indicates a microscopic reproduction of market responses. Economists have gone further and constructed also a theory of an actual household that is simply a microscopic reproduction of the market. Observed market behavior is used to infer unobserved household behavior without any recognition that a theory of the household need not simply reproduce the market because market rationality is consistent with household irrationality. If we may join the trend toward borrowing analogies from the currently glamorous field of physics, the theory of molecular motion does not simply reproduce the motion of large bodies: the smooth, "rational" motion of a macrobody is assumed to result from the erratic, "irrational" motions of a very large number of microbodies.

Patterning the theory of households after market responses was not only unnecessary, but also responsible for much bitter and rather sterile controversy. Confidence in market rationality misled some into stout defenses of rationality at all levels, while confidence in household irrationality misled others into equally stout attacks on all rationality. What has apparently been overlooked is that both views may be partly right and partly wrong: households may be irrational and yet markets quite rational. If this were generally recognized, critics might be more receptive to models implying rational market responses, and economic theorists to models permitting erratic and other irrational household responses.

Utility analysis does not imply that market demand curves necessarily have sizable elasticities; nevertheless, rational behavior is popularly believed to produce sizable responses in at least some markets. Perhaps, therefore, it would be useful to show that irrational households can produce sizable as well as negative elasticities. The market response of inert households depends on the dispersion among them, the change in prices, and the response of those forced to adjust. If the price of X rose by 10 percent, if households were uniformly distributed along the initial budget line, and if those forced to adjust reduced their average consumption to the midpoint of the new budget line, market demand would decline by about 30 percent, giving a high elasticity of -3.[13] A smaller price change or a larger dispersion would yield a still higher elasticity. It is also significant that a large group of erratic households must have unitary elastic market demand curves.[14] So the broad class of irrational behavior explicitly discussed in this paper can generate sizable market elasticities, and thus can reproduce this attribute of "rational" behavior as well.

Inert households in the region Ap in figure 2 were forced off the boundary and into the interior of the opportunity set by a shift of the budget line from AB to CD. Although "commodities" can sometimes be usefully defined, and usually are defined, so that households must necessarily be on the boundary, I would usually prefer to treat this as an additional implication of rational behavior. Thus utility-maximizing households would be on the boundary not because of a definition but because utility would be maximized (as long as the marginal utility of at least one commodity was positive). Even if "expenditures" were defined so that the entire income had to be spent, irrational households might not "consume" it all because some "purchases" might be lost, spoil, or accumulate unused. These households would be located in the interior of their opportunity sets if the commodity space referred to "consumption" rather than to "expenditures."

[13] Initially, average consumption of X would be $X_0 = 1/2P_x$; subsequently, it would decline to

$$X_1 = \frac{1}{2}\left(\frac{I}{4P_x}\right) + \frac{1}{2}\left(\frac{I}{2.2P_x}\right) = \frac{31}{88}\frac{I}{P_x},$$

so

$$\frac{X_1 - X_0}{X_0} = \frac{\frac{31}{88} - \frac{44}{88}}{\frac{44}{88}} = -.3.$$

[14] The amount of X consumed would be given by the function

$$X = k\,\frac{I}{P_x},$$

where X is market demand and I market income. A compensated change in the price of X would hold constant the ratio of market income to a Laspeyres price index. That is,

$$\frac{I}{P} = c,$$

hence

$$X = k' \cdot \frac{P}{P_x},$$

or

$$X \cdot \frac{P_x}{P} = k'.$$

Our assumption that opportunities are (at least initially) restricted to the budget line must go if the effect of "inefficient" consumption is to be investigated. Inefficient impulsive households might assign equal probabilities to all points in the opportunity set, not just to those on the boundary. The average consumption of a large number of these households would almost certainly be at the set's center of gravity, with households uniformly distributed around this point. Since a compensated change in prices would shift opportunity sets and thus centers of gravity away from commodities rising and toward those falling in price, these households would also have negatively inclined market demand curves. For example, point *c* in figure 2 would be the center of the set *OAB*, and *c'*, to the left and above *c*, would be the center of *OCD*.[15] Inefficient inert households would be initially distributed throughout the opportunity set. They too would tend to have negatively inclined market curves because a compensated change in prices would still force those consuming relatively large amounts of commodities rising in price to change, presumably toward a smaller consumption of these commodities. So an extension of irrational behavior to cover inefficient consumption does not alter the conclusion that irrational households would tend to have rational market responses to a change in prices.

3. Firms

The analysis can easily be extended to the demand for inputs by interpreting *X* and *Y* in figure 2 as inputs rather than commodities, and *AB* and *CD* as equal outlay rather than equal income lines. A fundamental theorem of rational behavior is that a compensated increase in the price of *X* would reduce the amount of *X* employed with a given outlay: less *X* would be employed with the outlay line *CD* than *AB*. The applicability of figure 2 is a hint that this theorem is derived not so much from rational behavior itself as from the general effect of a change in relative input prices on the distribution of employment opportunities. Even irrational firms would tend to respond "rationally" to a change in input prices; for example, a large number of impulsive firms would on the average be located at point *p* when faced with *AB* and at *p'*, to the left and above *p*, when faced with *CD*.[16]

---

[15] The set *OCD* differs from *OAB* only because *ApC* differs from *BpD* (*OApD* is common to both). Since *ApC* is to the left and above *BpD*, the center of *OCD* must be to the left and above that of *OAB*.

[16] Just as a group of impulsive households would produce compensated commodity demand curves having unitary elasticity, so impulsive firms would produce compensated input demand curves having unitary elasticity, or exactly the same as that produced by firms maximizing profits subject to Cobb-Douglas production functions. It is rather amazing that these implications of Cobb-Douglas functions, which have been extensively acclaimed, should also result from the simplest model of impulsive behavior.

Figure 2 could not be directly applied to the demand for inputs if total outlays were permitted to vary because outlay lines could not then serve as budget lines. More generally, since the traditional analytical distinction between households and firms is that firms are not supposed to be subject to budget constraints,[17] our analysis of irrational households would seem to have little relevance to irrational firms. As long as the assumption of profit maximization is maintained, firm decisions can legitimately be analyzed without recourse to budgetary constraints, and the traditional distinction is valid. But as soon as other decision rules are permitted, the existence and importance of a budget constraint become patently clear, and the traditional distinction is blurred and perhaps even vanishes.

In my judgment the great achievement of the "survival" argument advanced by Alchian and others[18] is not a demonstration that surviving firms must act as if they were trying to maximize profits, for counter-examples can easily be developed, but rather a demonstration that the decisions of irrational firms are limited by a budgetary constraint. Indeed, the survival argument is really simply a special case of a general argument, developed for households in section 2, linking the behavior of all economic units to the distribution of their opportunities. Thus firms could not continually produce, could not "survive," outputs yielding negative profits, as eventually all the resources at their disposal would be used up.[19] For exactly the same reason households could not continually consume, in this sense could not "survive," outside the region covered by incomes. In both cases the word "survive" simply refers to a resource constraint on behavior and does not literally distinguish "life" from "death," although some households and firms may actually die from trying to "live" beyond their means. Had the meaning of survival in this context been understood, numerous pointless discussions of the application of biological survival theories in economics could have been avoided.

Since the region inclosed by the income constraint is called the consumption opportunity set of households, the region of nonnegative profits can appropriately and naturally be called the production opportunity set of firms. For example, households with the budget line AB in figure 2 have the consumption opportunity set OAB, and firms with the average cost curve AC and demand curve dd shown in figure 3 have the production opportunity set Q_eQ_u. Just as households choose their consumption subject to the limitation that they spend no more than the available income, so firms can be assumed to choose their output subject to the limitation that they spend no more than the maximum profit which could have been earned. The entire amount, so to speak, would be spent at outputs yielding

---

[17] See, e.g., Hotelling (1935) and Samuelson (1947, p. 218).

[18] See, e.g., Alchian (1950) and Friedman (1953).

[19] More generally, firms could not survive if the sum of profits and net income from other sources was less than zero.

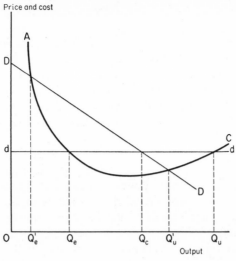

Fig. 3

zero profits; nothing would be spent if profits were maximized; and a positive but less than the entire amount would be spent at any other admissible output. The traditional conclusion that firms are not subject to a budget constraint is clearly valid when profits are maximized: nothing would be "spent" and so no constraint could be operative. With any other decision rule, however, a constraint on total expenditures might be operative because something would be spent.

A change in cost or demand conditions would change production opportunity sets and force even irrational firms to respond systematically. Many variables influence these sets, and I have not tried to determine the response of irrational firms to changes in all of them. It is instructive, however, to consider explicitly some differences between monopolistic and competitive outputs: a well-known theorem is closely associated with profit-maximizing behavior, and even skeptical readers might be impressed by a demonstration that a wide variety of irrational behavior would reproduce this theorem.

Industrial costs would be the same as a firm's, except for a difference in units, in industries having many independent, identical firms, but the industrial demand curve would be more elastic than the firm's. The *AC* curve in figure 3 can, therefore, measure both industry and firm average costs, *DD* industry and *dd* firm demand conditions. Line *DD* is drawn so that the competitive equilibrium of profit-maximizing firms occurs at a price of *od* and a per firm output of OQ_c, where presumably marginal costs equal price. If the industry became a completely monopolistic cartel, *DD* would measure firm as well as industrial demand and *dd* would no longer be relevant. A famous and ancient theorem states that, if profits were always maximized, output per firm under the cartel would be less than OQ_c.

Completely impulsive firms would assign an equal probability to all available outputs and select one at random: no marginal cost function would be consulted and certainly no attempt would be made to equate marginal cost and marginal revenue. If the industry was "competitive," these firms would be uniformly distributed along the opportunity set Q_e, Q_u, with an average output almost certainly at the midpoint. Let Od again be the equilibrium price and OQ_c average output, where OQ_c is now simply the midpoint of $Q_e Q_u$ and not necessarily a point equating marginal cost to price. Cartelization would shift the firm's demand curve to DD and shift the opportunity set to the left of $Q_e Q_u$ to $Q'_e Q'_u$. If outputs were again chosen randomly, firms would be uniformly distributed along $Q'_e Q'_u$ and average output would almost certainly be at its midpoint, which is to the left of OQ_c.

In the same way inert and many other kinds of irrational firms can be shown to reproduce this famous theorem of neoclassical economics. The fundamental explanation is that a change from competition to monopoly shifts the production opportunity set toward lower outputs, which in turn encourages irrational firms to lower their outputs. At best only of indirect importance is the effect on the marginal revenue function, the explanation always given for profit-maximizing firms.

Our discussion of changes in input prices and the degree of competition indicates that irrational firms can give very rational market responses, and this seeming paradox offers a solution to the heated and protracted controversy between marginalists and antimarginalists. Confidence in the irrationality of firms induced the latter to conclude that market responses were also irrational, while confidence in the rationality of markets induced the former to conclude that firms were also rational. Apparently few realized that both kinds of "evidence" could be valid and yet both inferences invalid, so that each side might be partly right and partly wrong. Basically, what is missing in the controversy is a systematic analysis of the responses of irrational firms; in particular, of how opportunity sets and thus the decisions of irrational as well as rational firms are affected by changes in different variables. For such an analysis reveals that irrational firms would often be "forced" into rational market responses. Consequently, antimarginalists can believe that firms are irrational, marginalists that market responses are rational, and both can be talking about the same economic world.

4. Summary and Conclusions

Economists have long recognized that consumption opportunities of households are limited to those costing no more than the income available, but not that production opportunities of firms are limited in *exactly the same way* to those yielding nonnegative profits—or to a somewhat larger set when income is also received from other sources. This neglect results from the almost exclusive concern with profit-maximizing firms, for they and they alone are not affected by the constraint on production opportunities. If firms maximized utility rather than profits[20] or behaved irrationally, the constraint on opportunities would be as real to firms as to households. The word "firm" in this context includes foundations and other private nonprofit organizations, governments, and persons choosing occupational and industrial employment as well as "commercial" organizations. Opportunity sets apply, then, to all decision units with limited resources.

Even irrational decision units must accept reality and could not, for example, maintain a choice that was no longer within their opportunity set. And these sets are not fixed or dominated by erratic variations, but are systematically changed by different economic variables: a compensated increase in the price of some commodities would shift consumption opportunities toward others; a compensated increase in the price of some inputs would shift production opportunities toward others; or a compensated decrease in the attractiveness of some occupations would shift employment opportunities toward others. Systematic responses might be expected, therefore, with a wide variety of decision rules, including much irrational behavior.

Indeed, the most important substantive result of this paper is that irrational units would often be "forced" by a change in opportunities to respond rationally. For example, impulsive households would tend to have negatively inclined demand curves because a rise in the price of one commodity would shift opportunities toward others, leaving less chance to purchase this one even impulsively. Other irrational households would likewise tend to have negatively inclined demand curves, irrational firms negatively inclined demand curves for inputs, and irrational workers positively inclined supply curves to occupations.

If irrational units, nevertheless, often respond rationally, what accounts for the deep and prolonged animosity between marginalists and anti-marginalists, Veblenites and neoclassicists, and other groups differing in the degree of rationality attributed to economic decision units? The major explanation undoubtedly is that formal models of irrational behavior have seldom been systematically explored—in particular, to determine how changes in opportunities impinge on irrational behavior. A subsidiary explanation is that little attention has been paid to the distinction between group or market and individual responses. This distinction is unnecessary in traditional theories of rational behavior because a market's response is usually simply the macro-version of an individual's response. A group of

[20] See Alchian and Kessel (1960) and my *The Economics of Discrimination* (1957), chap. 3.

irrational units would, however, respond more smoothly and rationally than a single unit would, and undue concentration at the individual level can easily lead to an overestimate of the degree of irrationality at the market level.

When market responses of irrational units differ substantially from the responses of rational units, empirical evidence on actual responses would be crucially important in assessing the extent of individual rationality. The kind of evidence traditionally used, the negative slope of market demand curves or the positive slope of market supply curves, is equally consistent with individual irrationality and cannot discriminate between them. Inadequate attention has been paid to gathering relevant evidence apparently because opportunity sets and their effect on the market responses of irrational units have been inadequately appreciated.

I explicitly analyzed only simple models of irrational behavior in which current choices were partly determined by past ones and partly by probability considerations. Much additional work is required to formulate rigorously other models and to determine their implications. Although many of these would surely differ, an important area of agreement would result from common responses to shifts in opportunities. Such is the main lesson to be learned from this paper.

Part 6   Marriage, Fertility, and the Family

The application of the economic approach to fertility, marriage, employment, and other interactions among family members continues to encounter open hostility. When the first paper in this section suggested at a conference on population that children could be treated as durable consumer goods, it was greeted with derision by many participants. However, studies using the economic approach to analyze fertility have steadily increased in number since then, and they are now becoming respectable in the economics profession.

Yet the paper on marriage (published almost 15 years later) was not much more favorably received than the first one on fertility. Are marital decisions less subject than fertility decisions to the calculus provided by the economic approach, or is the hostility again simply an expression of intellectual inertia? Although I believe that marriage is an even more promising subject for the economic approach than fertility, it is still too early to evaluate this claim because the approach has been applied to marriage only during the last few years.

The traditional theory of the household is essentially a theory of a one-person household, and it is almost, but not quite, sterile (the important theorem on negatively sloped demand curves saves it from complete sterility). In contrast, the new theory of the household is a theory of the multi-person family with interdependent utility functions, and focuses on the coordination and interaction among members with regard to decisions about children, marriage, the division of labor concerning hours worked and investments in market-augmenting and nonmarket-augmenting skills, the protection of members against hazards, intergenerational transfers among members, and so on. Economists are, therefore, only beginning to attribute to the family the same dominant role in society traditionally attributed to it by sociologists, anthropologists, and psychologists. Whereas the theory of the firm is basically no different than it was 30 years ago, the household has been transformed from a sterile field in economics into one of the most exciting and promising areas.

9   An Economic Analysis of Fertility

THE inability of demographers to predict western birth rates accurately in the postwar period has had a salutary influence on demographic research. Most predictions had been based either on simple extrapolations of past trends or on extrapolations that adjusted for changes in the age-sex-marital composition of the population. Socio-economic considerations are entirely absent from the former and are primitive and largely implicit in the latter. As long as even crude extrapolations continued to give fairly reliable predictions, as they did during the previous half century, there was little call for complicated analyses of the interrelation between socio-economic variables and fertility. However, the sharp decline in birth rates during the thirties coupled with the sharp rise in rates during the postwar period swept away confidence in the view that future rates could be predicted from a secularly declining function of population compositions.

Malthus could with some justification assume that fertility was determined primarily by two primitive variables, age at marriage and the frequency of coition during marriage. The development and spread of knowledge about contraceptives during the last century greatly widened the scope of family size decision-making, and contemporary researchers have been forced to pay greater attention to decision-making than either Malthus or the forecasters did. Psychologists have tried to place these decisions within a framework suggested by psychological theory; sociologists have tried one suggested by sociological theory, but most persons would admit that neither framework has been particularly successful in organizing the information on fertility.

Two considerations encouraged me to analyze family size decisions within an economic framework. The first is that Malthus' famous discussion was built upon a strongly economic framework; mine can be viewed as a generalization and development of his. Second, although no

Reprinted from *Demographic and Economic Change in Developed Countries*, a conference of the Universities–National Bureau Committee for Economic Research (Princeton University Press for the National Bureau of Economic Research, Inc., 1960).

single variable in the Indianapolis survey[1] explained more than a small fraction of the variation in fertility, economic variables did better than others. Section I develops this framework and sets out some of its implications. Section II uses this framework to analyze the actual effects of income on fertility. Section III speculates about some further implications of the discussion in I and II.

I. The Economic Framework

GENERAL CONSIDERATIONS

In societies lacking knowledge of contraception, control over the number of births can be achieved either through abortion or abstinence, the latter taking the form of delayed marriage and reduced frequency of coition during marriage. Since each person maintains some control over these variables, there is room for decision-making even in such societies. Other things the same, couples desiring small families would marry later and have more abortions than the average couple. Yet the room for decision-making would be uncomfortably small, given the taboos against abortion, the strong social forces determining the age of marriage, and the relative inefficiency of reductions in the frequency of coition. Chance would bulk large in determining the distribution of births among families.[2]

The growth of knowledge about contraception has greatly widened the scope of decision-making, for it has separated the decision to control births from the decision to engage in coition. Presumably, such a widening of the scope of decision-making has increased the importance of environmental factors, but which of the numerous environmental factors are most important? To simplify the analysis of this problem I assume initially that each family has perfect control over both the number and spacing of its births.

For most parents, children are a source of psychic income or satisfaction, and, in the economist's terminology, children would be considered a consumption good. Children may sometimes provide money income and are then a production good as well. Moreover, neither the outlays on children nor the income yielded by them are fixed but vary in amount with the child's age, making children a durable consumption and production good. It may seem strained, artificial, and perhaps even immoral to classify children with cars, houses, and machinery. This classification does not imply, however, that the satisfactions or costs associated with

---

[1] *Social and Psychological Factors Affecting Fertility*, ed. by P. K. Whelpton and C. V. Kiser, Milbank Memorial Fund, Vols. 1–4.

[2] The effect of chance will be fully discussed in a subsequent paper.

children are morally the same as those associated with other durables. The satisfaction provided by housing, a "necessity," is often distinguished from that provided by cars, a "luxury," yet both are treated as consumer durables in demand analysis. Abstracting from the kind of satisfaction provided by children makes it possible to relate the "demand" for children to a well-developed body of economic theory. I will try to show that the theory of the demand for consumer durables is a useful framework in analyzing the demand for children.

TASTES

As consumer durables, children are assumed to provide "utility." The utility from children is compared with that from other goods via a utility function or a set of indifference curves. The shape of the indifference curves is determined by the relative preference for children, or, in other words, by "tastes." These tastes may, in turn, be determined by a family's religion, race, age, and the like. This framework permits, although it does not predict, fertility differences that are unrelated to "economic" factors.

QUALITY OF CHILDREN

A family must determine not only how many children it has but also the amount spent on them—whether it should provide separate bedrooms, send them to nursery school and private colleges, give them dance or music lessons, and so forth. I will call more expensive children "higher quality" children, just as Cadillacs are called higher quality cars than Chevrolets. To avoid any misunderstanding, let me hasten to add that "higher quality" does not mean morally better. If more is voluntarily spent on one child than on another, it is because the parents obtain additional utility from the additional expenditure and it is this additional utility which we call higher "quality."

INCOME

An increase in income must increase the amount spent on the average good, but not necessarily that spent on each good. The major exceptions are goods that are inferior members of a broader class, as a Chevrolet is considered an inferior car, margarine an inferior spread, and black bread an inferior bread. Since children do not appear to be inferior members of any broader class, it is likely that a rise in long-run income would increase the amount spent on children.[3]

[3] This is also suggested by another line of reasoning. It is known that $\Sigma k_i n_i \equiv 1$, where k_i is the fraction of income spent on the ith commodity, and n_i is the income

For almost all other consumer durables, such as cars, houses, or refrigerators, families purchase more units as well as better quality units at higher income levels, with the quantity income elasticity usually being small compared to the quality elasticity.[4] If expenditures on children responded in a similar way, most of the increased expenditures on children would consist of an increase in the quality of children. Economic theory does not guarantee that the quantity of children would increase at all, although a decrease in quantity would be an exception to the usual case. Thus an increase in income should increase both the quantity and quality of children, but the quantity elasticity should be small compared to the quality elasticity.

Malthus, on the other hand, concluded that an increase in income would lead to a relatively large increase in family size. His argument has two major components. First, an increase in income would cause a decline in child mortality, enabling more children to survive childhood. If a decrease in births did not offset the decrease in child mortality, the number of children in the average family would increase. His second argument is less mechanical and takes greater account of motivation. An increase in income increases fertility by inducing people to marry earlier and abstain less while married.

My analysis has generalized that of Malthus by relating the quantity of children to the quality of children and by permitting small (even negative) quantity income elasticities as well as large ones. My conclusion that in modern society the quantity elasticity is probably positive but small differs from his for the following reasons. First, child mortality has fallen so low that the ordinary changes in income have little effect on the number of survivors out of a given birth cohort. Moreover, it is doubtful that even a large decline in child mortality would have much effect on family size, for parents are primarily interested in survivors, not in births per se. Therefore, a decline in child mortality would induce a corresponding decline in births.[5] Second, births can now be controlled without abstinence and this has greatly reduced the psychic costs of birth

---

elasticity of the amount spent on the ith commodity. Other things the same, the larger k_i is, the less likely it is that n_i is either very small or very large. In particular, the less likely it is that n_i is negative. In most families the fraction of income spent on children is quite large and this decreases the likelihood that the income elasticity for children is negative.

[4] Chow estimated the total income elasticity for automobiles at about $+2$. Cf. G. C. Chow, *Demand for Automobiles in the United States*, North Holland Publishing Co., Amsterdam, 1957; however, the quantity elasticity is only about $+0.31$. Cf. *Federal Reserve Bulletin*, August, 1956, p. 820.

[5] This will be discussed more fully in a future publication.

control. "Human nature" no longer guarantees that a growth in income appreciably above the subsistence level results in a large inadvertent increase in fertility.

COST

In principle the net cost of children can be easily computed. It equals the present value of expected outlays plus the imputed value of the parents' services, minus the present value of the expected money return plus the imputed value of the child's services. If net costs were positive, children would be on balance a consumer durable and it would be necessary to assume that psychic income or utility was received from them. If net costs were negative, children would be a producer durable and pecuniary income would be received from them. Children of many qualities are usually available, and the quality selected by any family is determined by tastes, income, and price. For most families in recent years the net expenditure on children has been very large. [6]

Real incomes per capita in the United States have increased more than threefold in the last 100 years, which must have increased the net expenditure on children. It is possible that in the mid-nineteenth century children were a net producer's good, providing rather than using income. However, the marginal cost of children must have been positive in families receiving marginal psychic income from children; otherwise, they would have had additional children. Even in 1850, the typical family in the United States was producing fewer children than was physically possible. Some more direct inferences can be drawn from the data on Negro slaves, an extreme example of a human producer's good. These data indicate a positive net expenditure on male slaves during their first eighteen years. [7] Slave raising was profitable because the high price that an eighteen-year-old could bring more than offset the net cost during the first eighteen years. Presumably, in most families expenditures on white children during their first eighteen years were greater than those on slaves. Moreover, after eighteen, white children became free agents and could decide

[6] See J. D. Tarver, "Costs of Rearing and Educating Farm Children," *Journal of Farm Economics*, February, 1956, pp. 144–153, and L. I. Dublin and A. J. Lotka, *The Money Value of a Man*, Ronald Press, 1946, ch. 4. Most studies consider only the costs and returns before age eighteen. It is possible that returns bulk larger than costs at later ages; but because these ages are heavily discounted and because costs are so large before age eighteen, there is little chance that a correction of this bias would substantially reduce the net cost of children.

[7] See A. H. Conrad and J. R. Meyer, "The Economics of Slavery in the Ante Bellum South," *Journal of Political Economy*, April, 1958, p. 108. At an 8 per cent discount rate (about the estimated rate of return on slaves), the present value of the net costs is + $35, or about one-third of the present value of gross costs. The data are subject to considerable error and are at best a rough indication of the magnitudes involved.

whether to keep their income or give it to their parents. The amount given to parents may have been larger than the costs before eighteen, but it is more likely that costs before eighteen dominated returns after eighteen. This conclusion does not imply that monetary returns from children were unimportant, and indeed, they are stressed at several points in this paper. It does imply, however, that a basic framework which treats children as a consumer's good is relevant not only for the present, but also for some time in the past.

A change in the cost of children is a change in the cost of children of *given quality*, perhaps due to a change in the price of food or education. It is well to dwell a little on this definition for it is widely misunderstood. One would not say that the price of cars has risen over time merely because more people now buy Cadillacs and other expensive cars. A change in price has to be estimated from indexes of the price of a given quality. Secular changes in real income and other variables have induced a secular increase in expenditures on children, often interpreted as a rise in the cost of children. The cost of children may well have risen (see pp. 227–28) but the increase in expenditure on children is no evidence of such rise since the quality of children has risen. Today children are better fed, housed, and clothed, and in increasing numbers are sent to nursery schools, camps, high schools, and colleges. For the same reason, the price of children to rich parents is the same as that to poor parents even though rich parents spend more on children.[8] The rich simply choose higher quality children as well as higher qualities of other goods.[9]

It is sometimes argued that social pressures "force" richer families to

[8] One qualification is needed because the rich may impute a higher value than the poor to the time spent on children. The same qualification is needed in analyzing the demand for other goods.

[9] As an example of how prevalent this error is, even among able economists, we refer to a recent discussion by H. Leibenstein in *Economic Backwardness and Economic Growth*, John Wiley, 1957, pp. 161–170. He tries to relate cost of children to level of income, arguing, among other things, that "The relation between the value of a child as a contributor to family income and changes in per capita income is fairly clear. As per capita income increases, there is less need to utilize children as sources of income. At the same time the level of education and the general quality of the population implied by a higher income per head mean that more time must be spent on child training, education, and development, and, therefore, less time is available to utilize the child as a productive agent. Therefore, the higher the income, the less the utility to be derived from a prospective child as a productive agent" and "The conventional costs of child maintenance increase as per capita income increases. The style in which a child is maintained depends on the position and income of the parents; therefore, we expect such costs to rise as incomes rise. . . ." (*ibid.*, pp. 163–164.)

By trying to relate cost to income Leibenstein confused cost and quality, and succeeded only in inadvertently relating quality to income. His technique would imply that the relative price of almost every group of goods rose over time because the quality chosen spend more on children, and that this increases the cost of children to the rich. This higher cost is supposed to explain why richer families have fewer children than others and why richer societies have fewer children than poorer ones. However, since the cost of different goods is given in the market place, social pressures cannot change this, but can only change the basket of goods selected. That is, social pressures influence behavior by affecting the indifference curve structure, not by affecting costs. To put this differently, social pressures may affect the income elasticity of demand for children by rich (and poor) families, but not the price elasticity of demand. Therefore, the well known negative relationship between cost (or price) and quantity purchased cannot explain why richer families have had relatively few children. Moreover, nothing in economic analysis implies that social pressures would make the quantity income elasticity of demand for children negative. Thus my conclusion that the quantity income elasticity is relatively small but positive and the quality elasticity relatively large is entirely consistent with an analysis which emphasizes social pressures.

Suppose there was an equal percentage decline in the price of all qualities of children, real income remaining constant. Although economic theory suggests that the "amount" of children consumed would increase, it does not say whether the amount would increase because of an increase in quantity, quality, or both—the last, however, being most likely. It also has little to say about the quantitative relationship between price and amount. There are no good substitutes for children, but there may be many poor ones.[10]

---

rose, an obvious impossibility. This flaw in his procedure greatly weakens his analysis of the secular decline in birth rates.

Bernard Okun also applied economic analysis to the population area, and explicitly assumed that the cost of children is higher to rich people because they spend more on children (see *A Rational Economic Model Approach to the Birth Rate*, Rand Corp. Series, P1458, August, 1958). His argument, like Leibenstein's, would imply that the cost of many (if not most) goods is greater to richer families than to poorer ones. Also see S. H. Coontz, *Population Theories and the Economic Interpretation*, Routledge, London, 1957, Part II.

[10] Let x be the quantity of children, p an expenditure measure of the quality of x, y an index of other goods, I money income, U a utility function, α a parameter shifting the cost of each quality of x by the same percentage, and π the price of y. A consumer maximizes $U(x, y, p)$ subject to the constraint $\alpha px + \pi y = I$. This leads to the equilibrium conditions

$$\frac{Ux}{\alpha p} = \frac{Up}{\alpha x} = \frac{Uy}{\pi}$$

The marginal utility from spending a dollar more on the quantity of children must equal the marginal utility from spending a dollar more on their quality.

After a draft of this paper was written I came across an article by H. Theil, "Qualities, Prices, and Budget Inquiries," *The Review of Economic Studies*, XIX, pp. 129–147, which

SUPPLY

By and large, children cannot be purchased on the open market but must be produced at home. Most families are no longer self-sufficient in any major commodity other than children. Because children are produced at home, each uncertainty in production is transferred into a corresponding uncertainty in consumption, even when there is no uncertainty for all families taken together. Although parents cannot accurately predict the sex, intelligence, and height of their children, the distribution of these qualities is relatively constant for the country as a whole. This uncertainty makes it necessary to distinguish between actual and expected utility. Thus suppose a group of parents received marginal utility equal to U_m from a male child and U_f from a female child. The expected utility from an additional child equals $EU = PU_m + (1 - P)U_f \cong \dfrac{U_m + U_f}{2}$, where P, the probability of a male is approximately equal to $1/2$. They would have additional children whenever the expected utility per dollar of expected cost from an additional child were greater than that from expenditures elsewhere. The actual utility is either U_f or U_m, which differs from EU as long as $U_f \neq U_m$. In fact, if U_f (or U_m) were negative, some parents would receive negative utility.

A second important consequence of uniting consumption and production is that the number of children available to a family is determined not only by its income and prices but also by its ability to produce children. One family can desire three children and be unable to produce more than two, while another can desire three and be unable to produce fewer than five.[11] The average number of live births produced by married women in societies with little knowledge of contraception is very high. For example, in nineteenth-century Ireland, women marrying at ages 20–24 averaged more than 8 live births.[12] This suggests that the average family more frequently had excess rather than too few children.

---

treats the interaction of quality and quantity in an elegant manner. Also see, in the same issue, H. S. Houthhakker, "Compensated Changes in Quantities and Qualities Consumed," pp. 155–164. Theil differentiates equations like these and shows that a compensated decrease in the price of a good of given quality must increase either the quantity of goods or the quality, or both.

[11] There is some ambiguity in the last part of this sentence since abstinence enables a family to produce as few children as desired. The terms "unplanned," "excess," or "unwanted" children refer to children that would not be conceived if there were perfect mechanical control over conception. No children are unplanned in terms of the contraceptive knowledge and techniques actually known.

[12] See D. V. Glass and E. Grebenik, *The Trend and Pattern of Fertility in Great Britain,* Paper of the Royal Commission on Population, Vol. VI, p. 271.

Relatively effective contraceptive techniques have been available for at least the last 100 years, but knowledge of such techniques did not spread rapidly. Religious and other objections prevented the rapid spread of knowledge that is common to other technological innovations in advanced countries. Most families in the nineteenth century, even in advanced Western countries, did not have effective contraceptive information. This information spread slowly from upper socio-economic groups to lower ones.[13]

Each family tries to come as close as possible to its desired number of children. If three children are desired and no more than two are available, two are produced; if three are desired and no fewer than five are available, five are produced. The marginal equilibrium conditions would not be satisfied for children but would be satisfied for other goods, so the theory of consumer's choice is not basically affected.[14] Families with excess children consume less of other goods, especially of goods that are close substitutes for the quantity of children. Because quality seems like a relatively close substitute for quantity, families with excess children would spend less on each child than other families with equal income and tastes. Accordingly, an increase in contraceptive knowledge would raise the quality of children as well as reduce their quantity.

II. An Empirical Application

Having set out the formal analysis and framework suggested by economic theory, we now investigate its usefulness in the analysis of fertility patterns. It suggests that a rise in income would increase both the quality and quantity of children desired; the increase in quality being large and the increase in quantity small. The difficulties in separating expenditures on children from general family expenditures notwithstanding, it is evident that wealthier families and countries spend much more per child than do poorer families and countries. The implication with respect to quantity is not so readily confirmed by the raw data. Indeed,

---

[13] For evidence supporting the statements in this paragraph see the definitive work by N. A. Himes, *Medical History of Contraception*, The Williams and Wilkins Company, Baltimore, 1936.

[14] A consumer maximizes a utility function $U = u(x_1, \ldots x_n)$ (neglecting quality considerations) subject to the constraints $\sum_{i=1}^{n} p_i x_i \equiv Y$, and $x_1 \geq$ or $\leq c$, where p_i is the price of the ith commodity, Y is money income, and x_1 refers to children. If the second constraint were effective, x_1 would equal c. Then the consumer would maximize $U = U(c, x_2, \ldots x_n)$ subject only to $\sum_{i=2}^{n} p_i x_i \equiv Y' \equiv Y - p_1 c$, and this gives the usual marginal conditions for $x_2, \ldots, x_n$.

most data tend to show a negative relationship between income and fertility. This is true of the Census data for 1910, 1940, and 1950, where income is represented by father's occupation, mother's education, or monthly rental; the data from the Indianapolis survey, the data for nineteenth century Providence families, and several other studies as well.[15] It is tempting to conclude from this evidence either that tastes vary systematically with income, perhaps being related to relative income, or that the number of children is an inferior good. Ultimately, systematic variations in tastes may have to be recognized; but for the present it seems possible to explain the available data within the framework outlined in section I, without assuming that the number of children is an inferior good. First, it is well to point out that not all the raw evidence is one way. In some studies, the curve relating fertility and income flattens out and even rises at the higher income classes, while in other studies the curve is positive throughout.[16] Second, tastes are not the only variable that may have varied systematically with income, for there is a good deal of general evidence that contraceptive knowledge has been positively related to income. Himes, in his history of contraception, indicates that the upper classes acquired this knowledge relatively early.[17] If such knowledge spread gradually from the upper classes to the rest of society, fertility differentials between classes should have first increased and then narrowed. This was clearly the pattern in England and was probably the pattern in the United States.[18]

Such evidence does little more than suggest that differential knowledge of contraceptive techniques might explain the negative relationship between fertility and income. Fortunately, the Indianapolis survey makes it possible, at least for 1941, to assess its quantitative importance. Table 1 presents some data from this study. In column (1) the native-white Protestant couples in the sample are classified by the husband's income, and column (2) gives the number of children born per 100 couples in each income class. The lowest income class was most fertile (2.3 children per couple) and a relatively high class least fertile (1.5

[15] U.S. Bureau of the Census, Census of Population, 1940; *Differential Fertility 1910 and 1940*, Government Printing Office, Washington, 1945; U.S. Bureau of the Census, Census of Population, 1950; *Fertility*, Government Printing Office, Washington, 1955; *Social and Psychological Factors Affecting Fertility*, by P. K. Whelpton and C. V. Kiser, eds., Milbank Memorial Fund, 1951; A. J. Jaffe, "Differential Fertility in the White Population in Early America," *Journal of Heredity*, August, 1940, pp. 407–411.

[16] K. A. Edin and E. P. Hutchinson, *Studies of Differential Fertility*, London, 1935; W. H. Banks, "Differential Fertility in Madison County, New York, 1865," *Milbank Memorial Fund Quarterly*, Vol. 33, April, 1955, pp. 161–186.

[17] Himes, *op. cit.*

[18] See the papers by C. V. Kiser and G. Z. Johnson in this volume.

children per couple), but the highest class averaged slightly more children than the next highest. This relationship between economic level and fertility was about the same as that shown by the 1940 Census.[19] Sterility did not vary systematically with income, so column (3), which is restricted to relatively fecund families, differs only slightly from column (2).

TABLE 1

Children Ever Born per 100 Couples in Indianapolis Classified by
Husband's Income and Planning Status
(native-white Protestants)

Income (1)	All Couples (2)	Relatively Fecund (3)	Number and Spacing Planners (4)	All Planners (5)	Desires of Relatively Fecund (6)
$3,000+	159	180	149	175	171
2,000–2,999	149	176	182	161	170
1,600–1,999	163	194	91	126	153
1,200–1,599	189	229	97	144	175
1,200 and less	227	266	68	146	193

Source: *Social and Psychological Factors Affecting Fertility*, P. K. Whelpton and C. V. Kiser, eds., N.Y., Milbank Memorial Fund, 1951, Vol. 2, part 9. Columns (2) and (3) from Table 4; columns (4) and (5) computed from Figure 8; column (6) computed from Figures 8 and 21.

It is well known that rich families use contraception earlier and more frequently than poor families. It has been difficult to determine whether poor families are ignorant of contraceptive methods or whether they desire more children than richer ones. The Indianapolis survey tried to separate ignorance from tastes by classifying couples not only by use of contraception but also by control over births. Column (4) gives the average number of children for "number and spacing planning" couples, including only couples who had planned all their children. A positive pattern now emerges, with the richest families averaging more than twice as many children as the poorest families. The income elasticity is about +0.42. Column (5) presents data for "number planned" couples, including all couples that planned their last child. These data also show a positive pattern, with an elasticity of +0.09, lower than that for number and spacing planners.

Fecund couples having excess children were asked questions about the number of such children. Column (6) uses this information and that in column (5) to relate income to the number of children desired by all

[19] Whelpton and Kiser, eds., *op. cit.*, Vol. 2, p. 364.

fecund couples. The elasticity is negative, being about -0.07.[20] After an intensive study, however, Potter found evidence that the number of desired children was overestimated; his own estimates of desired fertility show a positive relationship with income.[21] Thus evidence from the Indianapolis survey indicates that differential knowledge of contraception does convert a positive relation between income and *desired* fertility into a negative relation between income and *actual* fertility.[22]

Several other surveys provide information on desired fertility. For example, in 1954 a group at Michigan asked Detroit area families; "In your opinion what would be the ideal number of children for a young couple to have, if their standard of living is about like yours?" There was a distinct positive relationship between the ideal number of children and income of the family head.[23]

If knowledge of contraceptive techniques did not vary with income, the relation between actual fertility and income would equal that between desired fertility and income. Contraceptive knowledge is said to be diffused among all income classes in Stockholm, and the fertility of Stockholm families from 1917–1930 was positively related to income.[24] Contraceptive knowledge was said to be very primitive in *all* income

---

[20] These elasticities are estimates of the slope of the regression of the logarithm of fertility on the logarithm of income. The mean of the open end income class is assumed to be $4,000, and the mean of the other classes is assumed to be at their mid-points.

[21] R. G. Potter, *The Influence of Primary Groups on Fertility*, unpublished Ph.D. dissertation, Department of Social Relations, Harvard University, 1955, Appendix A, pp. 277–304.

[22] This conclusion must be qualified to allow for the possibility that tastes and costs also varied with income. Since all couples lived in the same city the cost of children was presumably the same. Age, religion, color, and nativity were held constant in an attempt to limit the systematic variation in tastes. Education did vary with income, but for number and spacing planners it was possible to separate the effect of income from the effect of education. The simple correlation coefficient between fertility and income is $+0.24$ and between fertility and education $+0.17$, with both significant at the 1 per cent level. The partial correlation coefficient between fertility and income, holding education constant is $+0.23$, about the same as the simple coefficient, and is also significant at the 1 per cent level. The partial correlation between fertility and education is only $+0.04$, not significant even at the 10 per cent level. (For these correlations see Whelpton and Kiser, eds., *op. cit.*, Vol. 3.) Holding education constant has little effect on the relationship between income and fertility.

[23] See R. Freedman, D. Goldberg, and H. Sharp, " 'Ideals' about Family Size in the Detroit Metropolitan Area, 1954," *Milbank Memorial Fund Quarterly*, Vol. 33, April, 1955, pp. 187–197. An earlier survey asked about the ideal family size for the average American couple, and found a negative relationship between ideal size and income of the head. But ideal size should be related to the income *assumed* by a respondent, rather than to his own income; and there is no way to do this. R. G. Potter has criticized both surveys because of their tendency to show larger ideal than realized families. See his "A Critique of the Glass-Grebenik Model for Indirectly Estimating Desired Family Size," *Population Studies*, March, 1956, pp. 251–270. It is not possible to determine whether this bias is systematically related to income.

[24] See Edin and Hutchinson, *op. cit.*

classes of prewar China, and a positive relation between fertility and income also seemed to prevail there.[25] Graduates in the same college class are probably relatively homogeneous in contraceptive knowledge and values as well as in formal education. I have the impression that income and fertility of these graduates tend to be positively related, but I have been able to examine only one sample. Some graduates from Harvard and Yale were classified by occupation and "degree of success." Within each occupation, the more successful graduates usually had more children.[26]

Information has been obtained on the family income, education, earners, and dependent children of a sample of the subscribers to Consumers Union.[27] This sample is particularly valuable for our purposes since it primarily consists of families with a keen interest in rational, informed consumption. If my analysis is at all relevant, fertility and income should be more positively related in this group than in the U.S. population as a whole. Table 2 presents the average number of dependent

TABLE 2

Average Number of Dependent Children for Single Earner Families with Head Age 35–44 in a Sample of Subscribers to Consumers Union, April, 1958

| | Average Number of Dependent Children by Education Class of Head | | | |
Income Class	High School Graduate or Less	Some College	Graduate of Four Year College	Graduate Degree
Less than $3,000	2.43	1.61	2.50	2.17
$ 3,000–3,999	2.15	2.47	2.18	2.23
4,000–4,999	2.70	2.40	2.04	2.18
5,000–7,499	2.68	2.73	2.88	2.67
7,500–9,999	2.80	2.94	3.00	3.03
10,000–14,999	2.89	3.03	3.12	3.23
15,000–24,999	2.85	3.04	3.04	3.31
25,000 and over	3.12	3.23	3.28	3.60

Source: Unpublished data from consumer purchases study by Thomas Juster at National Bureau of Economic Research.

[25] See H. D. Lamson, "Differential Reproductivity in China," *The Quarterly Review of Biology*, Vol. 10, no. 3, September, 1933, pp. 308–321. Abstinence, which is equally available to lower and upper classes, is the major form of birth control when contraceptive knowledge is limited.

[26] See E. Huntington and L. F. Whitney, *The Builders of America*, New York, Morrow, 1927, ch. xv. Although they did not clearly define "success," it appears that income was a major factor in ranking persons within an occupation and a less important factor in ranking occupations.

[27] This is part of a study by Thomas Juster on buying plans, and I am indebted to him for making the data available to me.

children for single earner families with the head aged 35–44, each family classified by its income and by the education of the head. There is a substantial positive relationship between income and children within each educational class; education *per se* has relatively little effect on the number of children. The income elasticity is about 0.09 and 0.14 for graduates of a four year college and of a graduate school respectively. These data, then, are very consistent with my analysis, and indicate that well-informed families do have more children when their income increases.

Contraceptive knowledge in the United States spread rapidly during the War, largely fostered by the military in its effort to limit venereal disease and illegitimacy. We would expect this to have reduced the relative fertility of low income classes, and Census Bureau studies in 1952 and 1957 confirm this expectation. Table 3 presents the data for urban and rural nonfarm families for 1952 and all families for 1957 with column (1) giving husband's income, column (2) the age-standardized number

TABLE 3

Fertility by Husband's Income

Husband's Income (1)	Children Under 5 per 100 Married Men 20–59 (age standardized) (2)	Children Born per 100 Wives 15–44 Years Old (age standardized) (3)	Children Born per 100 Wives over 45 (4)
Part I: In Urban and Rural Nonfarm Areas in the United States in 1952			
$7 000 +	53	189	194
6,000–6,999	52	188	210
5,000–5,999	50	188	210
4,000–4,999	52	177	217
3,000–3,999	52	184	240
2,000–2,999	51	189	256
1,000–1,999	40	181	279
1,000 and less	40	211	334
Part II: For the United States in 1957			
$7,000 +	—	216	213
5,000–6,999	—	220	230
4,000–4,999	—	221	240
3,000–3,999	—	236	279
2,000–2,999	—	247	304
1,000–1,999	—	289	341
1,000 and less	—	—	383

Source I. U.S. Bureau of the Census, *Current Population Reports*, Wash., Government Printing Office, 1953, no. 46, p. 20.

II. U.S. Bureau of the Census, *Current Population Reports*, Wash., Government Printing Office, 1958, no. 84, p. 12.

of children under 5 per 100 men aged 20 to 59, column (3) the age-standardized number of children ever born per 100 wives aged 15 to 44, and column (4) the number ever born per 100 wives aged 45 and older. Columns (2) and (3) deal primarily with childbearing since 1940 and show a much weaker negative relationship between fertility and income than does column (4), which deals primarily with childbearing before 1940.

The relationship between fertility and income can be investigated not only with cross-sectional income differences but also with time series differences. Cyclical fluctuations in income have regularly occurred in Western nations, and, if our analysis is correct, a change in income would induce a change in fertility in the same direction. For our purpose cyclical fluctuations in fertility can be measured by the cyclical fluctuations in births (although see p. 227). Some earlier studies presented evidence that births do conform positively to the business cycle, even when adjusted for fluctuations in the marriage rate.[28]

I have related some annual figures since 1920 on first and higher order birth rates—brought forward one year—to the National Bureau annual business cycle dates. Column (3) of Table 4 gives the percentage change per year in first and higher order birth rates from the beginning of one phase to the beginning of the next phase. The strong secular decline in births before World War II makes most of these entries negative before that time and hence obscures the effect of cyclical fluctuations in economic conditions. If economic conditions affected births they should have declined more rapidly (or risen less rapidly) during a downswing than during an upswing. This can be detected from the first differences of the entries in column (3), which are shown in column (4). Aside from the wartime period, 1938–1948, second and higher order births conform perfectly in direction to the reference dates and first births conform almost as well. So reference cycle analysis strongly indicates that business conditions affect birth rates. This effect is not entirely dependent on cyclical fluctuations in the marriage rate since second and higher order births conform exceedingly well.

The next step is to relate the magnitude of the movement in births to that in general business, and to compare this with corresponding figures for other consumer durables. Time series giving net national product and purchases of consumer durables were analyzed in the same way as birth

[28] V. L. Galbraith and D. S. Thomas, "Birth Rates and the Interwar Business Cycles," and D. Kirk, "The Relation of Employment Levels to Births in Germany," both in *Demographic Analysis*, J. J. Spengler and O. D. Duncan, eds., Free Press, Glencoe, 1956.

TABLE 4

Reference Cycle Pattern of Birth Rates for U.S. Since 1920

		Birth Rates per 1,000 Women 15–44 Years of Age, Brought Forward One Year at Reference Cycle Dates[2]		Annual Percentage Change During a Business		Excess of Annual Percentage Change During Business Expansion Over	
REFERENCE CYCLE DATES[1]							
Peak	Trough	At Peak	At Trough	Expansion	Contraction	Preceding Contraction	Succeeding Contraction
(1)		(2)		(3)		(4)	

FIRST BIRTHS

Peak	Trough	At Peak	At Trough	Expansion	Contraction	Preceding Contraction	Succeeding Contraction
1920		39					
	1921		34		−12.82		
1923		34		0.00		+12.82	
	1924		34		0.00		0.00
1926		32		−2.94		−2.94	
	1927		30		−6.25		−3.31
1929		30		0.00		+6.25	
	1932		25		−5.57		−5.57
1937		31		4.80		+10.37	
	1938		31		0.00		−4.80
1944		29		−1.06		−1.06	
	1946		46		28.33		+29.39
1948		36		−10.87		−39.20	
	1949		33		−8.33		+2.54
1953		34		0.76		+9.09	
	1954		33		−2.94		−3.70
1957		33*		0.00		+2.94	

HIGHER ORDER BIRTHS

Peak	Trough	At Peak	At Trough	Expansion	Contraction	Preceding Contraction	Succeeding Contraction
1920		82					
	1921		78		−4.88		
1923		78		0.00		+4.88	
	1924		74		−5.13		−5.13
1926		68		−4.05		+1.08	
	1927		64		−5.88		−1.83
1929		60		−3.12		+2.76	
	1932		52		−4.45		−1.33
1937		48		−1.53		+2.92	
	1938		47		−2.08		−0.55
1944		57		3.46		+5.54	
	1946		67		8.47		+5.01
1948		71		2.98		−5.49	
	1949		73		2.81		−0.17
1953		84		3.77		+0.96	
	1954		85		1.19		−2.58
1957		88*		3.53		+2.34	

* Last figure is for 1956.

Source: [1] See National Bureau of Economic Research Standard Reference Dates for Business Cycles.

[2] See Dudley Kirk, Appendix to "The Influence of Business Cycles on Marriage and Birth Rates," this volume.

rates were. The figures for birth rates in column (4) of Table 4 and corresponding figures for purchases of consumer durables were divided by corresponding figures for national product to obtain cyclical income elasticities for births and consumer durables. These figures, shown in Table 5, are positive for almost all phases, and this indicates that cyclical

TABLE 5

Cyclical Income Elasticities for Births and Consumer Durable
Purchases During Reference Cycle Phases

Reference Cycle Phases (1)		First Births (2)	Higher Order Births (3)	Purchases of Consumer Durables (4)
1920–1921	Down	0.81	0.31	2.48
1921–1923	Up	0.00	.58	2.96
1923–1924	Down	−1.55	.57	6.63
1924–1926	Up	.87	.48	5.26
1926–1927	Down	2.05	.90	4.05
1927–1929	Up	.37	.09	1.40
1929–1932	Down	.47	.13	1.51
1932–1937	Up	.26	.03	1.96
1937–1938	Down	− .09	.46	1.38
1938–1944	Up	4.26	.73	9.20
1944–1946	Down	3.89	.54	5.33
1946–1948	Up	− .44	.03	0.11
1948–1949	Down	.88	.09	0.01
1949–1953	Up	.78	.54	1.78
1953–1954	Down	1.19	.95	3.23
1954–1957	Up			
Simple Average excluding				
1938–1948		.56	.42	2.84
and negative figures		.77	.42	2.84

Source: Birth rates from column (4) of Table 4; similar figures were computed for consumer durable purchases and net national product. The durable figures were from Raymond W. Goldsmith, *A Study of Savings in the United States*, Vol. 1, Tables Q-6 and A-25 for 1920–1949 and from U.S. Dept. of Commerce, *Survey of Current Business*, July, 1958, Table 2, for 1949–1957. Net National Product figures were from Simon Kuznets, Technical Tables (mimeo), T-5, underlying series in *Supplement to Summary Volume on Capital Formation and Financing* for 1920–1955 and from U.S. Dept. of Commerce, *Survey of Current Business*, July, 1958, Table 4, for 1955–1957.

changes in births and purchases of consumer durables have been in the same direction as those in national output. The cyclical change in first births was usually greater than that in higher order births, and both were usually less than the change in output. Changes in first and higher order births were, however, far from insignificant, averaging 74 and 42 per cent of the corresponding change in output.

Cyclical changes in births are small compared to those in consumer durables. The latter averaged about 2.84 times the change in output, or about 4 and 7 times the change in first and higher order births respectively. This is consistent with our emphasis on inadequate knowledge of birth control; inadequate knowledge seems to explain much but not all of the difference between the average cyclical change in higher order births and in purchases of durables.[29] Some would be explained by the fact that the data for children include only fluctuations in numbers, while those for durables include both fluctuations in numbers and in quality. The rest may be explained by other differences between children and consumer durables.

For example, to purchase a consumer durable it is necessary to make a down payment with one's own resources and to finance the remainder either with one's own or with borrowed resources. The economic uncertainty generated by a depression increases the reluctance to use own or borrowed resources and induces creditors to raise standards and screen applicants more carefully.[30] Therefore some purchases of durables would be postponed until economic conditions improved. The "purchase" of children, however, is less apt to be postponed than the purchase of other durables. The initial cost of children (physician and delivery charges, nursery furniture, expenses, and so on) is a smaller fraction of its total cost than is the initial cost of most other durables because expenditures on children are more naturally spread over time. Hence children can be "purchased" with a smaller down payment and with less use of borrowed funds than can most other durables.

There is still another reason why the "purchase" of children is less apt to be postponed. *Ceteris paribus*, the demand for a good with a lengthy construction period is less sensitive to a temporary economic movement than the demand for more readily constructed goods, since delivery is likely to occur when this movement has passed. The construction and delivery period is very short for durables like cars and quite long for

[29] An estimate of the desired change in births of planned families can be readily obtained if we assume that the distribution of contraceptive knowledge among U.S. whites is the same as among families in the Indianapolis study, that for planned families the actual change in births equals the desired change, and that for other families the actual change is nil. Then the desired change equals the actual change (averaging 42 per cent of the change in output) divided by the fraction of all births in planned families (31 per cent), or about 136 per cent of output. This is about half of the change for consumer durables.

[30] For evidence relating credit conditions to cyclical fluctuations in the demand for housing, see J. Guttentag, *Some Studies of the Post-World War II Residential Construction and Mortgage Markets*, unpublished Ph.D. dissertation, Department of Economics, Columbia University, 1958.

children. It takes about 10 months on the average to produce a pregnancy and this period combined with a nine-month pregnancy period gives a total average construction period of nineteen months. This period is sufficiently long to reduce the impact on the demand for children of temporary movements in income.

There are also some reasons why the "purchase" of children is more apt to be postponed. For example, since children cannot be bought and sold they are a less "liquid" asset than ordinary durables, and the economic uncertainty accompanying a depression would increase the community's preference for liquid assets. A more complete analysis would also have to take account of other factors, such as the accelerator and the permanent income concept, which may have produced different cyclical responses in fertility and consumer durables. Our aim here, therefore, is not to present a definitive explanation of the relative cyclical movement in fertility but only to suggest that economic analysis can be useful in arriving at such an explanation.

Although the data on cyclical movements in fertility appears consistent with our analysis, another piece of time series data is in apparent conflict with it. Over time per capita incomes in the United States have risen while fertility has declined, suggesting a negative relationship between income and fertility. Of course, many other variables have changed drastically over time and this apparent conflict in the secular movements of fertility and income should not be taken too seriously until it can be demonstrated that these other changes were not responsible for the decline in fertility. Three changes seem especially important: a decline in child mortality; an increase in contraceptive knowledge; and a rise in the cost of children.

The number of children in the average completed urban white family declined by about 56 per cent from 1870 to 1940. The decline in child mortality explains about 14 percentage points or 25 per cent of this decline.[31] Some evidence already presented indicates that a large secular increase in contraceptive knowledge occurred in the United States. It is not possible, however, to estimate its magnitude precisely enough to compare it to the decline in fertility.

I have emphasized that the increase over time in expenditures on children is not evidence that the cost of children has increased since the quality of children has also increased. Changes in the relative cost of children have to be assessed from indexes of the relative cost of given

[31] Taken from my unpublished paper "Child Mortality, Fertility, and Population Growth."

quality children. There are several reasons why the relative cost of a given quality child may have changed over time. The decline in child mortality decreased the cost of a given quality child, although it may have only a small effect. The growth of legislation prohibiting child labor and requiring education may have raised the cost of children, but largely made compulsory only what was being done voluntarily by most parents.[32] This is another aspect of the increase in quality of children and does not imply any increase in their cost. If such legislation raised costs at all, it did so primarily for the poorest families since they would be less apt to give their children much education. Therefore, legislation may have been partly responsible for the narrowing of fertility differentials by income class in the last fifty years.[33] The movement from farm to urban communities raised the average cost of children to the population as a whole since it is cheaper to raise children on a farm, but did not appreciably affect the cost within urban communities. Because technological advance has probably been more rapid in the market place than in the home, the imputed cost of time and effort spent on children probably rose, perhaps by a substantial amount. This discussion suggests that there was a secular rise in the cost of children which also contributed to the secular decline in fertility.

Secular changes in educational attainment, religious attachment, discrimination against women, and so on, may also have decreased fertility, and presumably there were changes other than the growth of income which increased fertility. It would take a major study—and even that might be inconclusive—to determine whether the factors decreasing fertility were sufficiently strong to produce a secular decline in fertility in spite of the secular rise in income. At present, it seems that the negative correlation between the secular changes in fertility and income is not strong evidence against the hypothesis that an increase in income would cause an increase in fertility—tastes, costs, and knowledge remaining constant.

III. Some Further Implications

Section II tries to show that the economic analysis of section I is very useful in understanding the effect of income on fertility. This section sketches some additional implications. Our understanding of temporal

---

[32] See G. J. Stigler, *Employment and Compensation in Education*, National Bureau of Economic Research, Occasional Paper 33, 1950, Appendix B.

[33] This analysis casts doubt on the view that the sharp decline in British fertility during the 1870's and 1880's resulted from the introduction of compulsory education. The decline was greatest in the upper classes which were least affected by this legislation.

fluctuations in births would be deepened if it were more widely recognized that births are "flows" to the "stock" of children, just as new car purchases are flows to the stock of cars. Flows are determined not only by variables determining stocks, but also by depreciation rates, acceleration, savings, and, as shown in our discussion of cyclical movements in births, by considerations of timing. The recent work relating births to parity shows that demographers as well as economists are beginning to stress the interaction between stocks and flows.[34] This work needs to be extended in a systematic fashion.

The discussion in section I made it clear that the quantity and quality of children are intimately related. An increase in income or a decline in the cost of children would affect both the quantity and quality of children, usually increasing both. An increase in contraceptive knowledge would also affect both, but would increase quality while decreasing quantity. The quality of children is very important in its own right, for it determines the education, health, and motivation of the future labor force. It is a major contribution of an economic framework to bring out the mutual interaction of quantity and quality—an interaction that has been neglected all too often in writings both on population and on the quality of the labor force.

It is often said that farm families are larger than urban families because of a difference in tastes. Since farmers have a comparative cost advantage in raising children as well as in raising foodstuffs, they would tend to be more fertile even without any difference in tastes. The rural advantage may not be the same at all qualities and, indeed, presumably is less at higher qualities where child labor and food are less important. Over time, rural as well as urban families have moved to higher quality children, and this may have contributed to the narrowing of urban-rural fertility differentials in recent decades. The influence of differences in the cost of children deserves much more systematic study, for it may partly explain not only these urban-rural fertility differences but also the secular decline in fertility up to World War II and the apparent secular narrowing of fertility differentials among urban economic classes.

In the Western World, birth rates in the early postwar period were well above rates of the thirties. In some countries, including the United States and Canada, they have remained at about the early postwar level; in others, including Great Britain and Sweden, they have drifted down to about their 1940 level; in still others, including France, they have

[34] Both economists and demographers found that wartime effects on stocks had important consequences for postwar flows.

drifted down to a position intermediate between their immediate pre- and postwar levels. The analysis in this paper does not readily explain these differences, but it does explain why birth rates in all these countries are well above levels predicted from their secular trends. The secular decline in child mortality and the secular increase in contraceptive knowledge were important causes of the secular decline in births. By 1945 the level of child mortality was so low that little room remained for a further improvement. Although contraceptive knowledge was not well spread throughout every layer of society, the room for its further improvement was also more limited than it had been. With the weakening of these forces, much of the steam behind the secular decline in birth rates has been removed. Positive forces like the growth in income are now opposed by weaker negative forces, and it is not too surprising that fertility has ceased to decline and even has risen in some countries.

Several recent studies of consumption have used a measure of family size as an independent variable along with measures of income and price.[35] This procedure is justifiable if family size were a random variable or completely determined by "non-economic" factors.[36] If, on the other hand, family size were partly determined by economic factors, this procedure would result in misleading estimates of the regression coefficients for the other independent variables. Thus, suppose family size were positively related to income, and food consumption varied with income only because family size did. The regression coefficient between food consumption and income, holding family size constant, would be zero, an incorrect estimate of the long-run effect of an increase in income on food consumption. One would not estimate the effect of income on gasoline consumption by finding the regression coefficient between gasoline consumption and income, holding the number of cars constant. For gasoline consumption might increase with income largely because

[35] See, for example, Theil, *op. cit.*, S. J. Prais and H. S. Houthhakker, *The Analysis of Family Budgets*, Cambridge, Cambridge University Press, 1955. Measures of family size often include not only the inner core of parents and their children but also other relatives living in the same household. My discussion refers only to the inner core; a somewhat different discussion is required for "other relatives."

[36] Prais and Houthhakker appear to believe that family size is determined by non-economic factors when they say "It might be thought that since household size is, in a sense, a noneconomic factor. . . ." *ibid.*, p. 88.

the number of cars does, just as food consumption might increase because family size does. This discussion, brief as it is, should be sufficient to demonstrate that students of consumption economics need to pay more attention to the determinants of family size than they have in the past.

IV. Summary

This paper employs an economic framework to analyze the factors determining fertility. Children are viewed as a durable good, primarily a consumer's durable, which yields income, primarily psychic income, to parents. Fertility is determined by income, child costs, knowledge, uncertainty, and tastes. An increase in income and a decline in price would increase the demand for children, although it is necessary to distinguish between the quantity and quality of children demanded. The quality of children is directly related to the amount spent on them.

Each family must produce its own children since children cannot be bought or sold in the market place. This is why every uncertainty in the production of children (such as their sex) creates a corresponding uncertainty in consumption. It is also why the number of children in a family depends not only on its demand but also on its ability to produce or supply them. Some families are unable to produce as many children as they desire and some have to produce more than they desire. Therefore, actual fertility may diverge considerably from desired fertility.

I briefly explored some implications of this theory. For example, it may largely explain the postwar rise in fertility in Western nations, the relatively small cyclical fluctuation in fertility compared to that in other durables, some observed relations between the quantity and quality of children, and why rural women are more fertile than urban women.

I tested in more detail one important implication, namely that the number of children desired is directly related to income. Crude cross-sectional data show a negative relationship with income, but the crude data do not hold contraceptive knowledge constant. When it is held constant, a positive relationship appears. This view is supported by the positive correspondence between cyclical movements in income and fertility. The secular decline in fertility may also be consistent with a positive relationship since the secular decline in child mortality and the secular rise in both contraceptive knowledge and child costs could easily have offset the secular rise in income.

10 On the Interaction between the Quantity and Quality of Children

Students of human fertility have been aware for a long time that there may be some special relation between the number (quantity) of children ever born to a family and the "quality" of their children as perceived by others if not by the parents. One need only cite the negative correlation between quantity and quality of children per family so often observed in both cross-section and time-series data. One of us (Becker 1960) more than a decade ago stressed the importance for understanding fertility (quantity) of the interaction between quantity and quality, and we are pleased to note that this interaction is emphasized in most of the papers in this Supplement, especially those by De Tray and Willis.

Some economists have argued that the negative relation between quantity and quality often observed is a consequence of a low substitution elasticity in a family's utility function between parents' consumption or level of living and that of their children (see, e.g., Duesenberry 1960; Willis 1969). The approach followed by De Tray in this volume is different, but it makes equally special assumptions about the substitution between quantity and quality in the utility function and in household production.

We want to argue here that one can go a long way toward understanding data on the interaction between quantity and quality as well as on quantity or quality alone without assuming that, either in the utility function or in household production, quantity and quality are more closely related than any two commodities chosen at random. The analysis that follows is sketchy and incomplete, mainly because we have only recently developed this line of argument.

The key feature in our analysis is that the shadow price of children with respect to their number (i.e., the cost of an additional child, holding their quality constant) is greater the higher their quality is. Similarly, the shadow price of children with respect to their quality (i.e., the cost

Reprinted from the *Journal of Political Economy* 81, no. 2, part 2 (March/April 1973); S279–S288. © 1973 by The University of Chicago. Written with the collaboration of H. Gregg Lewis.

of a unit increase in quality, holding number constant) is greater, the greater the number of children. Furthermore, with appropriate change of language, the same may be said of the other commodities consumed by the family. However, to simplify the analysis in this paper, we make the quantity-quality distinction only for children. Thus, to illustrate our reasoning, we specify the following simple utility function:

$$U = U(n, q, y), \tag{1}$$

where n is the number of children, q their quality (assumed to be the same for all of the children), and y the rate of consumption of all other commodities. We start out with a simple budget restraint:

$$I = nq\pi + y\pi_y, \tag{2}$$

where I is full income, π is the price of nq, and π_y is the price of y. We make no special assumptions about the elasticities of substitution among n, q, and y, either in the utility function or in the household production functions that underlie the π's.

The first-order conditions for maximizing the utility function subject to the budget restraint are:

$$MU_n = \lambda q\pi = \lambda p_n; \; MU_q = \lambda n\pi = \lambda p_q; \; MU_y = \lambda \pi_y = \lambda p_y, \tag{3}$$

where the MU's are the marginal utilities, the p's are marginal costs or shadow prices, and λ is the marginal utility of money income. The important point is that the shadow price of children with respect to number (p_n) is positively related to q, the level of quality, and the shadow price with respect to quality (p_q) is positively related to n, the number of children. The economic interpretation is that an increase in quality is more expensive if there are more children because the increase has to apply to more units; similarly, an increase in quantity is more expensive if the children are of higher quality, because higher-quality children cost more.

These equilibrium conditions (3) together with the second-order conditions can be found in several places in the literature on quantity and quality (see, e.g., Houthakker 1952; Theil 1952; Becker 1960; and Willis's paper in this volume), but a number of their important implications for income and price effects apparently have not been explored.

1. Income Effects

Let the "true" income elasticities of demand for the number (n) and quality (q) of children and for all other commodities (y) be η_n, η_q, and η_y, respectively. These elasticities are derived in the usual way by changing "income" while holding constant the "prices" of n, q, and y. The appropriate prices for this purpose are the shadow prices (marginal costs)

p_n, p_q, and p_y, whose ratios in equilibrium (see eq. [3]) are equal to the marginal rates of substitution in the utility function. The appropriate income concept is the total "expenditure" on n, q, and y calculated at these shadow prices; that is, the correct measure of income for this purpose is

$$R = np_n + qp_q + yp_y = I + nq\pi. \qquad (4)$$

It is well known that the mean value of the true income elasticities is unity; that is:

$$1 = \frac{np_n}{R}\eta_n + \frac{qp_q}{R}\eta_q + \frac{yp_y}{R}\eta_y. \qquad (5)$$

Consider, however, the "observed" income elasticities, which we denote by $\bar{\eta}_n$, $\bar{\eta}_q$, and $\bar{\eta}_y$, derived by changing I while holding π and π_y constant. It follows directly from the budget restraint (2) and the definitions of the p's in (3) that the similarly weighted mean of the observed income elasticities is $I/R = I/(I + nq\pi)$, which is less than unity; that is:

$$1 > \frac{I}{R} = \frac{I}{I + nq\pi} = \frac{np_n}{R}\bar{\eta}_n + \frac{qp_q}{R}\bar{\eta}_q + \frac{yp_y}{R}\bar{\eta}_y. \qquad (6)$$

That is, on the average, the observed elasticities are smaller than the true elasticities in the ratio I/R. The economic explanation for this downward bias is simple. The direct effect of the increase in I, holding the π's but not the p's constant, in general is to increase n, q, and y. However, increases in n and q cause the shadow prices p_n and p_q to rise. Thus, the percentage increase in real income in the sense of R deflated by an index of the p's is less than the percentage increase in money income I.

This price effect of an increase in money income resembles somewhat the price effect resulting from a rise in money income caused by a rise in wage rates. The increase, in ratio terms, is less in real income than in money income, because the costs of producing commodities in the household are increased by the rise in the price of time (see Becker 1965).[1]

We think that it is plausible to assume that the true income elasticity with respect to quality (η_q) is substantially larger than that with respect to quantity (η_n). Because of the downward bias in the observed elasticities and the effect on prices, the observed elasticity for quantity ($\bar{\eta}_n$) may be negative even though the true elasticity (η_n) is not. Assume for simplicity

---

[1] This price effect, however, does offer a correction to the argument advanced by Becker (1960), and followed by many others, that the price of children is the same for the rich as for the poor (aside from the cost-of-time argument), even though the rich choose more expensive children. The relevant price of children with respect to their number *is* higher for the rich precisely because they choose more expensive children. Similarly, the relevant price of cars, houses, or other goods is higher for the rich because they choose more expensive varieties.

that $\eta_n = 0$. Let income I increase while holding π and π_y constant. The direct effect of the increase in I is to increase q (and y) while leaving n unchanged. But then the shadow price with respect to quantity ($p_n = q\pi$) will rise while the shadow price of quality ($p_q = n\pi$) and that of y ($p_y = \pi_y$) are unchanged, causing q and y to be substituted for n, and therefore n will decline.

More generally, when the utility function and budget restraints are those given above in equations (1) and (2), the observed income elasticities for quantity and quality are related to the corresponding true elasticities as follows:[2]

$$\frac{D\bar{\eta}_n}{1-k} = (1 - k\sigma_{nq})\eta_n - (1-k)\bar{\sigma}_n\eta_q;$$

$$\frac{D\bar{\eta}_q}{1-k} = (1 - k\sigma_{nq})\eta_q - (1-k)\bar{\sigma}_q\eta_n,$$

$$(7)$$

where

$$\left\{ \begin{aligned} & k \equiv \frac{nq\pi}{R} \; ; \; (1-k)\bar{\sigma}_n = k\sigma_{nq} + (1-2k)\sigma_{ny}; \; (1-k)\bar{\sigma}_q \\ & \quad = k\sigma_{nq} + (1-2k)\sigma_{qy}; \\ & D \equiv (1 - k\sigma_{nq})^2 - (1-k)^2\bar{\sigma}_n\bar{\sigma}_q. \end{aligned} \right. \quad (8)$$

The σ's are the familiar Allen partial elasticities of substitution in the utility function; the $\bar{\sigma}$'s are averages of the σ's, and they must be positive; D and $(1 - k\sigma_{nq})$ are positive by the second-order conditions. Equations (7) verify that the observed quantity elasticity ($\bar{\eta}_n$) may be negative even when the true quantity elasticity (η_n) is positive. Furthermore, if $\eta_q > \eta_n$, as we assume, $\bar{\eta}_q > \bar{\eta}_n$ unless q is a much better substitute than n for y, for it follows from (7) and (8) that

$$\frac{D}{1-k}(\bar{\eta}_q - \bar{\eta}_n) = \eta_q - \eta_n + (1-2k)(\sigma_{ny}\eta_q - \sigma_{qy}\eta_n). \quad (9)$$

Moreover, $\bar{\eta}_q$ may exceed $\bar{\eta}_n$ by more than η_q exceeds η_n; that is, the downward bias in $\bar{\eta}_q$ may be less than that in $\bar{\eta}_n$. This is easily seen for the case in which $\sigma_{nq} = \sigma_{ny} = \sigma_{qy} = \sigma$. Then D, which is positive, is equal to $(1-\sigma)[1 + \sigma(1-2k)]$ and $\bar{\eta}_q - \bar{\eta}_n = (1-k)(\eta_q - \eta_n)/(1-\sigma)$, so that $\bar{\eta}_q - \bar{\eta}_n > \eta_q - \eta_n$ if $\sigma > k$. Indeed, $\bar{\eta}_q$ may even exceed η_q, as may be seen from (7) and (8) by assuming $\eta_n = 0$ and $\sigma_{nq} = \sigma_{ny} = \sigma_{qy} = \sigma$. Then $\bar{\eta}_q = (1-k)(1-k\sigma)\eta_q/(1-\sigma)[1 + \sigma(1-2k)]$, which will exceed η_q if, for example, $k = \frac{1}{3}$ and $\sigma = \frac{3}{4}$.

[2] See the Mathematical Appendix to this paper.

Even if η_n were constant, $\bar{\eta}_n$ need not be, since the latter depends not only on η_n but also on the substitution elasticities and the share of $nq\pi$ in money income I $(nq\pi/I = k/(1 - k))$. For example, if η_q declines as income I rises—a plausible assumption, we think—$\bar{\eta}_n$ would tend to rise with income, even with constant η_n, and, of course, η_n may rise with income, contributing to the increase in $\bar{\eta}_n$. Indeed, $\bar{\eta}_n$ could be negative at lower levels of income and positive at higher levels, the pattern observed in some fertility data.[3]

2. Price Effects

Before discussing price effects, we generalize the budget constraint (2) slightly as follows:

$$I = n\pi_n + nq\pi + q\pi_q + yp_y \qquad (10)$$

so that the shadow prices or marginal costs are now

$$p_n = \pi_n + q\pi; \; p_q = \pi_q + n\pi; \; p_y = \pi_y. \qquad (11)$$

These shadow prices for n and q each contain a "fixed" component: π_n in p_n and π_q in p_q. The component $n\pi_n$ in child costs consists of costs that depend on quantity but not on quality. Contraception costs and prenatal child costs (such as maternity care) are moderately good examples. Similarly, the component $q\pi_q$ depends on quality but not quantity, and thus has the attributes of a "public good," or a better expression is a "family good." Perhaps some aspects of training in the home and the "handing down" of some clothing are reasonable examples. We assume that the fixed component is more important for quantity than for quality, that is, $n\pi_n > q\pi_q$.

a) First consider the pure substitution effects of an increase in π_n induced, say, by an exogenous improvement in contraceptive technique. Since this increases the shadow price of quantity (p_n) relative to both the shadow price of quality (p_q) and the shadow price of $y(p_y)$, n would fall. But the fall in numbers reduces the shadow price of quality $(p_q = \pi_q + n\pi)$, which induces substitution in favor of quality. The outcome would be not only a fall in quantity but also a relatively large rise in quality— relative, that is, to other commodities—without assuming that quantity and quality are better substitutes than any two commodities chosen at random. Exactly the same result holds if π_q falls, say, because of an increase in the education of parents. The fall in p_q induces an increase in quality, which in turn induces an increase in the shadow price of quantity $(p_n = \pi_n + q\pi)$ and thus a relatively large decrease in quantity.

Consequently, both De Tray's finding (in this Supplement) that an

---

[3] See the discussion and alternative explanation of this finding in Willis (1973).

increase in the education of mothers has a strong positive effect on the quality and a strong negative effect on the number of their children, and the common belief that important advances in birth control knowledge not only significantly reduce the number of children but also significantly increase their quality, are consistent with the preceding analysis. Quantity and quality are closely related, because the shadow price of quality depends on quantity and the shadow price of quantity depends on quality. We repeat that no special assumptions about substitution in household production or consumption are required to derive a special relation between quantity and quality.

b) Now consider the pure substitution effects of equal percentage increases in π_n, π_q, and π due, say, to increases in wage rates. To put the argument in extreme form, assume $\pi_q = 0$ and $\pi_n > 0$. The equal increases in π_n, π_q, and π relative to $\pi_y = p_y$ can be treated simply as a relative fall in $\pi_y = p_y$. A fall in p_y initially would induce equal percentage declines in n and q if they were equally good substitutes for y. However, since the equal percentage declines in n and q would lower p_q more than p_n, n would fall relative to q. Thus, the income-compensated elasticity of quantity with respect to equal percentage changes in π_n, π_q and π tends to be greater numerically than the corresponding elasticity for quality. De Tray finds that an increase in women's wage rates reduces the number of children by a much bigger percentage than the quality of children.

This difference is, of course, accentuated if quantity is a better substitute than quality for other commodities, which we think is a plausible, though special, assumption. For then a fall in p_y directly induces a fall in n relative to q, which accentuates the decline in p_q relative to p_n.

We conclude, therefore, that the observed price elasticity of quantity exceeds that of quality, just the opposite of our conclusion for observed income elasticities.[4] This reversal of the quantity-quality ordering for price and income elasticities is not only a somewhat unexpected implication of the analysis, but also gives a consistent interpretation to the findings of De Tray and others.

Of course, most of our discussion applies not only to the interaction between the quantity and quality of children, but also to the quantity and quality of cars, houses, food, tea, education, publications, and large numbers of other goods. The observed price and income elasticities of quantity and quality will differ in predictable directions from the "true" elasticities. A systematic analysis and reconsideration of the interaction between quan-

---

[4] This conclusion about income elasticities, derived from the budget restraint (2), is modified somewhat when the budget restraint is of the more general form (10), since the shadow price of quality is less sensitive to any given percentage change in quality than the price of quality is to a change in quantity. Conceivably then, $\bar{\eta}_n$ could be greater than $\bar{\eta}_q$ at the same time that $\eta_n < \eta_q$, but we consider this unlikely, since η_q is probably much greater than η_n.

tity and quality of all goods from the viewpoint of this paper should be quite rewarding.

Mathematical Appendix

The budget restraints specified in equations (2) and (10) are not linear in n and q. It is precisely this nonlinearity, of course, that leads to the "interaction between quantity and quality" that we discuss in this paper.

The derivation of the elasticities of the demand functions for number of children (n) and child quality (q) can be carried in a direct fashion by differentiating the budget restraint and the first-order conditions. Because of the nonlinearity of the budget restraint, however, if this direct mode of derivation is followed, it is all too easy to lose sight of the underlying income and substitution elasticities in the utility function. Hence, we follow an indirect approach that makes use of quite familiar propositions in demand theory.

First, we replace the curvilinear budget surface given in equation (10) by a plane surface by adding $nq\pi$ to both sides:

$$I + nq\pi = n(\pi_n + q\pi) + q(\pi_q + n\pi) + y\pi_y \qquad (A1)$$

$$R = np_n + qp_q + yp_y. \qquad (A2)$$

where

$$R = I + nq\pi = I/(1 - k); \; k \equiv nq\pi/R. \qquad (A3)$$

The two income concepts I and R differ by the nonlinear term $nq\pi$ in the budget restraint.

Define

$$k_i \equiv \frac{ip_i}{R}, i = n, q, y; \; k_n + k_q + k_y = 1. \qquad (A4)$$

It is well known that the true income elasticities (η_n, η_q, and η_y) must satisfy the relation

$$1 = k_n\eta_n + k_q\eta_q + k_y\eta_y. \qquad (A5)$$

The observed income elasticities ($\bar\eta_n$, $\bar\eta_q$, $\bar\eta_y$) obtained by changing full income I while holding the π's constant, however, must satisfy

$$1 - k = -\frac{I}{R} = k_n\bar\eta_n + k_q\bar\eta_q + k_y\bar\eta_y. \qquad (A6)$$

Equation (A6) may be verified by differentiating the budget restraint (10) logarithmically with respect to I, holding the π's constant, and then using equations (A3) and (A4). Thus, the observed elasticities, on the average, are smaller than the true elasticities in the ratio $1 - k = I/R$.

We now define two household price indexes $\bar\pi$ and $\bar p$ in differential form as follows:

$$E\bar\pi \equiv \frac{y\pi_y}{I} E\pi_y + \frac{n\pi_n}{I} E\pi_n + \frac{q\pi_q}{I} E\pi_q + \frac{nq\pi}{I} E\pi$$

$$= \frac{1}{1-k} [k_y E\pi_y + (k_n - k)E\pi_n + (k_q - k)E\pi_q + kE\pi], \qquad (A7)$$

$$E\bar{p} \equiv k_y Ep_y + k_n Ep_n + k_q Ep_q, \tag{A8}$$

where the symbol E denotes the natural logarithmic differential operator $d\ln$.

Since $p_y = \pi_y$, $p_n = \pi_n + q\pi$, and $p_q = \pi_q + \eta_\pi$, it follows that

$$Ep_y = E\pi_y; \; Ep_n = \frac{(k_n - k)E\pi_n + k(E\pi + Eq)}{k_n};$$

$$Ep_q = \frac{(k_q - k)E\pi_q + k(E\pi + En)}{k_q}. \tag{A9}$$

Substitute these results (A9) into (A8) and then use (A7) to obtain

$$E\bar{p} = (1 - k)E\bar{\pi} + kEnq\pi. \tag{A10}$$

Now differentiate (A3) logarithmically:

$$ER = (1 - k)EI + kEnq\pi. \tag{A11}$$

Subtract (A10) from (A11):

$$E(R/\bar{p}) = (1 - k)E(I/\bar{\pi}). \tag{A12}$$

When I is increased, holding the π's constant, real income $R/\bar{p}$ increases in the smaller ratio $1 - k = I/R$. This is the economic basis of the downward bias in the observed income elasticities relative to the true income elasticities.

We now turn to the derivation of the observed income and substitution elasticities. We make use of the well-known propositions that

$$\begin{cases} En = \eta_n E(R/\bar{p}) + k_y\sigma_{ny}Ep_y - (1 - k_n)\bar{\sigma}_n Ep_n + k_q\sigma_{nq}Ep_q, \\[2mm] Eq = \eta_q E(R/\bar{p}) + k_y\sigma_{qy}Ep_y + k_n\sigma_{nq}Ep_n - (1 - k_q)\bar{\sigma}_q Ep_q, \\[2mm] (1 - k_n)\bar{\sigma}_n \equiv k_y\sigma_{ny} + k_q\sigma_{nq}; \; (1 - k_q)\bar{\sigma}_q \equiv k_y\sigma_{qy} + k_n\sigma_{nq}, \end{cases} \tag{A13}$$

where the σ's are the Allen partial elasticities of substitution in the utility function. Notice that $\bar{\sigma}_n$ is the average elasticity of substitution of n against y and q and that $\bar{\sigma}_q$ is the similar elasticity for q against y and n.

We first derive the observed income elasticities $\bar{\eta}_n$ and $\bar{\eta}_q$ by letting I change while the π's are constant. Because the π's are constant, it follows from (A9) and (A12) that

$$Ep_y = 0; \; Ep_n = \frac{kEq}{k_n}, \; Ep_q = \frac{kEn}{k_q}; \; E(R/\bar{p}) = (1 - k)EI. \tag{A14}$$

Substitute (A14) into (A13) and collect terms to obtain

$$\begin{cases} (1 - k\sigma_{nq})\bar{\eta}_n + \dfrac{k(1 - k_n)\bar{\sigma}_n}{k_n}\bar{\eta}_q = (1 - k)\eta_n \\[4mm] \dfrac{k(1 - k_q)\bar{\sigma}_q}{k_q}\bar{\eta}_n + (1 - k\sigma_{nq})\bar{\eta}_q = (1 - k)\eta_q. \end{cases} \tag{A15}$$

Solve these two equations for $\bar{\eta}_n$ and $\bar{\eta}_q$:

$$\begin{cases} \dfrac{D\bar{\eta}_n}{1-k} = (1 - k\sigma_{nq})\eta_n - \dfrac{k(1 - k_n)\bar{\sigma}_n}{k_n}\eta_q, \\[2mm] \dfrac{D\bar{\eta}_q}{1-k} = (1 - k\sigma_{nq})\eta_q - \dfrac{k(1 - k_q)\bar{\sigma}_q}{k_q}\eta_n, \\[2mm] D \equiv (1 - k\sigma_{nq})^2 - \dfrac{k^2(1 - k_n)(1 - k_q)\bar{\sigma}_n\bar{\sigma}_q}{k_n k_q}, \end{cases} \quad (A16)$$

where D and $(1 - k\sigma_{nq})$ must be positive by the second-order conditions.

In the section on income effects, we used the simpler budget restraint (2) rather than (10), so that we assumed that $k_n = k_q = k$; equations (7) and (8) are simply equations (A16) when $k_n = k_q = k$. The only proposition in that section that needs qualification when the budget restraint is (10) is the proposition that $\bar{\eta}_q - \bar{\eta}_n$ has the sign of $\eta_q - \eta_n$ unless σ_{qy} is much larger than σ_{ny}. Let $\sigma_{ny} = \sigma_{qy} = \sigma_{nq} = \sigma$ in (A16). Then

$$\frac{D(\bar{\eta}_q - \bar{\eta}_n)}{1 - k} = (1 - 2k\sigma)(\eta_q - \eta_n) + \frac{k\sigma}{k_n k_q}(k_q\eta_q - k_n\eta_n),$$

$$(A17)$$

where $(1 - 2k\sigma)$ must be positive by the second-order conditions. In the section on price effects, we assume that $k_n - k_q = n\pi_n - q\pi_q/R$ is positive. But then if η_q/η_n is sufficiently smaller than k_n/k_q, $\bar{\eta}_q - \bar{\eta}_n$ will have a sign opposite that of $\eta_q - \eta_n$. We have noted this qualification and commented on it (see n. 4 above).

We turn now to the income-compensated elasticities of quantity and quality with respect to the π's, deriving them in essentially the same manner as the income elasticities. We consider first the elasticities with respect to π_n and π_q:

$$\begin{cases} D\bar{\eta}_{i\pi_i}^{(s)} = -\dfrac{(k_i - k)(1 - k_i)\bar{\sigma}_i}{k_i}, \ i = n, q, \\[3mm] D\bar{\eta}_{i\pi_j}^{(s)} = (k_j - k)\left[\sigma_{nq}(1 - k\sigma_{nq}) + \dfrac{k(1 - k_i)(1 - k_j)\bar{\sigma}_i\bar{\sigma}_j}{k_i k_j}\right], \\[3mm] \hspace{6cm} i \neq j = n, q. \end{cases}$$

$$(A18)$$

When $\sigma_{ny} = \sigma_{qy} = \sigma_{nq} = \sigma$, these simplify to

$$\begin{cases} D\bar{\eta}_{i\pi_i}^{(s)} = -\dfrac{(k_i - k)(1 - k_i)\sigma}{k_i}, \ i = n, q, \\[3mm] D\bar{\eta}_{i\pi_j}^{(s)} = \dfrac{(k_j - k)\sigma}{k_i k_j}(k_i k_j + k k_y \sigma), \ i \neq j = n, q, \quad (A19) \\[3mm] D = (1 - 2k\sigma) - \dfrac{k_y(k\sigma)^2}{k_n k_q}. \end{cases}$$

Both observed "own price" elasticities, $\bar{\eta}_{n\pi_n}^{(s)}$ and $\bar{\eta}_{q\pi_q}^{(s)}$ are negative, and the sign of $|\bar{\eta}_{n\pi_n}^{(s)}| - |\bar{\eta}_{q\pi_q}^{(s)}|$ is ambiguous even when it is assumed that

$\sigma_{ny} = \sigma_{qy} = \sigma_{nq} = \sigma$ and that $k_n - k_q > 0$. However, if π_q is small relative to p_q, $|\bar{\eta}_{n\pi_n}{}^{(s)}|$ will exceed $|\bar{\eta}_{q\pi_q}{}^{(s)}|$. The observed cross-elasticities, $\bar{\eta}_{n\pi_q}{}^{(s)}$ and $\bar{\eta}_{q\pi_n}{}^{(s)}$, are positive if $\sigma_{nq} > 0$, and $\bar{\eta}_{q\pi_n}{}^{(s)}$ exceeds $\bar{\eta}_{n\pi_q}{}^{(s)}$ if $k_n > k_q$, as we assume. The cross-partial derivatives, however, are equal:

$$\frac{\partial n}{\partial \pi_q} = \frac{\partial q}{\partial \pi_n} = \frac{nq}{R}\left[\sigma_{nq}(1 - k\sigma_{nq}) + \frac{k(1-k_n)(1-k_q)\bar{\sigma}_n\bar{\sigma}_q}{k_n k_q} \right]$$

(A20)

where the derivatives are income-compensated.

The observed elasticities with respect to $\pi_y = p_y$ are

$$\frac{D\bar{\eta}_{i\pi_y}}{k_y} = \sigma_{iy}(1 - k\sigma_{nq}) - \sigma_{jy}k(k_j\sigma_{nq} + k_y\sigma_{iy})/k_i, \; i \neq j = n, q,$$

(A21)

from which it follows that

$$\left\{ \begin{aligned} \frac{D}{k_y}(\bar{\eta}_{n\pi_y}{}^{(s)} - \bar{\eta}_{q\pi_y}{}^{(s)}) &= (\sigma_{ny} - \sigma_{qy}')(1 - k\sigma_{nq}) \\ &+ \frac{k\sigma_{nq}}{k_n k_q}(k_n{}^2\sigma_{ny} - k_q{}^2\sigma_{qy}) + \frac{kk_y\sigma_{ny}\sigma_{qy}}{k_n k_q}(k_n - k_q). \end{aligned} \right.$$

(A22)

Thus, if the σ's are equal and if $k_n > k_q$, the quantity elasticity ($\bar{\eta}_{n\pi_y}{}^{(s)}$) exceeds the quality elasticity ($\bar{\eta}_{q\pi_y}{}^{(s)}$); this difference is increased if $\sigma_{ny} > \sigma_{qy}$, a special, though plausible, assumption.

The observed elasticities with respect to equal percentage changes in π_n, π_q, and π are simply those with respect to π_y but with signs changed. Thus, the demand functions for n and q are homogeneous of degree zero in I and the π's, just as they are in the shadow income (R) and the shadow prices (p's).

11   A Theory of Marriage

I

1. Introduction

In recent years, economists have used economic theory more boldly to explain behavior outside the monetary market sector, and increasing numbers of noneconomists have been following their examples. As a result, racial discrimination, fertility, politics, crime, education, statistical decision making, adversary situations, labor-force participation, the uses of "leisure" time, and other behavior are much better understood. Indeed, economic theory may well be on its way to providing a unified framework for *all* behavior involving scarce resources, nonmarket as well as market, nonmonetary as well as monetary, small group as well as competitive.

Yet, one type of behavior has been almost completely ignored by economists,[1] although scarce resources are used and it has been followed in some form by practically all adults in every recorded society. I refer to marriage. Marital patterns have major implications for, among other things, the number of births and population growth, labor-force participation of women, inequality in income, ability, and other characteristics among families, genetical natural selection of different characteristics

Reprinted from *Economics of the Family: Marriage, Children, and Human Capital*, edited by Theodore W. Schultz (University of Chicago Press, 1975). © 1975 by The University of Chicago. An earlier version of the paper was published in the *Journal of Political Economy* 81, no. 4 (July/August 1973), and 82, no. 2 (March/April 1974), pt. 2.

[1]To the best of my knowledge, the only exception prior to my own work is an unpublished paper by Gronau (1970*a*). His paper helped stimulate my interest in the subject.

over time, and the allocation of leisure and other household resources. Therefore, the neglect of marriage by economists is either a major oversight or persuasive evidence of the limited scope of economic analysis.

In this essay, it is argued that marriage is no exception and can be successfully analyzed within the framework provided by modern economics. If correct, this is compelling additional evidence on the unifying power of economic analysis.

Two simple principles form the heart of the analysis. The first is that, since marriage is practically always voluntary, either by the persons marrying or their parents, the theory of preferences ' can be readily applied, and persons marrying (or their parents) can be assumed to expect to raise their utility level above what it would be were they to remain single. The second is that, since many men and women compete as they seek mates, a *market* in marriages can be presumed to exist. Each person tries to find the best mate, subject to the restrictions imposed by market conditions.

These two principles easily explain why most adults are married and why sorting of mates by wealth, education, and other characteristics is similar under apparently quite different conditions. Yet marital patterns differ among societies and change over time in a variety of ways that challenge any single theory. In some societies divorce is relatively common, in others, virtually impossible, and in Western countries it has grown rapidly during the last half-century. Some societies adjust to legal difficulties in receiving divorces by delaying marriage, whereas others adjust by developing more flexible "consensual," "common-law," or "trial" marriages. In many the bride brings a dowry, in others the groom pays a bride-price, and in still others couples marry for "love" and disdain any financial bargaining. In some the newly married usually set up their own household, in others they live with one set of parents.

I do not pretend to have developed the analysis sufficiently to explain all the similarities and differences in marital patterns across cultures or over time. But the "economic" approach does quite well, certainly far better than any available alternative.[2] It is hoped that the present essay will stimulate others to carry the analysis into these uncharted areas.

Section 2 of Part I considers the determinants of the gain from marriage compared to remaining single for one man and one woman. The gain is shown to be related to the "compatibility" or "complementarity" of their time, goods, and other inputs used in household production.

Section 3 of Part I considers how a group of men and women sort themselves by market and nonmarket characteristics. Positive assortive mating— a positive correlation between the values of the traits of husbands and wives —is generally optimal, one main exception being the sorting by the earn-

---

[2] Some of the best work has been done by Goode (1963), but there is no systematic theory in any of his fine work.

ing power of men and women, where a negative correlation is indicated. Empirically, positive assortive mating is the most common and applies to IQ, education, height, attractiveness, skin color, ethnic origin, and other characteristics.

Section 4 of Part I considers how the the total output of a household gets divided between the husband and wife. The division is not usually fixed, say at 50–50, or determined mechanically, but changes as the supply of and demand for different kinds of mates changes.

Part II develops various extensions and modifications of the relatively simple analysis in this part. "Caring" is defined, and some of its effects on optimal sorting and the gain from marriage are treated. The factors determining the incidence of polygamous marital arrangements are considered. The assumption that the characteristics of potential mates are known with certainty is dropped, and the resulting "search" for mates, delays in marriage, trial marriage, and divorce are analyzed. Divorce and the duration of marriage are also related to specific investments made during marriage in the form of children, attachments, and other ways. Also briefly explored are the implications of different marital patterns for fertility, genetical natural selection, and the inequality in family incomes and home environments.

2. The Gain from Marriage

This section considers two persons, M and F, who must decide whether to marry each other or remain single. For the present, "marriage" simply means that they share the same household. I assume that marriage occurs if, and only if, both of them are made better off—that is, increase their utility.[3]

Following recent developments in the theory of household behavior, I assume that utility depends directly not on the goods and services purchased in the market place, but on the commodities produced "by" each household.[4] They are produced partly with market goods and services and partly with the own time of different household members. Most important for present purposes, commodities are not marketable or transferable among households, although they may be transferable among members of the same household.

Household-produced commodities are numerous and include the quality of meals, the quality and quantity of children, prestige, recreation, companionship, love, and health status. Consequently, they cannot be

---

[3] More precisely, if they *expect* to increase their utility, since the latter is not known with certainty. Part II discusses some consequences of this uncertainty, especially for the time spent searching for an appropriate mate and the incidence of divorce and other marital separations.

[4] An exposition of this approach is given in Michael and Becker (1973).

identified with consumption or output as usually measured: they cover a much broader range of human activities and aims. I assume, however, that all commodities can be combined into a single aggregate, denoted by Z. A sufficient condition to justify aggregation with fixed weights is that all commodities have constant returns to scale, use factors in the same proportion, and are affected in the same way by productivity-augmenting variables, such as education. Then different commodities could be converted into their equivalent in terms of any single commodity by using the fixed relative commodity prices as weights.[5] These weights would be independent of the scale of commodity outputs, the prices of goods and the time of different members, and the level of productivity.

Maximizing utility thus becomes equivalent for each person to maximizing the amount of Z that he or she receives. Moreover, my concentration on the output and distribution of Z does not presuppose transferable utilities, the same preference function for different members of the same household, or other special assumptions about preferences.

Each household has a production function that relates its total output of Z to different inputs:

$$Z = f(x_1, \ldots, x_m; t_1, \ldots, t_k; E), \tag{1}$$

where the x_i are various market goods and services, the t_j are the time inputs of different household members, and E represents "environmental" variables. The budget constraint for the x_i can be written as:

$$\sum_{}^{m} p_i x_i = \sum_{}^{k} w_j l_j + v, \tag{2}$$

where w_j is the wage rate of the jth member, l_j the time he spends working in the market sector, and v property income. The l_j and t_j are related by the basic time constraint

$$l_j + t_j = T \qquad \text{all } j, \tag{3}$$

where T is the total time of each member. By substituting equation (3) into (2), the goods and time constraints can be combined into a single "full" income constraint:

$$\sum_{}^{m} p_i x_i + \sum_{}^{k} w_j t_j = \sum_{}^{k} w_j T + v = S, \tag{4}$$

where S stands for full income, the maximum money income achievable, if the w_j are constants.

I assume that a reduction in the household's total output of Z makes

[5] One serious limitation of these assumptions is that they exclude the output of commodities from entering the production functions of other commodities. With such "joint production," the relative price of a commodity would depend partly on the outputs of other commodities (Grossman 1971). Joint production can result in complementarity in consumption, and thereby affect the gain from marriage and the sorting of mates. See the brief discussion which follows in section 3.

no member better off and some worse off.[6] Consequently, each member would be willing to cooperate in the allocation of his time and goods to help maximize the total output of Z. Necessary conditions to maximize Z include

$$\frac{MP_{t_i} \equiv (\partial Z/\partial t_i)}{MP_{t_j} \equiv (\partial Z/\partial t_j)} = \frac{w_i}{w_j}, \qquad \text{for all } 0 < t < T. \tag{5}$$

If the household time of the kth member $= T$, then

$$\frac{MP_{t_k}}{MP_{t_j}} = \frac{\mu_k}{w_j}, \tag{6}$$

where $\mu_k \geq w_k$ is the "shadow" price of the time of k. Also

$$\frac{MP_{x_i}}{MP_{t_j}} = \frac{p_i}{w_j} \qquad \text{for all } x_i > 0 \text{ and } 0 < t_j < T. \tag{7}$$

Each member must cooperate and allocate his time between the market and nonmarket sectors in the appropriate proportions.

If M and F are married, their household is assumed to contain only the two time inputs t_m and t_f; for simplicity, the time of children and others living in the same household is ignored. As long as they remain married, $T_m = T_f = 24$ hours per day, 168 hours per week, and so forth, and conditions (5) to (7) determine the allocation of the time of M and F between the market and nonmarket sectors. More time would be allocated to the market sector by M than by F (less to the nonmarket sector) if $w_m > w_f$ and if $MP_{t_f} \geq MP_{t_m}$ when $t_f = t_m$. Indeed, F would specialize in the nonmarket sector ($l_f = 0$) if either w_m/w_f or MP_{t_f}/MP_{t_m} were sufficiently large.

A singles household is taken to be exactly the same as a married one except that $T_f = 0$ when M is single and $T_m = 0$ when F is single. A singles household allocates only its own time between the market and nonmarket sectors to satisfy equation (7). Single persons generally allocate their time differently than married persons because the former do not have time and goods supplied by a mate. These differences depend partly on the elasticities of substitution among the x_i, t_f, and t_m, and partly on the differences between the market wage rates w_m and w_f. For example, single F are more likely to "work" more than married F and single M less than married M, the greater the percentage excess of w_m over w_f. Empirically, single women clearly "work" more than married women and single men less than married men.[7]

If Z_{m0} and Z_{0f} represent the maximum outputs of single M and F, and m_{mf} and f_{mf} their incomes when married, a necessary condition for

---

[6] This assumption is modified in the following section and in Part II.

[7] See, e.g., *Employment Status and Work Experience* (U.S., Bureau of the Census 1963c), tables 4 and 12.

M and F to marry is that

$$m_{mf} \geq Z_{m0}$$
$$f_{mf} \geq Z_{0f}. \tag{8}$$

If $m_{mf} + f_{mf}$, the total income produced by the marriage, is identified with the output of the marriage,[8] a necessary condition for marriage is then that

$$m_{mf} + f_{mf} \equiv Z_{mf} \geq Z_{m0} + Z_{0f}. \tag{9}$$

Since most men and women over age 20 are married in all societies, equation (9) must generally hold because of fundamental reasons that are not unique to time or place. I have a useful framework for discovering these reasons.

The obvious explanation for marriages between men and women lies in the desire to raise own children and the physical and emotional attraction between sexes. Nothing distinguishes married households more from singles households or from those with several members of the same sex than the presence, even indirectly, of children. Sexual gratification, cleaning, feeding, and other services can be purchased, but not *own* children:[9] both the man and woman are required to produce their own children and perhaps to raise them. The physical and emotional involvement called "love" is also primarily between persons of the opposite sex. Moreover, persons in love can reduce the cost of frequent contact and of resource transfers[10] between each other by sharing the same household.

Economies of scale may be secured by joining households, but two or more males or females could equally well take advantage of these economies and do so when they share an apartment and cooking. Consequently, the explanation of why men and women live together must go beyond economies of scale.

The importance of own children and love implies that, even with constant returns to scale, M (now standing for a man) and F (now standing for a woman) gain from marriage because t_m and t_f are not perfect substitutes for each other or for goods and services supplied by market firms or households. When substitution is imperfect, single persons cannot produce small-scale equivalents of the optimal combination of inputs achieved by married couples.

Consequently, the "shadow" price of an hour of t_f to a single M—the price he would be willing to pay for t_f—would exceed w_f, and the "shadow" price of t_m to a single F—the price she would be willing to pay

---

[8] Income and output can differ, however, because some output may be jointly consumed. See the discussion in the following section and in Part II.

[9] The market in adoptions is used primarily by couples experiencing difficulties in having their own children and by couples paid to raise other persons' children.

[10] The relation between love and such transfers is discussed in Part II.

for t_m—would exceed w_m. Both gain from marriage because M then, in effect, can buy an hour of t_f at w_f and F can buy an hour of t_m at w_m, lower prices they then would be willing to pay. Of course, this is also why married households use positive amounts of t_f and t_m.

My explanation of the gain from marriage focuses on the complementarity between M and F. The gain from complementary can be illustrated in much-exaggerated measure by assuming that the production function relating Z to t_m, t_f, and x has the Cobb-Douglas form

$$Z = kx^a t_m{}^b t_f{}^c. \tag{10}$$

Clearly, $Z_{m0} = Z_{0f} = 0$ since both t_m and t_f are needed to produce Z ($Z = 0$ if t_m or $t_f = 0$), whereas Z_{mf} can take any value. Other functions have less extreme "complementarity" and permit positive production when some inputs are absent but less "efficiently" than when all are present.

Some sociological literature also suggests that complementarity between men and women is the major source of the gain from marriage (Winch 1958, 1967; Goode 1963), but the meaning of "complementarity" is left rather vague and ill defined. By building on the substantial economic literature that analyzes complementarity and substitution in production, I have shown how "complementarity" determines the gain from marriage.

Can this analysis also explain why one man is typically married to one woman, rather than one man to several women, several men to one woman, or several men to several women? The importance of own children is sufficient to explain why marriages of several men to one or several women are uncommon since it would be difficult to identify the father of a child if many men had access to the same woman, whereas the identity of the mother is always known. The marriage of several women to one man does not suffer from this defect, and, indeed, such marriages have been more common. However, if the sex ratio equalled about unity, each household having several women and one man would have to be balanced by households having only men. If I assume that all men and all women are identical, and if I make the rather plausible assumption of "diminishing returns" from adding persons to a household having one man and one woman, the total output from say two single male households and one household with three women and one man would be smaller than the total output from three households each having one man and one woman.[11] Consequently, monogamous unions—one man married to one woman—predominate because it is the most efficient marital form.

---

[11] For example, assume that singles households have an output of 5 units of Z, one man and one woman 13 units, one man and two women 20 units, and one man and three women 26 units. Three households each with one man and one woman would produce 39 units, whereas two single male households and one household having three women and one man would produce only 36 units.

Polygamy is encouraged when the sex ratio is significantly different from unity and when men or women differ greatly in wealth, ability, or other attributes.[12]

My definition of marriage in terms of whether a man and a woman share the same household differs from the legal definition because my definition includes persons in "consensual" and casual unions and excludes legally married persons who are separated. However, my analysis does have useful implications about the choice between legally recognized and other unions (Kogut 1972), as well as about the decisions to remain married, divorce, remarry legally, remarry "consensually," remain single, and so forth, that must be made in the course of a lifetime (see Part II).

The gain from marriage has to be balanced against the costs, including legal fees and the cost of searching for a mate, to determine whether marriage is worthwhile. The larger the gain is relative to costs, the larger the net gain from marriage; presumably, therefore, the larger too is the fraction of persons who marry. I now consider the more important determinants of this net gain.

The gain is greater the more complementary are the inputs: the time of spouses and market goods. Since I have argued that these inputs are complementary in good part because of the desire to raise own children, the gain would be positively related to the importance of children. Hence, persons desiring relatively few or low-"quality" children either marry later, end their marriages earlier, or do both.[13]

The gain from marriage also depends on market opportunities. The effect of a change in opportunities can be analyzed most easily by equating the maximum output of any household to its full income deflated by the average cost of producing a unit of output. For example, with constant returns to scale, the output of a married household with both members participating in the labor force can be written as

$$Z_{mf} = \frac{\text{full income}}{\text{average cost of production}} \equiv \frac{S_{mf}}{C_{mf}(w_m, w_f, p)} \equiv \frac{S_m + S_f}{C_{mf}},$$

$$(11)$$

where C_{mf} depends on the wage rates of t_m and t_f and the price of x.[14] The output of a singles household can be written in the same form except that only one price of time enters the average cost functions C_m and C_f.[15]

What is the effect of an increase in income on the incentive to marry? If only the property incomes of M and F, v_m and v_f, rose exogenously

[12] See the more extensive discussion of polygamy in Part II.
[13] A further discussion can be found in Keeley (1974).

[14] Duality theory shows that C is the dual of the production function.
[15] Or, alternatively, the shadow price of F to M enters C_m, and the shadow price of M to F enters C_f.

by the same percentage, and if $v_m/S_m = v_f/S_f$, then S_m, S_f, and S_{mf} would all rise by the same percentage. With constant returns to scale, Z_{m0}, Z_{0f}, and Z_{mf}, and thus the absolute gain from marriage, would also rise by the same percentage as full income since neither C_{mf}, C_m, nor C_f would be affected by the rise in property incomes, as long as both M and F continue to participate in the labor force,[16] and assuming that property income is unaffected by the allocation of time.[17] Since a rise in property income should not greatly affect the cost of getting married, the incentive to marry would also rise.

The effect of a rise in wage rates alone[18] on the incentive to marry is less clear-cut. A rise in the wage rates of M and F by the same percentage would increase outputs by smaller percentages than full incomes, even with constant returns to scale, because costs of production also rise.[19] Moreover, the cost of getting married rises to the extent that the own time of M and F enters into search and other marital costs. Consequently, the effect on the net gain from marriage is not clear a priori and depends on the relative importance of own time in marriage costs and in the production of output in single and married households.

Consequently, my analysis predicts that a rise in property income, necessarily, and a rise in wage rates, possibly, increase the incentive to marry. This implication runs counter to the popular opinion that poor persons marry earlier and divorce less than rich persons but is consistent with the empirical evidence. In the United States, at least, the probability of separation and divorce is negatively related to income (U.S., Bureau of the Census 1971). Keeley (1974) finds too that when years of schooling and a few other variables are held constant, higher-wage persons appear to marry earlier than others.

My analysis implies that a rise in w_f relative to w_m, F's wage rate relative to M's, with the productivity of time in the nonmarket sector held constant, would decrease the gain from marriage if w_f were less than w_m: the gain from substituting M's time in the market for F's time (and F's time in the household for M's time) is greater the lower w_f is relative to w_m. As a proof, consider an increase in w_f "compensated" by a sufficient decrease in w_m to maintain constant the combined output of the two singles households. The increase in w_f would not increase married output as

[16] Even if married F did not participate in the labor force, the percentage rise in Z_{mf} would still equal the share of property income in full income (see section 2, Part I of the Appendix).

[17] The gain from marriage would increase even more if the income from nonhuman capital, i.e., property income, was positively related to the time allocated to "portfolio management" (see the discussion in the following section).

[18] By alone is meant in particular that the productivity of time in household production or marital search is unchanged.

[19] The percentage rise in output equals the percentage rise in wage rates multiplied by the ratio of total earnings to full income. Although this relation holds whether or not married F is in the labor force (see section 2, Part I of the Appendix), the ratio of total earnings to full income can depend—positively or negatively—on her participation.

much as the decrease in w_m would decrease it if married F worked sufficiently fewer hours in the market sector than single F, and married M worked at least as much as single M. Since married women do work much less than single women and married men work more than single men, an increase in the wage rate of women relative to men would decrease the incentive to marry.[20] As supporting evidence, note that American states that have higher wage rates of women relative to men also have smaller fractions of men and women who are married (Santos 1970; Freiden 1972).

The gain from marriage also depends on traits, such as beauty, intelligence, and education, that affect nonmarket productivity as well, perhaps, as market opportunities. The analysis of sorting in section 3b implies that an increase in the value of traits that have a positive effect on nonmarket productivity, market productivity held constant, would generally increase the gain from marriage. Presumably this helps explain why, for example, less attractive or less intelligent persons are less likely to marry than are more attractive or more intelligent persons.[21]

3. The Marriage Market and Sorting of Mates

a) Optimal Sorting

I now consider not one M and F who must decide whether to marry or remain single, but many M's and F's who must decide whom to marry among numerous potential candidates, as well as whether to marry. If there are n M's and n F's (unequal numbers of M and F are discussed in section 4), each is assumed to know all the relevant[22] entries in an $n + 1 \times n + 1$ payoff matrix showing the maximum household commodity output that can be produced by any combination of M and F:

$$
\begin{array}{c|ccc}
 & F_1 & \cdots & F_n \\
\hline
M_1 & Z_{11} & \cdots & Z_{1n}\ Z_{10} \\
 & & Z_{ij} & \\
M_n & Z_{n1} & \cdots & Z_{nn}\ Z_{n0} \\
 & Z_{01} & \cdots & Z_{0n} \\
\end{array}
\qquad (12)
$$

The last row and column give the output of single M and F. Each person has $n + 1$ possibilities and the $2n$ persons together have $n^2 + 2n$ pos-

[20] A fortiori, if married women were not in the labor force, a compensated increase in their wage rate would decrease the incentive to marry since an increase in their wage rate would not affect married output, whereas a decrease in the male wage rate would decrease output. This footnote as well as the text assumes that compensated changes in w_f and w_m do not much affect the cost of getting married.

[21] Evidence on marriage rates by intelligence can be found in Higgins, Reed, and Reed (1962) and Bajema (1963). The statement on marriage rates by attractiveness is not based on any statistical evidence.

[22] That is, all the entries relevant to their decisions. This strong assumption of sufficient information is relaxed in Part II, where "search" for a mate is analyzed.

sibilities. I assume that each person gains from marriage, so that the singles row and column of the payoff matrix can be ignored.

There are $n!$ different combinations that permit each M to marry one F and vice versa; that is, there are $n!$ ways to select one entry in each married row and column. The total output over all marriages produced by any one sorting can be written as

$$Z^k = \sum_{i \in M, \, j \in F} Z_{ij}, \qquad k = 1, \ldots, n!. \qquad (13)$$

Number one of the sortings that maximizes total output so that its entries lie along the diagonal and write

$$Z^* = \sum_{i=1}^{n} Z_{ii} = \max_k Z^k \geq Z^k \qquad \text{all } k. \qquad (14)$$

If the total output of any marriage is divided between the mates,

$$m_{ij} + f_{ij} = Z_{ij}, \qquad (15)$$

where m_{ij} is the income of the ith M from marriage to the jth F, and similarly for f_{ij}. If each chooses the mate who maximizes his or her "income," the optimal sorting must have the property that persons not married to each other could not marry and make one better off without making the other worse off. In game theoretic language, the optimal sorting is in the "core" since no "coalition" outside the core could make any of its members better off without making some worse off.

Persons entering noncore marriages could not produce more together than the sum of their incomes in the core. For, if they could, and if any division of output between mates were feasible, they could find a division of their output that would make each better off, a contradiction of the definition of the core. If the sorting along the diagonal were in the core, this condition states that

$$m_{ii} + f_{jj} \geq Z_{ij} \qquad \text{all } i \text{ and } j. \qquad (16)$$

Conditions (15) and (16) immediately rule out any sorting that does not maximize the total output of commodities over all marriages, for at least one M and one F would then be better off with each other than with their mates.[23] Moreover, the theory of optimal assignments, which has

---

[23] If M_i married F_j and F_i married M_p in an optimal sorting that did not maximize total output, condition (16) requires that $m_{ij} + f_{pi} \geq Z_{ii}$, all ij, pi, or, by summation,

$$Z_p = \sum_{\text{all } ij, \, pi}^{n} m_{ij} + f_{pi} \geq \sum_i Z_{ii} = Z^*.$$

Since Z^* is the maximum total output, it must exceed Z_p, by assumption less than the maximum. Hence, a contradiction, and a proof that the optimal sorting cannot produce less than the maximum total output.

the same mathematical structure as the sorting of persons by marriage, implies the existence of a set of incomes that satisfy conditions (15) and (16) for sortings that maximize total output.[24]

The solution can be illustrated with the following 2×2 matrix of payoffs:

$$
\begin{array}{c}
\quad F_1 \quad F_2 \\
\begin{array}{c} M_1 \\ M_2 \end{array}
\begin{bmatrix} 8 & 4 \\ 9 & 7 \end{bmatrix}.
\end{array}
\tag{17}
$$

Although the maximum output in any marriage is between M_2 and F_1, the optimal sorting is M_1 to F_1 and M_2 to F_2. For, if $m_{11} = 3$, $f_{11} = 5$, $m_{22} = 5$, and $f_{22} = 2$, M_2 and F_1 have no incentive to marry since $m_{22} + f_{11} = 10 > 9$, and neither do M_1 and F_2 since $m_{11} + f_{22} = 5 > 4$. In other words, the marriage market chooses not the maximum household commodity output of any single marriage but the maximum sum of the outputs over all marriages, just as competitive product markets maximize the sum of the outputs over all firms. Let me stress again that the commodity output maximized by all households is not to be identified with national output as usually measured, but includes conversation, the quantity and quality of children, and other outputs that never enter or enter only imperfectly into the usual measures. Put still differently, the marriage market acts as if it maximizes not the gain from marriage compared to remaining single for any particular marriage, but the average gain over all marriages.[25]

Each marriage can be considered a two-person firm with either member being the "entrepreneur" who "hires" the other at the "salary" m_{ij} or f_{ij} and receives residual "profits" of $Z_{ij} - m_{ij}$ or $Z_{ij} - f_{ij}$. Another interpretation of the optimal sorting is that only it enables each "entrepreneur" to maximize "profits" for given "salaries" of mates because only the optimal sorting satisfies condition (16). With all other sortings, some "entrepreneurs" could do better by "hiring" different mates than those assigned to them.

---

[24] For a proof, see Koopmans and Beckman (1957).

[25] Clearly,

$$
\left[\sum_i^n Z_{ii} - \sum_{j=1}^n (Z_{0j} + Z_{j0}) \right] \bigg/ n = \left\{ \sum_i [Z_{ii} - (Z_{0j} + Z_{j0})] \right\} \bigg/ n
$$

is maximized if

$$
\sum Z_{ii}
$$

is, since Z_{0j} and Z_{j0} are given and independent of the marital sorting.

b) Assortive Mating

I now consider the optimal sorting when M and F differ in a trait, or set of traits, such as intelligence, race, religion, education, wage rate, height, aggressiveness, tendency to nurture, or age. Psychologists and sociologists have frequently discussed whether likes or unlikes mate, and geneticists have occasionally assumed positive or negative assortive mating instead of random mating. But no systematic analysis has developed that predicts for different kinds of traits when likes or unlikes are motivated to mate.[26] My analysis implies that likes or unlikes mate when that maximizes total household commodity output[27] over all marriages, regardless of whether the trait is financial (like wage rates and property income), or genetical (like height and intelligence), or psychological (like aggressiveness and passiveness).

Assume that M differs only in the quantitative trait A_m, and F only in A_f, that each trait has a monotonic effect on the output of any marriage, and that higher values have the larger effect:

$$\frac{\partial Z_{ij}(A_m, A_f)}{\partial A_m} > 0, \qquad \frac{\partial Z_{ij}}{\partial A_f}(A_m, A_f) > 0. \tag{18}$$

If increasing both A_m and A_f adds the same amount to output as the sum of the additions when each is increased separately, all sortings of M and F would give the same total output. On the other hand, if increasing both adds more to output than the sum of the separate additions, a sorting of large A_m with large A_f and small A_m with small A_f would give the greatest total output since an increase in A_m reinforces the effect of an increase in A_f. The converse holds if increasing both adds less to output than the sum of the separate additions. Mathematically, this states that positive or negative assortive mating—mating of likes or unlikes—is optimal as

$$\frac{\partial^2 Z(A_m, A_f)}{\partial A_m\, \partial A_f} \gtrless 0 \tag{19}$$

(proofs in Appendix, Part I, section 1).

Consider, as an example, a matrix of outputs when $n = 2$:

$$\begin{array}{c} \quad A_1 \quad\ \ A_2 \\ \begin{array}{c} A_1 \\ A_2 \end{array} \begin{bmatrix} Z_{11} & Z_{12} \\ Z_{21} & Z_{22} \end{bmatrix}, \end{array} \quad \text{with } A_2 > A_1. \tag{20}$$

---

[26] Winch (1958) essentially assumes that each person tries to maximize utility ("In mate selection each individual seeks within his or her field of eligibles for that person who gives the greatest promise of providing him or her with maximum need gratification" [pp. 88–89]) and stresses complementary needs as a prerequisite for mating (especially in chap. 4), but he only considers psychological traits, brings in "eligibles" as a deus ex machina, and nowhere shows how mating by complementary needs brings equilibrium into the marriage market.

[27] Let me emphasize again that commodity output is not the same as national product as usually measured, but includes children, companionship, health, and a variety of other commodities.

If $Z_{22} - Z_{12} > Z_{21} - Z_{11}$, if equality (19) is positive, then obviously $Z_{11} + Z_{22} > Z_{12} + Z_{22}$, and a positive correlation between A_m and A_f maximizes total output, as predicted from (19).

One tradition in production theory distinguishes substitution from complementarity by the sign of the cross-derivative of output with respect to different inputs into a production function. Although condition (19) is not defined in terms of household production functions, duality theory implies that the same condition holds when A_m and A_f are treated as inputs into these production functions.[28] Condition (19) says, therefore, that the association of likes is optimal when traits are complements and the association of unlikes is optimal when they are substitutes, a plausible conclusion since high values of different traits reinforce each other when they are complements, and offset each other when they are substitutes.

Economists have generally considered the sorting of different *quantities* of different traits, such as labor and capital, not different *qualities* of the same trait. Although sorting by quantity and quality are related analytically, many applications of sorting by quality are also directly available in economics, such as the optimal sorting of more able workers and more able firms,[29] more "modern" farms and more able farmers, or more informed customers and more honest shopkeepers. As already mentioned (n. 26 above), some sociologists have considered "complementarity" to be an important determinant of sorting, but have not given a rigorous analysis of the effects of "complementarity" or embedded their discussions in the context of a functioning marriage market.

Mating of likes—positive assortive mating—is extremely common, whether measured by intelligence, height, skin color, age, education, family background, or religion, although unlikes sometimes also mate, as measured, say, by an inclination to nurture or succor, to dominate or be deferential. This suggests that traits are typically but not always complements.

The determinants of complementarity and substitutability are best discovered by going explicitly to the household production function and the maximization process. All households are assumed to have the same production *function*; that is, if the inputs of time, goods, and *all* traits were exactly the same, the output of commodities would be exactly the same. Different families can, of course, produce different outputs from the same input of goods and time if their education, ability, and so forth, differ.

I consider a number of determinants in turn. First, if M and F differ *only* in their market wage rates—each M and each F are identical in all

---

[28] Wage rates or other monetary variables, however, cannot be treated as productive inputs.

[29] This sorting is discussed for Japanese firms by Kuratani (1972). Hicks (1948, chap. 2, sec. 3) asserts that more able workers work for more able firms without offering any proof. Black (1926) discusses the sorting of workers and firms with a few numerical examples.

other market and in nonmarket traits—according to equation (11), the optimal output between M and F who are both participating in the labor force can be written as

$$Z = \frac{S}{C(w_m, w_f, p)}, \tag{21}$$

where the subscripts on Z, S, and C have been omitted and constant returns to scale assumed. Then, by differentiation and by using equation (4),

$$Z^m = \frac{T}{C} - \frac{S}{C^2} C^m,$$

where

$$Z^m = \frac{\partial Z}{\partial w_m} \quad \text{and} \quad C^m \equiv \frac{\partial C}{\partial w_m} \tag{22}$$

Since

$$C^m = t_m Z^{-1}, \tag{23}$$

where t_m is the time spent by M in the household,

$$Z^m = l_m C^{-1} > 0 \tag{24}$$

if l_m, the time spent at work, is greater than zero. Similarly,

$$Z^f = \frac{T}{C} - \frac{S}{C^2} C^f = l_f C^{-1} > 0. \tag{25}$$

Positive or negative assortive mating by wage rates is optimal as

$$\frac{\partial^2 Z}{\partial w_m \, \partial w_f} \equiv Z^{mf} \equiv Z^{fm} \gtrless 0. \tag{26}$$

Differentiate Z^f with respect to w_m to get

$$Z^{fm} = -C^{-2} C^m l_f + C^{-1} \frac{\partial l_f}{\partial w_m}. \tag{27}$$

The first term on the right is clearly negative, so Z^{fm} will be negative if the second term, $\partial l_f / \partial w_m \leq 0$, is nonpositive, that is, if t_m and t_f are not gross complements, as these terms are usually defined.[30] Consequently, a perfectly negative rank correlation between w_m and w_f would maximize total commodity output if the time of M and F were not such gross

---

[30] This definition is different from the one given earlier in terms of the sign of the cross-derivative of profit or production functions. The definition in equation (28) is preferable, at least as a predictor of responses to changes in input prices. By "gross" rather than "net" complements is meant in the usual way that the income effect is included along with the substitution effect. Even if t_m and t_f were net complements they could still be gross substitutes since the income effect of an increase in w_m would tend to increase t_f.

complements as to swamp the first term in (27). Considerable empirical evidence supports the conclusion that t_m and t_f are not gross complements (Ofek 1972; Smith 1972*a*).

A negative correlation between w_m and w_f maximizes total output because the gain from the division of labor is maximized. Low-wage F should spend more time in household production than high-wage F because the foregone value of the time of low-wage F is lower; similarly, low-wage M should spend more time in household production than high-wage M. By mating low-wage F with high-wage M and low-wage M with high-wage F, the cheaper time of both M and F is used more extensively in household production, and the expensive time of both is used more extensively in market production.

All persons have been assumed to participate in the labor force. During any year, however, most married women in the United States do not participate, and a significant number never really participate throughout their married life. My analysis does predict that many women would have only a weak attachment to the labor force since low-wage women would be discouraged from participation both by their low wage and by the high wage of their husbands.[31]

If some women are not in the labor force, however, the wage rates of men and women need not be perfectly negatively correlated to maximize total output. For assume that all women with wage rates below a certain level would not participate in the labor force with a perfectly negative correlation between the wage rates of men and women. These women have $\partial Z / \partial w_f = 0,$[32] and, thus, $Z^{fm} = 0$; therefore, up to a point, they could switch mates without lowering total output. Consequently, other sortings having weaker negative, and conceivably even positive, correlations would also maximize total output; that is, many sortings would be equally good, and wage rates would not be a decisive determinant of the optimal sorting.

If M and F differ only in their stock of nonhuman capital, K_m and K_f, and if everyone participates in the labor force, $\partial C / \partial K_m = \partial C / \partial K_f = 0$ since the value of time is measured by the market wage rates. If the rate of return on K, denoted by r, depended positively on the amount of time allocated to "portfolio management," r would be positively related to K.[33] It then follows that

---

[31] Low-wage men also would be encouraged to work less both because of their low wage and the relatively high wage of their wives. They would not leave the labor force in large numbers, however, partly because average wage rates of men are so much higher than those of women and partly because the nonmarket productivity of women is higher than that of men.

[32] As long as they are not indifferent at the margin to working in the market sector.

[33] For this result and a more complete analysis of the allocation of time to portfolio management, see Ben-Zion and Ehrlich (1972).

$$\left. \begin{array}{c} \dfrac{\partial Z}{\partial K_m} = \dfrac{\partial Z}{\partial K_f} = rC^{-1} > 0 \\[18pt] \dfrac{\partial^2 Z}{\partial K_m\,\partial K_f} = \dfrac{dr}{dK} C^{-1} > 0 \end{array} \right\} \text{[34]}$$

and $\hspace{4cm}$ (28)

A perfectly positive correlation between the nonhuman capital of M and F would be optimal, an implication that is consistent with evidence on sorting by, say, parental wealth.

If some F did not participate in the labor force, the value of their time would be measured by a "shadow" price that exceeded their wage rate and was not constant but positively related to the sum of their nonhuman capital.[35] Moreover, a perfectly positive correlation of this capital is no longer necessarily optimal because of diminishing returns to an increase in the time of M and goods for a given amount of the time of F (for proof, see Appendix, Part I, section 2).

All differences in the output of commodities, by assumption the only determinant of behavior, not related to differences in wage rates or non-human capital are, by definition, related to differences in nonmarket productivity.[36] The widespread differences between men and women in nonmarket productivity are caused by differences in intelligence, educa-tion, health, strength, height, personality, religion, and other traits. I now consider the optimal sorting of traits that affect nonmarket pro-ductivity, while assuming that wage rates and nonhuman capital are the same for all M and for all F.

To demonstrate the tendency toward complementarity of nonmarket traits in the context of household commodity outputs, rewrite the optimal output equation given by (21) as

$$Z = \frac{S}{C(w_m, w_f, p, A_m, A_f)}, \qquad (29)$$

where A_m and A_f are the traits of M and F. Then using the assumption that w_m, w_f, and the rate of return on nonhuman capital are independent of A_m and A_f,

---

[34] If time is allocated to portfolio management, $S = wT + Kr(\ell_p) - w\ell_p$, where ℓ_p is the time so allocated. Then $\partial S/\partial K = r + (K\,dr/d\ell_p)(d\ell_p/dK) - w(d\ell_p/dK) = r + d\ell_p/dK[(K\,dr/d\ell_p) - w]$. Since, however, $K\,dr/d\ell_p = w$ is one of the first-order maximiza-tion conditions, then $\partial S/\partial K = r$.

[35] See the discussion in section 2, Part I of the Appendix.

[36] Differences in the earning power of children are assumed to be derived from differences in either the nonmarket productivity or incomes of their parents, and are not considered separately.

$$\left.\begin{array}{l} \dfrac{\partial C}{\partial A_m} \equiv C_{a_m} \\[2.2em] \dfrac{\partial C}{\partial A_f} \equiv C_{a_f} \end{array}\right\} < 0 \quad \text{and} \quad \dfrac{\partial S}{\partial A_f} = \dfrac{\partial S}{\partial A_m} = 0. \qquad (30)$$

Then,

$$\left.\begin{array}{l} \dfrac{\partial Z}{\partial A_m} = -SC^{-2}C_{a_m} \\[2.2em] \dfrac{\partial Z}{\partial A_f} = -SC^{-2}C_{a_f} \end{array}\right\} > 0, \qquad (31)$$

and

$$\frac{\partial^2 Z}{\partial A_m \, \partial A_f} > 0 \qquad \text{if } 2C^{-1}C_{a_m}C_{a_f} > C_{a_m,a_f}. \qquad (32)$$

Since the term on the left is positive, equation (32) necessarily holds if A_m and A_f have either independent or reinforcing effects on productivity, for then $C_{a_m,a_f} \leq 0$; moreover, (32) might hold even if they had offsetting effects. Therefore, perfectly positive assortive mating is definitely optimal if the traits have reinforcing effects; less obvious and more impressive, however, is the conclusion that positive assortive mating is also optimal if they have independent effects because C enters inversely in the equation for Z, or even if they have offsetting effects if these are weaker than a multiple of the direct ones.[37]

The reasons for the prevalence of a complementary relation between traits that raise nonmarket productivity can be seen more transparently by considering a couple of special cases. If the percentage effect on output of a trait were independent of the quantities of goods and time, the optimal output equation could be written as

$$Z = \frac{S}{b(A_m, A_f)K(w_m, w_f, p)}, \qquad (33)$$

where $\partial b/\partial A_m \equiv b_{a_m} < 0$, and $\partial b/\partial A_f \equiv b_{a_f} < 0$. Hence,

$$\frac{\partial^2 Z}{\partial A_m \, \partial A_f} > 0 \qquad \text{as } 2b^{-1}b_{a_m}b_{a_f} > b_{a_m,a_f}, \qquad (34)$$

---

[37] Equation (32) can be written as

$$2|\varepsilon_{c_{a_m}}| > \varepsilon_{c_{a_f},a_m},$$

where $\varepsilon_{c_{a_m}} = (C_{a_m} \cdot A_m)/C < 0$, and $\varepsilon_{c_{a_m},a_f} = C_{a_f,a_m} \cdot A_m/C_{a_f} > 0$ if the effects are offsetting. The cross-elasticity must be smaller than twice the absolute value of the direct elasticity.

which must hold if $b_{a_m,a_f} \leq 0$ and can easily hold even if $b_{a_m,a_f} > 0$. Positive assortive mating is optimal even when these productivity effects are independent because productivity is raised multiplicatively: higher A_m (or A_f) have bigger *absolute* effects when combined with higher A_f (or A_m). A fortiori, this multiplicative relation encourages the mating of likes when the effects are reinforcing and can do so even when they are offsetting.[38]

The effect of most traits on nonmarket output is not independent of goods and time, but generally operates through the time supplied to the household; for example, if the time supplied became zero, so would the effect. A simple way to incorporate this interaction is to assume that each trait affects outputs only by augmenting the effective amount of own household time. It is shown in section 3, Part I of the Appendix that positive assortive mating would still be optimal as long as the elasticity of substitution between the household time of M and F was not very high.[39] Negative assortive mating can be expected for own-time-augmenting traits only if they augment dimensions that are easily substitutable between M and F. Dominant and deferential persons tend to marry each other (Winch 1958), perhaps, therefore, because the dominant person's time can be used when households encounter situations calling for dominance and the deferential person's time can be used when they call for deference.

Note that it is shown in section 2 that the gain from marriage is also greater when substitution between the time of M and F is more difficult. Therefore, the mating of likes should be more common when marriage is more attractive, an important and subtle implication of the analysis.

How do the nonmarket traits of one sex combine with the market traits of the other? In particular, does my analysis justify the popular belief that more beautiful, charming, and talented women tend to marry wealthier and more successful men? Section 4 in Part I of the Appendix shows that a positive sorting of nonmarket traits with nonhuman wealth always, and with earning power usually,[40] maximizes commodity output over all marriages. The economic interpretation is basically that nonmarket productivity and money income tend to combine multiplicatively, so that higher values of a trait have larger absolute effects when combined with higher income.

Scattered references have been made to the empirical evidence on sorting, and this evidence is now considered a little more systematically. The simple correlations between the intelligence, education, age, race,

---

[38] Section 3, Part I of the Appendix shows that positive assortive mating of A_m and A_f is still optimal even when F do not participate in the labor force.

[39] The elasticity estimates of Ofek (1972) and Smith (1972a) are only of modest size.

[40] By "usually" is meant that a positive sorting with earnings always maximizes total output when an increase in a trait does not decrease the spouses' hours worked in the market sector and *could* maximize output even when they do decrease.

nonhuman wealth, religion, ethnic origin, height, and geographical propinquity of spouses are positive and strong.[41] A small amount of evidence suggests that the correlations between certain psychological traits, such as a propensity to dominate, nurture, or be hostile, are negative.[42] The correlation by intelligence is especially interesting since, although intelligence is highly inheritable, the correlation between mates is about as high as that between siblings (Alstrom 1961). Apparently, the marriage market, aided by coeducational schools, admissions tests, and the like, is more efficient than is commonly believed.

This evidence of positive simple correlations for a variety of traits, and of negative correlations for some, is certainly consistent with my theory of sorting. A more powerful test of the theory, however, requires evidence on partial correlations, when various other traits are held constant. For example, how strong is the correlation by intelligence, when years of schooling and family background are held constant? I do not yet have results on partial correlations by intelligence, but do have some on years of schooling, wage rates, and age, for samples of white and black families.[43] Even when age and wage rates are held constant, the correlation between years of schooling is high, $+.53$ for whites and virtually the same ($+.56$) for blacks. Although the partial correlations between wage rates are much lower, they are also positive, $+.32$ for whites and a bit lower ($+.24$) for blacks.

The strong positive partial correlation between years of schooling is predicted by the theory, but the positive correlation between wage rates is troublesome since the theory predicts a negative correlation when nonmarket productivity is held constant. Note, however, that the sample is biased because it is restricted to women in the labor force in a particular year. Since the higher the husband's wage rate the higher must be his wife's wage rate to induce her to enter the labor force, a negative correlation across all mates is consistent with a positive one for those having wives in the labor force.[44] Indeed, Gregg Lewis has shown[45] that a correlation of about $+.3$ for mates who are participating almost certainly implies a negative one (about $-.25$) for all mates, given the relatively small

[41] Many of the relevant studies are listed in Winch (1958, chap. 1).
[42] See Winch (1958, chap. 5). Deference is treated as negative values of dominance, succorance as negative values of nurturance, and abasement as negative values of hostility.
[43] A 20 percent random sample of the approximately 18,000 married persons in the 1967 Survey of Economic Opportunity was taken. Families were included only if the husband and wife both were less than age 65 and were employed, the wife for at least 20 hours in the survey week.
[44] Also, nonmarket productivity varies even when years of schooling and age are held constant. If investments that raise nonmarket productivity also raise, somewhat, market earning power (Heckman [1974] finds that the education of women raises their non-market productivity almost as much as their market earning power), the positive correlation between wage rates may really be picking up the predicted positive correlation between husband's wage rate and wife's nonmarket productivity.
[45] Via an unpublished memorandum extending some work of Gronau (1972).

fraction of married women who participate. If his calculations hold up, this would be striking confirmation of my theory since it is counter to common impressions and is one of the few examples (and a predicted one!) of negative associative mating.

Other evidence, probably less affected by unobserved differences in nonmarket productivity, does suggest that the gain from marriage is greater when differentials between male and female wage rates are greater. For example, a larger percentage of persons are married in American states that have higher wages of males and lower wages of females, even when age, years of schooling, the sex ratio, the fraction Catholic, and other variables are held constant (Santos 1970; Freiden 1972). Or a larger fraction of black households are headed by women in metropolitan areas with higher earnings of black women relative to black men (Reischauer 1970).

Quantitative evidence on the association of traits that affect nonmarket productivity with earnings and other income is scarce. The evidence I put together and referred to earlier indicates that husband's wage rate and wife's education are significantly positively correlated, even when husband's education and wife's wage rate are held constant.[46] One interpretation, stressed by Benham in his paper which follows, is that a wife's education contributes to her husband's earnings, just as a mother's education is said to contribute to her children's earnings (Leibowitz 1972). An alternative suggested by our theory of sorting is that a wife's education is a proxy for traits affecting her nonmarket productivity, especially when her wage rate is held constant[47] and that women with higher nonmarket productivity marry men with higher earning power. Although the relative importance of these alternative interpretations has not been determined, Benham does find that hours worked by husbands are positively related to wife's education, a sufficient condition for positive sorting (see n. 40 above).

My analysis of mating and sorting has assumed perfect certainty in the production of household commodities. Uncertainty surrounds the production of many commodities, but my concern here is only with uncertainty about the "quality" of own children since children are a major source of the gain from marriage. An important result in population genetics is that positive assortive mating of inheritable traits, like race, intelligence, or height, increases the correlation of these traits among siblings; the increase would be greater the more inheritable the trait is and the greater the degree of assortive mating (Cavalli-Sforza and Bodmer 1971, chap. 9, sec. 7). Therefore, inheritable traits of M and F

---

[46] In his more detailed analysis in this book, Benham finds similar results, after several additional variables are also held constant. Note, however, that the husband's wage rate is much more strongly related to his own than to his wife's education.

[47] I argued earlier that her wage rate also is a proxy for such traits, when her education is held constant.

can be said to be complements in reducing the uncertainty about one's children. Positive assortive mating of inheritable traits would increase the utility of total output if more certainty about the "quality" of children is desirable—perhaps because friction between siblings or the cost of raising them is increased by uncertainty.

My analysis of sorting is based on several other simplifying assumptions that ought to be modified in a fuller treatment. For example, the conclusion in section 2, that the gain from marriage is independent of preferences, assumes, among other things, no joint production and constant returns to scale in households. With beneficial joint production[48] or increasing returns, mating of persons with similar preferences would be optimal and conversely with detrimental production or decreasing returns. Similarly, the conclusion in section 2, that a monogamous union is always optimal, which is taken for granted in the discussion of sorting, should be modified to consider polygamy (I do this in Part II) and remaining single (see the discussion of search in Part II). Further, I have considered only one trait at a time, holding all other traits constant. But since people differ in many interdependent traits, optimal sortings should be determined for a set of traits, perhaps using the canonical correlation coefficient or related statistics as the measure of association.

Probably the assumption that would be most questioned is that any division of output between mates is feasible. Some of the output may not be divisible at all and may constitute a "public," or better still, a "family" commodity. Children might be said to be largely a family commodity, and, as shown in Part II, "caring" can convert the whole output into family commodities. Or some divisions may not be feasible because they are not enforceable. For example, even though the marriage market might dictate a 2/5 share for a particular husband, he may receive a 3/5 share because his wife cannot "police" the division perfectly.

Although the rigidities resulting from family commodities and enforcement problems can often be overcome (through dowries and other capital transfers), it is instructive to consider a model of sorting that incorporates these rigidities in an extreme fashion. How robust are the conclusions about optimal sorting when complete rigidity in the division of output replaces the assumption of complete negotiability?

Rigidity is introduced by assuming that M_i would receive a constant fraction e_i of commodity output in *all* marriages, and F_j receive d_j. Note that e_i and e_k ($k \neq i$) or d_j and d_k ($k \neq j$) need not be equal, and that

$$e_i + d_j \gtrless 1, \tag{35}$$

as family commodities or enforcement costs were dominant. The matrix showing the incomes for all combinations of M and F would then be

[48] Grossman (1971) distinguishes beneficial from detrimental production by the effect of an increase in output of one commodity on the cost of producing others.

$$
\begin{array}{c|ccc|}
 & F_1 & F_j & F_n \\
\hline
M_1 & e_1Z_{11}, d_1Z_{11} & \cdots\cdots\cdots & e_1Z_{1n}, d_nZ_{nn} \\
M_i & & e_iZ_{ij}, d_jZ_{ij} & \\
M_n & e_nZ_{nj}, d_1Z_{n1} & \cdots\cdots\cdots & e_nZ_{nn}, d_nZ_{nn} \\
\hline
\end{array} \qquad (36)
$$

If

$$
\hat{Z}_1 \equiv Z_{st} > Z_{ij}, \qquad \text{all } i \neq s, \text{ all } j \neq t, \tag{37}
$$

were the maximum output in any possible marriage and if each person tried to maximize his commodity income, M_s would marry F_t since they could not do as well in any other marriage.[49] Now exclude M_s and F_t from consideration, and if

$$
\hat{Z}_2 = Z_{uv} > Z_{ij}, \qquad \text{all } i \neq u \text{ or } s, \text{ all } j \neq v \text{ or } t, \tag{38}
$$

were the maximum output in all other marriages, M_u would marry F_v. This process can be continued through the $\hat{Z}_3, \ldots, \hat{Z}_n$ until all the M and F are sorted.

How does this sorting, which combines the various maxima, compare with that obtained earlier, which maximizes total output? As the example in (17) indicates, they are not necessarily the same: combining the maxima in that example sorts M_2 with F_1 and M_1 with F_2, whereas maximizing total output sorts M_1 with F_1 and M_2 with F_2. Yet, in perhaps the most realistic cases, they are the same, which means that the sum of the maxima would equal the maximum of the sums.

Assume that an increase in trait A_m or A_f always increases output and that M and F are numbered from lower to higher values of these traits. Then, $\hat{Z}_1$ is the output of M_n with F_n, $\hat{Z}_2$ is that of M_{n-1} with F_{n-1}, and $\hat{Z}_n$ that of M_1 with F_1. Consequently, when traits have monotonic effects on output, the most common situation, combining the various maxima implies perfectly positive assortive mating.

I showed earlier that, in a wide variety of situations, namely, where traits are "complementary," maximizing total output also implies perfectly positive assortive mating. In these situations, permitting the market to determine the division of output and imposing the division a priori gives exactly the same sorting. Therefore, the implication of the theory about the importance of positive assortive mating is not weakened, but rather strengthened, by a radical change in assumptions about the determinants of the division of output.

When maximizing total output implies negative assortive mating, as it does between wage rates (with nonmarket productivity held constant), and between own-time augmenting traits that are close substitutes, these assumptions about the division of output have different implications. The

[49] Clearly, $e_sZ_{st} > e_sZ_{sj}$, all $j \neq t$, and $d_tZ_{st} > d_tZ_{it}$, all $i \neq s$ by condition (37).

empirical evidence on sortings cannot yet clearly choose between these assumptions, however, because positive sortings are so common: perhaps the positive correlation between observed wage rates is evidence of rigidities in the division, but several alternative interpretations of this correlation have been suggested that are consistent with a negative "true" correlation, and some psychological traits are apparently negatively correlated. Moreover, dowries and other capital transfers provide more effective fluidity in the division than may appear to the casual observer.

4. The Division of Output between Mates

With complete negotiability the division of output is given by condition (15) and (16). The m_{ii} and f_{ii} are determined by their marginal productivity in the sense that if $Z_{ki} > Z_{kk}$, necessarily $f_{ii} > f_{kk}$,[50] and similarly for the m_{ii}. Also, if $f_{ii} > f_{kk}$, necessarily $Z_{ii} > Z_{ik}$.[51] The following limits are easily derived:

$$\left. \begin{array}{l} Z_{ii} - \text{Max}_k \, (Z_{ki} - Z_{kk}) \geq m_{ii} \geq \text{Max}_k \, (Z_{ik} - Z_{kk}) \\ Z_{ii} - \text{Max}_k \, (Z_{ik} - Z_{kk}) \geq f_{ii} \geq \text{Max}_k \, (Z_{ki} - Z_{kk}) \end{array} \right\} . [52] \qquad (39)$$

The division of output resulting from conditions (15) and (16) is not unique, however. For if a set of m_{ii} and f_{ii} satisfies these conditions with all $0 < m_{ii} < Z_{ii}$, a positive quantity λ exists, such that $m_{ii} + \lambda$ and $f_{ii} - \lambda$ also satisfy these conditions. The range of indeterminacy in the division would narrow as the sum of $\text{Max}_k \, (Z_{ik} - Z_{kk})$ and $\text{Max}_k \, (Z_{ki} - Z_{kk})$ approached closer to Z_{ii}.

Clearly, the indeterminacy would vanish if the distribution of Z_{ik} became continuous. It could also vanish in a second case to which I turn. Assume v_i identical M_i and u_i identical F_i; by identical is meant that they would produce the same output with any mate or while single, so that they would receive the same income in market equilibrium. If the number of v_i were sufficiently large for a competitive equilibrium, there would be a supply curve of M_i to the marriage market: it would be horizontal at the singles income Z_{io} until all v_i^o were married, and then would rise vertically (see S_o in fig. 1). Similarly, if the number of u_i were sufficiently large, there would be a market supply curve of F_i: it would be horizontal at Z_{oi} until all u_i^o were married, and then would rise vertically. If initially I assume, for simplicity, that the M_i and F_i either marry each other or remain single, the supply curve of F_i would

---

[50] Since $f_{kk} + m_{kk} = z_{kk}$, all k, and $f_{ii} + m_{kk} \geq z_{ki}$, all i and k, then $f_{ii} - f_{kk} \geq z_{ki} - z_{kk} > 0$ by assumption.

[51] That is, if $f_{ii} > f_{kk}$, then $Z_{ii} = m_{ii} + f_{ii} > m_{ii} + f_{kk} \geq Z_{ik}$.

[52] Given conditions (15) and (16), $m_{ii} - m_{kk} \geq Z_{ik} - Z_{kk}$, all k, or, since $m_{kk} \geq 0$, $m_{ii} \geq Z_{ik} - Z_{kk}$, all k. The other conditions in (39) can be proved in a similar way.

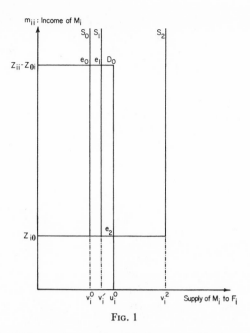

Fig. 1

also be a derived demand curve for M_i that would be horizontal at Z_{ii} − Z_{oi} until all $u_i{}^o$ were married, and then would fall vertically (D_o in fig. 1); moreover, the supply curve of M_i to the market would be its supply curve to F_i.

The equilibrium income to each M_i is given by point e_o, the intersection of S_o and D_o. If the sex ratio $(v_i{}^o/u_i{}^o)$ were less than unity, the equilibrium position is necessarily on the horizontal section of the derived demand curve, as is e_o. All the M_i would marry and receive the whole difference between their married output and the singles output of F_i. All the F_i would receive their singles output and, therefore, would be indifferent between marrying and remaining single, although market forces would encourage $v_i{}^o$ of them to marry.

An increase in the sex ratio due to an increase in the number of M_i would lengthen the horizontal section of the supply curve and shift the equilibrium position to the right, say, to e_1. All the M_i would continue to marry and a larger fraction of the F_i also would. If the sex ratio rose above unity, equilibrium would be on the horizontal section of the supply rather than the derived demand curve (see e_2). Now all the F_i would marry and receive the whole difference between their married output and the singles output of M_i; market forces would induce $u_i{}^o$ of the M_i to marry, and $v_i{}^2 − u_i{}^o$ to remain single.

The importance of sex ratios in determining the fraction of men and women who marry has been verified by numerous episodes and in several studies. An aftermath of a destructive war is many unmarried young women pursuing the relatively few men available, and men usually either marry late or not at all in rural areas that have lost many young women to cities. Statistical studies indicate that the fraction of women currently married at different ages is positively related to the appropriate sex ratio.[53]

I know of only highly impressionistic evidence on the effects of the sex ratio, or for that matter any other variable, on the division of output between mates. This division usually has not been assumed to be responsive to market forces, so that no effort has been put into collecting relevant evidence. Admittedly, it is difficult to separate expenditures of goods and time into those that benefit the husband, the wife, or both, but with enough will something useful could be done. For example, the information giving the separate expenditures on husband's and wife's clothing in some consumer surveys, or on the "leisure" time of husbands and wives in some time budget studies could be related to sex ratios, wage rates, education levels, and other relevant determinants of the division of output.

If I drop the assumption that all the M_i and F_i must either marry each other or remain single, M_i's supply curve to F_i would differ from its market supply curve because marriage to other persons would be substituted for marriage to F_i; similarly, F_i's supply curve to M_i would differ from its market supply curve. To demonstrate this, suppose that, at point e_o in figure 1, M_i does better by marrying F_i than by marrying anyone else; that is, condition (16) is a strict inequality for M_i. If M_i's income from marrying F_i were less than at e_o, the difference between the sum of M_i's income and that of other $F_j \neq F_i$, and what they could produce together would be reduced. At some income, this difference might be eliminated for an F, say, F_k: then all the M_i would be indifferent between marrying F_i and F_k.

At lower values of M_i's income from marrying F_i, some of the M_i would try to marry F_k. The increase in the supply of mates to F_k would raise M_i's income and reduce that of M_i's mates. In equilibrium, just enough M_i would marry F_k to maintain equality between the income M_i receives with F_i and F_k. The important point is that if some M_i marry F_k, the number marrying F_i would be less than the number supplied to the marriage market (v_i). Moreover, the number marrying F_i might fall still further as M_i's income with F_i fell further because some might marry, say, F_p, if they could then do as well with F_p as with F_i or F_k.

The net effect of these substitutions toward other F is a rising supply curve of M_i to F_i, shown by S_o in figure 2, with an elasticity determined both by the distribution of substitute F and by the effect on the income of

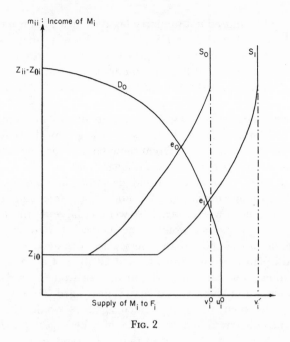

$$\text{F{\scriptsize IG}. 2}$$

these F of a given increase in the number of M_i available to marry them. Since F_i would also substitute toward other M, its derived demand curve for M_i would also fall, as D_o does in figure 2. The equilibrium position e_o determines both the division of output between M_i and F_i and the number marrying each other. The difference between the total number of M_i, $v_i{}^o$, and the number marrying F_i no longer measures the number of M_i remaining single, since at e_o all M_i marry, but rather it measures the number marrying other F and receiving the same income as the M_i marrying F_i; similarly, for the F_i.

An increase in the number of M_i from $v_i{}^o$ to v'_i would shift their supply curve to F_i to the right and lower the equilibrium position to e_1 in figure 2. The reduction in M_i's income (equal to the increase in F_i's income) is negatively related to the elasticities of the demand and supply curves, which are determined by the availability of substitute M and F. The additional M_i all marry, some to F_i and some to other F; a larger fraction of the F_i are induced to marry M_i by the increase in F_i's income.

An increase in the sex ratio between M_i and F_i would not necessarily increase the fraction of F_i or decrease the fraction of M_i who marry since all can marry if some marry other F or M. However, if all F_i and M_i married, an increase in their sex ratio would tend to decrease the number of other M or increase the number of other F who marry, if the quantity of other M and F were fixed. For an increase in the ratio of M_i to F_i not only lowers M_i's and raises F_i's income, but also lowers the incomes of substitute M and raises those of substitute F. Some of these M

would thereby be induced not to marry because their gain from marriage would be eliminated, and some F would be induced to marry because a gain from marriage would be created. Consequently, an increase in the ratio of M_i to F_i would still decrease the fraction of M and increase the fraction of F marrying, if substitute M and F as well as M_i and F_i were considered.

To illustrate these effects, assume an autonomous increase (perhaps due to selective immigration) in the size of a group of identical men, aged 24, who initially were indifferent between marrying women aged 22 and those slightly older or younger, although most married 22-year-olds. The increase in their numbers would decrease their income and the proportion marrying women aged 22. For if the percentage increase in the number marrying women aged 22 were as large as the increase in the number marrying other women, the income of those marrying 22-year-olds would fall by more than others, since men aged 24 are a larger fraction of all men marrying women aged 22 than of all men marrying women of other ages. Moreover, the income of women aged 22 would increase and more of them would marry men aged 24; the income of older or younger men marrying women aged 22 would fall and they would be encouraged to marry women of other ages; the income of women somewhat older or younger than 22 would increase too, and so on.[54]

5. Summary

In Part I above I have offered a simplified model of marriage that relies on two basic assumptions: (1) each person tries to find a mate who maximizes his or her well-being, with well-being measured by the consumption of household-produced commodities; and (2) the "marriage market" is assumed to be in equilibrium, in the sense that no person could change mates and become better off. I have argued that the gain from marriage compared to remaining single for any two persons is positively related to their incomes, the relative difference in their wage rates, and the level of nonmarket-productivity-augmenting variables, such as education or beauty. For example, the gain to a man and woman from marrying compared to remaining single is shown to depend positively on their incomes, human capital, and relative difference in wage rate.

The theory also implies that men differing in physical capital, education or intelligence (aside from their effects on wage rates), height, race, or many other traits will tend to marry women with like values of these traits, whereas the correlation between mates for wage rates or for traits of men and women that are close substitutes in household production will tend to be negative.

[54] The permanence of these effects depends on whether the immigration continues or is once and for all.

My theory does not take the division of output between mates as given, but rather derives it from the nature of the marriage market equilibrium. The division is determined here, as in other markets, by marginal productivities, and these are affected by the human and physical capital of different persons, by sex ratios, that is, the relative numbers of men and women, and by some other variables.

II

1. Introduction

In the discussion which follows I extend the simplified analyses in Part I in several directions. My purpose is both to enrich the analysis in Part I and to show the power of this approach in handling different kinds of marital behavior.

The effect of "love" and caring between mates on the nature of equilibrium in the marriage market is considered. Polygamy is discussed, and especially the relation between its incidence and the degree of inequality among men and the inequality in the number of men and women. The implications of different sorting patterns for inequality in family resources and genetic natural selection are explored. The assumption of complete information about all potential mates is dropped and I consider the search for information through dating, coeducational schools, "trial" marriages, and other ways. This search is put in a life-cycle context that includes marriage, having children, sometimes separation and divorce, remarriage, and so forth.

2. Love, Caring, and Marriage

In Part I, I ignored "love," that cause of marriage glorified in the American culture. At an abstract level, love and other emotional attachments, such as sexual activity or frequent close contact with a particular person, can be considered particular nonmarketable household commodities, and nothing much need be added to the analysis, in Part I, of the demand for commodities. That is, if an important set of commodities produced by households results from "love," the sorting of mates that maximizes total commodity output over all marriages is partly determined by the sorting that maximizes the output of these commodities. The whole discussion in Part I would continue to be relevant.

There is a considerable literature on the effect of different variables such as personality, physical appearance, education, or intelligence, on the likelihood of different persons loving each other. Since I do not have anything to add to the explanation of whether or why one person would love another, my discussion concentrates on some effects of love on marriage. In particular, since loving someone usually involves caring about what happens to him or her,[55] I concentrate on working out several implications, for marriage, of "caring."

An inclusive measure of "what happens" is given by the level of commodity consumption, and the natural way for an economist to measure "caring" is through the utility function.[56] That is, if M cares about F, M's utility would depend on the commodity consumption of F as well as on his own; graphically, M's indifference curves in figure 3 are negatively inclined with respect to Z_m and Z_f, the commodities consumed by M and F respectively.[57] If M cared as much about F as about himself (I call this "full" caring), the slopes of all the indifference curves would equal unity (in absolute value) along the 45° line;[58] if he cared more about himself, the slopes would exceed unity, and conversely if he cared more about F.

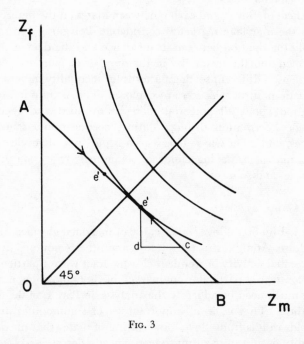

Fig. 3

[55] The *Random House Dictionary of the English Language* includes in its definitions of love, "affectionate concern for the well-being of others," and "the profoundly tender or passionate affection for a person of the opposite sex."

[56] This formulation is taken from my paper, "A Theory of Social Interactions" (1969).

[57] Since there is only a single aggregate commodity, saying that M's utility depends on F's consumption is equivalent to saying that M's utility depends on F's utility (assuming that F does not care about M). If many commodities $Z_1, \ldots, Z_q$, were consumed, M's utility would depend on F's utility if $U^m = U^m[Z_{1m}, \ldots, Z_{qm}, g(Z_{1f}, \ldots, Z_{qf})]$ where g describes the indifference surface of F. Hence $(\partial U^m / \partial Z_{if})/(\partial U^m / \partial Z_{jf}) = (\partial g / \partial Z_{if})/(\partial g / \partial Z_{jf})$; this ratio is F's marginal rate of substitution between Z_i and Z_j.

[58] "Full" caring might also imply that the indifference curves were straight lines with a slope of unity, that Z_f was a perfect substitute for Z_m.

Point c in figure 3 represents the allocation of commodities to M and F that is determined by equilibrium in the marriage market. Only if M were married to F could he transfer commodities to F, since household commodities are transferable within but not between households. If the terms of transfer are measured by the line AB, he moves along AB to point e: he transfers cd and F receives de. Presumably commodities can be transferred within a household without loss, so that AB would have a slope of unity. Then the equilibrium position after the transfer would be on the 45° line with full caring, and to the right of this line if M preferred his own consumption to F's.

Most people no doubt find the concept of a market allocation of commodities to beloved mates strange and unrealistic. And, as I have shown, caring can strikingly modify the market allocation between married persons. For example, the final allocation (point e) after the transfer from M to F has more equal shares than does the market allocation (point c).[59] Moreover, if F also cared about M, she would modify the market allocation by transferring resources to M from anywhere in the interval Ae' until she reached a point e',[60] generally to the left of e. The market completely determines the division of output only in the interval $e'e$: positions in Be are modified to e, and those in Ae' are modified to e'. Furthermore, if each fully cares for the other, points e and e' are identical and on the 45° line. Then the total amount produced by M and F would be shared equally, regardless of the market-determined division. This concept of caring between married persons, therefore, does imply sharing—equal sharing when the caring is full and mutual—and is thus consistent with the popular belief that persons in love "share."

Sharing implies that changes in the sex ratio or other variables considered in section 4 of Part I would not modify the actual distribution of output between married M and F (unless the market-mandated distribution were in the interval ee'). This is another empirical implication of caring that can be used to determine its importance.

I indicated earlier that total income would be less than total output in a marriage if resources were spent "policing" the market-mandated division of output, whereas total income would exceed total output if some output were a "family" commodity, that is, were consumed by both mates. Caring raises total income relative to total output both by reducing policing costs and by increasing the importance of family commodities.

Consider first the effect of caring on policing costs. "Policing" reduces the probability that a mate shirks duties or appropriates more output than is mandated by the equilibrium in the marriage market.[61] Caring reduces

[59] Provided it were in the interval Ae, M would not modify the market allocation.

[60] I assume that AB also gives the terms of transfer for F, and that e' is the point of tangency between AB and her indifference curves.

[61] Policing is necessary in any partnership or corporation, or, more generally, in any cooperative activity (see Becker 1971b, pp. 122–23; Alchian and Demsetz 1972).

the need for policing: M's incentive to "steal" from his mate F is weaker if M cares about F because a reduction in F's consumption also lowers M's utility. Indeed, caring often completely eliminates the incentive to "steal" and thus the need to police. Thus, at point e in the figure, M has no incentive to "steal" from F because a movement to the right along AB would lower M's utility.[62] Therefore, if M cares about F sufficiently to transfer commodities to her, F would not need to "police" M's consumption.[63] Consequently, marriages with caring would have fewer resources spent on "policing" (via allowances or separate checking accounts?) than other marriages would.

M's income at e exceeds his own consumption because of the utility he gets from F's consumption. Indeed, his income is the sum of his and F's consumption, and equals OB (or OA), the output produced by M and F. Similarly, F's income exceeds her own consumption if she benefits from M's consumption.[64] Caring makes family income greater than family output because some output is jointly consumed. At point e, all of F's and part of M's consumption would be jointly consumed. Since both e and e' are on the 45° line with mutual and full caring, the combined incomes of M and F would then be double their combined output: all of M's and all of F's consumption would be jointly consumed.

Love and caring between two persons increase their chances of being married to each other in the optimal sorting. That love and caring cannot reduce these chances can be seen by assuming that they would be married to each other in the optimal sorting even if they did not love and care for each other. Then they must also be married to each other in the optimal sorting if they do love and care for each other because love raises commodity output and caring raises their total income by making part of their output a "family" commodity. Hence, their incomes when there is love and caring exceed their incomes when there is not. Consider the following matrix of outputs:

$$
\begin{array}{c}
 & \begin{array}{cc} F_1 & \quad F_2 \end{array} \\
\begin{array}{c} M_1 \\ \\ M_2 \\ \\ \end{array} &
\left[\begin{array}{cc}
8 & 4 \\
(3, 5) & \\
9 & 7 \\
 & (5, 2)
\end{array} \right].
\end{array}
\tag{1}
$$

---

[62] A fortiori, a movement along any steeper line—the difference between AB and this line measuring the resources used up in "stealing"—would also lower M's utility.

[63] With mutual and full caring, neither mate would have to "police." On the other hand, if each cared more about the other than about himself (or herself), at least one of them, say M, would want to transfer resources that would not be accepted. Then F would "police" to prevent undesired *transfers from* M. This illustrates a rather general principle; namely, that when the degree of caring becomes sufficiently great, behavior becomes similar to that when there is no caring.

[64] F's income equals the sum of her consumption and a fraction of M's consumption that is determined by the slope of F's indifference curve at point e. See the formulation in section 1 of the Mathematical Appendix.

With no caring, this is also the matrix of total incomes,[65] and M_1F_1 and M_2F_2 would be the optimal sorting if incomes were sufficiently divisible to obtain, say, the division given in parenthesis. With mutual and full caring between M_1 and F_1, m'_{11}, the income of M_1, would equal $8 > 3$, and f'_{11}, the income of F_1, would equal $8 > 5$;[66] clearly, M_1 would still be married to F_1 in the optimal sorting.

That love and caring can bring a couple into the optimal sorting is shown by the following matrix of outputs:

$$
\begin{array}{c}
 \\
M_1 \\
 \\
M_2 \\
 \\
M_3 \\
\end{array}
\begin{array}{ccc}
F_1 & F_2 & F_3 \\
\begin{bmatrix} 10 \\ (4,6) \\ 9 \\ \\ 2 \end{bmatrix} & \begin{matrix} 6 \\ \\ 10 \\ (6,4) \\ 3 \end{matrix} & \begin{matrix} 5 \\ \\ 4 \\ \\ 10 \\ (5,5) \end{matrix}
\end{array}. \qquad (2)
$$

Without love and caring the optimal sorting is M_1F_1, M_2F_2, and M_3F_3, with a set of optimal incomes given in parenthesis. If, however, M_1 and F_2 were in love and had mutual and full caring, the optimal sorting would become M_1F_2, M_2F_1, and M_3F_3 because the incomes resulting from this sorting, $m_{12} = f_{21} = k > 6$,[67] and, say, $m_{21} = f_{21} = 4\frac{1}{2}$, and $m_{33} = f_{33} = 5$, can block the sorting along the diagonal.

Does caring per se—that is, as distinguished from love—encourage marriage: for example, couldn't M_1 marry F_1 even though he receives utility from F_2's consumption, and even if he wants to transfer resources to F_2? One incentive to combine marriage and caring is that resources are more cheaply transferred within households: by assumption, commodities cannot be transferred between households, and goods and time presumably also are more readily transferred within households. Moreover, caring partly results from living together,[68] and some couples marry partly because they anticipate the effect of living together on their caring.

Since, therefore, caring does encourage (and is encouraged by) marriage, there is a justification for the economist's usual assumption that even a multiperson household has a single well-ordered preference function. For, if one member of a household—the "head"—cares enough about all other members to transfer resources to them, this household would act *as if* it maximized the "head's" preference function, even if the preferences of other members are quite different.[69]

[65] I abstract from other kinds of "family" commodities because they can be analyzed in exactly the same way that caring is.

[66] The output of love raises these incomes even further.

[67] The difference between k and 6 measures the output of love produced by M_1 and F_2.

[68] So does negative caring or "hatred." A significant fraction of all murders and assaults involve members of the same household (see Ehrlich 1970).

[69] For a proof, see section 1, Part II of the Appendix; further discussions can be found in Becker (1969).

Output is generally less divisible between mates in marriages with caring than in other marriages[70] because caring makes some output a family commodity, which cannot be divided between mates. One implication of this is that marriages with caring are less likely to be part of the optimal sorting than marriages without caring that have the same total *income* (and thus have a greater total output).[71]

Another implication is that the optimal sorting of different traits can be significantly affected by caring, even if the degree of caring and the value of a trait are unrelated. Part I shows that when the division of output is so restricted that each mate receives a given fraction of the output of his or her marriage, beneficial traits are always strongly positively correlated in the optimal sorting. A negative correlation, on the other hand, is sometimes optimal when output is fully divisible. Caring could convert what would be an optimal negative correlation into an optimal positive one because of the restrictions it imposes on the division of output.

For example, assume that a group of men and women differ only in wage rates, and that *each* potential marriage has mutual and full caring, so that the degree of caring is in this case uncorrelated with the level of wage rates; then the optimal correlation between wage rates would be positive, although I showed in Part I that it is negative when there is no caring.[72] The (small amount of) evidence presented there indicating that wage rates are negatively correlated suggests, therefore, that caring does not completely determine the choice of marriage mates.

3. Polygamy

Although monogamous unions predominate in the world today, some societies still practice polygamy, and it was common at one time. What determines the incidence of polygamous unions in societies that permit them, and why have they declined in importance over time?

I argued in Part I that polyandrists—women with several husbands—have been much less common than polygynists—men with several wives—because the father's identity is doubtful under polyandry. Todas of India did practice polyandry, but their ratio of men to women was much above

[70] See the proof in section 2, Part II of the Appendix.

[71] See the example discussed in section 2, Part II of the Appendix.

[72] As an example, let the matrix of outputs from different combinations of wage rates be

$$
\begin{array}{c}
 & \begin{array}{cc} F_{w_1} & \quad F_{w_2} \end{array} \\
\begin{array}{c} M_{w_1} \\[6pt] M_{w_2} \end{array} &
\left[
\begin{array}{cc}
5 & 10 \\
(5, 5) & (10, 10) \\
12 & 15 \\
(12, 12) & (15, 15)
\end{array}
\right].
\end{array}
$$

If outputs were fully divisible, the optimal sorting would be $M_{w_1}F_{w_2}$ and $M_{w_2}F_{w_1}$, since that maximizes the combined output over all marriages. With mutual and full caring in all marriages, the income of each mate equals the output in his or her marriage; these incomes are given in parenthesis. Clearly, the optimal sorting would now be $M_{w_2}F_{w_2}$ and $M_{w_1}F_{w_1}$.

one, largely due to female infanticide.[73] They mitigated the effects of uncertainty about the father by usually having brothers (or other close relatives) marry the same woman.

I showed in Part I that if all men and all women were identical, if the number of men equaled the number of women, and if there were diminishing returns from adding an additional spouse to a household, then a monogamous sorting would be optimal, and therefore would maximize the total output of commodities over all marriages.[74] If the plausible assumption of diminishing returns is maintained, inequality in various traits among men or in the number of men and women would be needed to explain polygyny.

An excess of women over men has often encouraged the spread of polygyny, with the most obvious examples resulting from wartime deaths of men. Thus, almost all the male population in Paraguay were killed during a war with Argentina, Brazil, and Uruguay in the nineteenth century,[75] and apparently polygyny spread afterward.

Yet, polygyny has occurred even without an excess of women; indeed, the Mormons practiced polygyny on a sizable scale with a slight excess of men.[76] Then inequality among men is crucial.

If the "productivity" of men differs, a polygynous sorting could be optimal, even with constant returns to scale and an equal number of men and women. Total output over all marriages could be greater if a second wife to an able man added more to output than she would add as a first wife to a less able one. Diminishing marginal products of men or women within each household do not rule out that a woman could have a higher marginal product as a second wife in a more productive household than as the sole wife in a less productive household.

Consider, for example, two identical women who would produce 5 units of output if single, and two different men who would each produce 8 and 15 units, respectively, if single. Let the married outputs be 14 and 27 when each man has one wife, and 18 and 35 when each has two.[77] Clearly, total output is greater if the abler man takes two wives and the other remains single than if they both take one wife: $35 + 8 = 43 > 14 +$

[73] See Rivers (1906). Whether the infanticide caused polyandry, or the reverse, is not clear.

[74] An optimal sorting has the property that persons not married to each other could not, by marrying, make some better off without making others worse off. I show in Part 1 (1973) that an optimal sorting maximizes total output of commodities.

[75] After the war, males were only 13 percent of the total population of Paraguay (see *Encyclopaedia Britannica*, 1973 ed., s.v. "Paraguay"). I owe this reference to T. W. Schultz.

[76] See Young (1954, p. 124). The *effective* number of women can exceed the number of men, even with an equal number at each age, if women marry earlier than men and if widowed women remarry. The number of women married at any time would exceed the number of men married because women would be married longer (to different men— they would be sequentially polyandrous!). This apparently was important in Sub-Saharan Africa, where polygyny was common (see Dorjahn 1959).

[77] These numbers imply diminishing marginal products, since $18 - 14 = 4 < 6$, and $35 - 27 = 8 < 12$.

$27 = 41$. If the abler man received, say, 21 units and each wife received, say, 7 units, no one would have any incentive to change mates.

My analysis implies generally that polygyny would be more frequent among more productive men—such as those with large farms, high positions, and great strength—an implication strongly supported by the evidence on polygyny. For example, only about 10–20 percent of the Mormons had more than one wife,[78] and they were the more successful and prominent ones. Although 40 percent of the married men in a sample of the Xavante Indians of Brazil were polygynous, "it was the chief and the heads of clans who enjoyed the highest degree of polygyny" (Salzano, Neel, and Maybury-Lewis 1967, p. 473). About 35 percent of the married men in Sub-Saharan Africa were polygynous (Dorjahn 1959, pp. 98–105), and they were generally the wealthier men. Fewer than 10 percent of the married men in Arab countries were polygynous, and they were the more successful, especially in agriculture (Goode 1963, pp. 101–4).

I do not have a satisfactory explanation of why polygyny has declined over time in those parts of the world where it was once more common.[79] The declines in income inequality and the importance of agriculture presumably have been partly responsible. Perhaps the sex ratio has become less favorable, but that seems unlikely, wartime destruction aside. Perhaps monogamous societies have superior genetic and even cultural natural selection (see the next section). But since more successful men are more likely to be polygynous, they are more likely to have relatively many children.[80] If the factors responsible for success are "inherited," selection over time toward the "abler" might be stronger in polygynous than in monogamous societies. I have even heard the argument that Mormons are unusually successful in the United States because of their polygynous past! However, if the wives of polygynous males were not as able, on the average, as the wives of equally able monogamous males, selection could be less favorable in polygynous societies.

The decline in polygyny is usually "explained" by religious and legislative strictures against polygyny that are supposedly motivated by a desire to prevent the exploitation of women. But the laws that prevent men from taking more than one wife no more benefit women than the

---

[78] Young (1954, p. 441) says that "in some communities it ran as high as 20–25 percent of the male heads of families," but Arrington (1958, p. 238) says about 10 percent of all Mormon families were polygynous.

[79] Polygyny was more common in Islamic and African societies than in Western and Asian ones, although in China and Japan concubines had some of the rights and obligations of wives (see Goode 1963, chap. 5).

[80] Salzano, Neel, and Maybury-Lewis (1967, p. 486) found evidence among the Xavante Indians of "similar means but significantly greater variance for number of surviving offspring for males whose reproduction is completed than for similar females." This indicates that polygynous males (the more successful ones) have more children than other males.

laws in South Africa that restrict the ratio of black to white workers (see Wilson 1972, p. 8) benefit blacks. Surely, laws against polygyny reduce the "demand" for women, and thereby reduce their share of total household output and increase the share of men.[81]

4. Assortive Mating, Inequality, and Natural Selection

I pointed out in Part I that positive assortive mating of different traits reduces the variation in these traits between children in the same family (and this is one benefit of such mating). Positive assortive mating also, however, increases the inequality in traits, and thus in commodity income, between families. Note that the effects on inequality in commodity and money incomes may be very different; indeed, if wage rates, unlike most other traits, are negatively sorted (as argued in Part I), assortive mating would reduce the inequality in money earnings and increase that in commodity income.

Positive sorting of inherited traits, like intelligence, race, or height, also increases the inequality in these traits among children in different families, and increases the correlation between the traits of parents and children (see proofs in Cavalli-Sforza and Bodmer [1971, chap. 9]). Moreover, positive sorting, even of noninherited traits such as education, often has the same effect because, for example, educated parents are effective producers of "education-readiness" in their children (see Leibowitz [1972] and the papers by her and Benham in this volume). The result is an increase in the correlation between the commodity incomes of parents and children, and thereby an increase in the inequality in commodity income among families spanning several generations. That is, positive assortive mating has primary responsibility for noncompeting groups and the general importance of the family in determining economic and social position that is so relevant for discussions of investment in human capital and occupational position.

Since positive assortive mating increases aggregate commodity income over all families, the level of and inequality in commodity income are affected in different ways. Probably outlawing polygyny has reduced the

---

[81] An alternative interpretation of the religious and legislative strictures against polygyny is that they are an early and major example of discrimination *against* women, of a similar mold to the restrictions on their employment in certain occupations, such as the priesthood, or on their ownership of property. This hypothesis has been well stated by (of all people!) George Bernard Shaw: "Polygamy when tried under modern democratic conditions as by the Mormons, is wrecked by the revolt of the mass of inferior men who are condemned to celibacy by it; for the maternal instinct leads a woman to prefer a tenth share in a first rate man to the exclusive possession of a third rate." See his "Maxims for Revolutionists" appended to *Man and Superman* (Shaw 1930, p. 220). Shaw was preoccupied with celibacy; he has three other maxims on celibacy, one being "any marriage system which condemns a majority of the population to celibacy will be violently wrecked on the pretext that it outrages morality" (1930, p. 220).

inequality in commodity income among men at the price of reducing aggregate commodity income. Perhaps other restrictions on mating patterns that reduce inequality would be tolerated, but that does not seem likely at present.

Since positive assortive mating increases the between-family variance, it increases the potential for genetic natural selection, by a well-known theorem in population genetics.[82] The actual amount of selection depends also on the inheritability of traits, and the relation between the levels of the traits of mates and the number of their surviving children (called "fitness" by geneticists). For example, given the degree of inheritability of intelligence, and a positive (or negative) relation between number of children and average intelligence of parents, the rate of increase (or decrease) per generation in the average intelligence of a population would be directly related to the degree of positive assortive mating by intelligence.

Moreover, the degree of assortive mating is not independent of inheritability or of the relation between number of children and parental traits. For example, the "cost" of higher-"quality" children may be lower to more-intelligent parents, and this affects the number (as well as quality) of children desired.[83] In a subsequent paper I expect to treat more systematically the interaction between the degree of assortive mating and other determinants of the direction and rate of genetic selection.

5. Life-Cycle Marital Patterns

To life-cycle dimensions of marital decisions—for instance, when to marry, how long to stay married, when to remarry if divorced or widowed, or how long to stay remarried—I have paid little attention so far. These are intriguing but difficult questions, and only the broad strokes of an analysis can be sketched at this time. A separate paper in the not-too-distant future will develop a more detailed empirical as well as theoretical analysis.

A convenient, if artificial, way to categorize the decision to marry is to say that a person first decides when to enter the marriage market and then searches for an appropriate mate.[84] The age of entry would be earlier

---

[82] This theorem was proved by Fisher (1958, pp. 37–38) and called "the fundamental theorem of natural selection." For a more recent and extensive discussion, see Cavalli-Sforza and Bodmer (1971, sec. 6.7).

[83] For a discussion of the interaction between the quantity and quality of children, see Becker and Lewis in this book.

[84] This categorization is made in an important paper by Coale and McNeil, "The Distribution by Age of the Frequency of First Marriage in a Female Cohort" (1972). They show that the frequency distribution of the age at first marriage can be closely fitted in a variety of environments by the convolution of a normal distribution and two or three exponential distributions. The normal distribution is said to represent the distribution of age at entry into the marriage market, and the exponential distributions, the time it takes to find a mate.

the larger the number of children desired, the higher the expected lifetime income, and the lower the level of education.[85]

Once in the marriage market, a person searches for a mate along the lines specified in the now rather extensive search literature.[86] That is, he searches until the value to him of any expected improvement in the mate he can find is no greater than the cost of his time and other inputs into additional search. Some determinants of benefits and costs are of special interest in the context of the marriage market.

Search will be longer the greater the benefits expected from additional search. Since benefits will be greater the longer the expected duration of marriage, people will search more carefully and marry later when they expect to be married longer, for example, when divorce is more difficult or adult death rates are lower. Search may take the form of trial living together, consensual unions, or simply prolonged dating. Consequently, when divorce becomes easier, the fraction of persons legally married may actually *increase* because of the effect on the age at marriage. Indeed, in Latin America, where divorce is usually impossible, a relatively small fraction of the adult population is legally married because consensual unions are so important (see Kogut 1972); and, in the United States, a smaller fraction of women have been married in those states having more-difficult divorce laws (see Freiden [1972] and his paper in this volume).[87]

Search would also be longer the more variable potential mates were because then the expected gain from additional "sampling" would be greater. Hence, other determinants being the same, marriage should generally be later in dynamic, mobile, and diversified societies than in static, homogeneous ones.

People marry relatively early when they are lucky in their search. They also marry early, however, when they are unduly pessimistic about their prospects of attracting someone better (or unduly optimistic about persons they have already met). Therefore, early marriages contain both lucky and pessimistic persons, while later marriages contain unlucky and optimistic ones.

The cost of search differs greatly for different traits: the education, income, intelligence, family background, perhaps even the health of persons can be ascertained relatively easily, but their ambition, resiliency under pressure, or potential for growth are ascertained with much greater difficulty.[88] The optimal allocation of search expenditures implies that marital decisions would be based on fuller information about more-easily searched traits than about more-difficult-to-search traits. Presumably,

[85] For a theoretical and empirical study of these and other variables, see Keeley (1974).

[86] The pioneering paper is by Stigler (1961). For more recent developments, see McCall (1970) and Mortensen (1970).

[87] These results are net of differences in income, relative wages, and the sex ratio.

[88] In the terminology of Nelson (1970), education, income, and intelligence are "search" traits, whereas resiliency and growth potential are "experience" traits.

therefore, an analysis of sorting that assumes perfect information (as in Part I) would predict the sorting by more-easily searched traits, such as education, better than the sorting by more-difficult-to-search traits, such as resiliency.[89]

Married persons also must make decisions about marriage: should they separate or divorce, and if they do, or if widowed, when, if ever, should they remarry? The incentive to separate is smaller the more important are investments that are "specific" to a particular marriage.[90] The most obvious and dominant example of marriage-specific investment is children, although knowledge of the habits and attitudes of one's mate is also significant. Since specific investments would grow, at least for quite a while, with the duration of marriage, the incentive to separate would tend to decline with duration.

The incentive to separate is greater, on the other hand, the more convinced a person becomes that the marriage was a "mistake." This conviction could result from additional information about one's mate or other potential mates. (Some "search" goes on, perhaps subconsciously, even while one is married!) If the "mistake" is considered large enough to outweigh the loss in marriage-specific capital, separation and perhaps divorce will follow.

The analysis in Part I predicts sorting patterns in a world with perfect information. Presumably, couples who deviate from these patterns because they were unlucky in their search are more likely than others to decide that they made a "mistake" and to separate as additional information is accumulated during marriage. If they remarry, they should deviate less from these patterns than in their first marriage. For example, couples with relatively large differences in education, intelligence, race, or religion, because they were unlucky searchers, should be more likely to separate,[91] and should have smaller differences when they remarry. Subsequently, I plan to develop more systematically the implications of this analysis concerning separation, divorce, and remarriage, and to test them with several bodies of data.

6. Summary

The findings of Part II include:

a) An explanation of why persons who care for each other are more likely to marry each other than are otherwise similar persons who do not.

---

[89] See the discussion in section 3, Part II of the Appendix.

[90] The distinction between general and specific investment is well known, and can be found in Becker (1964, chap. 11). Children, for example, would be a specific investment if the pleasure received by a parent were smaller when the parent was (permanently) separated from the children.

[91] If they have relatively large differences because they were less efficient searchers, they may be less likely to separate.

This in turn provides a justification for assuming that each family acts as if it maximizes a single utility function.

b) An explanation of why polygyny, when permitted, has been more common among successful men and, more generally, why inequality among men and differences in the number of men and women have been important in determining the incidence of polygyny.

c) An analysis of the relation between natural selection over time and assortative mating, which is relevant, among other things, for understanding the persistence over several generations of differences in incomes between different families.

d) An analysis of which marriages are more likely to terminate in separation and divorce, and of how the assortative mating of those re-marrying differs from the assortative mating in their first marriages.

The discussion in this paper is mainly a series of preliminary reports on more extensive studies in progress. The fuller studies will permit readers to gain a more accurate assessment of the value of our economic approach in understanding marital patterns.

Mathematical Appendix

I

1. Optimal Sorting[92]

Given a function $f(x,y)$, I first show that if $\partial^2 f/\partial x \partial y < 0$,

$$\frac{\partial[f(x_2, y) - f(x_1, y)]}{\partial y} \equiv \frac{\partial Q(x_2, x_1, y)}{\partial y} < 0 \qquad \text{for } x_1 < x_2. \qquad (A1)$$

Since $\partial Q/\partial y = (\partial f/\partial y)(x_2, y) - \partial f/\partial y(x_1, y)$, $\partial Q/\partial y = 0$ for $x_2 = x_1$. By assumption, $(\partial/\partial x_2)(\partial Q/\partial y) = (\partial^2 f/\partial x \partial y)(x_2, y) < 0$. Since $\partial Q/\partial y = 0$ for $x_2 = x_1$ and $\partial Q/\partial y$ decreases in x_2, $\partial Q/\partial y < 0$ for $x_2 > x_1$; hence (A1) is proved. It follows immediately from (A1) that if $y_2 > y_1$,

$$f(x_2, y_1) - f(x_1, y_1) > f(x_2, y_2) - f(x_1, y_2). \qquad (A2)$$

A similar proof shows that if $\partial^2 f/\partial x \partial y > 0$,

$$f(x_2, y_1) - f(x_1, y_1) < f(x_2, y_2) - f(x_1, y_2). \qquad (A3)$$

I now am prepared to prove the following theorem: Let $f(x,y)$ satisfy $\partial^2 f/\partial x \partial y > 0$. Suppose $x_1 < x_2 < \cdots < x_n$ and $y_1 < y_2 < \cdots < y_n$. Then,

$$\left. \begin{array}{c} \displaystyle\sum_{j=1}^{n} f(x_j, y_{i_j}) < \sum_{i=1}^{n} f(x_i, y_i) \\[2mm] \text{for all permutations} \\[2mm] (i_1, i_2, \ldots i_n) \neq (1, 2, \ldots n) \end{array} \right\} . \qquad (A4)$$

[92] I owe the proofs in this section to William Brock.

Assume the contrary; namely, that the maximizing sum is for a permutation $i_1 \cdots i_n$, not satisfying $i_1 < i_2 < \cdots < i_n$. Then there is (at least) one j_o with the property $i_{j_o} > i_{j_o+1}$. Therefore,

$$f(x_{j_o}, y_{i_{j_o}}) + f(x_{y_o+1}, y_{i_{j_o}+1}) < f(x_{j_o}, y_{i_{j_o}+1}) + f(x_{j_o+1}, y_{i_{j_o}}), \quad \text{(A5)}$$

by (A3) since $y_{i_{j_o}+1} < y_{i_{j_o}}$. But this contradicts the optimality of $i_1, \ldots i_n \cdot QED$.

A similar proof shows that if $\partial^2 f / \partial x \partial y < 0$, then

$$\left.\begin{aligned} \sum_{j=1}^{n} f(x_j, y_{i_j}) &< \sum_{i=1}^{n} f(x_i, y_{n+1-i}) \\[2mm] \text{for all permutations} & \\[2mm] (i_1, i_2, \ldots i_n) &\neq (n, n-1, \ldots, 1) \end{aligned}\right\} . \quad \text{(A6)}$$

2. Women Not in the Labor Force

If F did not participate in the labor force,

$$S = Tw_m + T\hat{w}_f + r(l_{pm}, l_{pf})(K_m + K_f) - l_{pm}w_m - l_{pf}\hat{w}_f, \quad \text{(A7)}$$

where $\hat{w}_f$, the "shadow" price of F, is greater than w_f, her market wage rate, unless F is at the margin of entering the labor force,[93] and l_{pm} and l_{pf} are the time allocated to portfolio management by M and F, respectively. If the production function for Z were homogeneous of the first degree in time and goods, $Z = S/C(p, w_m, \hat{w}_f, A_f, A_m)$.

Then,

$$\frac{\partial Z}{\partial K_i} = C^{-1}\left[r + K\left(\frac{\partial r}{\partial l_{pm}}\frac{\partial l_{pm}}{\partial K_i} + \frac{\partial r}{\partial l_{pf}}\frac{\partial l_{pf}}{\partial K_i}\right) - \frac{\partial l_{pm}}{\partial K_i}w_m - \frac{\partial l_{pf}}{\partial K_i}\hat{w}_f\right]$$

$$+ TC^{-1}\frac{d\hat{w}_f}{dK_i} - SC^{-2}C^f\frac{d\hat{w}_f}{dK_i} - C^{-1}l_{pf}\frac{\partial \hat{w}_f}{\partial K_i} \quad \text{(A8)}$$

$$= rC^{-1} > 0, \quad i = m \text{ or } f \quad \text{(A9)}$$

since $C^f = t_f Z^{-1} = (T - l_{pf})Z^{-1}$, $K_m + K_f = K$, and $\hat{w}_f = (\partial r/\partial l_{pf})K$ and $w_m = (\partial r/\partial l_{pm})K$ with an optimal allocation of time. Similarly,

$$\frac{\partial Z}{\partial w_m} = TC^{-1} + \frac{TC^{-1}d\hat{w}_f}{dw_m}$$

$$+ C^{-1}\left(\frac{\partial r}{\partial l_{pm}}\frac{\partial l_{pm}}{\partial w_m}K + \frac{\partial r}{\partial l_{pf}}\frac{\partial l_{pf}}{\partial w_m}K - l_{pm} - \frac{\partial l_{pm}w_m}{\partial w_m} - l_{pf}\frac{d\hat{w}_f}{dw_m} - \frac{\partial l_{pf}}{\partial w_m}\hat{w}_f\right)$$

$$- SC^{-2}C^m - SC^{-2}C^f\frac{\partial \hat{w}_f}{\partial w_m} = l_m C^{-1} > 0, \quad \text{(A10)}$$

and

$$\frac{\partial Z}{\partial A_i} = -SC^{-2}C_{a_i} + TC^{-1}\frac{\partial \hat{w}_f}{\partial A_i} - SC^{-2}C^{\hat{f}}\frac{\partial w_f}{\partial A_i} - l_{pf}\frac{\partial \hat{w}_f}{\partial A_i}$$

$$+ \text{ terms whose sum is zero}$$

$$= -SC^{-2}C_{a_i} > 0 \quad i = m \text{ or } f, \quad \text{(A11)}$$

---

[93] An earlier draft of this section developed the analysis using the shadow price of F, but contained some errors. I owe the present formulation to H. Gregg Lewis.

if A_i does not directly affect r. Note that equations (A9)–(A11) are exactly the same as those when F does participate—equations (24), (28), and (31).

Then,

$$\frac{\partial^2 Z}{\partial K_f \, \partial K_m} = C^{-1} \left| \frac{\partial r}{\partial l_{pm}} \frac{\partial l_{pm}}{\partial K_m} + \frac{\partial r}{\partial l_{pf}} \frac{\partial l_{pf}}{\partial K_m} \right| - rC^{-2}C^f \frac{\partial \hat{w}_f}{\partial K_m}. \qquad (A12)$$

The first term is positive, but the second one is negative since

$$\frac{\partial w_f}{\partial K_m} > 0, \qquad \frac{\partial \hat{w}_f}{\partial K_f} > 0, \qquad \left(\text{and } \frac{\partial \hat{w}_f}{\partial w_m} > 0 \right). \qquad (A13)$$

A proof of (A13) follows from the derived demand equation for t_f. Of course,

$$\frac{\partial^2 Z}{\partial w_m \, \partial w_f} = 0. \qquad (A14)$$

Moreover,

$$\frac{\partial^2 Z}{\partial K_m \, \partial A_f} = -rC^{-2}C_{a_f} - C^{-2}C^f \frac{\partial \hat{w}_f}{\partial A_f}. \qquad (A15)$$

The first term is necessarily positive and the second would be nonnegative if $\partial \hat{w}_f / \partial A_f \leq 0$. It can easily be shown that $\partial \hat{w}_f / \partial A_f = 0$ if A_f has a factor-neutral effect on output and $\partial \hat{w}_f / \partial A_f < 0$ if A_f is own-time augmenting. Consequently, there is some presumption that

$$\frac{\partial^2 Z}{\partial K_m \, \partial A_f} > 0. \qquad (A16)$$

The general expression for the cross-derivative of Z with respect to A_m and A_f can be found by differentiating equation (A11). I consider here only the case where the effects are factor-neutral, so that

$$Z = g(A_m, A_f)f(x, t_m, t_f), \qquad (A17)$$

or the optimal Z is $Z = gS/[K(p, w_m, \hat{w}_f)]$, with

$$g_i = \frac{\partial g}{\partial A_i} > 0, \qquad \text{and} \qquad g_{mf} = \frac{\partial^2 g}{\partial A_m \, \partial A_f} > 0. \qquad i = m, f. \qquad (A18)$$

By substituting into (A11),

$$\frac{\partial Z}{\partial A_i} = Z \frac{g_i}{g} > 0. \qquad (A19)$$

Therefore,

$$\frac{\partial^2 Z}{\partial A_m \, \partial A_f} = \frac{g_m}{g^2} g_f Z + \frac{g_{mf} Z}{g} - \frac{g_m g_f Z}{g^2} = \frac{g_{mf} Z}{g} > 0. \qquad (A20)$$

3. Own-Time-Augmenting Effects

By own-time augmenting is meant that the household production function can be written as $Z = f(x, t'_f, t'_m)$, where $t'_f = g_f(A_f)t_f$, and $t'_m = g_m(A_m)t_m$ are the time inputs of F and M in "efficiency" units, and

$$\frac{dg_f}{dA_f} = g'_f > 0, \qquad \text{and} \qquad \frac{dg_m}{dA_m} = g'_m > 0, \qquad (A21)$$

indicates that an increase in the trait raises the number of efficiency units. The optimal Z can be written as $Z = S/C(p, w'_m, w'_f)$, where $w'_m = w_m/g_m$ and $w'_f = w_f/g_f$ are wage rates in efficiency units. Therefore,

$$\frac{\partial Z}{\partial A_m} = -t'_m C^{-1} \frac{\partial w'_m}{\partial A_m} > 0, \tag{A22}$$

since $\partial w'_m/\partial A_m < 0$. Hence,

$$\frac{\partial^2 Z}{\partial A_m \, \partial A_f} = -\frac{\partial w'_m}{\partial A_m} C^{-1} \left(\frac{\partial t'_m}{\partial A_f} - \frac{\partial w'_f}{\partial A_f} t'_m t'_f S^{-1} \right) \tag{A23}$$

The term outside the parenthesis and the second term in it are positive. The first term in the parenthesis might well be negative,[94] but Gregg Lewis has shown in an unpublished memorandum that $\partial^2 Z/\partial A_m \, \partial A_f$ is necessarily positive if the elasticity of substitution between the time of M and F is less than 2.

4. Sorting by Income and Nonmarket Productivity

If M differed only in K_m and F only in A_f, and if all M and F participated in the labor force, $\partial Z/\partial K_m = rC^{-1} > 0$, and

$$\frac{\partial^2 Z}{\partial K_m \, \partial A_f} = -rC^{-2} C_{a_f} > 0 \qquad \text{since } C_{a_f} < 0. \tag{A24}$$

If M differed only in w_m, $\partial Z/\partial w_m = C^{-1} l_m > 0$, and

$$\frac{\partial^2 Z}{\partial w_m \, \partial A_f} = -C^{-2} C_{a_f} l_m + C^{-1} \frac{\partial l_m}{\partial A_f}. \tag{A25}$$

The first term on the right is positive, and the second would also be if $\partial l_m/\partial A_f \geq 0$, that is, if an increase in A_f does not reduce the time M spends in the market sector. Even if it does, the cross-derivative is still positive if the first term dominates. In particular, equation (A25) is necessarily positive if the effect of A_f is independent of the input of goods and time. For, if A_f were independent, $C = b(A_f)K(p, w_m, w_f)$. Since $l_m = (\partial C/\partial w_m) Z = (\partial K/\partial w_m)SK^{-1}$, then,

$$\frac{\partial l_m}{\partial A_f} = 0. \tag{A26}$$

II

1. Formally, M (or F) maximizes his utility function

$$U_m = U_m(Z_m, Z_f) \tag{A1}$$

subject to the constraints

$$\left. \begin{array}{l} Z^0_m - C_m = Z_m \\ Z^0_f + C_m = Z_f \\ C_m \geq 0 \end{array} \right\}, \tag{A2}$$

where Z^0_m and Z^0_f are the market allocations of output to M and F, and C_m is the amount transferred by M to F. If $C_m > 0$, these constraints can be reduced to a single income constraint by substitution from the Z_f into the Z_m equation:

[94] There is some evidence suggesting, e.g., that men with more educated wives generally work more hours (see Benham's paper in this book).

$$m_{mf} = Z_{mf} = Z_f^0 + Z_m^0 = Z_m + Z_f, \tag{A3}$$

where Z_{mf} is the output produced by M and F, and m_{mf} is M's income. Maximization of U_m subject to this single income constraint gives

$$\frac{\partial U_m}{\partial Z_m} = \frac{\partial U_m}{\partial Z_f}. \tag{A4}$$

If $C_m = 0$, U_m is maximized subject to the two constraints $Z_m^0 = Z_m$ and $Z_f^0 = Z_f$. The equilibrium conditions are $\partial U_m/\partial Z_m = \lambda_m$, $\partial U_m/\partial Z_f = \mu_m$, where λ_m and μ_m are the marginal utilities of additional Z_m^0 and Z_f^0, respectively. The income of M would then be

$$m_{mf} = Z_m^0 + (\mu_m/\lambda_m)Z_f^0, \tag{A5}$$

where μ_m/λ_m is the "shadow" price of Z_f to M in terms of Z_m.
    Since $\mu_m/\lambda_m < 1$ (otherwise $C_m > 0$),

$$Z_m^0 + \frac{\mu_m}{\lambda_m} Z_f^0 < Z_{mf} = Z_m^0 + Z_f^0. \tag{A6}$$

If $C_m > 0$, the "family" consisting of M and F would act as if it maximized the single "family" utility function U_m subject to the single family budget constraint given by (A3), even if F's utility function were quite different from U_m. In effect, transfers between members eliminate the conflict between different members' utility functions.
    2. Total income in a marriage between M and F is

$$m_{mf} + f_{mf} = I_{mf} = Z_{mf} + p_m Z_{mf}^f + p_f Z_{mf}^m,$$

where I_{mf} is the total income in the marriage, Z_{mf}^m and Z_{mf}^f are the outputs allocated to M and F, Z_{mf} ($= Z_{mf}^f + Z_{mf}^m$) is total output, p_m is the shadow price to M of a unit of Z_m^f, and p_f is a shadow price to F of a unit of Z_{mf}^m. Their incomes must be in the intervals

$$Z_{mf}^m + p_m Z_{mf}^f = m_{mf} \leq Z_{mf},$$
$$Z_{mf}^f + p_f Z_{mf}^m = f_{mf} \leq Z_{mf}. \tag{A7}$$

If $p_m = p_f = 0$—no caring—m_{mf} and f_{mf} can be anywhere between 0 and Z_{mf}. But if $p_m = p_f = 1$—mutual and full caring—then $m_{mf} = f_{mf} = Z_{mf}$. And, more generally, if p_m and $p_f > 0$, then

$$Z_{mf}^m < m_{mf} \leq Z_{mf} < I_{mf},$$
$$Z_{mf}^m < f_{mf} \leq Z_{mf} < I_{mf}. \tag{A8}$$

Consider the following matrix of total *incomes*:

$$
\begin{array}{c}
 \\
M_1 \\
 \\
M_2 \\
 \\
\end{array}
\begin{array}{cc}
F_1 & F_2 \\
\left[\begin{array}{cc}
8 & 8 \\
 & (4, 4) \\
7 & 7 \\
(3, 4) & \\
\end{array}\right]
\end{array}. \tag{A9}
$$

On the surface, both sortings are equally optimal, but this is not so if only M_1 and F_2 have a marriage with caring, say full and mutual, so that $m_{12} = f_{12} =$

4.[95] The sorting M_1F_2 and M_2F_1 is not as viable as the sorting M_1F_1 and M_2F_2 because income is more divisible between M_1 and F_1 than between M_1 and F_2.[96] For if, say, $m_{11} = 4\frac{1}{2}, f_{11} = 3\frac{1}{2}, m_{22} = 4\frac{1}{2}$, and $f_{22} = 2\frac{1}{2}$, no two persons have an incentive to change mates and marry each other.[97] On the other hand, since $m_{12} = f_{12} = 4$, unless $m_{21} = 3$ and $f_{21} = 4$, either M_1 and F_1, or M_2 and F_2 would be better off by marrying each other. If $m_{21} = 3$ and $f_{21} = 4$, M_1 and F_1, and M_2 and F_2 could be just as well off by marrying each other. Therefore, this sorting is not as viable as the sorting that does not have any marriages with caring.

3. Assume that the gain from marriage of a particular person M is positively related to the expected values of two traits of his mate, as in $m = g(A_1, A_2)$, with $\partial g/\partial A_i = g_i > 0, i = 1, 2$. If the marginal costs of search were c_1 and c_2 for A_1 and A_2, respectively, equilibrium requires that

$$\frac{g_1}{g_2} = \frac{c_1}{c_2}. \tag{A10}$$

The lower c_1 is relative to c_2, the higher generally would be the equilibrium value of A_1 relative to A_2, since convexity of the isogain curves is a necessary condition for an internal maximum.

If g_1 and g_2 were invariant when search costs changed to all participants in the marriage market, not an innocuous assumption, then A_1^{max} and A_2^{max} would be the equilibrium values of A_1 and A_2 to M when everyone had perfect information about all traits. A reduction in the cost of searching A_1, therefore, would move the equilibrium value of A_1 to M closer to A_1^{max}, its value with perfect information.

[95] The *output* between M_1 and F_2 also equals four, half that between M_1 and F_1.
[96] Or, put differently, the output between M_1 and F_1 exceeds that between M_1 and F_2.
[97] F_2 would prefer to marry M_1, but could not induce M_1 to do so because m_{12} cannot exceed four, the output produced by M_1 and F_2 (see eq. [A7]), which is less than $m_{11} = 4\frac{1}{2}$.

Part 7   Social Interactions

The two papers in this section consider the interaction
between persons that results from the attitudes they have
about one another. The first develops a general analysis of
these "social interactions" and then considers several
applications, especially the interaction among members of
the same family. It shows, among other things, why even
selfish family members sometimes have an incentive to act
as if they were altruistic toward each other.

This incentive to simulate altruism is called the
"rotten-kid theorem," and is used in the second paper to
explain why altruistic behavior can be biologically selected
over time. Altruistic behavior can actually increase instead
of decrease own consumption and own survival prospects.
Since altruism is more likely to increase them when it is
directed toward family members, altruism—real or
simulated—is more strongly selected biologically within a
family than across families.

12   A Theory of
Social Interactions

No man is an island
John Donne

Man is a social animal
Seneca

This essay uses simple tools of economic theory to analyze interactions between the behavior of some persons and different characteristics of other persons. Although these interactions are emphasized in the contemporary sociological and anthropological literature, and were considered the cornerstone of behavior by several prominent nineteenth-century economists, they have been largely ignored in the modern economic literature. The central concept of the analysis is "social income," the sum of a person's own income (his earnings, etc.) and the monetary value to him of the relevant characteristics of others, which I call his social environment. By using the concept of social income, I can analyze the effect on these expenditures of changes in different sources of income and in different prices, including the "price" of the social environment. Interactions among members of the same family receive the greatest attention. The "head" of a family is defined not by sex or age, but as that member, if there is one, who transfers general purchasing power to all other members because he cares about their welfare. A family with a head is a highly interdependent organization that has the following properties: A redistribution of income among members does not affect the consumption or welfare of any member because it simply induces offsetting changes in transfers from the head. Not only the head but other members too act "as if" they "loved" all members, even when they are really selfish, in the sense that they maximize not their own income alone but family income. Transfers from parents to children in the form, say, of schooling, gifts, and bequests tend to be negatively related to what the income of children would be relative to their parents in the absence of these transfers. Therefore, the relative income of children *inclusive* of transfers could be unrelated or

Reprinted from the *Journal of Political Economy* 82, no. 6 (1974): 1063–1091. © 1974 by The University of Chicago.

even negatively related to these transfers. Consequently, one cannot infer anything about the stability across generations of economic or social positions simply from knowing the relation between parental position and the amount transferred.

1. Introduction

Before the theory of consumer demand began to be formalized by Jevons, Walras, Marshall, Menger, and others, economists frequently discussed what they considered to be the basic determinants of wants. For example, Bentham (1789, chap. 5) discusses about 15 basic kinds of pleasures and pains—all other pleasures and pains are presumed to be combinations of the basic set—and Marshall (1962, bk. 3, chap. 2) briefly discusses a few basic determinants of wants before moving on to his well-known presentation of marginal utility theory. What is relevant and important for present purposes is the prominence given to the interactions among individuals.

Bentham mentions "the pleasures . . . of being on good terms with him or them," "the pleasures of a good name," "the pleasures resulting from the view of any pleasures supposed to be possessed by the beings who may be the objects of benevolence," and "the pleasures resulting from the view of any pain supposed to be suffered by the beings who may become the objects of malevolence." Nassau Senior said that "the desire for distinction . . . is a feeling which if we consider its universality, and its constancy, that it affects all men and at all times, that it comes with us from the cradle and never leaves us till we go into the grave, may be pronounced to be the most powerful of all human passions" (quoted by Marshall 1962, p. 87.) Marshall also stresses the desire for distinction and illustrates its influence by discussing food, clothing, housing, and productive activities.[1]

As greater rigor permeated the theory of consumer demand, variables like distinction, a good name, or benevolence were pushed further and further out of sight. Each individual or family generally is assumed to have a utility function that depends directly on the goods and services it con-

---

[1] He limits his discussion of consumer demand to the largely formal theory of marginal theory because of the importance he attaches to the interaction between activities, consumer behavior and the basic wants: "Such a discussion of demand as is possible at this stage of our work must be confined to an elementary analysis of an almost purely formal kind" (1962, p. 90). He never developed the more complicated and less formal analysis.

sumes. This is not to say that interactions between individuals have been completely ignored. Pigou (1903), Fisher (1926, p. 102), and Panteleoni (1898)[2] included attributes of others in utility functions (but did nothing with them). In recent literature, "demonstration" and relative income" effects on savings and consumption,[3] "bandwagon" and "snob" influences on ordinary consumption theory,[4] and the economics of philanthropic contributions[5] have been discussed. But these efforts have not been unified and, more significantly, have not captured the dominance attributed to social interactions by nineteenth-century economists.

Of course, sociologists have for a long time emphasized the central role of interactions and their importance in the basic structure of wants or personality. Veblen's conspicuous consumption and conspicuous leisure (if for this purpose he is classified as a sociologist) have entered ordinary discourse. At one point he said: "But it is only when taken in a sense far removed from its naive meaning that the consumption of goods can be said to afford the incentive from which accumulation invariably proceeds. The motive that lies at the root of ownership is emulation," and "the usual basis of self-respect is the respect accorded by one's neighbors" (Veblen 1934, pp. 25, 30). Interactions were also emphasized by Durkheim, Simmel, Freud, and Weber, as well as in modern discussions of "social exchange" and the "theory of action" (see Blau 1968; Parsons 1968).

My interest in interactions can probably be traced to a study of discrimination and "prejudice" where I analyzed discriminatory behavior by incorporating the race, religion, sex, or other personal characteristics of employees, fellow workers, customers, dealers, neighbors, etc., into utility functions (Becker 1971 [1st ed., 1957]). Subsequently, in order to provide a theoretical framework for a study of philanthropy by the National Bureau of Economic Research, I incorporated the standard of living of "poorer" persons into the utility functions of "richer" ones (Becker 1961). Further reflection gradually convinced me that the emphasis of earlier economists deserved to be taken much more seriously because social interactions had significance far transcending the special cases discussed by myself[6] and others.

---

[2] I owe this reference to George Stigler.
[3] See, e.g., Brady and Friedman (1947), Duesenbery (1949), or Johnson (1952).
[4] See Leibenstein (1950).
[5] See Vickery (1962), Schwartz (1970), Alchian and Allen (1967, pp. 135–42), and Boulding (1973).
[6] Other drafts that were also circulated include Becker (1968).

This essay incorporates a general treatment of interactions into the modern theory of consumer demand. In Section 2, various characteristics of different persons are assumed to affect the utility functions of some persons, and the behavioral implications are systematically explored. Section 3 develops further implications and applications in the context of analyzing intrafamily relations, charitable behavior, merit goods and multiperson interactions, and envy and hatred. The variety and significance of these applications is persuasive testimony not only to the importance of social interactions but also the feasibility of incorporating them into a rigorous analysis.

2. Theoretical Framework

A. *Equilibrium for a Single Person*

According to the modern (and very old!) theory of household behavior,[7]

$$U_i = U_i(Z_1, \ldots, Z_m) \qquad (2.1)$$

is the utility function of the ith person, and $Z_1, \ldots, Z_m$ are the basic wants or commodities. As indicated earlier, Bentham mentions about 15 basic wants, whereas Marshall and Senior stress an even smaller number. Each person also has a set of production functions that determine how much of these commodities can be produced with the market goods, time, and other resources available to him:

$$Z_j = f_j^i(x_j, t_j, E^i, R_j^1, \ldots, R_j^r), \qquad (2.2)$$

where x_j are quantities of different market goods and services; t_j are quantities of his own time, E^i stands for his education, experience, and "environmental" variables; and $R_j^1, \ldots, R_j^r$ are characteristics of other persons that affect his output of commodities. For example, if Z_1 measures i's distinction in his occupation, $R_1^1, \ldots, R_1^r$ could be the opinions of i held by other persons in the same occupation. Presumably, characteristics of others affect the production of a significant fraction of commodities.

If the R_j were completely outside i's control—that is, unaffected by what he does with his resources—i would maximize U taking the R_j as given. This is one way to justify the usual neglect of interactions. They are considered beyond the control of the persons being studied and are therefore taken as given when one is analyzing their reactions to changes in resources and prices.

The point of departure of my approach is to assume the contrary, namely, that i can change R_j by his own efforts. For example, he can avoid social opprobrium and perhaps ostracism by not engaging in criminal activities; achieve distinction by working diligently at his occu-

---

[7] For an exposition of this theory, see Michael and Becker (1973).

pation, giving to charities, or having a beautiful house; or relieve his envy and jealousy by talking meanly about or even physically harming his neighbors. These effects can be formalized in a production function for the $(R_j^1, \ldots, R_j^r)$ that depends partly on the efforts of i and partly on other variables.

To simplify the discussion,[8] I follow Senior and assume only a single commodity (distinction?) that is produced with a single good (the input of time is ignored) and a single characteristic of others. Then maximizing utility is equivalent to maximizing the output of this commodity, and one can write

$$U_i = Z(x, R). \tag{2.3}$$

I assume also (until Section 3C) that the effect of other variables (including the efforts of others) on this characteristic is not dependent on i's own efforts. Therefore, R can be written as the additive function

$$R = D_i + h, \tag{2.4}$$

where h measures the effect of i's efforts, and D_i the level of R when i makes no effort; that is, D_i measures i's "social environment."

His budget constraint for money income can be written as

$$p_x x + p_R h = I_i, \tag{2.5}$$

where I_i is his money income, $p_R h$ is the amount he spends on R, and p_R is the price to him of a unit of R. Substitute $R - D_i$ for h in equation (2.5) to get

$$p_x x + p_R R = I_i + p_R D_i = S_i. \tag{2.6}$$

The right-hand side gives the sum of i's money income and the value to him of his social environment, and will be called his social income. The left-hand side shows how his social income is "spent": partly on his "own" goods (x) and partly on the characteristics of others (R).[9]

If i maximizes the utility-output function given by equation (2.3) subject to the constraint on social income given by equation (2.6), the equilibrium condition is [10]

$$\frac{\partial U_i}{\partial x} \bigg/ \frac{\partial U_i}{\partial R} = \frac{p_x}{p_R}. \tag{2.7}$$

---

[8] I have also developed the analysis assuming many commodities and many characteristics.

[9] Sociologists sometimes assert that variables like social approval and respect "do not have any material value on which a price can be put" (see Blau 1968). But prices measure only scarcity and have nothing intrinsically to do with "material value"; p_R, for example, only measures the resource cost to i of changing social approval, respect, etc.

[10] I assume for simplicity in this formula that p_R measures the marginal as well as average price of R.

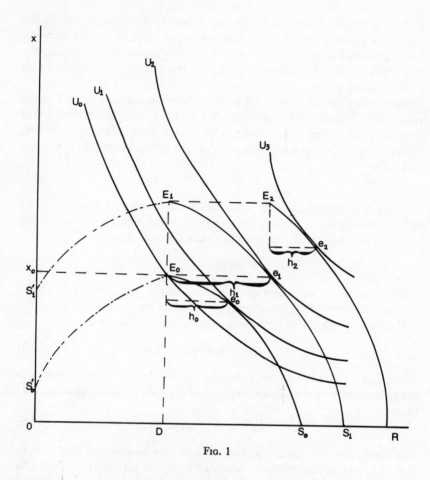

FIG. 1

If I did not want to purchase any R, p_R would be a "shadow" price, measured by the monetary equivalent of the marginal utility (equal to the marginal product) of R to i when $R = D_i$ (or when $h = 0$).

His equilibrium position is shown in figures 1 and 2. The first figure assumes that R has a positive marginal product in the production of Z (a positive marginal utility); that R refers, for example, to the respect accorded i rather than to his envy of others. The quantity $0D$ measures his social environment, and $0x_0$ his own income (measured in terms of x), so that the "endowed" point E_o gives his utility when he spends nothing on R. If E_oS_o measures the opportunities available for purchasing additional R,[11] he would maximize his utility by moving along E_oS_o to point e_o, where the slope of this opportunity curve equaled the slope of his

---

[11] If he can also reduce R by giving up own goods, the curve E_oS_o would continue in the southwest direction (see ES'_o in the figure). However, this section would be irrelevant if R had positive marginal utility.

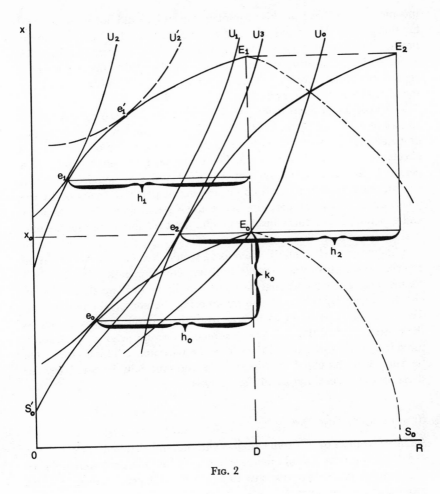

Fig. 2

indifference curve. His equilibrium purchase of R is measured by the line segment h_o.

Figure 2 assumes that R has a negative marginal product (or utility) because, say, it measures the income or prestige of persons that i envies. The section of the opportunity curve to the southeast of point E_o is now irrelevant, and he moves along the southwest section E_oS_o' to point e_o. He is willing to give up resources to reduce R because his utility is raised by a reduction in R; at point e_o, he spends enough resources to reduce R by h_o.

Note that since the marginal (and average) price of R is negative in figure 2, i's social income is *less* than his own income because the value of his social environment is subtracted from his own income. That is, he is made worse off by his social environment if it is dominated by character-istics of others that are distasteful to him. Note too that as long as the marginal utility of R is not zero at the socially endowed position, his social income would differ from his own income even if he did not want to spend anything on R. He would add to (or subtract from) his own income the product of D and the (monetary equivalent of the) marginal utility of R at the endowed position E_o. In other words, the traditional income concept is incomplete even when no resources are spent trying to influence the attitudes or situation of others.

The analysis developed for social interactions in these figures and in equations (2.3), (2.6), and (2.7) is also applicable whenever there is a physical environment that either can be altered directly or can have its effects augmented or diminished. For example, the human capital of a person is the sum of the amount inherited and that acquired through investments; moreover, the amount invested is partly determined by the inheritance. Or the temperature in a house is determined by the weather and expenditures on fuels, insulation, etc., that reinforce or offset the natural environment.

A more general analysis, therefore, would assume that every term entering the utility function has both an environmental and acquired component. The general analysis could readily be developed, but I have chosen to simplify the discussion by ignoring the nonsocial environment. The results are consistent with those from the general analysis as long as the contribution of the social environment is, on the whole, significantly more important than that of the physical environment. This is assumed to be true. (I am indebted to Gilbert Ghez and especially Robert Barro for stressing the general nature of the analysis.)

B.   Income and Price Effects

An increase in i's own income alone—without any change in prices or the social environment—would increase both x and R unless one were inferior. The average percentage response in x and R per 1 percent change in his own income is not unity, but is less by the fraction α, where α is the share of the social environment in his social income.[12] Therefore, the effect of a change in his own income on his utility-output is smaller the more important his social environment is.

Put differently, the greater the contribution of his social environment to his social income, the more his welfare is determined by the attitudes and behavior of others rather than by his own income. Traditional models

---

[12] By differentiating equation (2.6) with respect to I_t alone, $\bar{n} \equiv w_x n_x + w_R n_R = 1 - \alpha$, where

$$w_x = \frac{p_x x}{S_t}, \, w_R = \frac{p_R R}{S_t} = 1 - w_x, \, n_x = \frac{dx}{dI_t} \cdot \frac{I_t}{x}, \, n_R = \frac{dR}{dI_t} \cdot \frac{I_t}{R}, \, \alpha = \frac{p_R D_t}{S_t},$$

and I am assuming that p_R is given (not dependent on h, x, etc.). Of course, the weighted average of income elasticities with respect to a change in S_t must equal unity, as in the usual analysis.

of choice by economists assume that own efforts and access to property income and transfer payments determine welfare. On the other hand, those who stress the social environment, its normative requirements and sanctions for compliance and noncompliance, and the helplessness of the individual in the face of his environment naturally see society dominating individual efforts and, consequently, see little scope for important choices by individuals.

The relative importance of the social environment, as well as other implications of the theory of social interactions, can be empirically estimated from information on expenditures motivated by these interactions. If i's social environment did not change when his own income changed, the induced absolute change in the characteristics of others would equal the change in his contribution to these characteristics. However, the relative change in his contribution would differ from the relative change in these characteristics because the level of the latter is partly determined by the social environment.

Consider again figures 1 and 2, where an increase in i's own income with no change in the environment is shown by a vertical increase in the endowed position from E_o to E_1. Since his equilibrium position changes from e_o to e_1, the change in R is exactly equal to $h_1 - h_o$, the change in i's contribution to R. The percentage change in R in figure 1 is clearly less than that in h, since R is the sum of h and (a fixed) D. Since the percentage change in R in figure 2 is negative, it is also less than the percentage change in h, which is positive (since h is negative). However, if R had been increased by the increase in i's own income—if, say, the new equilibrium position was at point e_1'—the percentage change in R would be positive and would clearly exceed in algebraic value the negative percentage change in h.

The own-income elasticity of demand for contributions is related to the elasticity of demand for characteristics by the following formula:[13]

$$n_h \equiv \frac{dh}{dI_i} \cdot \frac{I_i}{h} = \frac{n_R}{\bar{n}(=1-\alpha)}\left[1 + \alpha\left(\frac{1}{\beta} - 1\right)\right], \qquad (2.8)$$

where $0 \leq \beta \leq 1$ is the fraction of own income that is spent on contributions to R. If $\alpha > 0$, if the social environment adds to i's social income,

---

[13] Since $dh/dI_i = dR/dI_i$,

$$n_h = \frac{dh}{dI_i} \cdot \frac{I_i}{h} = \frac{dR}{dI_i} \cdot \frac{I_i}{R} \cdot \frac{R}{h} = n_R \cdot \frac{R}{h}. \qquad (2.8')$$

But

$$\frac{R}{h} = \frac{p_R R}{p_R h} = 1 + \frac{p_R D_i}{p_R h} = 1 + \frac{S_i - I_i}{\beta I_i} = 1 + \frac{1/(1-\alpha) - 1}{\beta} = \frac{(1-\alpha) + \alpha/\beta}{1-\alpha}.$$

Since $1 - \alpha = \bar{n}$ (see n. 12 above), $n_h = (n_R/\bar{n})(\alpha/\beta + 1 - \alpha)$.

then clearly $n_h > n_R$.[14] Moreover, if $n_R \geq \bar{n} = 1 - \alpha < 1$, necessarily $n_h > 1$ even when $n_R < 1$; that is, contributions to the characteristics of others could have a "high" income elasticity even when the characteristics themselves had a "low" elasticity. Of course, if $n_h > 1$, the own-income elasticity of demand for own consumption (n_x) would be less than unity. That is, social interaction implies a relatively *low* income elasticity for own consumption even without introducing transitory changes in income, errors in variables, and the like.

Equation (2.8) further implies that an increase in α, an increase in the social environment, with no change in the own-income elasticity of demand for characteristics relative to the average elasticity $(n_R/\bar{n})$,[15] would increase the own-income elasticity of demand for contributions.[16] In other words, the more that i's social income was determined by his social environment, the greater would be the percentage change in his contributions to the characteristics of others as his own income changed.

If, on the other hand, $\alpha < 0$—the social environment subtracted from i's social income—then equation (2.8) implies that $n_h < n_R$ when $n_R > 0$, and $n_h > n_R$ when $n_R < 0$ (these different cases are shown in fig. 2). His demand for characteristics would probably be reduced by an increase in his own income (i.e., $n_R < 0$) if these characteristics have a negative marginal utility to him. Again, an increase in α, with $n_R/\bar{n}$ held constant, would raise n_h (the argument in n. 16 fully applies).

Since the social environment to any person cannot be readily observed, an indirect method of estimating at least its sign would be useful. If $n_R/\bar{n}$ were known, that is, if the relative income elasticity of demand for characteristics were known, the sign of α could be estimated simply from information on the own-income elasticity of demand for contributions to the environment, and its magnitude from additional information on the fraction of own income spent on these contributions. Equation (2.8) implies that

$$\alpha = \frac{n_h(\bar{n}/n_R) - 1}{1/\beta - 1}. \tag{2.9}$$

Therefore, $\alpha \gtreqless 0$ as $n_h(\bar{n}/n_R) \gtreqless 1$, and information on n_h, $\bar{n}/n_R$, and β would be sufficient to estimate α.

An increase in a social environment that adds to i's social income would increase his demand for own goods if they had positive income elasticities.

[14] For $[1 + \alpha(1/\beta - 1)]/(1 - \alpha) > 1$, since $1/\beta > 1$, and $1 - \alpha < 1$.

[15] An increase in α lowers $\bar{n}$ because the relative contribution of own income to social income is reduced.

[16]
$$\frac{dn_h}{d\alpha}\left(\frac{n_R}{\bar{n}} = \text{constant}\right) = \frac{n_R}{\bar{n}}\left(\frac{1}{\beta} - 1\right) - \frac{n_R}{\bar{n}}\,\alpha\,\beta^{-2}\frac{d\beta}{d\alpha}.$$

Both terms are greater than zero because $\beta < 1$, and $d\beta/d\alpha < 0$ (this is shown shortly); therefore, $dn_h/d\alpha > 0$.

If his own income were unchanged, his increased expenditure on own goods would have to be "financed" by reduced contributions to the characteristics of others. Similarly, an increase in a social environment that subtracts from his social income would increase his expenditures on others and reduce his expenditures on own goods. Consequently, the effect of a change in the environment is always (i.e., as long as own goods are not inferior) partly offset by induced changes in i's contributions in the opposite direction, regardless of whether the environment adds to or subtracts from i's social income.

Geometrically, a change in the social envirnment is shown by a horizontal movement of the endowed position. An increase in the environment shifts the endowment in figure 1 from point E_1 to E_2; the equilibrium position is changed from point e_1 to a point on a higher indifference curve (e_2), and i's contribution declines from h_1 to h_2. In figure 2, the equilibrium is changed from point e_1 to a point on a lower indifference curve (e_2), and i's contribution increases from h_1 to h_2.[17]

If both the own and environment incomes of i changed, the effect would be a combination of those when each alone changed. For example, if both incomes increased, the effect on his contributions of the increase in the environment would at least partly offset the effect of the increase in his own income. In particular, if both incomes increased by the same percentage, the percentage change in contributions would be greater than, equal to, or smaller than that percentage as his demand for characteristics exceeded, equaled, or was less than unity.

Through the assumption that p_R is constant, I have been assuming, in effect, that expenditures and the social environment are perfect substitutes in producing characteristics of others. However, the qualitative implications of this assumption can also be derived if they are simply better substitutes for each other than for own consumption—if p_R rises as h rises, but not "too" rapidly. For example, a rise in the environment would reduce contributions, and a rise in own income would increase contributions by a relatively large percentage if the environment and expenditures on these characteristics are simply relatively close direct substitutes.

A rise in the cost of changing the characteristics of others (p_R) would induce the usual substitution (and perhaps income) effects away from these characteristics. If the environment were given, the absolute change in contributions would equal the absolute change in these characteristics,

---

[17] The endowment-income elasticity of demand for contributions can easily be shown to equal

$$N_h = \frac{dh}{dD} \cdot \frac{D}{h} = (N_R - 1) \left\{ \frac{1}{1-\alpha} \left[1 + \alpha \left(\frac{1}{\beta} - 1 \right) \right] \right\} + 1.$$

Clearly, when $\alpha > 0$, $N_h < 0$ if $N_R \leq \alpha = \overline{N}$, the average endowment-income elasticity of demand; and when $\alpha < 0$, $N_h > 0$ if $N_R \geq \alpha$.

while the percentage changes would differ according to equation (2.8) in the following way:

$$E_h = -\frac{dh}{dp_R}\frac{p_R}{h} = E_R\left[\frac{1 + \alpha(1/\beta - 1)}{1 - \alpha}\right] \qquad (2.10)$$

(same proof as in n. 13 above). Therefore, when $\alpha > 0$, E_h would exceed E_R by an amount that would be greater, the greater α and the smaller β. Similarly, when $\alpha < 0$, E_h would be less than E_R[18] by an amount that would be greater, the greater the absolute value of α and the smaller β.

3. Applications

Three specific applications of the general analysis of social interaction are now considered: interactions among members of the same family, charity, and envy and hatred. These applications not only provide empirical support for the income and price implications just derived, but also bring out a number of other implications of social interaction.

A. The Family

Assume that i cares about his spouse j in the sense that i's utility function depends on j's welfare.[19] I assume until much later in this section that j does not care positively or negatively about i. For simplicity, define the variable measuring this dependence, R_i, as follows:

$$R_i = \frac{I_j + h_{ij}}{p_x} = \frac{S_j}{p_x} = x_j, \qquad (3.1)$$

where I_j is j's own income, h_{ij} are the contributions from i to j, S_j is j's social income, and x_j are the goods consumed by j. The social income of i can be derived by substituting equation (3.1) into equation (2.6):

$$p_x x_i + p_R R_i = S_i = I_i + \frac{p_R I_j}{p_x}, \qquad (3.2)$$

where p_R is the price to i of transferring resources to j. If i can transfer resources to j without any "transactions" costs—presumably, these costs are reduced by sharing a common household—and if i cares sufficiently about j to have $h_{ij} > 0$, then $p_R = p_x$, and

$$S_i = p_x x_i + p_x x_j = I_i + I_j = I_{ij}. \qquad (3.3)$$

[18] I assume that an increase in the absolute value of p_R reduces the demand for R, so that $E_h > 0$.

[19] Caring is not simply a *deus ex machina* introduced to derive the following implications, since I have shown elsewhere (Becker 1974) that the marriage market is more likely to pair a person with someone he cares about than with an otherwise similar person that he does not care about.

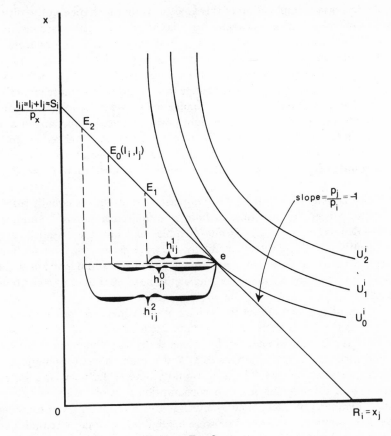

FIG. 3

The social income of i equals the combined own incomes of i and j, or the "family's" own income. Moreover, the equilibrium condition given by equation (2.7) implies that

$$\frac{\partial U_i}{\partial x_i} \bigg/ \frac{\partial U_i}{\partial (R_i = x_j)} = \frac{p_x}{p_R} = 1, \qquad (3.4)$$

or i would receive equal marginal utility from j's and his own consumption.

Conditions (3.3) and (3.4) are shown in figure 3. Resources can be transferred from i to j by moving along i's budget line in a southeast direction from the endowed position at point E_o. The equilibrium position is at point e, where the slope of i's indifference curves equals the slope of his budget line (= to − 1). The vertical (or horizontal) intercept gives the family's own income—i's social income—deflated by the price of x.

An important implication of this analysis is that a change in the distribution of family income between i and j has no effect at all on the consumption or welfare of either, as long as i continues to transfer resources to j. A change in the distribution would be on the same budget line as E_o if total family income is unchanged: the change from E_o to E_1 is nominally more favorable to j, whereas the change to E_2 is nominally more favorable to i. Since there is only one point of tangency between i's budget line and an indifference curve, the equilibrium position must be unchanged at e. A shift in favor of j's income to E_1 simply induces an equal reduction in i's contributions to j (from h_{ij}^o to h_{ij}^1 in the figure), whereas a shift against j's income to E_2 induces an equal increase in his contributions (from h_{ij}^o to h_{ij}^2).[20]

This discussion has assumed a two-person family but is equally applicable to larger families that include grandparents, parents, children, uncles, aunts, or other kin. If one member, call him the "head," cares sufficiently about all other members to transfer general resources to them,[21] redistribution of income among members would not affect the consumption of any member, as long as the head continues to contribute to all.

The head's concern about the welfare of other members provides each, including the head, with some insurance against disasters. If a disaster reduced the income of one member alone, k, by say 50 percent, the head would increase his contributions to k, and thereby offset to some extent the decline in k's income. The head would "finance" his increased contribution to k by reducing his own consumption and his contributions to other members; in effect each member shares k's disaster by consuming less. If k's share of family income were negligible, he would essentially be fully insured against his own disasters because even a 50 percent decline in his income would have a negligible effect on family income, and thus on the consumption of each member. Since the share contributed by any member would tend to be inversely related to family size, large families, including the extended kinship family found in certain societies, can provide self-insurance especially when old-age, health, and other kinds of market insurance are not available or are very costly.[22] Note that insurance is automatically provided when resources are voluntarily transferred,

[20] If the utility of i also partly depended directly on the amounts he transferred to j, perhaps because i's "prestige" or "approval" partly depended on these transfers, then redistribution of family income *would* have a net effect on the consumption of both i and j.

[21] A somewhat weaker assumption is that the family is "fully connected" through a series of transfers between members; for example, a transfers resources to b because a cares about b, b transfers to c because b cares about c, and so on until m transfers to the last member, n, and n transfers to no one (this assumption is made in an intergenerational context by Barro 1974). Indirectly, a (or any other member but n) would be transferring to all members because an increase in his contributions to b would induce an increase in the contributions to all other members.

[22] The interaction between self and market insurance is analyzed in Ehrlich and Becker (1972).

without the need for any member to have dictatorial control over the family's allocation of resources.

The result on the unimportance of the distribution of income among persons linked by transfers can also be used to understand the interaction among generations.[23] Suppose that the resources of the present generation are changed at the expense of or to the benefit of the resources accruing to future generations. For example, increased government debt or social security payments are financed by increased taxes on future generations, or increased public investment, perhaps in schools, with benefits accruing to future generations is financed by taxes on the present generation. If present and future generations are fully connected by a series of intergenerational transfers, called "bequests," then each of these apparent changes in the relative resources of present and future generations would tend to be offset by equal but opposite changes in bequests. In particular, increased public debt would not raise the real wealth or consumption of the present generation or reduce that of future generations because increased taxes on future generations would be matched by increased bequests to them. Similarly, increased public investment in education would be matched by reduced private investment in education.[24]

The budget constraint of the head is determined by total family income, not his own income alone—equation (3.3) for a two-person family can be readily generalized to many persons. Since the head maximizes his utility subject to his budget constraint, anything that increased family income would increase his utility. Therefore, the head would consider the effect on total family income of his different actions, and would forfeit own income if the incomes of other family members were increased even more. For example, he would not move to another city if his spouse's or children's income would be decreased by more than his own income would be increased. Or, although children usually eventually set up their own households and fully control their own incomes, the head would guide and help finance their investments in education and other human capital to maximize the present value of the real income yielded by these investments.[25]

Put differently, the head automatically internalizes the "external" effects of his actions on other family members.[26] Indeed, because the

[23] This application is taken from the detailed discussion in Barro (1974).

[24] The empirical evidence does strongly suggest that most of the investment in higher education by state governments has been offset by reduced private investment (see Peltzman 1973; McPherson, in preparation).

[25] The incentive that parents have to invest in their children is discussed in several places (see, e.g., De Tray 1973; Parsons 1974).

[26] The Coase Theorem proves that when "bargaining costs" are negligible, each family member could always be induced to maximize family opportunities through bargaining with and side payments from other members. I have proved that the head (and, as shown later, other members too) has this incentive and, in effect, makes or receives "side payments" without bargaining with other members. The word "automatically" is used to distinguish this theorem from the Coase Theorem.

head maximizes family income, he *fully* internalizes these externalities not only when the income of different members but also when their consumption, the other side of the budget constraint, is directly affected. He would take an action directly affecting consumption only when either the value of any increase in his consumption exceeded the value (to him) of any decrease in other members' consumption, or when any decrease in his own was less valuable than the increase in theirs.[27]

For example, he would read in bed at night only if the value of reading exceeded the value (to him) of the loss in sleep suffered by his wife, or he would eat with his fingers only if its value exceeded the value (to him) of the disgust experienced by his family. The development of manners and other personal behavior "rules" between family members well illustrates how apparent "external" effects can be internalized by social interaction between members.

Note too that not only is the head better off when his utility is raised, but so too are other members of his family, even if his actions directly reduce their consumption or increase their discomfort and disgust. For if his utility is raised and if their welfare has a positive income elasticity to him, he would increase his contributions to them by more than enough to offset their initial losses. For example, if he benefits from reading at night, his wife does too because he more than compensates her for her loss of sleep.[28]

The head maximizes a utility function that depends on the consumption of all family members subject to a budget constraint determined by family

[27] Although this is a rather immediate implication of his interest in maximizing family opportunities, a direct proof may be instructive. Suppose that a particular action changed the utility of the head by

$$dU_h = mu^h dx_h + \sum_{j=1, \neq h}^{n} mu^j dx_j, \qquad (1')$$

where $mu^j = \partial U_h/\partial x_j$, and dx_j measures the change in consumption of the jth family member. If the head can transfer resources to other members dollar for dollar, in equilibrium,

$$mu^j = \lambda_h p_j \qquad \text{all } j, \qquad (2')$$

where λ_h is the marginal utility of income to the head, and p_j is the cost of x_j. Substitution of eq. (2') into (1') gives

$$dU^h = \lambda_h(p_h dx_h + \sum_{j=1, \neq h}^{n} p_j dx_j) = \lambda_h \sum_{\text{all } j} p_j dx_j. \qquad (3')$$

Since the head takes an action if and only if $dU_h > 0$, eq. (3') implies (since $\lambda_h > 0$) that he takes an action if, and only if,

$$\sum_{\text{all } j} p_j dx_j > 0, \qquad (4')$$

which was to be proved.

[28] Recall that I have been assuming that only a single good is consumed by each person, although this analysis presupposes many goods. The transition to many goods is straightforward if the head's utility depends on a function of the various goods consumed by another member that is monotonically related to the utility function of that member (see the discussion later in this section).

income and family consumption. Therefore, the effect of a change in relative prices of goods, or in aggregate family income (as well as in its distribution) on a family's consumption of different goods, could be predicted solely from the head's utility function and a budget constraint on family variables. The usual substitution and income effects of demand theory would be fully applicable.

In this sense, then, a family with a head can be said to maximize "its" consistent and transitive utility function of the consumption of different members subject to a budget constraint defined on family variables. The "family's" utility function is identical with that of one member, the head, because his concern for the welfare of other members, so to speak, integrates all the members' utility functions into one consistent "family" function.

That is, a "family's" utility function is the same as that of one of its members not because this member has dictatorial power over other members, but because he (or she!) cares sufficiently about all other members to transfer resources voluntarily to them. Each member can have complete freedom of action; indeed, the person making the transfers would not change the consumption of any member even with dictatorial power! For example, if i had dictatorial power, he could move the equilibrium position e in figure 3 to the vertical axis (or anywhere else), but would not choose to move it because his utility partly depends on j's consumption.[29]

Nothing much has yet been said about the preferences of members who

---

[29] It is difficult to contrast my derivation of a "family" utility function with a traditional derivation, since explicit derivations are rare. The most explicit appears to be in a well-known article on social indifference curves by Samuelson (1956). He considers the problem of relating individual and family utility functions, but his discussion is brief and the arguments sometimes are not spelled out. Without sufficient elaboration, he refers to a consistent "family welfare function" being grafted onto the separate utility functions of different family members (p. 10). In addition, he says that a family member's "preferences among his own goods have the special property of being independent of the other members' consumption. But since blood is thicker than water, the preferences of the different members are interrelated by what might be called a 'consensus' or 'social welfare function' which takes into account the deservingness or ethical worths of the consumption levels of each of the members." How are these preferences interrelated by a "consensus," and should not the "deservingness" of the consumption levels of different members simply be incorporated into different members' preferences (as in my approach)? Incidentally, at one point (p. 9), Samuelson appears to believe that if the family utility function is the same as the head's, he must have sovereign power, which I have shown is not necessary. He later (p. 20) says that "if within the family there can be assumed to take place an optimal reallocation of income so as to keep each member's dollar expenditure of equal ethical worth, then there can be derived for the whole family a set of well-behaved indifference contours relating the totals of what it consumes: the family can be said to *act as if* it maximizes such a group preference function" (italics in original). In my analyses, the "optimal reallocation" results from interdependent preferences and voluntary contributions, and the "group preference function" is identical with that of the "head."

are not heads. The major, and somewhat unexpected, conclusion is that if a head exists, *other members also are motivated to maximize family income and consumption, even if their welfare depends on their own consumption alone.* This is the "rotten kid" theorem (I owe this name to the Barro family). For consider a selfish member j who can take an action that would reduce his income by b, but increase that of another member k by c. Initially, j would be worse off by b, since the gain to k is of no direct concern to him. However, if $c = b$, the head would transfer enough additional resources to j from k to leave him (and k) equally well off, since intrafamily reallocations of income do not affect the consumption of any member. Moreover, if $c > b$—if family income were raised by j's action—and if j's welfare were a superior "good" to the head, then he would transfer enough additional resources to j to make j better off. Consequently, even a selfish j would only undertake actions that raised family income or consumption, regardless of the initial impact on him.

In other words, when one member cares sufficiently about other members to be the head, all members have the same motivation as the head to maximize family opportunities and to internalize fully all within-family "externalities," regardless of how selfish (or, indeed, how envious) these members are. Even a selfish child receiving transfers from his parents would *automatically* consider the effects of his actions on other siblings as well as on his parents. Put still differently, sufficient "love" by one member guarantees that all members act as if they loved other members as much as themselves. As it were, the amount of "love" required in a family is economized: sufficient "love" by one member leads all other members by "an invisible hand" to act as if they too loved everyone.

Armed with this theorem, I do not need to dwell on the preferences of nonheads. Of course, just as there may be no head if all members are sufficiently selfish, so there may be none if they are all sufficiently altruistic. Each would want to transfer resources to other members, but no one would want to accept transfers. Aside from that, mutual interaction or mutual interdependence of welfare raises no particular problems.[30]

---

[30] It frequently has been alleged to me that mutual interaction of the form

$$U_i = U_i[x_i, g_i(U_j)]$$
$$U_j = U_j[x_j, g_j(U_i)],$$

where x_i and x_j are the own consumption of i and j, and g_i and g_j are monotonic functions of the utility indexes U_i and U_j, results in instability and unbounded utility levels. For it is argued, an increase in x_i by one unit directly raises i's utility, which raises j's utility through g_j, which in turn further raises i's utility, and so on, until U_i and U_j approach infinity. Mathematically, there is an infinite regress, since, by substitution,

$$U_i = U_i[x_i, g_i\{x_j, g_j\{x_i, g_i\{x_j, g_j\{\ldots\}\}] .$$

However, with appropriate restrictions on the magnitude of the interactions, the infinite regress has a finite effect, and the "reduced forms" of U_i and U_j on x_i and x_j

By assuming in figure 3 and in the formal development given by equations (3.1)–(3.4) that only a single good is consumed by each person, I eliminated any distinction between transferring general purchasing power and transferring particular goods to another member. If each member consumes many goods, the conclusions in this section about family utility functions, internalization of within-family externalities, and so on fully hold only if the head is content to transfer general purchasing power. He would transfer in this form if his utility function depended on the utility of other members—that is, if his utility function could be written in the form

$$U_h = U_h[x_{h1}, \ldots, x_{hm}, g_1(x_{21}, \ldots, x_{2m}), \ldots, g_n(x_{n1}, \ldots, x_{nm})] \,, \quad (3.5)$$

where x_{ij} is the quantity of the jth good consumed by the ith person, and

$$dg_i = 0 \left(= \sum_{j-1}^{m} \frac{\partial g_i}{\partial x_{ij}} \, dx_{ij} \right)$$

implies that the utility of the ith person is unchanged. If he is concerned not about the utility of other members but about their consumption of particular "merit" goods, the conclusions can be quite different. The systematic discussion of merit goods is postponed to Section 3C.

If parents are transferring resources to their children in the form, say, of gifts and expenditures on education and other human capital or after they die in the form of bequests, then an increase in the income of parents by a given percentage would tend to increase contributions to children by a still larger percentage, certainly by one exceeding the increased welfare of their children (see the discussion in Section 2). In other words, contributions to children can be very responsive to a change in parental income without the welfare of children being so responsive.

Empirical evidence on bequests, gifts, and many other transfers to children is seriously deficient. The general impression is, however, that

---

are well defined. Consider, for example, the Cobb Douglas functions

$$U_i = x_i^{a_i} U_j^{b_i}$$

$$U_j = x_j^{a_j} U_i^{b_j},$$

where a_i and a_j presumably are greater than zero, and b_i and b_j can either be greater than or less than zero. By substitution,

$$U_i = x_i^{a_i/(1-b_i b_j)} x_j^{a_j b_i)/(1-b_i b_j)} = x_i^{\alpha_i} x_j^{\beta_i}$$

$$U_j = x_i^{a_i b_j)/(1-b_i b_j)} x_j^{a_j/(1-b_i b_j)} = x_i^{\alpha_j} x_j^{\beta_j},$$

where $b_i b_j$ is independent of monotonic transformations on U_i and U_j. A finite sum to the regress requires that $|b_i b_j| < 1$; essentially, that the marginal utilities or disutilities due to interdependence are less than unity. Note that although it is possible for $a_i = b_i$ and $a_j = b_j$, for own consumption and the welfare of the other person to be equally "important," the condition $|b_i b_j| < 1$ implies that either $|\alpha_i| > |\beta_i|$, or $|\beta_j| > |\alpha_j|$, or both; that is, for at least one of the persons, own consumption has to be more important than the other person's consumption in the "reduced forms."

bequests have a very high income elasticity. Moreover, the elasticity of expenditures on children's education with respect to parental income does appear to be above unity (Schultz 1967, p. 9), which is consistent with the implications of the theory.

The responsiveness of expenditures on children's education and other training and skills to parental income has often been noted, and lamented as evidence of immobility and rigid "class" structure. Yet my analysis implies that the welfare of children—a measure of their "class"—rises by a smaller percentage than parent expenditures on them, and possibly even by a smaller percentage than parental income. Put differently, considerable regression toward the mean across generations—that is, the expected income or other measure of the position of children would be much closer to the average position than is that of their parents—can be observed at the same time that contributions to children are very responsive to parental income.[31]

The crucial point is that considerable regression toward the mean across generations would occur partly because of genetic factors and luck if all parents spent an equal amount on their children. As a result of this, and given interdependent preferences, higher-income parents tend to spend considerably more on their children than lower-income ones. However, these expenditures would only tend to dampen but not eliminate the

---

[31] In one study, the elasticity of children's years of schooling with respect to parental income is a sizeable $+1.2$, at the same time that the elasticity of children's *income* with respect to parental income is only $+0.3$, or a 70 percent regression toward the mean (unpublished calculations by Jacob Mincer from the Eckland Sample). Note in this regard, however, that parents cannot easily prevent considerable regression toward the mean by investing in their children. For let the relation between the human capital invested in children and parental income be

$$S_c = a + b \log I_p + u,$$

where b is the elasticity of parental response, and u represents other determinants of S_c. According to the theory of investment in human capital (Mincer 1974; Becker 1975 [in press]),

$$\log I_c = \alpha + rS_c + v,$$

where r is the rate of return on human capital, and v represents other determinants of $\log I_c$. Then by substitution,

$$\log I_c = (\alpha + ra) + rb \log I_p + (ru + v).$$

Even if r were as large as 0.2, and b as large as 2.0, rb would only be 0.4: the regression toward the mean would be 60 percent. If $v = c \log I_p + v'$, where $1 - c$ measures the degree of "intrinsic" regression to the mean, then by substitution,

$$\log I_c = (\alpha + ra) + (rb + c) \log I_p + (ru + tv').$$

Since the analysis in the text implies that b would be positively related to $1 - c$ as parents try to offset the "intrinsic" regression, the "observed" regression to the mean,

$$1 - \gamma = 1 - (c + rb) = (1 - c) - rb,$$

may be only weakly related to and also is less than the "intrinsic" regression $1 - c$. I am indebted to discussions with Jacob Mincer on the issues sketchily covered in this footnote.

regression toward the mean. Therefore, the elastic response of contributions to children can give a very biased picture of the degree of immobility or inheritance of "class" position. Indeed, contributions would be more responsive to parental income the stronger are the basic forces producing mobility because parents attempt to offset these forces. In other words, an elastic response of contributions to parental income may be evidence of sizeable *mobility*![32]

B.   Charity

If someone makes contributions of time or goods to unrelated persons or to organizations, he is said to be "charitable" or "philanthropic." The discussion of contributions within a family indicates that charitable behavior can be motivated by a desire to improve the general well-being of recipients.[33] Apparent "charitable" behavior can also be motivated by a desire to avoid the scorn of others or to receive social acclaim. Not much generality is sacrificed, however, by only considering charity motivated by a desire to improve well-being.[34]

The numerous implications about family behavior developed in the previous section fully apply to the synthetic "family" consisting of a charitable person i and all recipients of his charity. For example, no member's well-being would be affected by a redistribution of income among them, as

[32] It is generally believed that the United States has a more mobile "open" society than European countries do; yet (admittedly crude) comparisons of occupational mobility between fathers and sons do not reveal large differences between the United States and several Western European countries (Lipset and Bendix 1959). Since the analysis in this paper suggests that parents' contributions to their children's education and other training is more responsive to parental position in "open" societies, more responsive parental contributions are probably offsetting the greater "openness" of American society.

[33] *The Random House Dictionary of the English Language* (unabridged, 1967) defines charity as "the benevolent feeling, especially toward those in need or in disfavor."

[34] The utility function of a charitable person who desires to improve the general well-being of recipients can be written as

$$U_i = U_i \left[x_i, x_j \left(= \frac{I_j + h}{p_j} \right) \right],$$

where h is his charitable giving, x_j measures the well-being of recipients, and $\partial U_i / \partial I_j = \partial U_i / \partial h > 0$; that is, a unit increase in the own income of recipients has the same effect on the utility of a charitable person as a unit increase in his giving. The utility function of a person who makes "charitable" contributions to win social acclaim can be written as

$$U_i = U_i \left(x_i, \frac{I_j}{p_j}, \frac{h}{p_j} \right),$$

where still $\partial U_i / \partial h > 0$—an increase in his contributions would increase his acclaim—but now the sign of $\partial U_i / \partial I_j$ is not so obvious. If, however, contributions and the income of recipients were much closer substitutes for each other than for the own consumption of the contributor, which is plausible, then these utility functions have similar implications. Not much generality is sacrificed, therefore, by only considering charity motivated by a desire to improve the well-being of recipients.

long as i continued to give to all of them. For he would simply redistribute his giving until everyone losing income was fully compensated and everyone gaining was fully "taxed." Moreover, all members, not simply i, would try to maximize "family" opportunities and "family" consumption, instead of their own income or consumption alone. In addition, each member of a synthetic "family" is at least partly "insured" against catastrophes because all other members, in effect, would increase their giving to him until at least part of his loss were replaced. Therefore, charity is a form of self-insurance that is a substitute for market insurance and government transfers. Presumably, the rapid growth of these latter during the last 100 years discouraged the growth of charity.

According to the analysis in Section 2, an increase in the income of a charitable person would increase his charitable giving by a greater percentage than the increase in the well-being of recipients. Indeed, his income elasticity of demand for giving would exceed unity, possibly by a substantial amount, as long as his elasticity of demand for their well-being (which I will call his demand for charity) was not much below his average income elasticity. The available evidence on charitable giving clearly supports this implication of the theory: income elasticities estimated by Taussig (1965) from giving in different income classes in 1962 are all well above unity, ranging from a low of $+1.3$ in the under \$25,000 class to a high of $+3.1$ in the \$100,000–\$200,000 class.[35]

A crucial implication of charitable giving in terms of social interaction between the giver and others is that an increase in the incomes of recipients would reduce giving. Therefore, an increase in the incomes of both recipients and givers should not increase giving by as much as an increase in the incomes of givers alone. These implications are tested and confirmed by Schwartz (1970), who analyzes aggregate time series on incomes and charitable giving in the United States between 1929 and 1966 and also compares his findings with the cross-sectional findings of Taussig (1965) reported above.[36]

The usual theory of consumer choice ignores social interactions, and would consider charitable giving simply as a "good" that enters the

[35] These estimates are net of differences in tax rates. Note, however, that charitable giving is estimated from itemized deductions in personal income tax returns. Since only giving to (certain) institutions and not to individuals can be deducted, since many taxpayers, especially with lower incomes, do not itemize their deductions, and since others inflate their deductions, the response of tax-reported giving may not accurately describe the response of actual giving.

[36] Schwartz's study, like Taussig's, is based on personal income tax returns. Both studies also estimate the price elasticity of giving, where price is measured by one minus the marginal tax rate. Schwartz finds considerable response to price, elasticities generally exceeding -0.5, which is consistent with the implications of the theory of social interactions. Taussig, on the other hand, finds only a weak response to price; but Schwartz argues that Taussig's findings are biased downward.

giver's utility function along with his other goods:

$$U_i = U_i(x_i, h) \,, \tag{3.6}$$

where h measures the amount given by i, and x_i are the other goods that he consumes. This "conventional" approach does not imply that an increase in i's income would increase his giving by a particularly large percentage, or that an increase in the income of recipients would lower his giving. Therefore, considerable ad hocery would be required if the "conventional" approach were to explain the evidence on charitable giving that is more readily explained by an approach that incorporates social interactions.

These findings can be used to make very crude, but instructive, calculations of the share of recipient's own incomes in the social incomes of contributors. If the own-income elasticity of demand for giving is taken from Taussig as $+2.0$, the share of own income spent on giving as 0.04 (see Schwartz 1970, p. 1278), and the income elasticity of demand for charity as equal to the average income elasticity (actually, Schwartz's findings suggest that it may be lower than the average), then, according to equation (2.9), charity's share in social income would be $(2 - 1)/(1/ 0.04 - 1) \eqsim 0.4$. If the own-income elasticity of giving were taken as $+3.0$ rather than $+2.0$, charity's share would double to 0.08; if, in addition, the income elasticity of charity were only four-fifths of the average elasticity, its share would increase further to 0.11 (a tithe?).

C. Merit Goods and Multiperson Interactions

Contributors are content to transfer general purchasing power to recipients if they are concerned about the general welfare or utility of recipients—as seen by recipients. They want to restrict or earmark their transfers, on the other hand, if they are concerned about particular "merit" goods consumed by recipients. For example, parents may want transfers to their children spent on education or housing, or only the money incomes rather than "full" incomes of children may be of concern to parents, or contributors to beggars may not want their giving spent on liquor or gambling.

Assume, therefore, that i transfers resources to j that are earmarked for particular goods consumed by j because the utility function of i depends not only on his own goods but also on these goods of j. If j were permitted to spend his own income as he wished, an assumption modified shortly, he would spend less on these goods as a result of the earmarked transfers from i. Clearly, the reduction in his own spending would be greater, the greater the transfer, the smaller the fraction of his social income spent on these goods, and the smaller their income elasticity. For example, if they take 20 percent of his social income and have an income elasticity equal to 2.0, he would reduce his own spending by $0.60 for each dollar earmarked by i.[37]

As long as j continues to spend on the merit goods, earmarked transfers are worth as much to j as a transfer of general purchasing power with equal monetary value. Moreover, i would not have a greater effect on j's consumption of these goods with earmarked transfers than with general transfers. Therefore, as long as j continues to spend on these goods, earmarked transfers are equivalent to general transfers; and the results derived for the latter fully hold for the former. For example, a redistribution of income between i and j would have no effect on the consumption of either as long as both continue to spend on the merit goods, or both i and j want to maximize their combined incomes, not their own incomes alone.

On the other hand, if j did not want to spend anything on the merit goods because earmarked transfers were sufficiently large, such transfers would be worth less to j and more to i than would general transfers with equal money value. Moreover, various results derived for general transfers no longer hold: for example, a redistribution of income to j and away from i would reduce j's consumption of merit goods and increase his consumption of other goods.

If i were aware that j reduced his spending on merit goods when transfers increased, i would be discouraged from giving because j's reaction raises i's private price of merit goods to

$$p_m^i = p_m \frac{1}{1 - r_j} = p_m \frac{1}{v_m n_m}, [38] \qquad (3.7)$$

where p_m is the market price of merit goods, and the other terms are defined in note 37. Similarly, if j were aware that i reduced his transfers when j increased his spending on merit goods, j would also be discouraged from spending because i's reaction raises the price to j. Indeed, j could end up consuming fewer merit goods than he would if i were not concerned! That these induced reactions are not simply hypothetical or always minor is persuasively shown in a recent study of higher education (Peltzman 1973). States earmark transfers to higher education mainly through highly subsidized public institutions. Private spending was apparently reduced by (at least) $0.75 per dollar of public spending in 1966–67; private spending may have been reduced by more than $1.00 per dollar of public spending in 1959–60, so that *total* spending on higher education in that year would have been reduced by public spending.

[37] It is easily shown that $r_j = 1 - v_m n_m$, where v_m is the share spent on merit goods; n_m, their income elasticity; and r_j, the reduction in j's own spending per unit increase in i's contribution. Therefore, if $v_m = 0.2$, and $n_m = 2.0$, $r_j = 0.6$.

[38] For example, if j spent $0.60 less for each dollar transferred by i, the price to i would be $p_m^i = p_m(1/0.4) = 2.5\, p_m$, or more than twice the market price.

Both i and j want to limit the induced reactions of the other because such reactions reflect the incentive to "underreveal" preferences about merit goods and "free-ride" in their consumption. Since equation (3.7) shows that these reactions raise the price of merit goods to i and j, in effect, both want to lower these prices. Indeed, it is well known from the theory of public goods, and a merit good is a particular kind of "public" good, that efficient prices to i and j would be less than the market price; indeed, these efficient prices would *sum* to the market price of the merit good.[39] Efficient prices might be achieved, for example, by i and j matching each other's spending in specified proportions, or each might be given a spending quota.

I intentionally say "might" be achieved because any agreement has to be "policed" to insure that each lives up to his commitment. Policing is relatively easy for the consumer of the merit goods, j, since he usually automatically knows how much is spent by i, but is much more difficult for i, since he does not automatically know how much is spent by j.[40] Parents may use their children's grades in school to measure the input of time and effort by children that presumably "matches" the money contribution by the parents.[41] Or parents may save a large part of their total transfer to children for a bequest when they die in order to provide an incentive for children to spend "appropriately," at least while their parents are alive.[42] This may explain why the inheritance tax on bequests apparently has induced relatively little substitution toward gifts to children (see Shoup 1966; Adams 1974).

The "underrevealing," "free-riding," coordination of efforts, and "policing" discussed for merit goods are common to all multiperson interactions—that is, all situations where two or more persons are affected by the consumption, attitudes, or other behavior of the same person. The analytical issues for multiperson interactions are the same as for other "public" goods: is public intervention desirable—for example, should charitable giving be deductible from personal income in arriving at tax liabilities in order to lower the private price of giving—and do private equilibria without government intervention more closely approximate joint maximization, a Nash noncooperative game solution, or something quite different? Since space is limited, I refrain from discussing further these and related issues.

[39] A proof of this well-known summation formula can be found in Samuelson (1954).

[40] The difficulty of policing "merit" goods is shown amusingly in a recent Wizard of Id cartoon. Two drunks meet, and one says, "Could you spare a buck for a bottle of wine?" The other answers, "How do I know you won't buy food with it?"

[41] I owe this example to Lisa Landes.

[42] This conclusion about the incentives provided by large bequests is a special case of a more general result proven elsewhere (see Becker and Stigler 1974) that relatively large pensions discourage employees from acting contrary to the interests of their employers (a bequest serves the same purpose as a pension).

D. Envy and Hatred

An envious or malicious person presumably would feel better off if some other persons become worse off in certain respects. He could "harm" himself (i.e., spend his own resources) in order to harm others: in figure 2, he gives up k_o units of his own consumption in order to harm others by h_o units. The terms of trade between his own harm and the harm to others, given by the curve $E_o S_o^1$ in figure 2, is partly determined by his skill at "predatory" behavior and partly by public and private expenditures to prevent crime, libeling, malicious acts, trespass, and other predatory behavior. Since an increase in these expenditures would increase the cost to him of harming others, he would be discouraged from harming them. The limited evidence available on predatory expenditures supports this implication of the theory. Crimes against persons provide some evidence on predatory behavior, since most assaults and murders probably are motivated by the harm to victims.[43] The frequency of assaults and murder (and also crimes against property) apparently is strongly negatively related to the probability of conviction, punishment, and other measures of the cost of committing these crimes (see Ehrlich 1973).

Section 2 suggests that a rise in own income would tend to reduce predatory expenditures. An increase in the social environment,[44] on the other hand, would necessarily increase these expenditures, unless own consumption were an inferior good. Therefore, a rise in the social environment and own income by the same percentage would reduce predatory expenditures by less than would a rise in own income alone, and might even increase them.

Again, the implications of the theory can be tested with evidence on crimes against persons. Since assaults and murders have been more frequent at lower income levels,[45] an increase in own income appears to reduce crimes against persons, if differences in own income alone are measured by differences in the incomes of individuals at a moment in time (as in the discussion of charity in Section 3B). As predicted by the theory, an increase in own income that is accompanied by an increase in the social environment (as measured by the income of others) does not have such a negative effect on these crimes. Indeed, the frequency of assaults and murders has not been reduced by the sizeable growth in aggregate incomes during the last 40 years, nor do higher-income states presently have fewer crimes against persons than other states.[46]

[43] Most robberies, burglaries, and larcenies, on the other hand, probably are motivated by the prospects of material gain.

[44] That is, in that part of the social environment that motivates predatory expenditures.

[45] Persons committing crimes against other persons as well as against property are much more likely to live in low income areas (see Crime Commission 1967a, table 9).

[46] The rate of assaults grew significantly from 1933 to 1965 in the United States, and the murder rate remained about the same (Crime Commission 1967b, figs. 3, 4). Higher-

Over the years, even acute observers of society have differed radically in their assessment of the importance of envy and hatred. Two hundred years ago, for example, Adam Smith recognized these "passions" but shunted them aside with the comment: "Envy, malice, or resentment, are the only passions which can prompt one man to injure another in his person or reputation. But the *greater part of men are not very frequently under the influence of those passions*, and the very worst men are so only occasionally. As their gratification too, how agreeable soever it may be to certain characters, is not attended with any real or permanent advantage it is in the greater part of men commonly restrained by prudential considerations. Men may live together in society with some tolerable degree of security, though there is no civil magistrate to *protect them from the injustice of those passions*" (Smith 1937; my italics).[47] To Thorstein Veblen, on the other hand, writing many years later, there motives are the very stuff of life that dominate everything else: "The desire for wealth can scarcely be satiated in any individual instance, and evidently a satiation of the average or general desire for wealth is out of the question. However widely, or equally, or 'fouly,' it may be distributed, no general increase of the community's wealth can make any approach to satiating this need, the ground of which is the desire of everyone to excel everyone else in the accumulation of goods" (Veblen 1934, p.32).[48]

In principle, the importance of envy and hatred can be measured using equation (2.9) by the contribution of the relevant social environment to social income; this is done in a crude way in Section 2B for charity. Unfortunately, not enough information is available either on the own-income elasticity of demand or on the fraction of own income spent on "predatory" behavior to make even crude estimates of the relative contribution of envy and hatred.

Still, it may be useful to note several implications of the differing views about the significance of envy and hatred. For example, Veblen's belief that the welfare of a typical person primarily depends on his relative income position implies that social income essentially is zero: that the value of the social environment causing envy would exactly offset the value of own income.[49] For then, and only then, would a rise in this

---

income states do not have fewer crimes against persons even when the probability of conviction, the punishment, and several other variables are held constant (Ehrlich 1973, tables 2–5). Note that Ehrlich's study, unlike the evidence from the Crime Commission, holds the "price" of crime constant when estimating the effects of income (and holds income constant when estimating the effects of price).

[47] Not much later, Jeremy Bentham reached a similar conclusion: "The pleasure derivable by any person from the contemplation of pain suffered by another, is in no instance so great as the pain so suffered" (Bentham 1952–54).

[48] Similarly, a sociologist recently has argued that envy is a powerful motive in primitive as well as advanced societies, communist as well as capitalist ones, and is critical in determining economic progress and public policy (see Schoeck 1966).

[49] "Own" income here includes the value of other aspects of the social environment.

social environment and own income by the same percentage, prices held constant, not affect social income or welfare. That is, a rise in all incomes in a community by the same percentage would not improve anyone's welfare in Veblen's world.[50]

If social income were negative, if the environment causing envy were more important than own income, a rise in the environment and own income by the same percentage would lower social income and welfare. That is, a general rise in incomes in a more extreme Veblenian world would actually lower welfare![51]

On the other hand, Smith's belief that envy is a relatively minor determinant of welfare implies that social income is positive: the environment causing envy is less important than own income. A rise in the environment and own income by the same percentage would then raise social income and welfare. That is, Veblen's general rise in the community's income would raise the welfare of the typical person.

4. Summary

This essay uses simple tools of economic theory to analyze interactions between the behavior of some persons and different characteristics of other persons. Although these interactions are emphasized in the contemporary sociological and anthropological literature, and were considered the cornerstone of behavior by several prominent nineteenth-century economists, they have been largely ignored in the modern economic literature.

The central concept of the analysis is "social income," the sum of a person's own income (his earnings, etc.) and the monetary value to him of the relevant characteristics of others, which I call his social environment. The optimal expenditure of his own income to alter these characteristics is given by the usual marginal conditions. By using the concept of social income, I can analyze the effect on these expenditures of changes in different sources of income and in different prices, including the "price" of the social environment. Perhaps the most important implication is that a change in own income alone would tend to cause a relatively large change in these expenditures; in other words, the own-income elasticity of demand for these expenditures would tend to be "large," certainly larger than the elasticity resulting from equal percentage changes in own income and the social environment.

[50] If $U_i = U_i(I_i/\bar{I})$, where $\bar{I}$ is the average community income, then $S_i = I_i - p_r\bar{I}$, where S_i is i's social income, and p_r is the price of $\bar{I}$ in terms of I_i. If i did not engage in predatory behavior, p_r would simply equal the slope of his indifference curve: slope = $dI_i/d\bar{I} = I_i/\bar{I} = p_r$. Hence $S_i = I_i - I_i/\bar{I} \cdot \bar{I} = 0$.

[51] When envy is so important, economic development is undesirable because it lowers welfare. See Schoeck's (1966) discussion of what he calls "the envy-barrier of the developing countries."

Interactions among members of the same family receive the greatest attention. The "head" of a family is defined not by sex or age, but as that member, if there is one, who transfers general purchasing power to all other members because he cares about their welfare. A family with a head is a highly interdependent organization that has the following properties:

A redistribution of income among members does not affect the consumption or welfare of any member because it simply induces offsetting changes in transfers from the head. As a result, each member is at least partially insured against disasters that may strike him.

Not only the head but other members too act "as if " they "loved" all members, even when they are really selfish, in the sense that they maximize not their own income alone but family income. As it were, the existence of a head economizes on the amount of true love required in a family.

A family acts "as if " it maximized a consistent and transitive utility function subject to a budget constraint that depended only on family variables. This utility function is the same as the head's not because he has dictatorial power, but because his concern for the welfare of other members integrates all their utility functions into one consistent "family" function.

Transfers from parents to children in the form, say, of schooling, gifts, and bequests tend to be negatively related to what the income of children would be relative to their parents in the absence of these transfers. Therefore, the relative income of children *inclusive* of transfers could be unrelated or even negatively related to these transfers. Consequently, one cannot infer anything about the stability across generations of economic or social positions simply from knowing the relation between parental position and the amount transferred.

More briefly treated are charity and envy, with special attention to the effects of different kinds of income change on charitable contributions and expenditures to alleviate envy. For example, the much higher income elasticity of demand for charitable contributions estimated from differences in individual incomes at a moment in time than from aggregate changes in incomes over time is shown to be implied by this theory of social interactions, but not readily by the traditional theory of choice.

From a methodological viewpoint, the aim of the paper is to show how another relation considered important in the sociological and anthropological literature can be usefully analyzed when incorporated into the framework provided by economic theory. Probably the main explanation for the neglect of social interactions by economists is neither analytical intractability nor a preoccupation with more important concepts, but excessive attention to formal developments during the last 70 years. As a consequence, even concepts considered to be important by earlier economists, such as social interactions, have been shunted aside.

Altruism, Egoism, and Genetic
Fitness: Economics and
Sociobiology

1. Introduction

Economists generally take tastes as "given," and work out the consequences of changes in prices, incomes, and other variables under the
assumption that tastes do not change. When pressed, either they engage in
ad hoc theorizing or they explicitly delegate the discussion of tastes to the
sociologist, psychologist, or anthropologist. Unfortunately, these disciplines have not developed much in the way of systematic, usable
knowledge about tastes.

Although economists have been reluctant to discuss systematically
changes in the structure of tastes, they have long relied on assumptions
about the basic and enduring properties of tastes. Self-interest is assumed
to dominate all other motives,[1] with a prominent place also assigned to
benevolence toward children[2] (and occasionally others), and with self-
interest partly dependent on distinction and other aspects of one's position
in society.[3] The dominance of self-interest and the persistence of some
benevolence have usually been explained by "human nature," or an
equivalent evasion of the problem.

Reprinted from the *Journal of Economic Literature* 14, no. 3 (September 1976). © 1976
by The American Economic Association.

[1] For example, Adam Smith said "We are not ready to suspect any person of being
defective in selfishness" (1968, p. 446), and "it is not from the benevolence of the
butcher, the brewer, or the baker, that we expect our dinner, but from their regard to
their own interest" (1937, p. 14).

[2] According to Alfred Marshall, "men labor and save chiefly for the sake of their
families and not for themselves" (1922, p. 228).

[3] Nassau Senior said, "the desire for distinction . . . may be pronounced to be the
most powerful of all human passions" (1938, p. 12).

The development of modern biology since the mid-19th century and of population genetics in the 20th century made clear that "human nature" is only the beginning, not the end of the answer. The enduring traits of human (and animal) nature presumably were genetically selected under very different physical environments and social arrangements as life on earth evolved during millions of years. It is not difficult to understand why self-interest has high survival value under very different circumstances,[4] but why should altruistic behavior, sometimes observed among animals as well as human beings also survive?

This kind of question has been asked by some geneticists and other biologists especially during the last two decades. Their work has recently been christened "sociobiology" by Edward Wilson in an important book that organizes and develops further what has been done. According to Wilson, "the central theoretical problem of sociobiology [is]: how can altruism, which by definition reduces personal fitness, possibly evolve by natural selection?" (1975, p. 3).

Sociobiologists have tried to solve their central problem by building models with "group selection"; these models can be illustrated with the particular variant called "kin selection." Suppose that a person is altruistic toward his brother, and is willing to lower his own genetic fitness[5] in order to increase his brother's fitness. If he lowers his own fitness by b units as a result of his altruistic behavior, he increases his brother's fitness by, say, c units. Since they have about $\frac{1}{2}$ of their genes in common, his altruism would increase the expected fitness of his own genes if $c > 2b$. In particular, it would then increase the expected fitness of the genes that contribute to hic altruism. Therefore, altruism toward siblings, children, grandchildren, or anyone with common genes could have high survival value, which would explain why altruism toward kin is one of the enduring traits of human and animal "nature."

The approach of sociobiologists is highly congenial to economists since they rely on competition, the allocation of limited resources—of, say, food and energy—efficient adaption to the environment, and other concepts also used by economists. Yet sociobiologists have stopped short of developing models having rational actors who maximize utility functions subject to limited resources. Instead they have relied solely on the "rationality" related to genetic selection: the physical and social environ-

---

[4] Ronald Coase (1976) argues convincingly that Adam Smith, especially in his *Moral Sentiments*, was groping toward an explanation of the importance of self-interest in terms of its contribution to viable social and economic arrangements.

[5] Genetic selection is defined as "the change in relative frequency in genotypes due to differences in the ability of their phenotypes to obtain representation in the next generation" (Wilson 1975, p. 67). Genetic fitness is the relative contribution of one genotype to the next generation's distribution of genotypes, where a genotype is "the genetic constitution of an organism" and a phenotype is "the observable properties of an organism" (Wilson 1975, pp. 585, 591).

ment discourages ill-suited behavior and encourages better-suited behavior. Economists, on the other hand, have relied solely on individual rationality, and have not incorporated the effects of genetic selection.[6]

I believe that a more powerful analysis can be developed by joining the individual rationality of the economist to the group rationality of the sociobiologist. To illustrate the potential, the central problem of sociobiology—the biological selection of altruistic behavior—is analyzed using recent work by economists on social interactions (see chap. 12, above, and Becker and Tomes 1976). I will show that models of group selection are unnecessary since altruistic behavior can be selected as a consequence of individual rationality.

2. An Economic Model of Altruism

Consider first the effect of altruism on consumption and wealth, the usual focus of economists. Essentially by definition, an altruist is willing to reduce his own consumption in order to increase the consumption of others. Two considerations suggest that the own consumption of egoistic persons (or animals) would exceed that of equally able altruistic persons (or animals).[7] The own consumption of egoists would be greater if the wealth of egoists and altruists were equal because altruists give away some of their wealth to be consumed by others. Moreover, the wealth of egoists apparently also would tend to be greater because egoists are willing to undertake all acts that raised their wealth, regardless of the effects on others, whereas altruists voluntarily forego some acts that raise their wealth because of adverse effects on others.

These forces are potent, but they are not the whole story, and a fuller analysis shows that the consumption and wealth of altruistic persons could exceed that of egoistic persons, even without bringing in social controls on the behavior of egoistic persons. Let us consider systematically the behavior of h, who is altruistic toward an egoist i. By definition of altruism, h is willing to give some of his wealth to i, but how much is he willing to give? That surely depends on his degree of altruism, his and i's wealth, the "cost" of giving, and other considerations.

The economic approach assumes that all behavior results from maximizing utility functions that depend on different commodities. If, to simplify, the allocation and transfer of time is neglected, and both h and

---

[6] Of course, economic analysis has sometimes been related to biological evolution: Alfred Marshall believed that economic systems evolve in the same way as biological systems do, and maximizing behavior has been said to be prevalent essentially because of the selection and survival of maximizers (see Alchian 1950). However, biological selection has not been integrated into and combined with the main body of economic analysis: it has been an occasional appendage rather than an integral part.

[7] Although the following discussion might be as applicable to animals as to persons, I simplify the presentation by referring only to persons.

i consume a single aggregate of market goods and services, the utility
function of an altruist *h* can be written as

$$U^h = U^h(X_h, X_i),^8 \tag{1}$$

where X_h and X_i are the own consumptions of *h* and *i* respectively. The
budget constraint of *h* can be written as

$$pX_h + h_i = I_h, \tag{2}$$

where h_i is the dollar amount transferred to *i*, and I_h is *h*'s own income.
If *h* transfers to *i* without any monetary loss or gain—"dollar for dollar"—
the amount received by *i* equals the amount transferred by *h*, and *i*'s
budget constraint would be

$$pX_i = I_i + h_i, \tag{3}$$

where I_i is *i*'s own income. By substitution of (3) into (2), the basic budget
constraint for *h* is derived:

$$pX_h + pX_i = I_h + I_i = S_h, \tag{4}$$

where *S* is called *h*'s "social income."[9]

The equilibrium condition for maximizing the utility function given by
equation (1) subject to the social income constraint given by (4) is

$$\frac{\partial U^h / \partial X_h}{\partial U^h / \partial X_i} = \frac{MU_h}{MU_i} = \frac{p}{p} = 1. \tag{5}$$

Then *h* would transfer just enough resources to *i* so that *h* would receive
the same utility from increments to his own or to *i*'s consumption. Put
differently, *h* would suffer the same loss in utility from a small change in
his own or *i*'s consumption.

Clearly, *h*'s altruism is relevant not only to transfers of income but also
to the production of income. He would pursue all actions that raised his
(real) social income and refrain from all that lowered it, because his utility
would be increased by all increases in his social income. Since the latter is
the sum of his own and *i*'s own income, he would, in particular, refrain
from actions that raised his own income at the expense of a greater
reduction in *i*'s own income. This was referred to earlier when it was said
that altruists have lower personal income (or wealth) than egoists because

---

[8] With many market goods and services, his utility function can be written as

$$U^h = U^h\{X_{h_1}, \ldots, X_{h_m}, g(X_{i_1}, \ldots, X_{i_m})\},$$

where X_{h_j} and X_{i_j} are the consumptions of the *j*th good by *h* and *i* respectively, and *g*
is a function that would have the same indifference curves as *i*'s utility function if *h*'s
welfare partly depended on *i*'s welfare.

[9] See chap. 12, above. The essentials of the economic analysis of altruism in the
present section are taken from that paper.

altruists do not take advantage of all opportunities to raise their own income.

Note, however, that some actions of altruistic h could increase his utility and own consumption while reducing his own income, a combination that is impossible for an egoist. Suppose that h could increase his social income by actions that lowered his own income and raised i's even more. Since h's utility would increase, he would increase both his own and i's consumption, as long as neither were an inferior good. He could increase his own consumption only by reducing his transfers to i because his own income declined; this is consistent with an increase in i's consumption because i's own income increased. Therefore, h's own consumption would increase even though his own income declined, and i's own consumption would increase even though transfers from h declined. Consequently, if an egoist and altruist began with the same consumption—the own income of the altruist necessarily being greater—events could raise the consumption of the altruist above that of the egoist at the same time that they lowered the difference in their incomes.

The most important consideration benefiting altruists, however, and one that seems puzzling and paradoxical at first, is that egoistic i has an incentive to act "as if" he too were altruistic—toward h—in the sense that it would be to i's advantage to raise the combined incomes of i and h. In particular, i would refrain from actions that lowered h's own income unless i's was raised even more, and i would lower his own income if h's were raised even more.

Why should egoist i act as if he were altruistic? Consider the consequences to him (all that he cares about) of doing the contrary; for example, let i raise his own income at the expense of lowering h's even more. Since h's social income and utility decline because the sum of his own and i's income declines, h would want to reduce his own and i's own consumption. Then h would have to reduce his transfers to i by more than the increase in i's income. Therefore, as long as h's transfers remained positive, i's own consumption and welfare would be reduced by h's response. If i anticipated correctly h's reaction, i would refrain from these actions. A similar argument shows that i would benefit from his own actions even if they lowered his income, as long as they raised h's income even more: for h would increase his transfers to i by more than the reduction in i's income.

In other words, by linking i's consumption with his own, the altruistic h discourages egoistic i from actions that lower h's consumption because then i's consumption would also be lower. Moreover, i would not refrain from harming other egoistic persons not linked to h. Therefore, the intuitively appealing conclusion that the own consumption of egoistic persons exceeds that of equally able altruistic persons is seriously qualified when interaction with others is incorporated. Even though an altruist gives away part of his income and refrains from some actions that raise his own income, his own consumption might not be less than that of an egoist because the beneficiaries of his altruism would consider the effect of their behavior on his consumption. These beneficial indirect effects on the behavior of others may dominate the direct "disadvantages" of being altruistic. Moreover, these indirect effects need not be minor, and could greatly exceed the amount transferred to i. For example, assume that h transfers \$1,000, and that i could increase his own income by \$800 at the cost of harming h by \$5,000. Since i would not take these actions, h's altruism has increased his income by \$5,000, or by five times the amount transferred to i.

The analysis is easily extended to incorporate altruism by h toward egoistic persons $j, k, \ldots$, as well as i. Then h would transfer resources to $j, k, \ldots$, as well as i, and maximize a utility function of all these consumptions subject to a social income constraint equal to the sum of all these own incomes. Following the previous analysis, it can be shown that h would refrain from actions that raised his own income if the combined incomes of $i, j, k, \ldots$, were lowered even more. Moreover, he would lower his own income if their combined incomes were raised even more.

Furthermore, not only i but each of the others would lower his own income if h's were raised more, and would refrain from raising his own income if h's were lowered still more. Therefore, h may give away more of his income, and refrain from more actions that raise his own income, yet he would benefit more too because more people would consider the effects of their behavior on him. Consequently, although the direct effects reducing his own consumption are stronger for an altruist toward many persons than toward a single person, the indirect effects are also stronger. The own consumption of an altruist toward many persons also need not be less than that of an equally able egoist.

The most important new consequence of multiperson altruism relates to the behavior of recipients toward each other. Although $i, j, k, \ldots$, are all egoistical and do not give or receive transfers from each other, each has an incentive to consider the effects of his behavior on the others. For example, j would not raise his own income if the sum of the incomes of $i, k, \ldots$, were reduced still more, and j would lower his own income if their incomes were raised still more. Elsewhere I have called this the "rotten kid" theorem (see chap. 12, above), although its applicability is not restricted to interaction among siblings.

To prove this theorem, assume the contrary; for example, let j raise his income and lower k's still more. Then h's social income (and utility) would be reduced because it is the sum of j's, k's, and the other's own incomes. Consequently, h would reduce the consumption of both j and k, assuming that these consumptions are superior goods to him, and would reduce his transfers to j by more than j's increase in income, and raise his transfers to k by less than k's decrease in income. In the end, j as well as k (and everyone else) would be worse off; if j could anticipate h's reaction, he would refrain from raising his income at greater expense to k.

Even though $i, j, k, \ldots$ are completely egoistical, they are linked together through h's altruism. Their own interest, not altruism, motivates them to maximize the sum of their own and h's incomes—that is, to maximize h's social income. This provides another reason why an altruist's own consumption may not be less than an egoist's consumption: beneficiaries of his altruism consider all indirect as well as direct effects of their behavior on his own consumption. They do not consider the effect of their behavior on the consumption of other persons not linked to this altruist.

Note that a sufficiently large redistribution of income away from h and toward $i, j, k, \ldots$, would make h unwilling to transfer resources to some of these persons, say to k. Then k and h would continue to be interested in maximizing the same social income only if the income redistribution induced k to transfer resources to h (or induced someone else, like j, to transfer to k). That is, k's (or someone else's) altruism—h's altruism toward k and k's toward h is an example of "reciprocal altruism"[10]— would increase the robustness of the conclusions with respect to large redistributions of income within the group initially related through h's altruism.

Each person in the group linked by an altruist's transfers has an incentive to maximize the group's total income, even if most are egoistical. The group's income could be maximized in the absence of altruism if the "government" imposed appropriate taxes and subsidies, or if members bargained with each other only to take actions that benefited the group as a whole. However, appropriate voluntary agreements and government action often are not achieved, especially when governments are primitive or subject to many pressure groups, contract law is not well developed, or other private transactions costs are sizable. Therefore, whereas the private behavior induced by the "rotten kid" theorem in an altruistic situation *automatically* maximizes group income, government responses or the Coase theorem (on private bargaining)[11] do not.

Recipients of h's transfers are encouraged to act "as if" they are altruistic to each other and to h by the adverse reaction from h when they act egoistically. Therefore, the "rotten kid" theorem is essentially a theorem about the incentive egoists have to *simulate* altruism when they benefit from someone else's altruism. More generally, an egoist has an incentive to try to simulate altruism whenever altruistic behavior increases his own consumption through its effect on the behavior of others. For

[10] The term "reciprocal altruism" is used in a different and misleading way in sociobiology. It refers not to true altruism but to one type of simulated altruism: a person helps others in the expectation or hope that he will be helped by them in the future (see Wilson 1975, pp. 120–21). This is more appropriately called "social exchange" by sociologists (see Blau 1968).

[11] The rotten kid theorem, therefore, is a powerful substitute for the Coase theorem when there is altruism.

example, egoist *n* may have an incentive to act as if he were altruistic toward *j*, in the sense that he would voluntarily transfer resources to *j*, maximize their combined own incomes, reduce his transfers when their combined own income fell, etc., if this discourages *j* from actions that harm *n*.

If egoists can always perfectly simulate altruism whenever altruistic behavior raises their own consumption, then, of course, the own consumption of true altruists would not exceed that of true egoists; they would be equal when egoists perfectly simulated altruism. We could still conclude, however, that "apparent" altruistic behavior—either true or simulated altruism—could increase own consumption, and that is important. Moreover, if altruism could be perfectly simulated, transactions and negotiation costs must be sufficiently small so that the Coase theorem could prevail. Conversely, if the Coase theorem broke down, say because of sizable bluffing and other bargaining costs, altruism could not be perfectly simulated, for otherwise the Coase theorem would prevail. When altruism cannot be perfectly simulated, the own consumption of altruists could exceed, perhaps by a good deal, the consumption of equally able egoists.

3. Genetic Fitness and the Economic Model of Altruism

Since sociobiologists are more concerned with selection and genetic fitness than with consumption and wealth per se, I can bring out sharply the relationship between this economic analysis of altruism and the central problem of sociobiology by reformulating the utility function to depend only on genetic fitness. Then altruistic *h* would have the function

$$U^h = U^h(f_h, f_i), \tag{6}$$

where f_h and f_i measure the fitness of *h* and *i* respectively, and the utility function of egoist *i* would depend only on his own fitness. Since genetic fitness depends directly on birth and death rates of offspring, and on own life expectancy only to the extent that it influences the number of offspring, even an egoist must be somewhat concerned about the well-being of mates and children.

In the language of the household production approach to consumer behavior (*see* Michael and Becker 1973), genetic fitness is a commodity produced by households using their own time and goods, their skills, experience and abilities, and the physical and social environment. For example, the fitness of *h* would be produced according to

$$f_h = f_h(X_h, t_h,; S_h, E_h), \tag{7}$$

where t_h is the time he directly[12] uses to produce fitness—as in the care and protection of children—S_h is his stock of skills and other human capital, and E_h is the environment.

If t, S and E were exogenous, fitness could be changed only by changing the input of goods. With the exception of a small part of the human population during the last 100 years or so, access to food and perhaps some other goods has been the main determinant of fitness throughout the biological world. The close relation between fitness and goods can be made transparent by writing the production function for fitness as

$$f = aX, \tag{8}$$

where a depends on the biological species and also on the parameters t, S, and E.[13] Fitness does not have a market price since it is not directly purchased, but does have a "shadow" price, defined as the value of the goods used in changing fitness by one unit:

$$\pi = \frac{\partial(pX)}{\partial f} = \frac{p}{a}, \tag{9}$$

where p is the (constant) price or cost of X.

Altruistic h is willing to transfer some of his goods to i because he is willing to reduce his own fitness in order to improve i's fitness. This is precisely the definition of altruism in sociobiology: "When a person (or animal) increases the fitness of another at the expense of his own fitness, he can be said to have performed an act of *altruism*" (see Wilson 1975, p. 117).

The budget constraint for h can be derived by substituting equation (8) into equation (4):

$$\frac{pf_h}{a_h} + \frac{pf_i}{a_i} = I_h + I_i = S_h, \tag{10}$$

or by equation (9),

$$\pi_h f_h + \pi_i f_i = S_h.$$

Therefore, h's social income is partly spent on his own and partly on i's fitness: the sum of the shadow values placed on their fitnesses equals his social income.

[12] A brief but suggestive discussion of the allocation of time (and energy) in the biological world can be found in Wilson (1975, pp. 143–43).

[13] A more appropriate formulation might be

$$f = \alpha X,$$

where α depends on the species, and X is produced by the function

$$X = \psi(t, S, E).$$

For present purposes, however, this formulation and the one in the text are essentially equivalent.

The equilibrium condition for maximizing h's utility function (6) subject to his budget constraint (10) is, with positive transfers,

$$\frac{\partial U^h/\partial f_h}{\partial U^h/\partial f_i} = \frac{\pi_h}{\pi_i} = \frac{a_i}{a_h}. \tag{11}$$

If h and i were equally efficient producers of fitness, $a_h = a_i$, and h would transfer goods to i until he was indifferent between equal increments to his own and to i's fitness. If h were a more efficient producer of fitness, $a_h > a_i$, and he would be discouraged from promoting i's fitness: he would receive more utility from an increment to i's fitness than from an equal increment to his own fitness because his own fitness is cheaper to produce.

The important point is that all the earlier results on the consumption of goods apply equally to this analysis of fitness. Both the altruist h and the egoistical recipient i maximize the *sum* of their real incomes, and would raise one of them only when the other were not reduced even more. In terms of fitness, they maximize the sum of the values placed on fitness, and would increase the fitness of one only if the shadow value of its increase were not less than the shadow value of the decrease in the other's fitness:

$$\pi_h \, df_h + \pi_i \, df_i \geq 0. \tag{12}$$

For example, if $\pi_i > \pi_h$ because h is more efficient at producing fitness, any increase in h's fitness will have to be at least π_i/π_h times as large as the decrease in i's fitness.

I concluded earlier that although an altruist foregoes some own consumption to raise the consumption of others, and foregoes some opportunities to raise his own income to avoid lowering the income of others, his own consumption may exceed that of an equally able egoist because the beneficiaries of his altruism are discouraged from harming him. Reasoning along the same lines, one can reach the same conclusion for altruism with regard to genetic fitness: although an altruist foregoes some own fitness to raise the fitness of others, and so forth, his own fitness may exceed that of an equally able egoist because the beneficiaries of his altruism are discouraged from harming him.

Therefore, two apparently equivalent statements about altruism by Wilson are in fact quite different. He says "altruism . . . *by definition* reduces personal fitness" (1975, p. 3, my italics), yet simply defines an act of altruism as "when a person (or animal) increases the fitness of another at the expense of his own fitness" (1975, p. 117). Using the latter definition, I have shown that altruism may actually increase personal fitness because of its effect on the behavior of others. Consequently, altruism does not by (Wilson's or my) definition necessarily reduce personal fitness.

This conclusion is highly relevant in answering the central question of sociobiology: "How can altruism . . . evolve by natural selection?"

(Wilson 1975, p. 3). If altruism, on balance, raises own genetic fitness, then natural selection would operate in its favor. A central focus of sociobiology would be to identify when biological and social conditions have a sufficient effect on the behavior of the beneficiaries of altruism so that own fitness is increased by altruism.

Note that the extensive evidence among animals of what appears to be altruistic behavior (see Wilson 1975, pp. 121–28)—for example, baboons expose themselves to danger to protect relatives—is not inconsistent with altruism's increasing personal fitness because the effects of altruism on the behavior of beneficiaries have not been considered. Note, moreover, the incentive to try to simulate altruism whenever true altruism raises personal fitness, and sociobiologists have found it difficult to distinguish simulated altruism from true altruism.[14]

Even if altruism lowers fitness, and the sociobiologist's group selection must be used to explain how altruism evolves by selection, the actual tradeoff between an altruist's and a beneficiary's fitness may be much more favorable to selection of altruism than the apparent tradeoff. For example, if h were altruistic toward a brother i with about half his genes in common, kin selection would favor h's altruistic (and other) genes only if he could increase i's fitness by at least two units for every unit reduction in his own fitness. Since according to equation (12) he would be willing to exchange a unit of his own fitness for at least π_h/π_i units of i's, apparently his altruistic genes can be selected only if $\pi_h > 2\pi_i$, or only if his brother is more than twice as efficient in producing fitness as he is.

Yet when all the effects of his altruism on i are considered, his genes may be strongly selected even when i is much less than twice as efficient as he is. Assume, for example, that the total loss in h's fitness from his altruism would be 5 units if he and i were equally efficient producers of fitness. Assume further that the total gain to his brother would be 15 units—the gain to his brother *must* be at least as large as his own loss since his altruism cannot decrease their combined fitness (by equation [12] when $\pi_h = \pi_i$). Instead of the apparent rate of exchange of one unit of his brother's fitness for one unit of his own, or the 2 to 1 minimum rate required to select his altruistic genes, he adds three units to his brother's fitness for each unit of his own loss.

The utility function (6) and the analysis can again be generalized to include altruism by h toward $j, k, \ldots$, as well as i. He would try to maximize the sum of his own and their real incomes, and would affect different fitnesses only if the sum of the shadow values of the changes were nonnegative:

$$\pi_h \, df_h + \pi_i \, df_i + \pi_j \, df_j + \pi_k \, df_k + , \cdots, \geq 0. \tag{13}$$

[14] The literature on altruism among animals reveals how difficult it is to distinguish true from simulated and other apparent altruism (see Wilson 1975, pp. 123–25).

Each beneficiary of h's altruism also maximizes the group's total real income, and is constrained in his behavior by equation (13); in particular, each would reduce the fitness of another member of the group only if the value of the reduction were less than the value of the increase in his own fitness.

The sociobiological literature contends that a major conflict arises between parents and children because the altruism of parents toward children exceeds the altruism of children toward each other: "There is likely to evolve a conflict between parents and offspring in the attitudes toward siblings: the parents will encourage more altruism than the youngster is prepared to give" (Wilson 1975, p. 343), or, "Conflict during socialization need not be viewed solely as conflict between the culture of the parent and the biology of the child; it can also be viewed as conflict between the biology of the parent and the biology of the child" (quoted in Wilson 1975, p. 343, from Trivers 1974). My analysis denies that such a conflict exists if parents are altruistic, because children have an incentive to act as altruistically toward each other as their parents want them to, even if children are really egoistical. This application of the more general result on the simulation of altruism by beneficiaries led to the name "the rotten kid" theorem.

Of course, the substitution between the fitness of parents and children that is due to the parent's altruism might not maximize the selection of his altruistic genes. However, the actual substitution may be much more favorable to the selection of his genes than substitution given by the shadow prices of fitness. For example, if these prices were equal, a parent would be willing to give up a unit of his fitness to increase the fitness of each child by a unit; yet his altruism might be strongly selected: both his and his children's fitness might actually exceed what they would be if he were not altruistic, or the reduction in his fitness might be much less than the increase in their's.[15]

4. Conclusion

Sociobiologists have explained the strong survival throughout most of the biological world of altruism toward children and other kin by group selection operating through the common genes of kin. Using an economic model of altruism, I have explained its survival by the advantages of

---

[15] If $\pi_h = \pi_i = \pi_j = \pi_k, \ldots$, then necessarily by equation (13)

$$G_c + L_h \geq 0,$$

where L_h is the total change in the parent's (h) fitness that results from his altruism, and G_c is the total change in his children's fitness. It could also be that

$$G_c > -2L_h,$$

or even that L_h as well as $G_c > 0$.

altruism when there is physical and social interaction: kin have had much interaction with each other because they have usually lived with or near each other. Since the economic model requires interaction, not common genes, it can also explain the survival of some altruism toward unrelated neighbors or coworkers, and these are not explained by the kin selection models of sociobiologists (but perhaps can be explained by their other models of group selection).

I have argued that both economics and sociobiology would gain from combining the analytical techniques of economists with the techniques in population genetics, entomology, and other biological foundations of sociobiology. The preferences taken as given by economists and vaguely attributed to "human nature" or something similar—the emphasis on self-interest, altruism toward kin, social distinction, and other enduring aspects of preferences—may be largely explained by the selection over time of traits having greater survival value.[16] However, survival value is in turn partly a result of utility maximization in different social and physical environments. To demonstrate this I have shown how the central problem of sociobiology, the natural selection of altruism, can be resolved by considering the interaction between the utility-maximizing behavior of altruists and egoists.

[16] A few years ago Michael and I already suggested that "if genetical natural selection and rational behavior reinforce each other in producing speedier and more efficient responses to changes in the environment, perhaps that common preference function has evolved over time by natural selection and rational choice as that preference function best adopted to human society" (see chap. 7, above).

References

Adams, James D. 1974. "Asset Transfers at Deathtime." Department of Economics, University of Chicago.

Adelman, I. 1963. "An Econometric Analysis of Population Growth." *American Economic Review* 53 (June): 314–39.

Alchian, A. A. 1950. "Uncertainty, Evolution and Economic Theory." *Journal of Political Economy* 58 (June).

Alchian, A. A., and Allen, W. R. 1967. *University Economics.* 2d ed. Belmont, Cal.: Wadsworth.

Alchian, A. A., and Demsetz, H. 1972. "Production, Information Costs, and Economic Organization." *American Economic Review* 62 (December).

Alchian, A. A., and Kessel, R. A. 1960. "Competition, Monopoly, and the Pursuit of Pecuniary Gains." In Universities–National Bureau Conference for Economic Research, *Aspects of Labor Economics.* Princeton University Press.

Allport. 1955. *The Nature of Prejudice.* Cambridge, Mass.: Addison-Wesley Press.

Alstrom, C. H. 1961. "A Study of Inheritance of Human Intelligence." *Acta Psychiatrica et Neurologica Scandinavica.*

Aptheker, H. 1946. *The Negro Problem in America.* New York: International Publishers.

Arrington, L. J. 1958. *Great Basin Kingdom.* Lincoln: University of Nebraska Press.

Arrow, K. J. 1962. "Economic Welfare and Allocation of Resources for Invention." In National Bureau Committee for Economic Research, *The Rate and Direction of Inventive Activity: Economic and Social Factors.* Princeton: Princeton University Press.

Azzi, C., and Ehrenberg, R. 1975. "Household Allocation of Time and Church Attendance." *Journal of Political Economy* 83 (February).

Bajema, C. J. 1963. "Estimation of the Direction and Intensity of Natural Selection in Relation to Human Intelligence by Means of the Intrinsic Rate of Natural Increase." *Eugenics Quarterly* 10 (December).

Banks, W. H. 1955. "Differential Fertility in Madison County, New York, 1865." *Milbank Memorial Fund Quarterly* 33 (April).

Barro, R. 1974. "Are Government Bonds Net Wealth?" *Journal of Political Economy* 82 (November/December).

Becker, G. S. 1957 (1st ed.), 1971 (2d ed.). *The Economics of Discrimination.* University of Chicago Press.

———. 1960. "An Economic Analysis of Fertility." In *Demographic and Economic Change in Developed Countries,* a conference of the Universities–National Bureau Committee for Economic Research. Princeton University Press for the National Bureau of Economic Research. Reprinted as chapter 9 of this book.

———. 1961. "Notes on an Economic Analysis of Philanthropy." Mimeographed. National Bureau of Economic Research.

———. 1962. "Irrational Behavior and Economic Theory. *Journal of Political Economy* 70: 1–13. Reprinted as chapter 8 of this book.

———. 1964 (1st ed.), 1975 (2d ed.). *Human Capital: A Theoretical and Empirical Analysis.* New York: Columbia University Press for the National Bureau of Economic Research.

———. 1965. "A Theory of the Allocation of Time." *Economic Journal* 75. Reprinted in this volume as chapter 5.

———. 1967. *Human Capital and the Personal Distribution of Income: An Analytical Approach.* Ann Arbor: Institute of Public Administration, University of Michigan.

———. 1968. "Interdependent Preferences: Charity, Externalities, and Income Taxation." Mimeographed. University of Chicago.

———. 1969. "A Theory of Social Interactions." Manuscript. Printed in 1974 in the *Journal of Political Economy* 82 (November/December) and reprinted as chapter 12 of this book.

———. 1971a. *See* Becker 1957.

———. 1971b. *Economic Theory.* New York: Knopf.

———. 1973. "A Theory of Marriage, Part I." *Journal of Political Economy* 81 (July/August). *See* chapter 11 of this book.

———. 1974. "A Theory of Marriage, Part II." *Journal of Political Economy* 82 (March/April), pt. 2. *See* chapter 11 of this book.

———. 1975. *See* Becker 1964.

———. N.d. "Child Mortality, Fertility, and Population Growth." Mimeographed.

Becker, G. S., and Landes, W. M., eds. 1974. *Essays in the Economics of Crime and Punishment.* New York: Columbia University Press for the National Bureau of Economic Research.

Becker, G. S., and Stigler, G. J. 1974. "Law Enforcement, Malfeasance, and Compensation of Enforcers." *Journal of Legal Studies* 3, no. 1 (January): 1–18.

Becker, G. S., and Tomes, N. 1976. "Child Endowments and the Quantity and Quality of Children." *Journal of Political Economy* 84 (August).

Benham, L. 1974. "Benefits of Women's Education Within Marriage." *Journal of Political Economy* 82 (March/April).

Ben-Porath, Y. 1973. "Economic Analysis of Fertility in Israel: Point and Counterpoint." *Journal of Political Economy* 81 (March/April). Supplement.

———. 1967. "The Production of Human Capital and the Life Cycle of Earnings." *Journal of Political Economy* 75 (August).

Bentham, J. 1931*a*. *An Introduction to the Principles of Legislation*. New York: Harcourt, Brace.

———. 1931*b*. *Theory of Legislation*. New York: Harcourt, Brace.

———. 1952–54. "The Philosophy of Economic Science." In *J. Bentham's Economic Writings*, ed. Stark. 3 vols. New York: Franklin.

———. 1963. *An Introduction to the Principles of Morals and Legislation*. New York: Hafner.

Ben-Zion, U., and Ehrlich, I. 1972. "A Model of Productive Saving." Unpublished. For a revised, published version, see Ehrlich and Ben-Zion (1976).

Black, J. D. 1926. *Introduction to Production Economics*. New York: Henry Holt.

Blau, P. M. 1968. "Social Exchange." In *International Encyclopedia of the Social Sciences* ed. D. E. Sills. Vol. 7. New York: Macmillan and Free Press, 1968.

Boulding, K. 1966. *Economic Analysis*. New York: Harper and Row.

———. 1973. *The Economy of Love and Fear*. California: Wadsworth.

Brady, D., and Friedman, R. 1947. "Savings and the Income Distribution." In *Studies in Income and Wealth*, vol. 10. New York: National Bureau of Economic Research.

Bureau of the Budget. 1967. *The Budget of United States Government, 1968, Appendix*. Washington: U.S. Government Printing Office.

Bureau of Prisons. 1960. *Prisoners Released From State and Federal Institutions*. National Prisoner Statistics. Washington: U.S. Department of Justice.

———. 1961. *Federal Prisons, 1960*. Washington: U.S. Department of Justice.

———. n.d. *Characteristics of State Prisoners, 1960*. National Prisoner Statistics. Washington: U.S. Department of Justice.

Cairncross, A. K. 1958. "Economic Schizophrenia." *Scottish Journal of Political Economy* (February).

Cagan, P. 1965. *Determinants and Effects of Changes in the Stock of Money, 1875–1960*. New York: Columbia University Press for the National Bureau of Economic Research.

Cavalli-Sforza, L. L., and Bodmer, W. F. 1971. *The Genetics of Human Populations*. San Francisco: Freeman.

Chow, G. C. 1957. *Demand for Automobiles in the United States*. Amsterdam: North-Holland.

Coale, A. S., and McNeil, D. R. 1972. "The Distribution by Age of the Frequency of First Marriage in a Female Cohort." *Journal of the American Statistical Association* 67 (December).

Coase, R. H. 1974. "The Market for Goods and the Market for Ideas." *American Economic Review* 64 (May).

———. 1976. "Adam Smith's View of Man." *Journal of Law and Economics* 19 (October).

Conrad, A. H., and Meyer, J. R. "The Economics of Slavery in the Ante Bellum South." *Journal of Political Economy* 66 (April).

Coontz, S. H. 1957. *Population Theories and the Economic Interpretation, Part II*. London: Routledge.

Corbett, W. J., and Hague, D. C. 1953–54. "Complementarity and the Excess Burden of Taxation." *Review of Economic Studies* 21.

Cox, D. R., and Smith, W. I. 1961. *Queues*. New York: Wiley.

Cox, O. C. 1948. *Caste, Class, and Race*. Garden City, N.J.: Doubleday.

Cramer, J. S. 1964. "Efficient Grouping, Regression and Correlation in Engel Curve Analysis." *Journal of the American Statistical Association* 59.

Crime Commission. *See* President's Commission.

"Criminal Safeguards and the Punitive Damages Defendant." 1967. *University of Chicago Law Review* 34.

Dean, E. 1966. *The Supply Responses of African Farmers: Theory and Measurement in Malawi*. Amsterdam: North-Holland.

DeTray, D. 1973. "Child Quality and the Demand for Children." *Journal of Political Economy* 81, no. 2, pt 2. (March/April): 70–95.

"Differential Fertility 1910 and 1940." 1945. Washington: Government Printing Office.

Director, A. 1964. "The Parity of the Market Place." *Journal of Law and Economics* (October).

Dollard, J. 1937. *Caste and Class in a Southern Town*. New Haven: Yale University Press.

Dorjahn, V. R. 1958. "The Factor of Polygyny in African Demography." In *Continuity and Change in African Cultures*, ed. W. R. Bascom and M. J. Herskovits. University of Chicago Press.

Downs, A. 1957a. *An Economic Theory of Democracy*. New York: Harper.

———. 1957b. "An Economic Theory of Political Action in a Democracy." *Journal of Political Economy* 67: 135.

Dublin, L. I., and Lotka, A. J. 1946. *The Money Value of a Man*. New York: Ronald Press.

Duesenberry, J. S. 1949. *Income, Savings, and the Theory of Consumer Behavior*. Cambridge: Harvard University Press.

————. 1960. Comment on "An Economic Analysis of Fertility" (*see* Becker 1960).

Easterlin, R. A. 1961. "The American Baby Boom in Historical Perspective." *American Economic Review* (December).

"Economics." 1963. *Columbia Encyclopedia.* New York: Columbia University Press.

Edin, K. A., and Hutchinson, E. P. 1935. *Studies of Differential Fertility.* London.

Edwards, W. 1954, 1960. "The Theory of Decision Making." *Psychological Bulletin* 51 (July). Reprinted in *Some Theories of Organization,* ed. A. Rubenstein and C. J. Haberstroh. Homewood, Ill.: Irwin.

Ehrlich, I. 1967. "The Supply of Illegitimate Activities." Manuscript. Columbia University.

————. 1970. "Participation in Illegitimate Activities: An Economic Analysis." Ph.D. dissertation, Columbia University.

————. 1973. "Participation in Illegitimate Activities: A Theoretical and Empirical Investigation." *Journal of Political Economy* 81 (May/June).

————. 1975. "Capital Punishment: A Case of Life or Death." *American Economic Review* (June).

Ehrlich, I., and Becker, G. S. 1972. "Market Insurance, Self-Insurance, and Self-Protection." *Journal of Political Economy* 80, no. 4 (July/August): 623–48.

Ehrlich, I., and Ben-Zion, U. 1976. "Asset Management, Allocation of Time, and Returns to Saving." *Economic Inquiry* (September).

Federal Bureau of Investigation. 1960. *Uniform Crime Reports for the United States.* Washington: U.S. Department of Justice.

————. 1961. Ibid.

Federal Reserve Bulletin. August 1956.

"Fertility." 1955. Washington: Government Printing Office.

Finnegan, A. 1962. "A Cross-Sectional Analysis of Hours of Work." *Journal of Political Economy* 70 (October).

Fisher, I. 1892, 1926. *Mathematical Investigations in the Theory of Value and Price.* Reprinted New Haven: Yale University Press.

————. 1930. *The Theory of Interest.* New York: Macmillan.

Fisher, R. A. 1958. *The Genetical Theory of Natural Selection.* 2d ed. New York: Dover.

Freedman, R.; Goldberg, D.; Sharp, H. 1955. " 'Ideals' about Family Size in the Detroit Metropolitan Area, 1954." *Milbank Memorial Fund Quarterly* 33 (April).

Freedman, D. 1963. "The Relation of Economic Status to Fertility." *American Economic Review* (June).

Freiden, A. 1972. "A Model of Marriage and Fertility." Ph.D. dissertation, University of Chicago.

————. 1974. "The United States Marriage Market." *Jonrnal of Political Economy* 82 (March/April), pt. 2.

Friedman, M. 1953. "The Methodology of Positive Economics." In *Essays in Positive Economics*. Chicago: University of Chicago Press.

Fuchs, Victor. 1968. *The Service Economy*. New York: Columbia University Press for the National Bureau of Economic Research.

Galbraith, V. L., and Thomas, D. S. 1956. "Birth Rates and the Interwar Business Cycles." In *Demographic Analysis*. Edited by J. J. Spengler and O. D. Duncan. Glencoe: Free Press.

Ghez, G. 1970. "A Theory of Life Cycle Consumption." Ph.D. dissertation, Columbia University.

Ghez, G. R., and Becker, G. S. 1975. *The Allocation of Time and Goods over the Life Cycle*. New York: Columbia University Press for the National Bureau of Economic Research.

Glass, D. V., and Grebenik, E. 1954. "The Trend and Pattern of Fertility in Great Britain." Papers of the Royal Commission on Population, vol. 6, London: H.M. Stationery Office.

Goode, W. 1963. *World Revolution and Family Patterns*. New York: Free Press.

De Grazia, S. 1962. *Of Time, Work and Leisure*. New York: Twentieth Century Fund.

Griliches, Z. 1957. "Hybrid Corn: An Exploration in the Economics of 'Technical Change'." *Econometrica* 25 (October).

———. 1961. "Hedonic Price Indexes for Automobiles: An Econometric Analysis of Quality Change." In *The Price Statistics of the Federal Government*. National Bureau of Economic Research, General Series no. 73.

Gronau, R. 1970*a*. "An Economic Approach to Marriage: The Intrafamily Allocation of Time." Paper presented at the Second World Congress of the Econometric Society, Cambridge, England.

———. 1970*b*. *The Value of Time in Passenger Transportation: The Demand for Air Travel*. New York: National Bureau of Economic Research, Occasional Paper 109.

———. 1972. *The Wage Rates of Women: A Selectivity Bias*. New York: National Bureau of Economic Research.

———. 1975. "Wage Comparison: A Selectivity Bias." *Journal of Political Economy* 83 (November/December).

Grossman, M. 1971. "The Economics of Joint Production in the Household." Report 7145, Center for Mathematical Studies in Business and Economics, University of Chicago.

———. 1972. *The Demand for Health: A Theoretical and Empirical Investigation*. New York: Columbia University Press for the National Bureau of Economic Research.

Guttentag, J. 1958. "Some Studies of the Post-World War II Residential Construction and Mortgage Markets." Ph.D. dissertation, Department of Economics, Columbia University.

Hall, Edward T. 1959. *The Silent Language*. New York: Doubleday.

Hammermesh, D., and Soss, N. M. 1974. "An Economic Theory of Suicide." *Journal of Political Economy* 82 (January/February).

Harberger, A. C. 1964. "Taxation, Resource Allocation and Welfare." In the *Role of Direct and Indirect Taxes in the Federal Revenue System*. Princeton University Press.

Harper, F. V., and James, F. 1956. *The Law of Torts*. Vol. 2. Boston: Little, Brown & Co.

Heckman, J. 1971. "Three Essays on Household Labor Supply and the Demand for Market Goods." Ph.D. dissertation, Princeton University.

———. 1974. "Shadow Prices, Market Wages, and Labor Supply." *Econometrica* 42, no. 4 (July).

Henderson, J. M. 1958. *The Efficiency of the Coal Industry: An Application of Linear Programming*. Cambridge: Harvard University Press.

Henderson, J. M., and Quandt, R. E. 1958. *Microeconomic Theory*. New York: McGraw-Hill.

Hicks, J. R. 1948. *The Theory of Wages*. New York: Peter Smith.

Higgins, J. V.; Reed, W. E.; and Reed, S. C. 1962. "Intelligence and Family Size: A Paradox Resolved." *Eugenics Q.* 9 (March).

Himes, N. A. 1936. *Medical History of Contraception*. Baltimore: The Williams and Wilkins Company.

Hotelling, H. 1935. "Demand Functions with Limited Budgets." *Econometrica* (January), pp. 66–78.

Houghton, D. H., and Philcox, D. 1950. "Family Income and Expenditure in a Ciskei Native Reserve." *South African Journal of Economics* 18 (December).

Houthhakker, H. S. 1952. "Compensated Changes in Quantities and Qualities Consumed." *Review of Economic Studies* 29, no. 3: 155–64.

———. 1961. "The Present State of Consumption Theory." *Econometrica* 29: 704–40.

Huntington, E., and Whitney, L. F. 1927. *The Builders of America*. New York: Morrow.

Jaffe, A. J. 1940. "Differential Fertility in the White Population in Early America." *Journal of Heredity* (August).

Jencks, C. 1972. *Inequality*. New York: Basic Books.

Johnson, H. 1952. "The Effect of Income-Redistribution on Aggregate Consumption with Interdependence of Consumers' Preferences." *Economica* (May).

Johnson, Thomas. 1967. "The Effects of the Minimum Wage Law." Ph.D. dissertation, Columbia University.

Juster, F. T. 1971. "A Framework for the Measurement of Economic and Social Performances." Mimeographed. New York: National Bureau of Economic Research.

Kain, J. F. 1963. *Commuting and the Residential Decisions of Chicago and Detroit Central Business District Workers*. New York: National Bureau of Economic Research.

Kaplan, A., and Lasswell, H. 1950. *Power and Society*. New Haven: Yale University Press.

Keeley, M. C. 1974. "A Model of Marital Formation: The Determinants of the Optimal Age of First Marriage and Differences in Age of Marriage." Ph.D. dissertation, University of Chicago.

Keynes, J. M. 1962. *The General Theory of Employment, Interest, and Money*. Harcourt, Brace and World.

Kirk, D. 1956. "The Relation of Employment Levels to Births in Germany." In *Demographic Analysis*. Edited by J. J. Spengler and O. D. Duncan. Glencoe: Free Press.

Kiser, C. V. 1960. "Differential Fertility in the United States. In *Demographic and Economic Change in Developed Countries*, a conference of the Universities–National Bureau Committee for Economic Research. Princeton University Press for the National Bureau of Economic Research.

Kleinman, E. 1967. "The Choice between Two 'Bads'—Some Economic Aspects of Criminal Sentencing." Mimeographed. Hebrew University, Jerusalem.

Kogut, E. L. 1972. "An Economic Analysis of Demographic Phenomena: A Case Study of Brazil." Ph.D. dissertation, University of Chicago.

Komesar, N. K. 1973. "Economic Analysis of Criminal Victimization." *Journal of Legal Studies* 2 (June).

Koopmans, T. C., and Beckman, M. 1957. "Assignment Problems and the Location of Economic Activities." *Econometrica* 25 (January): 53–76.

Kuratani, M. 1972. "Earnings Distribution and Specific Training: The Case of Japan." Ph.D. dissertation, Columbia University.

Lamson, H. D. 1933. "Differential Reproductivity in China." *The Quarterly Review of Biology* 10, no. 3 (September).

Lancaster, K. J. 1966. "A New Approach to Consumer Theory." *Journal of Political Economy* 74.

————. 1966. "Change and Innovation in the Technology of Consumption." *American Economic Review* 56.

————. 1971. *Consumer Demand*. New York: Columbia University Press.

Landes, William. 1966. "The Effect of State Fair Employment Legislation on the Economic Position of Nonwhite Males." Ph.D. dissertation, Columbia University, 1966.

Laws of New York. 1965. Vol. 2.

Leibenstein, H. 1950. "Bandwagon, Snob, and Veblen Effects in the Theory of Consumers' Demand." *Quarterly Journal of Economics* 64 (May): 183–207.

————. 1957. *Economic Backwardness and Economic Growth*. New York: Wiley.

Leibowitz, A. S. 1972. "Women's Allocation of Time to Market and Nonmarket Activities: Differences by Education." Ph.D. dissertation, Columbia University.

————. 1975. "Education and the Allocation of Women's Time." In *Education, Income and Human Behavior*, edited by F. Juster, pp. 171–198. New York: McGraw-Hill for the Carnegie Commission on Higher Education.

Leontief, W. 1947, 1966. "Introduction to a Theory of the Internal Structure of Functional Relationships." *Econometrica* 15, no. 4. Reprinted in his *Essays in Economics, 1947*. New York: Oxford University Press.

Linder, S. 1970. *The Harried Leisure Class*. New York: Columbia University Press.

Lipset, S. M., and Bendix, R. 1959. *Social Mobility in Industrial Societies*. Berkeley: University of California Press.

Marris, R. L. 1957. "Professor Hicks' Index Number Theorem." *Review of Economic Studies* 25 (October): 25–39.

Marschak, J. 1965. "Economics of Language." *Behavioral Science* 10 (April).

Marshall, Alfred. 1922, 1961, 1962. *Principles of Economics* 8th ed. New York, London: Macmillan.

McCall, J. J. 1970. "Economics of Information and Job Search." *Quarterly Journal of Economics* 84 (February).

McPherson, M. 1974. "The Effects of Public on Private College Enrollment." Ph.D. dissertation, University of Chicago.

McWilliams, C. 1948. *A Mask for Privilege: Anti-Semitism in America*. Boston: Little, Brown.

Merton, R. K. 1968. *Social Theory and Social Structure*. New York: Free Press.

————. 1973. *The Sociology of Science*. University of Chicago Press.

————. 1975. "Structural Analysis in Sociology." In *Approaches to the Study of Social Structure*, ed. P. M. Blau. New York: Free Press.

Michael, R. T. 1972. *The Effect of Education on Efficiency in Consumption*. National Bureau of Economic Research.

————. 1973a. "Education and the Derived Demand for Children." *Journal of Political Economy* 81 (March/April), pt. 2.

————. 1973b. "Education in Nonmarket Production." *Journal of Political Economy* 81 (March/April).

Michael, R. T., and Becker, G. S. 1973. "On the New Theory of Consumer Behavior." *The Swedish Journal of Economics* 75, no. 4. Reprinted in this volume as chapter 7.

Mincer, J. 1963a. "Labor Force Participation of Married Women." In *Aspects of Labor Economics*. New York: National Bureau of Economic Research.

————. 1963b. "Market Prices, Opportunity Costs, and Income Effects." In *Measurement in Economics*, ed. C. Christ. Stanford University Press.

————. 1974. *Schooling, Experience, and Earnings*. New York: Columbia University Press for the National Bureau of Economic Research.

Mitchell, W. C. 1937. *The Backward Art of Spending Money and Other Essays.* New York: McGraw-Hill.

Mohring, H. 1961. "Land Values and the Measurement of Highway Benefits." *Journal of Political Economy* 69 (June).

Moore, W. 1963. *Man, Time and Society.* New York: Wiley.

Morgan, J. N.; David, M. H.; Cohen, W. J.; and Brazer, H. E. 1962. *Income and Welfare in the United States.* New York: McGraw-Hill.

Mortensen, D. T. 1970. "Job Search, the Duration of Unemployment, and the Phillips Curve." *American Economic Review* 60: 847–62.

Moses, L. N., and Williamson, H. F. 1963. "Value of Time, Choice of Mode, and the Subsidy Issue in Urban Transportation." *Journal of Political Economy* 71 (June).

Muth, R. 1961. "Economic Change and Rural-Urban Conversion." *Econometrica*, vol. 29, no. 1 (January).

———. 1966. "Household Production and Consumer Demand Functions." *Econometrica* 34.

Nelson, P. J. 1970. "Information and Consumer Behavior." *Journal of Political Economy* 78 (March/April).

———. 1975. "The Economic Consequence of Advertising." *Journal of Business* 48 (April).

Nerlove, M., and Schultz, T. P. 1970. "Love and Life between the Censuses: A Model of Family Decision Making in Puerto Rica 1950–1960." RM-6322-AID, RAND, Santa Monica, California.

Ofek, H. 1972. "Allocation of Goods and Time in a Family Context." Ph.D. dissertation, Columbia University.

Okun, Bernard. 1958*a*. "A Rational Economic Model For the Birth Rate." RAND Corporation Series, P1458, August.

———. 1958*b*. *Trends in Birth Rates in the United States Since 1870.* Baltimore: The Johns Hopkins Press.

Owen, J. D. 1969. *The Price of Leisure.* Rotterdam University Press and McGill-Queens University Press.

Pantaleoni, M. 1892, 1898. *Pure Economics.* Clifton, N.J.: Kelley, 1892; London: Macmillan, 1898.

Parsons, D. O. 1974. "Intergenerational Wealth Transfers and the Educational Decisions of Male Youth." Mimeographed. Ohio State University.

Parsons, T. 1968. "Social Interactions." In *International Encyclopedia of the Social Sciences,* ed. D. S. Sills. Vol. 7. New York: Macmillan and Free Press.

Peltzman, S. 1973. "The Effect of Government Subsidies-in-Kind on Private Expenditures: The Case of Higher Education." *Journal of Political Economy* 81 (January/February).

Pigou, A. 1903. "Some Remarks on Utility." *Economic Journal* 13: 19–24.

———. 1962. *The Economics of Welfare.* 4th ed. London: Macmillan.

Plant, A. 1934. "The Economic Theory Concerning Patents for Inventions." *Economica* 1 (February).

Pollock, F., and Maitland, F. W. 1952. *The History of English Law*. Vol. 2. 2d ed. Cambridge University Press.

Posner, R. 1973. *Economic Analysis of Law*. Boston: Little, Brown.

Potter, R. G. 1955. "The Influence of Primary Groups on Fertility." Ph.D. dissertation, Department of Social Relations, Harvard University.

———. 1956. "A Critique of the Glass-Grebenik Model for Indirectly Estimating Desired Family Size." *Population Studies* 9 (March).

Prais, S. J., and Houthhakker, H. 1955. *The Analysis of Family Budgets*. Cambridge University Press.

President's Commission on Law Enforcement and Administration of Justice. 1967*a*. *The Challenge of Crime in a Free Society*. Washington: U.S. Government Printing Office.

———. 1967*b*. "Task Force Reports." *Corrections*. Washington: U.S. Government Printing Office.

———. 1967*c*. "Task Force Reports." *The Courts*. Washington: U.S. Government Printing Office.

———. 1967*d*. "Task Force Reports." *Crime and Its Impact—an Assessment*. Washington: U.S. Government Printing Office.

———. 1967*e*. "Task Force Reports." *Science and Technology*. Washington: U.S. Government Printing Office.

Radzinowicz, L. 1948. *A History of English Criminal Law and Its Administration from 1750*. Vol. 1. London: Stevens.

The Random House Dictionary of the English Language. 1967. Unabridged ed. New York: Random House.

Rees, Albert. 1968. "Economics." In *International Encyclopedia of the Social Sciences*, ed. D. E. Sills. New York: Macmillan and Free Press.

Reid, M. G. 1934. *Economics of Household Production*. New York: Wiley.

———. 1962. Housing and Income. University of Chicago Press.

———. 1963. "Consumer Response to the Relative Price of Store versus Delivered Milk." *Journal of Political Economy* 71 (April).

Reischauer, R. 1970. "The Impact of the Welfare System on Black Migration and Marital Stability." Ph.D. dissertation, Columbia University.

Reiss, A. J. 1968. "Sociology." In *International Encyclopedia of the Social Sciences*, ed. D. E. Sills. New York: Macmillan and Free Press.

Rivers, W. H. 1906. *The Todas*. London: Macmillan.

Robbins, L. 1930. "On the Elasticity of Demand for Income in Terms of Effort." *Economica* 10 (June).

———. 1962. *The Nature and Significance of Economic Science*. London: Macmillan.

Rockwell, G. R. 1959. "Income and Household Composition: Their Effects on Food Consumption." Marketing Research Report No. 340. Washington: U.S. Department of Agriculture.

Roper, E. 1948. "The Price Business Pays." In *Discrimination and the National Welfare*, edited by R. M. MacIver. New York: Harper.

Rose, A. 1951. *The Costs of Prejudice*. Paris: UNESCO.

Saenger, G. 1953. *The Social Psychology of Prejudice*. New York: Harper.

Salzano, F. M.; Neel, J. V.; and Maybury-Lewis, D. 1967. "Further Studies on the Xavante Indians." *American Journal of Human Genetics* (July): 463–89.

Samuelson, P. A. 1947. *The Foundations of Economic Analysis*. Cambridge: Harvard University Press.

———. 1954. "The Pure Theory of Public Expenditures." *Review of Economics and Statistics* 36 (November).

———. 1956. "Social Indifference Curves." *Quarterly Journal of Economics* 70 (February).

Santos, F. P. 1970. "Marital Instability and Male-Female Complementarity." Ph.D. dissertation, Columbia University.

Schilling, T. C. 1967. "Economic Analysis of Organized Crime." In President's Commission on Law Enforcement and Administration of Justice. *Organized Crime*. ("Task Force Reports"). Washington: U.S. Government Printing Office.

Schnore, L. F. 1963. "The Socio-Economic Status of Cities and Suburbs." *American Sociological Review* 68 (February).

Schoeck, H. 1966. *Envy*. New York: Harcourt, Brace and World.

Schultz, T. W. 1960. "The Formation of Human Capital by Education." *Journal of Political Economy* 68 (December). Reprinted in Becker (1975).

———. 1967. *The Economic Value of Education*. New York: Columbia University Press.

———. 1972. "Human Capital: Policy Issues and Research Opportunities." In *Human Resources*. New York: National Bureau of Economic Research, Colloquium VI.

———, ed. 1973. "New Economic Approaches to Fertility." *Journal of Political Economy* 81 (March/April), pt. 2.

———, ed. 1975. *Economics of the Family: Marriage, Children, and Human Capital*. University of Chicago Press for the National Bureau of Economic Research.

Schumpeter, J. 1942. *Capitalism, Socialism, and Democracy*. Reprinted New York: Harper, 1950.

Schwartz, R. 1970. "Personal Philanthropic Contributions." *Journal of Political Economy* 78 (November/December).

Senior, N W. 1965. *An Outline of the Science of Political Economy*. New York: Sentry Press.

———. 1938. *Political Economy*. Library of Economics Edition.

Shaw, G. B. 1930. *Man and Superman*. In *The Collected Works of Bernard Shaw*. Vol. 10. New York: Wise.

Shawness, Lord. 1965. "Crime Does Pay because We Do Not Back up the Police." *New York Times Magazine*, 13 June.

Shoup, C. 1966. *Federal Estate and Gift Taxes*. Washington, D.C.: The Brookings Institution.

Silver, M. 1965. "Birth Rates, Marriages, and Business Cycles in the U.S." *Journal of Political Economy* 73 (November/December).

Simons, H. 1934, 1948. *A Positive Program for Laissez-faire: Some Proposals for a Liberal Economy.* University of Chicago Press. Reprinted in H. Simons, *Economic Policy for a Free Society.* University of Chicago Press.

Smigel, Arleen. 1965. "Crime and Punishment: An Economic Analysis." Master's thesis, Columbia University.

Smith, Adam. 1937. *The Wealth of Nations.* New York: Modern Library.

———. 1968. *The Theory of Moral Sentiments,* ed. E. G. West. New Rochelle, N.Y.: Arlington House.

Smith, J. 1972. "The Life Cycle Allocation of Time in a Family Context." Ph.D. dissertation, University of Chicago.

Smith, V. 1975. "The Primitive Hunter Culture, Pleistocene Extinction, and the Rise of Agriculture." *Journal of Political Economy* 83 (August).

Stigler, G. J. 1945. "The Cost of Subsistence." *Journal of Farm Economics* 27.

———. 1950. "Employment and Compensation in Education." National Bureau of Economic Research, Occasional Paper 33.

———. 1961. "The Economics of Information." *Journal of Political Economy* 69 (June).

———. 1962. "What Can Regulators Regulate? The Case of Electricity." *Journal of Law and Economics* 5 (October).

———. 1964. "A Theory of Oligopoly." *Journal of Political Economy* 72 (February).

———. 1966. "The Economic Effects of the Antitrust Laws." *Journal of Law and Economics* 9 (October).

———. 1971. "Smith's Travels on the Ship of State." *History of Political Economy* (Fall).

———. 1974. "Do Economists Matter?" Mimeographed. University of Chicago. Published in 1976 in the *Southern Economic Journal* 42 (January).

Stigler, G. J., and Becker, G. S. 1974. "De Gustibus Non Est Disputandum." Mimeographed. University of Chicago.

Sutherland, E. H. 1960. *Principles of Criminology.* 6th ed. Philadelphia: J. B. Lippincott Co.

Tarver, J. D. 1956. "Costs of Rearing and Educating Farm Children." *Journal of Farm Economics* 38 (February).

Taussig, M. 1965. "The Charitable Contribution in the Federal Personal Income Tax." Ph.D. dissertation, Massachusetts Institute of Technology.

Theil, H. 1952. "Qualities, Prices, and Budget Inquiries." *Review of Economic Studies* 19, no. 3.

Tobin, J. 1950. "A Statistical Demand Function for Food in the U.S.A." *Journal of the Royal Statistical Society* 113, Series A.

———. 1952. "A Survey of the Theory of Rationing." *Econometrica* 20, no. 4 (October).

Trivers, R. L. 1974. "Parent-Offspring Conflict." *American Zoologist.*

United Nations Statistical Office. 1950. "National and per Capita Incomes in Seventy Countries, 1949." New York: United Nations Statistical Office.

U.S. Bureau of the Census. *Census of Population, 1940*: Washington, D.C.: U.S. Government Printing Office.

———. 1952. *Census of Population, 1950*: Washington, D.C.: U.S. Government Printing Office.

———. 1953. *Census of Population, 1950: Special Report on Non-White Populations by Race.* Washington, D.C.: U.S. Government Printing Office.

———. 1954. *Statistical Abstract of the United States, 1953.* Washington, D.C.: U.S. Government Printing Office.

———. 1963. *Census of Population: 1960.* Washington, D.C.: U.S. Government Printing Office.

———. 1971. *Social and Economic Variations in Marriage, Divorce, and Remarriage: 1967.* Current Population Reports, series P-20, no. 223. Washington, D.C.: U.S. Government Printing Office.

Vance, Rupert B. 1952. "Is Theory for Demographers?" *Social Forces* 31.

Veblen, T. 1934. *The Theory of the Leisure Class.* New York: Modern Library.

Vickery, W. S. 1962. "One Economist's View of Philanthropy." In *Philanthropy and Public Policy*, ed. F. Dickinson. New York: National Bureau of Economic Research.

Walsh, B. M. 1972. "Trends in Age at Marriage in Postwar Ireland." *Demography* 9 (May).

Waters, R. H., and Brunnell, B. N. 1968. "Comparative Psychology." In *International Encyclopedia of the Social Sciences*, ed. D. E. Sills. New York: Macmillan and Free Press.

Weintraub, R. 1962. "The Birth Rate and Economic Development: An Empirical Study." *Econometrica* 30, no. 4 (October).

Whelpton, P. K. 1947. *Forecasts of the Population of the United States 1945–1975.* Bureau of the Census. Washington, D.C.: U.S. Government Printing Office.

Whelpton, P. K., and Kiser, C. V., eds. 1951. *Social and Psychological Factors Affecting Fertility.* New York: Milbank Memorial Fund, 1951.

Wilburn, J. 1967. "A Contrast in Productivity Trends within Personal Services: The Barber and Beauty Shop Services." In *Productivity Differences within the Service Sector*, ed. V. Fuchs and J. Wilburn. New York: National Bureau of Economic Research, Occasional Paper 102.

Willis, R. J. 1969, 1971, 1973. "A New Approach to the Economic Theory of Fertility." Mimeographed 1969 and revised 1971, National Bureau of Economic Research. Printed 1973 in *Journal of Political Economy* 81 (March/April), pt. 2.

309   *References*

Wilson, E. O. 1975. *Sociobiology*. Cambridge: Harvard University Press.
Wilson, F. 1972. *Labor in the South African Gold Mines, 1911–1969*. Cambridge University Press.
Winch, R. E. 1958. *Mate Selection*. New York: Harper.
———. 1967. "Another Look at the Theory of Complementarity Needs in Mate Selection." *Journal of Marriage and the Family* 29 (November).
Young, K. 1954. *Isn't One Wife Enough?* New York: Holt.

Index